SAVAGE SYSTEMS:
Colonialism and Comparative Religion
in Southern Africa

DAVID CHIDESTER

SAVAGE SYSTEMS
Colonialism and Comparative
Religion in Southern Africa

University Press of Virginia
Charlottesville and London

THE UNIVERSITY PRESS OF VIRGINIA
© 1996 by the Rector and Visitors
of the University of Virginia

First published 1996

∞ The paper used in this publication meets the minimum requirements of the American National Standard for Information Sciences—
Permanence of Paper for Printed Library Materials, ANSI Z39.48-1984.

Library of Congress Cataloging-in-Publication Data

Chidester, David.
  Savage systems : colonialism and comparative religion in southern
Africa / David Chidester.
    p.   cm. — (Studies in religion and culture)
  Includes bibliographical references and index.
    ISBN 0-8139-1664-X (alk. paper). — ISBN 0-8139-1667-4 (pbk. : alk.
paper)
    1. Africa, Southern—Religion—Study and teaching—History.   2.
Colonies—Africa.   3. Colonies.   4. Religion—Study and teaching—
History.   I. Title.   II. Series: Studies in religion and culture (Char-
lottesville, Va.)
  BL2463.C45   1996
  291′.0968—dc20   96-12909
                                                              CIP

Printed in the United States of America

For Ninian Smart and Charles Long

CONTENTS

ILLUSTRATIONS

PREFACE

All kinds of reasoning consist in nothing but a *comparison*.
— DAVID HUME

All higher knowledge is acquired by comparison, and rests on comparison.
— F. MAX MÜLLER

The study of religion cannot pretend to find its way until it can relate to its past in narrative form.
— WALTER CAPPS

There is a complex relationship between the meaning and nature of religion as a subject of academic study and the reality of people and cultures who were conquered and colonized during the same period.
— CHARLES LONG

If there is one story-line that runs through the various figures and stratagems briefly passed in review, it is that this has been by no means an innocent endeavour.
— JONATHAN Z. SMITH

MY EPIGRAPHS hint at a new kind of history for the academic study of religion. By invoking David Hume and Friedrich Max Müller, I recall individuals who have been identified in previous histories as founders of the study of religion. The philosopher David Hume held that comparison was a basic feature of human thought. When applied to religion, comparison could support a rational explanation of its origin and persistence as a human phenomenon. Rationality, in Hume's sense, required a conceptual reduction of the diversity of religion to two interrelated causes, ignorance and fear of the unknown. According to J. Samuel Preus, who placed David Hume at the center of his history, *Explaining Religion: Criticism and Theory from Bodin to Freud*, Hume's rational explanation marked a crucial turning point in the history of the study of religion. Although anticipated by previous naturalistic explanations of religion, Hume's rationalism was developed into a science by subsequent thinkers, especially by Auguste Comte, Edward B. Tylor, Émile Durkheim, and Sigmund Freud. By the twentieth century, therefore, the academic study of religion could find its roots in the rationalism, naturalism, and skepticism of the European Enlightenment.[1]

In contrast, the linguist Friedrich Max Müller, who was celebrated by Eric Sharpe in his *Comparative Religion: A History* as the founder of comparative religion, drew more directly on the resources of early-nineteenth-century German romanticism and idealism in developing his "science of religion." As a result, Müller showed a greater interest in the poetic flights, emotional depths, and moral imperatives of religion. Nevertheless, he also insisted that specialized knowledge about religion depended upon comparison. Borrowing from Goethe, Müller applied the aphorism "He who knows one, knows none" to the study of religion in order to insist that its foundation and extensions were thoroughly comparative. Knowledge about religion only began and developed with the exploration of two or more religions. Through the practice of disciplined comparison, Müller promised that a higher, scientific knowledge of religion could be attained. In spite of his romantic impulses, therefore, Max Müller was also the progenitor of a comparative religion attuned to an Enlightenment ideal of reason.[2]

Is the Enlightenment, therefore, the historical heritage of Religious Studies? The question is important. Walter Capps proposed that the study of religion must find ways to relate to its past in narrative form if it is to develop any self-understanding as an academic discipline. Religious Studies needs a shared perspective on those efforts that have been made in the past to reflect on and make sense out of religion as a human product, a human project, or a human problem. Unavoidably, any disciplinary history of the academic study of religion will be invented rather than merely discovered. Its narrative sequences inevitably will be devised in the present to serve present intellectual or institutional interests. Nevertheless, as Capps suggested, the project of recovering a history of the academic study of religion is of critical importance to the identity and future of the field of study. If past is prologue, the academic study of religion requires a past that will serve as a frame of reference for charting a future. As we look to the future of an international, intercultural, and interdisciplinary study of religion, the invention of a new history of comparative religion should be a priority for historical research and critical reflection.[3]

As noted, recent histories have been provided. They have identified founders, successors, and intellectual heroes who pioneered the general trends of thought and movements of ideas that have led to the modern study of religion. But what kind of histories are these? What kind of a narrative leaves out all the dramatic tension, human conflict, or human comedy that makes for a good story? Obviously, these are "internal" histories. They might recognize that the very category of religion, in its modern sense, emerged out of a specific historical situation, the European struggle with religious pluralism that was intensified by increased exposure to an expanding range of human evidence from the "exotic" or "primitive" societies encompassed under colonial rule. However, in spite of this recognition, standard histories of the study of religion have been almost exclusively preoccupied with the questions, issues, or modes of analysis that were internal to the development of a set of European academic disciplines. As a result, the real story remains untold. As Charles Long observed, the history of the study of religion is the dramatic story of the complex relationship between European Enlightenment concepts about the nature of religion and the violent reality experienced by people and cultures all over the world who were conquered and colonized by Europeans.[4]

The discipline of comparative religion emerged, therefore, not only out of the Enlightenment heritage but also out of a violent history of colonial conquest and domination. Accordingly, the history of comparative religion is a story not only about knowledge but also about power. The disciplinary history of the study of religion is also a history of discipline, a dramatic narrative of the discourses and practices of comparison that shaped subjectivities on colonized peripheries and at European centers. To borrow a phrase from Jonathan Z. Smith, the discipline of comparative religion was by no means an innocent endeavor.[5] Whether practiced on the colonized periphery or at the colonizing center, the study of religion was entangled in the power relations of frontier conflict, military conquest and resistance, and imperial expansion. This book tells that story, thereby retelling the story of the academic study of religion from the vantage point of one colonized periphery, southern Africa. On southern African frontiers, as in other colonized regions all over the globe, a comparative religion was born.

From a southern African perspective, previous histories of the

study of religion might be useful, but they are ultimately inadequate as representations of the actual historical conditions under
which comparative religion emerged. In one respect, their Eurocentric bias has inhibited any consideration of the importance of
a peripheral region such as southern Africa in the development of
theory and method in the study of religion. Although it was on
the front lines of the human encounter out of which the modern
categories of *religion* and *religions* originated, southern Africa,
like other peripheral regions, has been relegated to a subordinate
status that is dependent upon the productions of European intellectual centers. Standard disciplinary histories create the impression that a place like southern Africa was an "undeveloped"
region from which raw religious materials could be extracted, ex-
ported, and eventually transformed into intellectual manufac-
tured goods in the metropolitan capitals of theory production in
Europe. Certainly, such a process occurred. However, relations between center and periphery in the history of comparative religion
were much more complex and revealing than this model of raw
materials and theory manufacture might suggest. A colonized
periphery, such as southern Africa, was also an arena of theory
production, with the conquering and colonizing center itself
colonized by reports about religion from missionaries, travelers,
colonial administrators, and others on the periphery.

Since conventional histories of comparative religion have con-
centrated upon what their authors perceived as enduring questions of category formation, interpretation, and explanation, they
have tended to foreclose the exploration of issues that are regarded as no longer relevant in the modern academic study of religion. As a result, these histories run the risk of ignoring aspects
of the story of comparative religion that might be of greatest historical interest. In southern Africa, for example, comparative religion was practiced, not by intellectuals aloof from the world, but
by human beings engaged in religious conflicts on the ground.
Principles of comparison were hammered out on frontier battlefields. Interpretive and explanatory strategies of comparative religion were inevitably entangled in the social, economic, and political conflicts of colonial situations. On the southern African
periphery, a frontier comparative religion emerged that was crucial to the development of the academic study of religion. Therefore, if the history of comparative religion is truly to be a history,
it must be a narrative of historically situated discourses and practices of comparison that is sensitive to their practical impli-

cations in the world. The study of religion must find itself, once again, on the frontier.

Although I address my own discipline—the academic study of religion—most directly in this book, I cover ground that I think should be of interest in the fields of African history, anthropology, and the emerging disciplines of colonial and postcolonial studies. I also think that the case studies I develop in southern Africa have wider significance for other colonized regions of the world. In every field and in every region, cultural analysis is currently confronting the problems and prospects of understanding human relations in frontier situations. As Homi Bhabha has observed, cultural relations are based, "not on the exoticism of multiculturalism or the *diversity* of cultures, but on the inscription and articulation of culture's *hybridity.*" Bhabha concludes, "it is the 'inter'—the cutting edge of translation and negotiation, the *in-between* space—that carries the burden of the meaning of culture."[6] In this formulation, Bhabha implicitly invokes the frontier—the cutting edge, the in-between space. Notice, however, the mixture of metaphor. Is the frontier a "cutting edge"? Is it a line to be advanced or a border to be crossed? Or is the frontier a spatial zone to be entered, an "in-between space" of unexpected contacts, exchanges, and interchanges? That inherent ambiguity in the governing metaphor of this book—the frontier—recurs in the specific case studies that I examine.

When I started this project, I did not expect to find what I found. As everyone knows, European observers entered southern Africa and declared that the indigenous people had no religion. I wanted to investigate that denial as a point of departure for a localized, contextualized history of comparative religion in southern Africa. I did not know, however, what it took for Europeans to recognize the existence of indigenous religions in southern Africa. It required systems of colonial administration—the "savage systems" of the commando system, the magisterial system, the location system, and the reserve system—to discover that Africans had a religious system. Furthermore, I did not know that comparative religion in the nineteenth century provided terms for distinguishing among local people—the Xhosa were Arabs, the Zulu were Jews, and the Sotho-Tswana were ancient Egyptians—in ways that both transposed the Middle East onto the southern African landscape and conceptually displaced the indigenous people of southern Africa to the Middle East. In these containments and displacements, a comparative religion was forged

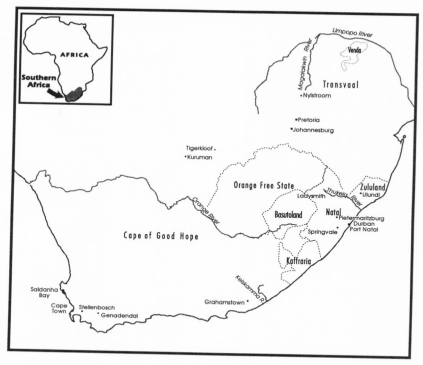

Southern Africa

on frontiers. Although I suspected that travelers, missionaries, traders, settlers, and colonial agents would provide evidence of a history of comparative religion, I did not fully appreciate the contributions of indigenous comparativists. Acting as more than merely informants or assistants, African comparative religionists also advanced comparisons in frontier situations. Certainly, there is more that I did not expect to find. How could I have anticipated the importance to the history of comparative religion of a forger from Poland, a pissing ceremony, a shipwrecked anchor, a pile of stones, a cattle killing, a group of prisoners, a mission station, a wooden crocodile, a goat, a wagon, or the undercurrent of laughter reverberating through the interplay of comparison? All these and more are recounted in this history of frontier comparative religion in southern Africa.

Over the past twelve years, I have found myself living in South Africa and working at the University of Cape Town. Although I have not exactly been in a frontier situation, I have encountered the kinds of conflict and cooperation that characterize an open frontier zone. As a result, this has been an exciting, challenging place to work. In 1991 it became a better place with the founding of the Institute for Comparative Religion in Southern Africa. ICRSA was launched with an inaugural lecture delivered by Professor Ninian Smart. During 1993 ICRSA hosted a six-week visit by Professor Charles Long. In many respects, these two friends of the institute represent its dual focus. With Ninian Smart's inspiration, we have embarked on constructive work in the fields of comparative religion and religion education in southern Africa. While Smart encourages us to imagine that anything is possible, Charles Long reminds us that everything is much more problematic than we imagined. During a crucial point in writing this book, my extended conversations with Long helped clarify the questions I was addressing. Long observed that he does not solve problems—he makes problems. The problems he created for me made this a better book. In dedicating this book to Ninian Smart and Charles Long, a traditional Xhosa praise poet might put it something like this:

Ninian Smart. *Sekukokuka—Smart! Uyinkosi yeenkosi eyazi nkonke itsho imbongi.*
Smart Knows! He is the Supreme Chief among those who Know says the Poet.

Charles Long. *NguZanengxaki! NguZanengxak' elibizwa yimbongi.*
Bringer of Problems! Bringer of Problems he is called by the Singer of Praises.

Growing out of a long-term ICRSA research project, this book has benefited from the aid and support provided by a team of talented research assistants. First and foremost, in friendship and gratitude, I acknowledge my debt to Senior Researcher Darrel Wratten. Over the course of five years, I have become increasingly dependent upon his research and editorial skills. I can honestly say that this book would not exist if it were not for our collaboration. As we collected material for what I thought would be a chapter in a book, he found so much rich, exciting evidence for a history of comparative religion that the chapter turned into this book. In this project, therefore, Darrel Wratten has been as much a coauthor as a research assistant.

Researchers working on this project have also included Ann-Marie Leatt, Sibusiso Masondo, Michael Mbokazi, Robert Petty, Sa'diyya Shaikh, and Judy Tobler. Although they have been working out of a different wing of ICRSA, I would also like to acknowledge the assistance of Nokuzola Mndende, A. Rashied Omar, Isabel Apawo Phiri, and Janet Stonier. They have all made the institute a reality.

Among the many debts I have incurred in producing this book, I acknowledge the following: Gene Klaaren provided a careful reading and proved a congenial conversation partner; Karel Schoeman and Jackie Loos graciously opened the resources of the South African Library; Susan Sayer created a map; Cathie Brettschneider guided the manuscript into and out of the press; Ivan Strenski almost convinced me that the crimes I have recounted in this book are not ours; Edward Linenthal maintained a reality check on the entire proceedings; Deborah Sills provided an opportunity to test some of these crazy ideas in front of an American audience; and James McNamara supported this project by ensuring that academic standards were maintained. There are some debts, however, about which I cannot speak. How could I tell those stories? We have a "New South Africa." The reality of that changing, transforming society must speak for itself.

Now, a word for our sponsors. As James Frazer observed in 1904 in a letter to his donor, Edmund Gosse of the Royal Literary Fund, "few people care to give their money for such a very unpractical subject as comparative religion, which puts nothing in anybody's pocket and only makes people uncomfortable by unsettling their beliefs."[7] Remarkably, however, the Centre for Science Development and the University Research Committee of the University of Cape Town have generously supported this unpractical project on comparative religion. I extend my thanks, but I also acknowledge that the opinions expressed and conclusions arrived at in this book are those of the author and are not necessarily to be attributed to the Centre for Science Development or the University of Cape Town. Of course, I also absolve all donors, assistants, colleagues, friends, and family of any responsibility for whatever unsettling effects this book might produce. However, since I think that unsettling beliefs can have practical benefits, I am willing to assume that responsibility. Finally, I pay tribute to the Board of Directors for existing, and to my wife, Careen, for sharing a life together.

SAVAGE SYSTEMS

Colonialism and Comparative Religion

in Southern Africa

1

FRONTIERS OF
COMPARISON

THIS BOOK is not a history of religious beliefs and practices. It is a critical analysis of the emergence of the conceptual categories of *religion* and *religions* on colonial frontiers. By documenting the practices of comparative religion on contested southern African frontiers, I try to show how this particular human science, with its techniques of observation, conversation, and description, and its procedures of analogical reasoning and theoretical generalization, can be resituated in the historical context of colonial conflict. Although I develop case studies from southern Africa, I am convinced that my findings have wider relevance. In general, the human sciences in Europe were born out of the vast intercultural exchanges that attended the age of exploration. With the rise of mercantile capitalism in northern Europe during the sixteenth century, authentic and reliable knowledge about human beings became a commodity that was valued for its utility in the work of trading or fighting with unfamiliar people all over the world.[1] However, the human sciences, in their constitution as authoritative and, eventually, professional knowledge, disguised their origin in this reality of intercultural contact and exchange, even preventing any recognition that their foundational notion of the human depended upon the new interchanges of an expanding global order. As I hope to demonstrate, comparative religion was at the forefront of the production of knowledge within these new power relations.

My basic approach to the history of comparative religion has been informed by critiques of the human sciences, particularly in the work of Michel Foucault and Edward Said, that have shown them to be historical constructions of both knowledge and power.

While Foucault proposed that the human sciences of life, labor, and language produced a European self, which was self-referentially universalized as "Man," Said analyzed the complex and subtle ways in which that European subjectivity was sustained and reinforced at the expense of conquering, dominating, and objectifying a world of colonized "Others."[2] On southern African frontiers, comparative religion was a discourse and practice that produced knowledge about religion and religions, and thereby reconfigured knowledge about the human, within the power relations of specific colonial situations. For European travelers, missionaries, settlers, and colonial agents, who all operated, at one time or another, as comparative religionists, this human science was a powerful knowledge to the extent that it contributed to establishing local control. In this respect, frontier comparative religion was a "rhetoric of control," a discourse about others that reinforced their colonial containment.[3] However, indigenous comparativists on southern African frontiers also played crucial roles in the production, and sometimes counterproduction, of knowledge about religion and the religions of the world. Since local control was at stake in southern Africa, at least until the destruction of the last independent African polity in the 1890s, the local knowledge about human identity and origins, similarities and differences, that was produced by comparative religion on the frontier remained a contested field of knowledge and power.

Following a trail pioneered by Edward Said, therefore, I explore the entangled relations between knowledge and domination in European human sciences, while occasionally trying to catch the brief glimpse of cognitive resistance or alternative knowledge advanced by indigenous comparativists. However, I have not forgotten Foucault's insight into the dramatic historical discontinuities that can be observed in the formation of European academic disciplines. Accordingly, I propose to distinguish three phases, or domains, or *epistemes*, in the history of comparative religion. With particular attention to my own local context, I identify them as frontier, imperial, and apartheid comparative religion.

First, as already suggested, frontier comparative religion, the specific subject of this book, was a human science of local control. During its long history, which stretched from the beginning of the seventeenth century to the end of the nineteenth century in southern Africa but varied according to local circumstances in other parts of the world, this comparative religion was practiced by travelers, missionaries, and colonial agents. At the furthest peripheries of the known world, European comparativists inquired about the existence or nature of local religions. Initially, they issued surprising reports about the absence of religion in the Americas, Australia, the Pacific Islands, or Africa. By the nineteenth century, however, discoveries of indigenous religions had been authenticated all over the world. The governing rhetorical figure in the discourse and practice of nineteenth-century frontier comparative religion was the local system. The notion of a coherent, integrated, and bounded system was crucial. Significantly, it resonated in southern Africa with the discourse and practice of colonial administration that produced the commando system, the village system, the magisterial system, the location system, and the reserve system for the containment and control of indigenous populations. The discovery of local religious systems in southern Africa can be precisely correlated with the establishment of local control over Africans. Frontier comparative religion was a human science that advanced regional domination. Always contested, frontier comparative religion nevertheless produced a knowledge that was embedded in local colonial situations.

Second, by contrast, imperial comparative religion, as practiced in European metropolitan centers from the 1850s into the twentieth century, showed no concern with religions as coherent, integrated systems. Rather, theorists in Europe, especially during the last quarter of the nineteenth century, arranged disparate evidence from all over the world into a single, uniform temporal sequence, from primitive to civilized, that claimed to represent the universal history of humanity. Knowledge about religion, therefore, reinforced a global control over the entire expanse of human geography and history. Rarely, as in the case of F. D. Maurice in the 1840s, a theoretician recognized that this knowledge was important for a European nation that was trading with, conquering, or administering people adhering to different religions. By the 1850s, however, the imperial science of comparative religion had completely obscured its entanglement in global conquest. Not only divorcing itself from its own origins—the dependence of its very existence upon the violent reality of colonial frontiers—this imperial comparative religion erased all of the historical, geographical, social, and political contexts in which its data had been embedded. As a result, all that remained for analysis in the disembodied evidence accumulated by imperial comparative religion was a mentality, whether that mentality was designated as religious, magical, superstitious, or primitive. Ironically, however, this human science dedicated to global knowledge and power also had local effects. In isolating a primitive religious mentality, which was attributed to "savages" all over the colonized world, imperial comparative religion brought its analysis home by asserting that the same mentality was shared by animals, children, women, rural peasants, the urban working class, the deaf and dumb, criminals, and the insane in Europe.[4] By developing a universal discourse about otherness, therefore, imperial comparative religion established a discursive regime of sameness that served the interests of global control over "primitives" at home and abroad.

Third, and finally, apartheid comparative religion sought local control in global terms. Whether we use the specific South African designation, *apartheid*, or the more generic English word, *separation*, this approach to comparative religion has been committed to identifying and reifying the many languages, cultures, peoples, and religions of the world as if they were separate and distinct regions. Each religion has to be understood as a separate, hermetically sealed compartment into which human beings can be classified and divided. In South Africa, apartheid ideologues reinforced those divisions and separations during the twentieth century by relying on the findings of European human and social sciences. In the study of religion, they used the global terms of imperial comparative religion, including *primitive mentality, fetishism, animism, totemism,* and the evolutionary trajectory from *primitive magic* to *civilized science,* in order to reinforce control over the people and the land of the region. By odd coincidence, the leading expert on indigenous African religion in the 1920s, W. M. Eiselen, turned out to be the assistant to H. F. Verwoerd at the Bantu Affairs Administration during the brutal implementation of the oppressive regime of "Grand Apartheid" during the 1950s. Eiselen was not alone. Many other human and social scientists drew upon European resources in fashioning academic justifications for apartheid. The pass laws, forced removals, racial segregation, and violent suppression of any mixing across reified racial, ethnic, or religious boundaries defined the hallmarks of apartheid in South Africa. However, I would suggest, apartheid comparative religion has not been unique to South Africa. It has surfaced wherever religious systems are classified, reified, and separated in the terms of a global theory of religion. In other words, apartheid comparative religion has appeared in principle, if not in practice, although its basic principles have adhered to practice in a place like South Africa, in the modern study of religion and religions at the end of the twentieth century in Europe and North America.

STUDY OF RELIGION, SCIENCE OF CONTACT

As an academic discipline, comparative religion was professionalized in Europe during the last three decades of the nineteenth century. Professorial chairs in the comparative history of religions were established at major universities: at Geneva in 1873; in Holland in 1876, with the launching of four chairs; at the Collège de France in 1880; and in Brussels in 1884. British enthusiasm for the subject was stimulated by the lectures on the "science of religion" delivered at Oxford by F. Max Müller in 1870. According to Eric Sharpe, it was Müller's lectures that marked the birth of comparative religion. One of the discipline's founders, however, the Dutch historian of religions C. P. Tiele, proposed that the science of religion began about 1850. Although European interest in religion and religions was certainly evident before then, the midpoint of the nineteenth century saw the emergence of a scientific comparative religion, in conversation with developments in other academic disciplines, including comparative philology, ethnology, anthropology, and folklore, that organized European reflection on religion into a science.[5]

However, as anthropologist Edmund Leach has observed, this dating of the origin of comparative religion in the 1850s has effectively erased all the European scholarship on religion and religions that flourished during the first half of the nineteenth century. Since much of that research and writing on religion was devoted to identifying the importance of sexuality, phallic cults, and the erotic dimensions of stone, tree, or serpent worship in the history of religions, Leach has argued that comparative religionists, subject to late Victorian sensibilities, suppressed its contributions. If European comparativists at the end of the nineteenth century repressed sexuality, only allowing it to appear in their research under the euphemism of "fertility," they also repressed violence, the violent context of colonialism under which their primary data for a science of religion was collected. During the second half of the nineteenth century, comparativists distanced themselves not only from their immediate predecessors in

Europe but also from the travelers, missionaries, and government agents who were conducting research on comparative religion all over the world. Although totally dependent upon their findings, European comparativists nevertheless denigrated travelers, missionaries, and colonial officials as unscientific collectors of raw materials. For example, while absorbing and assimilating an imposing array of such reports, John Lubbock doubted "whether travellers have correctly understood the accounts given to them." Lacking proper scientific definition and terms for analysis, European observers on the colonized peripheries of the world could not possibly understand the people they encountered. Scientific understanding could only be achieved at the metropolitan center through disciplined standards of comparison. Therefore, comparative religionists in Europe appropriated the reports but dismissed the reporters, as they distinguished themselves from travelers, missionaries, and colonial agents.[6]

More recently, however, all three have been recognized as pioneers of ethnographic knowledge. Travelers opened a world of knowledge by stimulating the circulation of new ideas about humanity in Europe. From the massive collections of voyages by Hakluyt, Astley, Purchas, and Pinkerton, to the more intimate narratives of personal adventure and reflection on difference in the nineteenth century, the genre of travel literature both focused and broadened European ethnographic knowledge. In travel reports, images of monsters and wild men, noble savages and earthly paradises, generated strange and contradictory ways of imagining other human beings and other possibilities of being human. Indigenous people in strange lands appeared in travel literature as objects for conquest and subjects for representation. Their discovery, or invention, reinforced—or perhaps actually constituted—the notion of Europe by centering and surrounding it with a strange periphery.[7]

In that process, travel literature developed a style and assembled an archive of ethnographic knowledge. As Mary Louise Pratt has suggested, travelers developed rhetorical strategies for representing foreign or exotic "others" that persisted in the modern practice of ethnography. Every "portrait of manners and customs," Pratt has argued, contributed to the formation of a "normalizing discourse" designed "to fix the Other in a timeless present." As travel reports multiplied and were avidly assimilated in Europe, they supported the emergence of what Pratt has called a "planetary consciousness" that underwrote European global expansion.[8]

That planetary consciousness, however, displayed some distinctive and curious local features in relation to the people and places of the colonized world. The published travel reports of Francis Galton, the British founder and popularizer of the "science" of eugenics, are instructive in this regard. Having explored southern African in the 1850s, Galton became an expert not only in the science of population control but also in a scientific discipline of travel that merged sexual desire, violence, and an awkward self-consciousness of European domination in foreign lands. One incident in Galton's travels became an emblem for this mix of desire and domination. While observing the "manners and customs" of people in the northwestern Cape, Galton noticed a young "Hottentot" woman, "a Venus among Hottentots," who was standing at some distance from him under a tree. Intrigued by the woman's features, especially by "the beautiful outline that her back affords," he used his sextant to take a reading of her dimensions, calculating her exact measurements, only after she had gone, by pacing out the distance between his point of observation and the tree. With this scientific sublimation of sexual desire, Galton also channeled the violent confrontations occasioned by travel into a practical science. While a gun was essential equipment, he advised, a traveler must also have sufficient rope to bind any recalcitrant natives. For the benefit of his readers, Galton provided detailed instructions on how to tie up natives with rope. In this context of covert sex and implicit violence, Galton advised travelers that it was essential that they adopt a particular disposition of command, showing, in every situation, more confidence in themselves than they might naturally feel.

Following his own advice, Francis Galton pursued ethnographic investigations as a traveler in southwestern Africa. Certainly, his ethnographic gaze, as well as his rope, "fixed" the Other. But what kind of a "normalizing discourse" was produced when Galton observed that his dog displayed more intelligence than the natives? Entangled in local situations of repressed desire and structural violence, European travelers generated a strange and impossible kind of ethnographic knowledge. Nevertheless, for European readers, travel reports created the conditions for imagining a global ethnographic field of knowledge about the world.[9]

Likewise, Christian missionaries have more recently been recognized for their role in the formation and expansion of ethnographic knowledge. While they tended to be disregarded as interested parties by scientists in Europe, missionaries were crucial to the emergence of local fieldwork and research traditions among indigenous people all over the world.[10] Like travelers, Christian missionaries also developed a "planetary consciousness" in framing and pursuing their work. For example, when the London Missionary Society was organized in 1795, its leaders had to develop a cognitive map of the world in order to carry out their mandate to evangelize all the nations. In a sermon delivered on 24 September of that year, Dr. Romaine Haweis gave some indication of the global framework in which this emerging missionary enterprise was located. A suitable field for mission work, Dr. Haweis proposed, could be identified by a process of elimination that required a survey of the entire world.

First, the mission could not be established in any place with an inhospitable climate. Not only concerned with the discomfort of extreme heat or cold, or the prospect of life-threatening diseases, missionaries often adhered to an environmental theory in which climate was held partly responsible for shaping human dispositions. In southern Africa, for example, J. W. D. Moodie complained about the "damp and cloudy atmosphere which depresses the mind, and disposes it for the reception of melancholy and superstitious impressions." Moodie noted that the "natives" and the Dutch immigrants were both susceptible to the "gloomy imaginings" of superstition as a result of living in such a climate. Concern about climate, therefore, could contain an implicit theory of religion. Second, Romaine Haweis ruled out any place in the world where absolute, tyrannical governments had been established, such as China and Japan. Since those absolute regimes also had a religious character, they were imagined to be inimical to the designs of the Christian mission. Third, Haweis ruled out India or Muslim lands where missionaries would encounter the "established prejudices of false religion." Established religions, like tyrannical governments, would block the progress of the mission. Fourth, and finally, Haweis eliminated any region, especially Africa, where missionaries could expect to have serious difficulties in acquiring local languages. Although he ignored the Americas in drawing this map, Haweis eliminated Africa, China, Japan, India, and the entire Muslim world in the process of narrowing the mission field to the one and only place that fulfilled all his requirements—Tahiti.[11]

Eighteen months later, on 5 March 1797, the first London Missionary Society representatives landed in Tahiti. In 1799, apparently overcoming worries about climate and language, the society began its work in southern Africa. For all their aversion to foreign climates and native customs, however, the missionaries devoted considerable time and effort to observing and recording the details of indigenous life. In Tahiti, as Christopher Herbert has shown, the missionaries immersed themselves in the meticulous documentation and description of local culture to the extent that they actually developed the ethnographic concept of a cultural system. Long before theorists in Europe discovered this notion of culture as an integrated, coherent system, Christian missionaries were representing local cultural systems in the remote Pacific Islands.[12]

Receiving less attention in recent research than travelers or missionaries, colonial officials were also ethnographers. Certainly, in many cases, the distinction between travelers, missionaries, and agents of an advancing colonialism was blurred, especially when emissaries of European governments traveled to the ends of the earth to conquer in the name of Christianity. The Virginia Company, established in 1607 for the colonization of North America, declared that "our primary end is to plant religion, our secondary and subalternate ends are for the honour and profit of our nation." On behalf of the Dutch East India Company, which had just established its colonial settlement in 1652, Jan van Riebeeck proclaimed a colonial mission "in which the name of Christ may be extended, the interests of the Company promoted." In such pronouncements, travel, mission, and colonial intervention were interwoven in a single project.[13]

Nevertheless, by the nineteenth century, professional civil servants, from colonial governors to local magistrates, were generating ethnographic knowledge through their regular reports on local customs. In rare cases, a colonial official received particular recognition for advancing the cause of ethnography. As colonial governor of Australia, New Zealand, and the Cape Colony in southern Africa, Sir George Grey achieved that distinction through his researches on local customs in three colonized regions of the British Empire. While in Australia, Grey initiated investigations into aboriginal language and customs. In New Zealand he supervised the collection of Maori myths and traditions. During his time of service in southern Africa, he commissioned a thorough research report on "native laws and customs" in support of the implementation of his system of magisterial rule in the eastern Cape. Employing the services of the philologist, folklorist, and comparative religionist W. H. I. Bleek as his librarian, Sir George Grey built his extensive personal collection on the languages, customs, and religions of the world into the nucleus for the South African Library in Cape Town. In all this ethnographic activity, however, Grey adopted a missionary theory of history that assumed the languages and customs he was recording were destined to disappear along with the "savages" who held them. The advance of "Christian civilization," Grey promised, would "sweep away ancient races; antique laws and customs moulder into oblivion. The strongholds of murder and superstition are cleansed, and the Gospel is preached amongst ignorant and savage men. The ruder languages disappear successively, and the tongue of England alone is heard around."[14]

Although their own contributions as ethnographers have been largely ignored, colonial officials have been recently regarded as co-conspirators in the history of the human sciences to the extent that research on indigenous people was only feasible and effective within the power relations that they established between dominating and dominated cultures.[15] Colonial policy, from this perspective, enabled ethnographic practice, but it also influenced the development of anthropological theory. In simple terms, recent analysts have argued that the theory of evolution served conquest, while the theoretical agenda of functionalism conformed to the political and practical interests of colonial administration. Unfortunately, however, this critique of the colonial entanglements of anthropology, and the human sciences in general, has for the most part maintained a Eurocentric focus on theorists and policymakers in metropolitan centers. On colonized peripheries, local government officials, such as Sir George Grey, were much more inclined than the imperialists or theorists in London to push the frontier of colonial advance. At the same time, local governors, magistrates, and other colonial agents on the periphery were more likely to demonstrate the complex and precise nature of the entanglement of ethnographic theory with the military and administrative practices of colonialism.

These observations about ethnography and the work of travelers, missionaries, and colonial agents also apply to comparative religion. If we allow the repressed to return, we must recognize that voyagers and traders, missionaries and government officials, were European observers on the front lines of intercultural contact that generated knowledge about religion and religions. Certainly, their reports can be questioned. They might not have been reliable witnesses about religious beliefs and practices. But they provided invaluable evidence for a history of comparison. Situated in regions of intercultural contact, they practiced comparisons that mediated between the familiar and the strange, producing knowledge about the definition and nature, the taxonomy, genealogy, and morphology, of the human phenomenon of religion. Therefore, the history of comparative religion must include not only European Enlightenment concepts but also the procedures of comparison that were practiced in situations of cross-cultural contact.

THE ABSENCE OF RELIGION

The initial comparative maneuver under intercultural conditions was most often denial, the assertion that people had been found who lacked any religion. Ironically, therefore, the historical origin of the academic discipline of comparative religion can be traced back to European discoveries of the absence of religion.[16] From the earliest explorations of the Atlantic world, European travelers testified to the remarkable finding that there were people who had no religion. In his first report about the indigenous people of the New World, Christopher Columbus observed in a letter that was widely circulated in Europe that the Arawak Indians "do not hold any creed nor are they idolaters." In his *Mundus Novus* (1504–5), Amerigo Vespucci reinforced this point. "Beyond the fact that they have no church, no religion and are not idolaters," Vespucci asked, "what can I say?"[17]

The identification of people with no religion already said quite a lot. At the very least, it called into question the humanity of the Indians, a question that the conquerors answered in performative terms by their brutal treatment and eventual extermination of the Arawaks. This denial of religion, the discovery of an absence, was almost endlessly repeated in reports from voyages to the Americas. The earliest reports from South America testified that the natives lived entirely "without religion." A missionary in California learned that "idols, temples, religious worship or ceremonies were unknown to them, and they neither believed in the true and only God, nor adored false deities." Throughout North America, this discovery of the absence of any religion, whether a true or false religion, among indigenous people was repeated by Spanish, Portuguese, Italian, French, and English observers. The explorer Verrazzano reported that the Indians "have no religion." French Jesuits held that the Indians had no religion, "only super-stitions, which we hope by the grace of God to change into true Religion." And the English settler Thomas Morton, who was a relatively sympathetic observer, insisted that "the Natives of New England have no worship nor religion at all." When the exis-tence of a religion could not be categorically denied, as in the case of the Aztecs or Incas, it could be demonized by being explained as the worship of the Devil. For the most part, however, the initial European reports from the Americas reinforced the conclusion that the indigenous people lacked any trace of religion.[18]

As a global enterprise, travel literature, with its penchant for repetition and plagiarism, proliferated the denial of religion all over the world. In the Pacific Islands, Jacques le Maire reported in 1624 that he had found people, who were "rather beasts than men," living without religion. "There is not the least spark of religion or policy to be observed amongst them," he noted; "on the contrary, they are, in every respect, brutal." A century later, the Spanish Father Juan Antonio Contova discovered that the in-habitants of the Caroline Islands in Micronesia "have no notion of religion." Subsequent voyagers found no religion on the Sa-moan, Solomon, or Andaman Islands. Even Tahiti, which would register in the travel literature as an island paradise, sometimes occasioned denials of religion. In Australia, well into the nine-teenth century, observers insisted that aboriginals had "nothing whatever of the character of religion, or of religious observance, to distinguish them from the beasts that perish."[19]

Reports from Africa consistently testified to a similar absence of religion. In antiquity, Graeco-Roman historians and ethnogra-phers might have imagined, as Diodorus Siculus recorded, that Ethiopians were "pioneers in religion." They were acknowledged as the first to perform religious rites in honor of the gods. In the age of European explorations, however, comparative religion had only the most tenuous connection to practices of observation and generalization in antiquity. Although European comparativists might occasionally refer back to Greek or Roman precedents to provide ancient warrant for their present practice, they advanced entirely new strategies of comparison within their expanding ho-rizons of intercultural contact.

On the west coast of Africa, a mercantile trading zone emerged in which Portuguese, Dutch, and English Christians, Arab and African Muslims, African Christians, and African practitioners of local indigenous religions entered into new relations of economic and social exchange. Out of that context, European travelers and traders reported on the local African worship of fetishes, which, in the words of Godefroy Loyer in 1714, was neither a cult, nor a religion, nor rational, because "not one of them knows his religion." The trader William Smith, having described the religion of Muslims and Christians on the coast of Gambia, dismissed the fetishists as people "who trouble themselves about no religion at all." Rather than a discovery of religion, or even of the origin of religion, as fetishism would eventually be regarded in the imperial comparative religion of the end of the nineteenth century, fetishism appeared to the eighteenth-century travelers and traders on the west coast of Africa as another way of designating the absence of religion. This lack of religion was verified by Richard Burton in the lake regions of central Africa, by James Grant on his "walk across Africa," and by René Caillié on his "travels to Timbuctoo." This same absence was repeatedly observed in southern Africa by travelers and settlers, by missionaries and government officials, throughout the nineteenth century. As the Wesleyan missionary William J. Shrewsbury put it, the indigenous people of southern Africa lived "without any religion, true or false."[20]

As a preliminary orientation to a more precise and contextualized investigation of frontier comparative religion in southern Africa, which pays particular attention to the transition from the denial to the discovery of religion, two questions must be put to this global litany of denial. First, what did the absence of religion signify? And second, under what conditions would the presence of religious beliefs and practices, or a religion, or a religious system, be discovered by European comparative religionists? At the risk of proposing extremely broad generalizations, an outline of answers to these two questions can be suggested here, although new aspects of both the questions and the answers recur throughout this book as we explore the specific dynamics of frontier comparative religion in southern Africa.

In trying to explain these denials of religion, we might suppose that they resulted from the briefness of contact, the limited opportunities for observation, the unfamiliarity of strange customs, or the incomprehensibility of local languages that prevented Europeans from discovering the existence of other religions. At the same time, we might wonder whether European observers employed an implicitly Christian definition of religion that prejudiced their findings. While all these factors certainly contributed, they did not constitute the significance of European assertions about the absence of religion. The discovery of that absence developed layers of strategic value in European encounters with others. Although the denial of religion carried a significance that varied according to the specific context in which it was issued, the assertion that people lacked a religion signified, in general terms, an intervention in local frontier conflicts over land, trade, labor, and political autonomy.

During the sixteenth and seventeenth centuries, travel reports frequently coupled the lack of religion with the absence of other defining human features, such as the institution of marriage, a system of law, or any formal political organization. In many cases, the diagnosis of an alien society without religion was delivered bluntly in the assertion that such people were brutes or beasts. As animals by comparison to Europeans, therefore, indigenous people who lacked religion also lacked any recognizable human right or entitlement to the land in which they lived. Even when this implication was not explicitly stated, a theological, philosophical, and legal tradition of European reflection on the status and rights of animals was implied in comparative observations about people who were indistinguishable from "the beasts that perished" precisely because they had no religion.

By the beginning of the seventeenth century, the status of animals had been formalized in European thought. Animals "can have no right of society with us," according to the seventeenth-century English theologian Lancelot Andrewes, "because they want reason." With respect to land, animals had no rights, Andrewes concluded on biblical grounds, because God had given the earth to humans, rather than to sheep or deer. Since they had no human rights, animals could be exterminated, both in the sense of being driven from land settled by humans and in the sense of being killed, because biblical commandments against theft or murder did not apply to nonhumans. Independent of biblical or theological basis, the philosopher Thomas Hobbes concluded that human beings had no moral or legal obligations to animals because "to make covenants with brute beasts is impossible." Animals, therefore, had no human rights to life or land; neither did the indigenous people in the Americas, Australia, Africa, or the Pacific Islands, who were classified as beastly or brutal because they lacked religion. In the first decade of the seventeenth century, this implication in the correlation between animals and indigenous people was made explicit in 1609 by the Reverend

Robert Gray. Most of the earth was "possessed and wrongfully usurped by wild beasts," Gray complained, "or by brutish savages, which by reason of their godless ignorance, and blasphemous idolatry, are worse than those beasts."[21]

During the eighteenth century, however, with the expansion of mercantile trading networks in the Atlantic and eventually the Pacific, the denial of religion assumed a new significance that was perhaps most evident on the west coast of Africa. As *fetishism* emerged as a new term for the absence of religion, many of the earlier stereotypes—brutality, irrationality—persisted, but they were reconfigured in a new context. In trading relations, the absence of religion signified a context in which relations of exchange were arbitrary or capricious, rather than predictable and regulated. African lack of religion, which was demonstrated by their vain, fanciful regard for fetish objects, assumed a specific significance within the intercultural network of mercantile exchange. According to Portuguese, Dutch, and English traders, Africans had no religion to organize relations among human beings or relations between humans and material objects. Without religion, Africans were unable to evaluate objects. They overvalued trifling objects—a bird's feather, a pebble, a bit of rag, or a dog's leg—by treating them as fetishes, but they undervalued trade goods. In the context of trade on the west coast of Africa, therefore, this alleged inability to assess the value of material objects became the defining feature of African ignorance, childishness, capriciousness, and lack of any organized religion.[22]

By the nineteenth century, as the European colonization of Africa was underway, the denial of religion assumed another layer of significance by representing Africa paradoxically as both an empty space and also an obstacle to conquest, colonization, and conversion. Drawing upon earlier representations of indigenous people as animals with no rights to life or land, or as children out of touch with the real world because they could not evaluate objects, European comparativists added a third implication to the denial of religion by asserting that people who had no religion lacked industry. The notion of the "lazy savage" was an immediate correlate of the absence of religion. This stereotype arose, however, to explain the widespread indigenous resistance to being incorporated as labor in an expanding colonial economy. Not only signifying a conflict over land and trade, therefore, the denial of religion was an aspect of colonial efforts to extract a native labor supply. Since they apparently refused to work because they lacked the discipline and industry that came with religion, the natives had to be converted to a "gospel of work" before they could be made into productive laborers. In the meantime, however, indigenous people without religion—who, as a result of that lack, illegitimately occupied the land, frustrated the development of regulated trading relations, and refused to engage themselves as laborers—stood as an obstacle to the advance of the colonial project.

As this brief review can only suggest, the long history of denial in the European comparative religion of maritime and colonial contact produced a multilayered discourse about otherness that identified the absence of religion with images of indigenous people as animals or children, as irrational, capricious, and lazy, as both blankness and barrier to European interests. In the analysis of African religion, as Christopher Miller has observed, European interests and desires produced a discourse that obscured more than it revealed. "The real contours of African religion have little importance to the functioning of this discourse," Miller has observed, "which proceeds through the centuries to project onto Africa a monstrous impossibility whose only existence is on paper."[23] On paper this impossible discourse certainly proliferated. But it also extended, not only as discourse but also as practice, on colonial frontiers in conflicts over land and wealth, over trade and labor, and in the violence of colonial conquest and domination. Knowledge on the frontier configured local control, a local rhetoric of control that was a significant component of colonial administration. In the colonial situation, knowledge about religion and religions, which certainly claimed authoritative status as knowledge about the "real contours" of indigenous religion, was produced through procedures of comparison and generalization. We cannot assume that some "real" religion waited to be discovered, since the very terms *religion* and *religions* were products of the colonial situation. Rather, we can only document and analyze the process of discovery, or, more accurately, the practice of invention, through which knowledge about religion and the religions of the world was fashioned on colonial frontiers.

FROM DENIAL TO DISCOVERY

This concern brings us to the question of the conditions under which Europeans arrived at the "discovery" of indigenous religions. The transition from denial to discovery, I submit, was not the result of prolonged exposure, increased familiarity, acquired linguistic competence, intercultural dialogue, or participant observation. Rather, the discovery of religion arose out of the practice of comparison itself. Making sense out of the strange in terms of the familiar, frontier comparativists resorted to analogies between indigenous customs and known religions. During the eighteenth century, European comparativists generally assumed that there were four religions in the world—Christianity, Judaism, Islam, and Paganism, with the last sometimes divided into ancient, heathen, and diabolical forms.[24] In other words, they presumed a taxonomy in which the *genus* of religion could be divided into four *species*. When comparativists denied the presence of an indigenous religion in some region of the world, therefore, they were not merely making the obvious assertion that the people were not Christian, since European comparativists recognized the existence of a diversity of religions. Europeans had little trouble in expanding the scope of religious diversity to include literate and priestly religions of India, China, and Japan because the identification of textual and ritual traditions in Asia provided convenient analogies with familiar forms of religion. However, the inclusion of Native American, Australian, Tahitian, or African religions within that recognized world of religious diversity depended upon similar comparative procedures of analogy and generalization.

In the discovery of indigenous religions, the two most prominent comparative procedures can be identified as genealogy and morphology. In the first procedure, the beliefs and practices of indigenous people were found to be derived from ancient sources, most often from the religion of ancient Israel as it was familiar to Christian comparativists from their reading of the Old Testament. In North America, for example, comparativists occasionally proposed conjectural histories that traced the Indians back to ancient Israel. Gregorio Garcia reported that they still observed aspects of the biblical law of Moses, while John Eliot insisted that Indians were descendants of ancient Jews. The derivation of American Indian beliefs and customs from ancient Israel was formulated by Thomas Thorowgood in 1650 in his publication *Jews in America, or Probabilities that the Americans are of that Race.*

As a matter of course, frontier comparativists presumed that such a historical derivation from an ancient religion was also a degeneration. During the course of history, the genealogical origin of indigenous religions had become distorted and corrupted. Sometimes, comparativists insisted that the "natives" had en-

tirely forgotten their ancient religion. As Johann Reinhold Forster observed on his voyage around the world, Indians and Africans were so "degenerated, debased, and wretched" that they had
forgotten their "ancient systems." Nevertheless, genealogy did
provide a comparative vocabulary for identifying the religious
roots of indigenous beliefs and practices. As we see in southern
Africa, theories of degeneration were prominent in the repertoire
of frontier comparative religion. Broadening the historical frame
of reference, comparativists proposed genealogies that traced indigenous beliefs and practices not only to ancient Israel but also
to ancient Arabia, Egypt, or China. In the process of construct-
ing genealogies, even if those derivations and degenerations
seemed extremely unlikely, the basic terms for a history of religions that included indigenous religions emerged on colonial
frontiers.[25]

More important to the discovery of indigenous religions was
the practice of morphological comparison that established analogies between the strange and the familiar. Morphology did not
depend upon reconstructing historical links between ancient
and contemporary religions. Rather, morphological comparison
relied exclusively on the observation of formal or functional resemblances. Forms or functions of religion could thereby be
compared without assuming any necessary cultural contact or
historical connection between the people compared. To cite one
prominent example of morphological comparison from North
America, in 1724 the Jesuit father Joseph Lafitau published an
analysis of Iroquois religion, *Moeurs des sauvages Amériquains
comparée aux moeurs des premiers temps*, that must be considered a pioneering text in the comparative study of religion. Drawing analogies between current Iroquois customs and ancient
Israelite and Greek religion, Lafitau advanced a morphological
approach to comparison in which the basic forms of an indigenous religion could be identified with reference to ancient precedents. Through comparison, therefore, the beliefs and practices
of "savages" could be reconfigured as religion. At the same time,
however, this procedure of morphological comparison reconstitu-
ted the religions of ancient Israel and Greece, reproducing them
through comparison as forms of "savage" religion. "I confess that,
if the ancient authors have given me information on which to
base happy conjectures about the Indians," Lafitau noted, "the
customs of the Indians have given me information on the basis of
which I can understand more easily and explain more readily

many things in the ancient authors."[26] On southern African frontiers, morphological comparison was practiced as a technique for
making strange beliefs and practices comprehensible by analogy
with some more familiar religion. As Lafitau suggested, however,
the familiar religions of ancient Israel, Greece, and Rome, of Judaism, Islam, and even forms of Christianity, were made strange by
their juxtaposition with "savage" religion. In the process of discovering indigenous religions, therefore, frontier comparativists
effectively reinvented all the religions of the world.

These comparative procedures—taxonomy, genealogy, morphology—were necessary for the discovery of indigenous religions. In
southern Africa, however, they were not sufficient. Although
these techniques of comparison were certainly practiced, they
did not necessarily result in the discovery of indigenous religions
or religious systems. That discovery was long delayed. By the
middle of the eighteenth century, religious diversity in Africa had
been recognized. The eighteenth-century *philosophe* Diderot
observed in the *Encyclopédie* that there were Christians in Egypt
and Abyssinia, Muslims in North and East Africa, and many
places throughout Africa where local forms of idolatry were practiced. In the southern African territory of "Cafreria," however,
"there are people who have no idea of religion and whose entire
view is limited to present life, with no inkling of a future state."
A century later, John Lubbock assumed that it was still the
case that indigenous southern Africans had "no appearance of any
religious worship whatever." Many parts of the world produced
indigenous terms that became part of the international vocabulary of comparative religion, terms such as *fetish* from West
Africa, *totem* from North America, or *mana* from Melanesia.
Southern Africa produced no such indigenous terms for the
study of religion. Rather, the region's distinction was to mark
an absence of religion in the world long after religion had been
discovered in West Africa, North America, and the Pacific
Islands.[27]

As I argue, the discovery of an indigenous religious system on
southern African frontiers depended upon colonial conquest and
domination. Once contained under colonial control, an indigenous population was found to have its own religious system. Ironically, however, the religion discovered was the same as the religion denied. A definitional shift occurred in the establishment
of colonial control. Evidence that had been used to deny the existence of any religion among southern Africans, such as their sup-

posed ignorance, fear, and superstitious regard for objects and the
dead, became the defining features that constituted European
representations of indigenous southern African religion. So what
changed? In identifying the conditions under which Europeans in
southern Africa discovered indigenous religious systems, I high-
light the historical dynamics of conquest and domination on
colonial frontiers. The discovery of a religious system depended
upon the establishment of local control. This historical correlation can be stated in stark terms: Before coming under colonial
subjugation, Africans had no religion. After local control was
established, however, they were found to have had a religious
system after all. Although this formula sounds like a causal explanation, I explore its significance as a historical correlation by
recovering the configuration of forces and discourses that produced discoveries of religion in southern Africa. The theory of the
discovery of religion that I propose, therefore, is not intended as
a simple deterministic explanation. The discovery or invention of
religion did not result solely from its functional utility to colonialism; nor did indigenous efforts to recast their ways of life as
religion only serve the cause of either accommodation or resistance to colonialism. Although it depended upon both comparison and containment, the discovery of religion in frontier comparative religion was "the product of an historically layered
colonial encounter."[28] The complex dynamics of that intercultural encounter can only be understood by returning to the
frontier.

FRONTIERS

This book recovers the history of the discovery of religion on four
frontiers: the western Cape, the eastern Cape, the southeastern
frontier of Natal and Zulu territory, and the northern frontiers of
what became the Orange Free State and the Transvaal. Following
recent comparative research, I define a frontier as a zone of contact, rather than a line, a border, or a boundary. By this definition,
a frontier is a region of intercultural relations between intrusive
and indigenous people. Those cultural relations, however, are also
power relations. A frontier zone opens with the contact between
two or more previously distinct societies and remains open as
long as power relations are unstable and contested, with no one
group or coalition able to establish dominance. A frontier zone

closes when a single political authority succeeds in establishing its hegemony over the area.[29]

In an open frontier zone, contact can produce conflict, but it can also occasion new forms of cooperation and exchange. In the study of southern African frontiers, attention to conflict has been most prominent. Research has documented the often violent competition over land, livestock, and labor in frontier situations. More recently, historians have also tried to identify areas of cooperative innovation in frontier social and economic relations. For our interests, however, the open frontier can be reexplored not only as a zone of conflict and cooperation but also as a contested arena for the production of knowledge about religion and religions. As the psychologist I. D. MacCrone suggested, religion, rather than race or ethnicity, provided the basic vocabulary of difference in the intercultural human relations of the frontier.[30] The practices of comparative religion in frontier situations tracked the presence or absence of religion, and the similarities and differences among religions, within an open, contested zone of intercultural contact.

On southern African frontiers, as historian Martin Legassick noted, "Enemies and friends were not divided into rigid, static categories." Nevertheless, in general terms, conflict between European intruders and indigenous people defined the frontier situation. Neither intruders nor indigenes, colonizers nor colonized, formed a unified front. European intruders were divided by national origin or allegiance, whether British, Dutch, French, German, or Portuguese; they were visitors and settlers, missionaries and administrators, herders, farmers, and workers. They were divided by gender, class, and social interests. Likewise, indigenous people were divided by a variety of political allegiances, by a gendered division of labor, by social class, and by varying degrees of interaction with an emerging market economy and expanding colonial administration. In spite of all this human complexity, however, observers of southern Africa sought clarity in simplicity. By the early nineteenth century, a British visitor could simplify intercultural relations in southern Africa as "three distinct exhibitions of hatred—first, the Dutch hate the English; next the Dutch and English hate the natives; and lastly, the natives hate the Dutch and English." In part, the practice of comparative religion on southern African frontiers was an effort to gain some understanding of an open and fluid intercultural zone through a similar process of simplification.[31]

The conceptual organization of human diversity into rigid,

static categories was one strategy for simplifying, and thereby achieving some cognitive control over, the bewildering complexity of a frontier zone. On each frontier, the production of knowledge about religion and religions provided colonial terms for comprehending particular groups of people as if, in the words of Eric Wolf, they were "internally homogeneous and externally distinctive and bounded objects."[32] Objectified, they could be not only comprehended but also contained within definite boundaries. In the process of identifying the languages and superstitions, the manners and customs, of indigenous people on southern African frontiers, boundaries were drawn around human groupings that came to be designated as "Hottentots" and "Bushmen," "Kafirs" and "Zulus," "Basutos" and "Bechuanas."

Since the tribal, ethnic, or national identities of indigenous people were produced in and through the process of establishing those colonial boundaries, we cannot employ the standard terminology that emerged from the nineteenth century without caution, especially since it was reified and employed to enforce the apartheid system of ethnic separation. In this book, I have retained the designations that appear in the historical record. However, we must not forget the arbitrary and invented nature of these terms. Certainly, some of the terms are antiquated; some are extremely offensive when deployed as racist epithets. All of these terms for African groupings, however, are deeply embedded in the history of comparative religion in southern Africa. Nevertheless, they should all be read as if they appear in quotation marks. Since they were produced as colonial constructions, we cannot suppose that these terms, whether "Bushmen," "Hottentots," "Kafirs," "Zulus," "Basutos," "Bechuanas," or "Bantus," refer in any unproblematic way to real or natural groupings of people who lived in the region prior to contact with Europeans. Although we can certainly assume that there were real indigenous people on the frontiers, the terms by which they were represented were thoroughly European inventions. Likewise, although they had beliefs and practices that by any modern definition were religious, their religions or religious systems were also European inventions.

As noted, we explore these processes of designation and representation, of discovery and invention, within the context of the historical dynamics of four southern African frontiers. In the Cape, the indigenous people who, from the time of the early European voyages, were called Hottentots, lived within an economic, social, and ritual order that was based on cattle. Known by modern scholarship as Khoi or Khoikhoi, meaning "humans," or "humans of humans," these pastoralists have been distinguished from the indigenous people known as Bushmen, who lived by hunting and gathering. Although modern scholars have designated these hunters and gatherers as San, that term originated as a derogatory epithet or class distinction applied to them by Khoikhoi. Nevertheless, the herders and the hunters have often been designated collectively by the term Khoisan.

These indigenous people were occupying the Cape region when the Dutch East India Company established its refreshment station at the Cape of Good Hope in 1652. Frontier relations fluctuated with the expansion of the colony, as competition and conflict intensified over the resources of land, livestock, and, eventually, labor. For our purpose, the frontier zone of the Cape opened with the earliest contacts by European navigators, beginning with Bartolemeu Dias in 1488 and increasing in frequency and regularity during the seventeenth century. As a constant feature of travelers' reports, the Hottentots of the Cape were characterized as brutes without religion.

I intend to show, however, that the discovery of Hottentot religion can be correlated with the closing, reopening, and final closure of the frontier zone in the Cape. In anticipation of a more detailed development, I can only suggest the broad outline of that correlation here. After the establishment of the Dutch station in 1652, the Hottentots who were engaged in trading with the company, supplying much of its meat and produce, were suddenly discovered to have a religion, one based on the worship of the moon. In the 1680s, however, when the boundaries of the initial Dutch settlement began to expand, the Hottentots on a new, contested frontier were once again characterized as lacking any trace of religion. By the beginning of the 1700s, when their resistance had largely been contained and their population had been drastically diminished by disease, the Hottentots were again credited with a religion. In fact, they were even found to have a coherent, integrated religious system. However, when they again mounted resistance in the 1770s, as the Cape settlers embarked upon a campaign of genocidal warfare against them, the Hottentots were consistently described, by all reports, as lacking religion. This absence of religion continued to be noted in accounts of the Hottentots until the beginning of the nineteenth century, when their scattered remnants, many of whom had taken refuge at mission stations, were described as having a religion—Christianity.

In the eastern Cape region, Xhosa-speaking people, who were organized into many different political groupings but who were designated in colonial discourse by the single label *Kafirs*, also pursued a pastoral lifestyle. Although they had maintained intercultural relations and exchanges with the Khoikhoi, Xhosa contact with the Cape Colony began and intensified during a period of transition in European political control. The British, having seized the Cape as a maneuver of war against France, established British administration of the region in 1795, briefly relinquished control to the Batavian Republic between 1803 and 1806, and then restored and extended their power throughout the nineteenth century. As the eastern Cape frontier opened, therefore, the Xhosa had to contend, not only with the hunters, traders, farmers, and settlers of Dutch, German, or French extraction but also with British colonists who were committed to expanding the scope of colonial settlement and administration.

Christian missionaries also advanced into this frontier zone, representing Protestant organizations—such as the London Missionary Society, the Wesleyan Methodist Missionary Society, and the Glasgow Missionary Society—that were engaged in the work of extending Christian civilization. Largely drawn from the artisan, manufacturing, or skilled laboring classes in England, these British missionaries became experts in the field of comparative religion on every southern African frontier. In the eastern Cape during the first half of the nineteenth century, missionaries consistently reported that Xhosa-speaking people had no religion whatsoever. They were echoed in this assessment by travelers, settlers, and magistrates in the region. While the frontier remained an open zone, and a region of almost constant colonial warfare, every report about the Xhosa certified this absence of religion. After the destruction of their political independence in 1857, however, the Xhosa were finally found to have an indigenous religion. As they were incorporated into the magisterial system, or "village system," of the British colonial administration, the Xhosa of the eastern Cape were credited with having a religious system.

In the area of southeast Africa that came to be known as Natal and Zululand, Zulu-speaking people, with a language and lifestyle that had much in common with the Xhosa, were also described as lacking a religion in the earliest reports of travelers and missionaries in the 1820s and 1830s. Annexed by Britain in 1843 and placed under the colonial administration of the "location system" designed by Theophilus Shepstone, the Zulu were found to have an indigenous religious system at a slightly earlier date than the Xhosa. Under colonial control, the religious system of the Zulu was inventoried and analyzed by three European immigrants who arrived in 1855, the biblical scholar J. W. Colenso, the philologist W. H. I. Bleek, and the folklorist Henry Callaway. Although they disagreed with each other on a number of points, these scholars agreed that the Zulu had an indigenous religion. Their research findings on the Zulu religious system became well known in Europe, contributing to the tendency of British academics to regard the Zulu as uniquely representative of the nature of African or "savage" religion in general.

On the northern frontiers, nineteenth-century colonial discourse designated Sotho-Tswana-speaking people by a variety of terms, but most often as Basutos and Bechuanas. Whether the Sotho polity of Chief Moshoeshoe, or the Tswana polities of the Tlhaping, Tlharo, and Rolong between the Vaal and Molopo Rivers, or the Pedi polity, all Sotho-Tswana people lived in a frontier zone that opened with the entry of the Dutch-speaking trekkers and settlers who established their independent republics in the 1850s. Leaving the Cape in the 1830s to escape British rule, these Voortrekkers, the ancestors of modern Afrikaners, established fluid alliances and engaged in recurring warfare with African polities in the region. Their republics in the Orange Free State and Transvaal were unstable and contested, resisted not only by Africans but also by the British administration in the Cape. The discovery of diamonds in 1867 and gold on the Witwatersrand in 1886 raised the stakes in the contest. During the last three decades of the nineteenth century, the British and the Boers, but also the Germans and the Portuguese, engaged in a struggle for colonial domination in the region. The period between 1890 and 1895, which brought to a culmination this European colonial scramble for southern Africa, marked the closing of the last frontier. From that point, European colonial control, under British hegemony, extended throughout the entire region of southern Africa.

As on other southern African frontiers, the indigenous people on northern frontiers were described by travelers, missionaries, and colonial administrators as lacking religion when the frontier zone opened. However, as the northern frontier remained a contested zone of conflict throughout the nineteenth century, the Sotho-Tswana were not credited with having a religion until the 1890s. Their political independence shattered, Africans in the region were by that point all placed under the administrative con-

trol of the "reserve system." Only then were they found to have
an indigenous religious system, as the Reverend John Mackenzie,
who had campaigned for years to bring the Bechuanas under direct imperial rule, finally used the term *religion*, for the first time
in 1899 to refer to the beliefs and practices of the Sotho-Tswana.
At the turn of the century, however, when white supremacy
seemed firmly established throughout southern Africa, and all
Africans in the region had in principle, if not in practice, been
placed under either an urban "location system" or a rural "reserve
system," comparative religionists on the closed frontier made a
remarkable discovery. They found that all Africans in southern
Africa, simply by virtue of birth, actually had a religion, a common, generic religious system that could be identified as Bantu
religion. On the closed frontier, therefore, African people, who
supposedly lacked any religion at the beginning of the nineteenth
century, all were credited with having the same religious system
at the century's end.

On every southern African frontier, an open zone of intercultural contact closed with the establishment of some form of European colonial hegemony. As I suggest, these acts of closure were
matters of both power and knowledge. Colonial containment established boundaries that both delimited and defined African
populations in frontier comparative religion. From the drawing of
boundaries, knowledge followed. As historian Fernand Braudel
has proposed, "The question of boundaries is the first to be encountered; from it all others flow. To draw a boundary around anything is to define, analyse and reconstruct it."[33] In frontier comparative religion, the discovery that Africans had a religion and
had beliefs and practices that could be defined, analyzed, and
reconstructed as a religious system was made precisely in the
context of establishing colonial borders around Africans. When a
frontier closed, as indigenous resistance was broken or contained,
and European hegemony was more or less established, a religion,
or a religious system, was discovered that could be defined and
inventoried.

COMPARISONS

This correlation between the discovery of religion and the closure
of a colonial frontier is by no means the entire story of frontier
comparative religion in southern Africa. If the discovery of a reli-

gion depended upon conquest and containment, the analysis of its nature or character emerged out of localized practices of comparison and generalization. Beginning with denial, frontier comparative religion proceeded to invent religious systems for various people—Hottentots, Kafirs, Zulus, and Bechuanas. In order to define unfamiliar African religions, frontier theorists resorted to comparisons with more familiar religions of Christianity, Judaism, Islam, Hinduism, and Buddhism, as well as with the ancient religions of Israel, Egypt, Arabia, Greece, Rome, and Europe. In the process of inventing specific African religious systems, frontier comparative religion also produced and reproduced knowledge about all the religions of the world.

In this comparative enterprise, a new taxonomy of world religions was forged on the frontier. For the missionaries in particular, the search for the "unknown God" in Africa provided a charter for comparative religion. Defining the genus of religion in terms of worship, they found three species of religion in the world—the God worship of Christianity, Judaism, and Islam; the object worship of Pagans, whether it assumed the form of the idol worship of Asia or the fetish worship of West Africa; and the ancestor worship of southern Africa, a species of religion defined by contrast with the other two. Without any worship of a Supreme Being, and without any idols or fetishes, indigenous religions in southern Africa were defined as a unique type of religion devoted to the worship of deceased ancestors. After the closure of frontiers, however, European comparativists eventually found indigenous evidence of the "unknown God." J. W. Colenso found it among the Zulu in the 1850s, Henry Callaway among the Xhosa in the 1870s, and D. F. Ellenberger among the Sotho-Tswana at the beginning of the twentieth century. Once they were conquered and dispossessed, therefore, African people were discovered to have a God.

By the beginning of the twentieth century, as I have indicated, all Africans in southern Africa were found to have the same generic Bantu religion. On contested frontiers, however, differences among the beliefs and practices of various African political groupings were clarified by the invention of imaginary genealogies. Comparativists traced southern Africans back to cultural centers in the ancient Near East. Khoikhoi had migrated from China via Egypt; the Xhosa had been Arabs; the Zulu had been Jews; and the Sotho-Tswana had been ancient Egyptians. In this fanciful genealogy of religions, frontier comparative religion was used to distinguish among different African peoples, but also to suggest that they did not really belong in southern Africa because their original homelands were in the distant, ancient Near East.

In addition to taxonomy and genealogy, frontier comparative religion developed new approaches to the morphology of religion. In representing African superstition or religion, basic elements of a European Protestant polemic against Roman Catholics, which attacked pagano-papism as ignorance, fear, magic, the deification of objects, and the deification of the dead, were transposed onto indigenous people in southern Africa. These forms defined the basic structure of African religions. On closed frontiers, when European comparativists discovered that Africans had religious systems, they identified recognizable structures and functions that could be compared with other religions. Accordingly, methods of structural and functional analysis were forged on the frontier. During the second half of the nineteenth century in Europe, this discovery of integrated, coherent religious systems was almost entirely ignored, as comparative religionists in London, Amsterdam, Paris, or Berlin were preoccupied with arranging diverse religious elements into an evolutionary sequence from primitive to civilized. On the frontier, however, the discovery of religious systems was essential to colonial management and control of African populations. Knowledge about indigenous religious systems was useful knowledge, useful for missionary intervention and conversion but also for efficient colonial administration. The discovery and analysis of religious systems, therefore, belonged, not to the emerging academic discipline of comparative religion in Europe, but to frontier comparative religion.

As already noted, comparativists in European metropolitan centers of theory production appropriated southern African evidence in building a science of religion. While frontier comparative religion produced knowledge about religion and religions to master specific local regions, an imperial comparative religion emerged in Europe that produced global knowledge. Imperial comparative religion reinforced power relations over colonized peripheries, but also over subclassed people at home. From the metropole, southern African evidence was useful in legitimating a domain of power that was global in scope but also local in its effects in Europe. Back in southern Africa, however, frontier and imperial theories of comparative religion reemerged during the twentieth century with a vengeance in apartheid to reinforce the denial, subclassification, and exclusion of Africans. Apartheid comparative religion assumed a dual mandate: It reified "tribal" differences among Africans. But it also distilled and abstracted a "primitive mentality" that supposedly unified all Africans in southern Africa. Like frontier comparative religion it contained, but like imperial comparative religion it dismissed, the people under its domain of knowledge and power.

What would a postapartheid comparative religion look like? Perhaps it would entail the recovery of indigenous voices that were suppressed in frontier, imperial, and apartheid comparative religion. However, the traces left in the historical record by African comparativists are also entangled in frontier situations and conflicts. No pure, precontact position can be recovered for our return. Instead, the ground for a postapartheid comparative religion might be cleared, not by finding new ways to define religion and compare religions, but by journeying back through the frontiers on which these categories were asserted, constituted, and contested. This book initiates a postapartheid comparative religion that does not compare religions. It compares comparisons.

2

INVENTING RELIGION

A EUROPEAN IMMIGRANT of Greek extraction by the name of Stephanos came from Poland at the end of the 1700s and settled among a Hottentot (Khoikhoi) community just beyond the northern frontier of the Cape Colony. There he built a temple by a grove of mimosa trees. He set up an altar for animal sacrifices. He convinced the local people to present the best of their cattle and sheep as offerings. Special sacrifices for protection were performed during thunderstorms or floods. Burning part of the sacrificial victims, Stephanos kept the rest of the offerings for himself. He was attended by young women at the temple, and his power and influence over this community grew. Every morning the people witnessed the supernatural source of his power as they watched Stephanos go out alone to climb a nearby mountain. Looking up, they beheld Stephanos standing on the summit, enveloped in clouds of smoke, receiving, as he would explain, special instructions from heaven. Through these ritual sacrifices and divine revelations, as the British traveler John Barrow recounted, Stephanos the Pole became the "high priest of his own constituted religion."[1]

Stephanos had already pursued a remarkable career in the Cape before founding his religion. He initially arrived as a mercenary. After completing the term of service, Stephanos found employment as a shop assistant in Cape Town. There he learned to forge the paper currency of the colony. When the forgery was discovered, Stephanos was arrested, convicted, and sentenced to death. However, he escaped from prison by using a rusty nail to break through its teakwood wall, eating the sawdust and replacing it with bread at night. Heading north, Stephanos sought refuge at the new mission station of the London Missionary Society agent Johannes Jacobus Kicherer. Fearing that Stephanos meant to kill him, the missionary banished the Pole from his station but showed Christian kindness by providing him with a Bible, meat, and gunpowder for his journey. As Kicherer later complained, however, he never should have given Stephanos a Bible because he read it only as a manual for forging a false religion that turned out to be more popular than the mission.

The traveler John Barrow was even more blunt in his assessment of Stephanos the Pole, maintaining that his practices were not religious at all. They were "religious mockeries"—false shows of religion designed to deceive and despoil the Hottentots. The sacrifices fed his greed, and the young women served his lust, and Stephanos faked his daily Mount Sinai revelations by surrounding himself in the smoke of burning dry grass that he set alight with gunpowder. Even the purpose of this daily ascension was suspect. It was not for heavenly inspiration, Barrow revealed, but to enable Stephanos to survey the plains to the south to see if any law-enforcement agents from the Cape Colony were coming to get him. At the urging of outraged Christian missionaries, officers of the colony did set out to capture Stephanos. Abandoning his temple and his following, Stephanos fled to the north, where he was recognized and taken prisoner by a Dutch-speaking farmer. Pretending to surrender, Stephanos killed his captor at the first opportunity and headed off to the lower Orange River, where he joined Afrikaner, the notorious leader of armed, cattle-raiding horsemen known as Griqua. Although local settlements suffered under the depredations of the "two robbers," nothing more was heard of the religion of Stephanos the Pole.[2]

In the same region, at roughly the same time, a story was told about another European immigrant. The Swedish naturalist Anders Sparrman, on a tour of the Cape in 1775, learned that Khoikhoi people held vague recollections of a German immigrant who had been banished from the country by the Cape government. This German had also introduced a new religion. But he had been banished for illegally establishing himself as a Hottentot chief. According to the popular account, the German had exercised absolute political control over the local people. He had exploited their labor. He had enriched himself not only through their hard work but also through the wealth in cattle that he had taken from them. It was widely supposed that the German was guilty of the charges that had led to his expulsion, because from that time it had been illegal for Europeans to acquire Hottentot cattle. Sparrman had no reason to doubt this story until he returned home to Europe and learned that the German in question had been the Moravian missionary George Schmidt, who had established his station between 1737 and 1744 at Genadendal in the Cape. Sparrman realized that rather than being chief and high priest of a new religion, Schmidt had been a pioneer of European Christian missions in southern Africa. Schmidt had been largely unsuccessful in his attempts to convert the Khoikhoi during his stay in the Cape. Adding to his problems, the company and ministers of the Dutch Reformed Church insisted that Schmidt lacked the proper authority to perform baptisms. They forced him to leave Africa and take his case to Amsterdam. Unsuccessful in his appeals, Schmidt never returned. Only much later, after Khoikhoi had been converted to Christianity on a large scale, would George Schmidt be remembered as the heroic forerunner of an advancing Christian mission.[3]

These two eighteenth-century European immigrants—Stephanos the Pole, George the German—were innovators in the field of religion in southern Africa. From a certain European perspective, one was a fake, the other genuine. By juxtaposing their stories, however, the question of authenticity can be refocused. As anthropologist Rodney Needham has suggested, even a fake religion, like the fabricated account of the religion of Formosa widely advertised in London at the beginning of the eighteenth century by the literary confidence man George Psalmanaazaar, has to look like religion in order to be a good fake. In the case of Stephanos the Pole, as Barrow noted, his "new and motley religion" successfully wove together recognizable elements of religion. Barrow identified aspects of religion that were familiar to him from accounts of the beliefs and practices of ancient Israel, Greece, and Rome. Another contemporary commentator, William Somerville, found that the religion of Stephanos was "composed of the Jewish, Mahomedan—and Roman Catholic." The missionary Kicherer compared Stephanos's new religion to Islam, noting that he was "apprehensive that his doctrine, like that of Mahomet, might widely diffuse its baneful influences among the neighbouring heathen." While these European commentators compared the religion of Stephanos to familiar forms of religion, the Khoikhoi must also have found recognizable religious beliefs and practices. The local Khoikhoi people who participated must have recognized echoes of their own indigenous religion—in the sacrifices, in the promise of protection from natural disaster, and even in the ecstatic converse with the heavens—that made the new religion of Stephanos the Pole a viable construction. If not for the intervention of the missionaries and the Cape government, Barrow observed, this new religion, "partly Hebrew and partly Greek," might have been established among the Khoikhoi, and the memory of Stephanos, as its *Pater Deorum*, would have been revered by subsequent generations. If that had happened, Barrow wondered, "what learned speculations on the origin of this society might not the future discovery of so heterogeneous a mixture of religions have given rise?"[4]

Although Barrow left this question rhetorical, its answer could have been suggested by the actual history of "learned speculations" about indigenous Khoikhoi religion that had been advanced during the seventeenth and eighteenth centuries by European travelers and scholarly tourists. Once they had recognized the existence of a Khoikhoi religion, a recognition long delayed, and occasionally contested, European commentators drew upon familiar analogies to describe the religion of the Hottentots. If, as it was widely assumed in Europe during the period, there were four religions in the world—Christian, Jewish, Muslim, and Pagan—then the religion of the Hottentots must have been some form of barbaric paganism. Its precise description and analysis, however, set new challenges and established new agendas for the practice of comparative religion in Europe and in southern Africa.

John Barrow drew a final moral from the story of Stephanos the Pole. "Such is the danger of being led astray, to which the unthinking multitude of all nations is exposed," Barrow concluded, "if once they foresake the customs and opinions of their forefathers, and commit themselves to the impostures of artful and designing men." This moral, however, contained an unintended irony that could be turned against the work of the Christian missions. Obviously, the missions were designed to convince people to abandon the customs and opinions of their ancestors. Certainly, Barrow did not think that Christian missionaries were necessarily artful and designing impostures. Neither did Anders Sparrman. However, the government and established church at the Cape did perceive the missionary George Schmidt as a fake to the extent that he lacked the proper authority to perform authentic Christian baptisms. Furthermore, representatives of the Cape establishment were adamant that Schmidt was a fraud. As one reported, "He was definitely a hypocrite and a sham; sometimes climbing on the low roof of the house of Captain Rhenius, with whom he lived for a while after his arrival; there he knelt so that all the inhabitants of the Castle could see him, and pretended to pray." Apparently, there were also Khoikhoi in the 1770s who remembered the German missionary as an artful and designing fraud. From their perspective, the mission was not "religion." Rather, the mission represented the arbitrary exercise of political power, exploitation of labor, and extraction of wealth. Ironically, therefore, the fakery of Stephanos looked like religion; the Christian mission of George Schmidt did not.[5]

This particular way of recollecting the mission suggests that comparative religion was practiced on both sides of the line that divided European intruders and "others" in southern Africa. European comparativists made their observations and drew their conclusions. They distinguished between authentic religion and artificial fraud or ignorant deception. They made sense out of the strange by drawing upon a cultural repertoire of familiar images and forms of religion. For their part, however, indigenous people also assessed the religious interchanges and innovations of the frontier zone. They also reflected on the play of difference in intercultural contact by juxtaposing the familiar and the strange. As a result, the missionary might appear strange, the forger familiar. This contest of comparison continued on the open frontier. However, the perspectives of indigenous comparativists are difficult to recover, as they are buried under the weight of testimony from travelers, missionaries, settlers, and administrators of colonial governments. Even the alternative perspective of the forger, Stephanos the Pole, was suppressed by force. In the historical record, indigenous Khoikhoi voices were silenced, while Europeans were busy inventing their religion.

CALLERS AT THE CAPE

The first accounts of Hottentot religion were issued in the context of European explorations of new worlds. Reports about the Cape, like similar reports from the Americas, circumscribed the familiar, centered world of Europe with a strange periphery. Until the 1650s, when the Dutch established a refreshment station at the Cape, every report about the indigenous inhabitants of the Cape denied the existence of any Hottentot religion. After the establishment of the Dutch settlement in 1652, however, the Khoikhoi gained the recognition that they had a religion. Most reports specified that religion as moon worship. Within the se-

cured boundaries of the Dutch station, therefore, European observers found that the indigenous people had a kind of religion.

This recognition of a Hottentot religion continued until the
1680s, when the Cape Colony expanded beyond its initial borders.
Historians have identified the opening of three frontier zones in
this expansion of the Dutch settlement: the frontiers represented
by colonial officials and traders, the settlements established by
Dutch, German, and French farmers, and the appropriation of
grazing lands by Dutch cattle herders. The colony's initial frontier
contact with the Khoikhoi through trade continued, but it receded in importance before the advance of the farming and cattle-
herding frontiers that intensified conflict over land and livestock.
In 1679 the new governor, Simon van der Stel, arrived with specific instructions for enlarging the Dutch settlement in the Cape.
He issued land grants to Dutch farmers and herders in Stellenbosch in 1679 and in the Drakenstein in 1687. The area around
the Hottentot's Holland range was ceded for European settlement.
In 1688 the influx of Huguenot settlers gave further impetus to
the advancing farming and cattle-herding frontiers. By the 1680s,
therefore, the Cape had become an expanding frontier zone. As
the frontiers moved out, and local resistance increased, reports
about the religion of the Hottentots returned to their earlier
denial, even dismissing the religious character of any Hottentot
observances of the moon. During this period, according to almost
all accounts, the Khoikhoi simply had no religion.[6]

By 1700, however, the Cape region had been brought under
Dutch control. Most Cape Khoikhoi had become dependent for
their lives upon the Colony. In this new context, reports about
the religion of the Hottentots observed that although they lacked
"revealed" religion, they nevertheless held a "natural" religion.
In 1713 a small pox epidemic, coupled with an outbreak of cattle
disease, further plagued the Khoikhoi. Destroyed and dominated,
the indigenous people of the Cape were once again credited by
European observers with having a religion. Beginning with the
earliest explorers, therefore, the Cape was a frontier zone for the
denial and discovery of the indigenous religion of the Hottentots.

No Religion (1610–1654)

The earliest reports about the religion of the people of the Cape
took the form of categorical denial. According to these accounts,
Hottentots had no religion. As Pyrard de Laval reported in 1610,

they "live without law or religion, like animals." In their wild
state, they ate human flesh, raw meat, and the unwashed guts
and intestines of animals that only dogs would eat. Like animals,
Hottentots lacked any sign of human intellectual capacity. "The
people who live along this coast," Pyrard de Laval concluded, "are
very brutish and savage, as stupid as can be and without intelligence." Callers at the Cape almost endlessly repeated these judgments. The indigenous people were represented by remarkable
absences. Although by 1612 they were no longer alleged to be
cannibals, the Hottentots still lacked basic human features. They
were "bruitt and savadg, without Religion, without languag, without Lawes or gouernment, without manners or humanittie." Although they were said to lack any human institutions, the people
of the Cape were most often distinguished by the absence of religion. In 1612 they had "little or no Religion." In 1614 they were
"most miserable, destitute of Religion in any kind." In 1615 it
was asserted that they "know noe kind of god or religion." In 1620
a traveler was "unable to discover in them any religion." In 1629
it was observed that "no laws, policies, religions or ordinances
can be discerned to exist among them." In 1634 a traveler reported
that they were "without any Religion, Lawe, Arte or Civility that
we could see." And in 1644 they had "hideous Countenance,
scarce any use of Reason, and less of Religion."[7]

The cumulative effect of these categorical denials during the
first half of the seventeenth century was overwhelming, representing the unanimous judgment of all European observers,
whether Protestant or Roman Catholic, whether English, Dutch,
German, French, or Portuguese. Even the testimony of an indigenous Khoikhoi, Coree, who was taken to England in 1613, only
to reject and abandon European ways upon his return to Saldanha
Bay in the Cape, was enlisted in this chorus of denial. "I asked
Coree," recalled the chaplain of the fleet, Edward Terry, "who was
their God?" Lifting up his hands, Coree reportedly responded,
"England God, great God, Souldania no God." Coree did not bring
"England God" back from his stay overseas. But he did return
with a new appreciation of the value of trade goods that altered
the European trading advantage in the Cape. For all his apparent
resistance to European dominance, however, Coree was simply
incorporated as an indigenous informant who could corroborate
the Hottentot lack of religion.[8]

Without God or religion, the indigenous inhabitants of the
Cape appeared in all these accounts as less than fully human be-

ings. The denial of Hottentot religion was often coupled with assertions that they lacked a recognizable human language. Speaking a language laced with clicks unfamiliar to European ears, the
people of the Cape were frequently described as producing animal
sounds rather than human speech. John Milward reported in 1614
that "their speech [is] a chattering rather than language." Edward
Terry, who recorded his conversation with Coree, claimed that
"their speech it seemed to us inarticulate noise, rather than language, like the clucking of hens, or gabbling of turkeys." Thomas
Herbert stated in 1627 that their language "is rather apishly than
articulately sounded." Chattering, gabbling, and clucking, rather
than speaking a human language, the Hottentots were represented by such reports in bestial terms, signifying an "uncivilized" rudeness perhaps most abruptly formulated by Jean-
Baptiste Tavernier, who observed in 1649 that "when they speak
they fart with their tongues in their mouths." If they lacked a
human language, how could Hottentots articulate a religion of
any kind? Accordingly, many reports issued a sweeping, generic
denial of Hottentot religion that was consistent with their supposed lack of other basic human characteristics.[9]

Occasionally, however, the denial of Hottentot religion was formulated in more specific terms as an absence of Christian doctrines and practices. Lack of a belief in God, for example, began
to be specified as a particular Christian absence in their lives. The
assertion that "they know nothing of God or the Devil" added a
second aspect of Christian absence to the denial of any religion
among the Hottentots. An even more specific catalog of absences,
however, was provided in the 1630s by Thomas Herbert, who observed that, in addition to no God, they had "no spark of Devotion, no symptome of Heaven or Hell, no place set apart for Worship, no Sabbath for rest." In a revised edition, Herbert added that
they had "no shame, no truth, no ceremony in births, or burials."
In compiling such an inventory of absences, the observer not only
denied a Hottentot religion. He also reproduced a certain kind of
Christian construction of religion, reinforcing its precise speci-
fications against the blank backdrop of southern Africa. In this
respect, the discovery of "no religion" among the Hottentots became an occasion for the reproduction and reinforcement of a certain kind of Christianity.[10]

A nascent Christian comparative religion, however, did not
only appear in the tracking of absences. It also surfaced in two
other forms—genealogy and morphology—that would have a

long history in struggles to understand religion in southern Africa. On the one hand, the Hottentots could be located in terms of a biblical chronology as descendants of Noah and, more specifically, as cursed offspring of Ham. "The Natives being propagated from Cham," Thomas Herbert insisted, "both in their Visages and Natures seem to inherit his malediction." Attempts to track the historical origins, migrations, and diffusion of the indigenous people of southern Africa, even when those efforts abandoned a specifically biblical frame of reference, persisted as a dominant approach to comparative religion in southern Africa. On the other hand, but often simultaneously, this tracing of historical origins was combined with efforts to make sense out of indigenous practices in terms of biblical analogy. In 1612, for example, the visitor Patrick Copland noticed signs of scarification on people's faces, perhaps resulting from ritual initiation. Having only a biblical frame of reference to rely upon, he concluded that "they cut their skinnes like Baals priests." Even this comparative observation, however, recognizing the possibility of a "religious" motive, even though, in biblical terms, it was drawn from a false religion, was extremely rare during the first half of the seventeenth century. Rather than developing theories of biblical history or morphology, most observers were content to issue categorical denials of the existence of any religion at all among the Hottentots of the Cape of Good Hope.[11]

As a subtext to all these denials, European commentators concluded that people so depraved and bestial as to lack religion had no right to possess such a land and agreed, in principle, as one journal recorded in 1612, that it was "a greatt pittie that such creattures as they bee should injoy so sweett a counttrey." In Europe, the influential cosmographer Peter Heylen repeated this sentiment in 1621 by observing, "pity 'tis that so beautiful and rich a country should be inhabited by so barbarous and rude a people." As travelers found in other regions during the seventeenth century, most of the world was inhabited by people who appeared more bestial than human. Since animals had no recognized rights to life, liberty, or property, the "creatures" who occupied those rich and beautiful countries could be dispossessed or displaced with impunity. In the Cape, travel reports about the absence of religion among the Hottentots were a prelude to European settlement. Without religion, like animals, the indigenous people of the Cape had no right to the land.[12]

Religion of the Moon (1654–1685)

Two years after the establishment of a Dutch settlement at the Cape, the first report to affirm the existence of a Hottentot religion was submitted by the Dutch traveler Johan Nieuhof. In 1654 Nieuhof published the remarkable observation that although the Hottentots were "the most savage folk in the whole earth, yet in my opinion those seem to err who will assert that among them there is no Knowledge or even any trace of religion." Suddenly, the Hottentots had a religion. All previous denials were found to have been mistaken. In support of this unexpected discovery Nieuhof not only relied upon the new opportunities for local observation that had been made possible by settlement. He also drew upon a shift in international opinion. Nieuhof referred to an emerging consensus in learned European thinking about the universality of "natural religion." Owing much to the work of Edward Herbert of Cherbury, whose *De veritate* (1624) had identified five basic religious doctrines supposedly held by all people, this assumption had by the 1650s become commonplace in European discussions of religion. Herbert had proposed that "Religion is a common notion; no period or nation is without religion." As a matter of principle, therefore, Nieuhof held that the Hottentots had to have a religion, "since, according to the unanimous opinion of all theologians, no folk in the world is so barbarous that it does not honour some Godhead, be it true or false." Although this opinion was not in fact unanimous in Europe, it did provide Nieuhof with a new theoretical framework in which to identify the religion of the Hottentots.[13]

That religion, according to Nieuhof, whose finding on this point was endorsed by most commentators for the next thirty years, was the worship of the moon. They honored the moon, Nieuhof reported, greeting it at regular celebrations with shouting and song. This ritual attention to the moon began to emerge as the dominant feature of Hottentot religion. In addition, however, they also honored the sun, migrating with their cattle to follow the sun's trajectory across the heavens. While this reverence for the moon and sun was most prominent in their religious life, the Hottentots reportedly also distinguished between a celestial "Great Captain," who was an "eternal Being" located in the sky, and an evil spirit that resided underground. They did not pray to either being, but remained silent out of respect. Although they were not worshiped, these supernatural beings seemed to have an effect on the forces of nature by causing rain or drought. Concerning beliefs in an afterlife, Nieuhof noted that Hottentots expected a kind of resurrection, that they thought they would rise up again beyond the hills after death. However, he supposed that they learned this notion of resurrection from the Portuguese or Dutch. Since their religion was a natural religion that was most evident in their apparent worship of the moon, Nieuhof concluded, any specific "revealed" doctrines, such as the resurrection of the dead, must have been acquired from European Christians.

Through the 1670s, reports about Hottentot religion continued to focus upon their worship of the moon. In 1655 Gijsbert Heeck testified that "they know nothing of *God* or His Commandments, living in the wilds little better than beasts." Lacking revealed religion, the Hottentots nevertheless did have a kind of religion, because, as Heeck observed, when "the New Moon shows itself, they seem to have a certain pleasure in singing, dancing and making a noise in honour of the same." In 1669 Albrecht Herport reported that their "religion or divine service is addressed to the sun and the moon, which they honour and pray to." On full or new moons, Herport noted, they came together, built a large fire, and danced around it all night, paying tribute to the moon with drums, song, and shouting. Sometimes commentators contrasted this religious celebration of the moon with Christian religion. As Georg Meister observed in 1677, the Hottentots were immersed in the "darkness of heathen atheism" and lacked basic Christian beliefs, yet "they revere certain created things, such as the moon when it is full, which they worship as a god." Likewise, Johan Wilhelm Vogel reported that "of God and His Knowledge they know little or nothing; yet it may be detected, that they have some veneration of the moon, since when this is new they come together and shriek and rave all night, and dance in a circle, in such dancing clapping their hands." Even a skeptic, such as Johan Christian Hoffmann, who observed in 1672 that "no one, however much I enquired, has been able to detect any sign of a Religion," recognized the possibility that the religion of the Hottentots could be found in their dances. Hoffmann reported: "They came together in their horrible cloaks in front of their Krales, and the men passed the whole night doing strange and wonderful posturings, with leaping, hopping and dancing; but the women made a continual hand-clapping and did other such rare antics, and sang only ha, ho, HO, HO, until one almost lost

hearing and sight because of the terrible noise." As Hoffman concluded, "Whether this now is a part of their religion, I do not
know." But if any religion were to be found among people in
whom "nothing in the least human is to be detected," Hoffmann
suggested, that religion consisted, not in any worship of God, but
in these dramatic, all-night dances under the moon. Even attempts to deny the religion of the Hottentots ended up affirming
the existence of this religion of the moon. "They have no manner
of Religion, Prayers, or Laws," Christophorus Schweitzer asserted
in 1676, "only they Worship the Moon."[14]

Between 1654 and 1685, few commentators demurred from this
discovery of a lunar religion among the Hottentots. As William
Ambrose Cowley observed, they worshiped "Dame Luna." Only
the Dutch author, Olfert Dapper, maintained the earlier categorical denial, observing in 1668 that Hottentots lacked "any trace of
religion or any show of honour to God or the devil." Furthermore,
Dapper elaborated this denial of religion in specifically Christian
terms by noting that "they have no churches or any congregation." Dapper, however, relied exclusively on the earlier literary
tradition, having never personally visited the Cape. Therefore, he
perpetuated the conventional denial of religion long after it had
been dropped from reports about southern Africa. As in the earlier period prior to Dutch settlement, most commentators, while
finding the Hottentot religion of the moon, also presumed a basically Christian comparative framework. They tracked specific
Christian absences. They placed the Hottentots in a biblical chronology as descendants of Adam. Occasionally, they drew comparisons with familiar forms of religion. For example, in 1688 Johan
Schreyer, who spent eight years at the Cape as company surgeon,
commented upon the much-publicized Hottentot custom of removing one testicle from boys at eight years of age. As a rite of
passage, Schreyer proposed, this custom was comparable to the
Christian ritual of baptism.[15]

Demonstrating a continuing Christian interest in comparison,
therefore, commentators persisted in searching for the Hottentot
God, who, if not the moon, was sometimes identified, following
Johan Nieuhof, as the "Great Captain," or the "one above," who
created and ruled the world. They also looked for a Hottentot
Devil, which was described by Nieuhof as the spirit beneath the
ground, and by Frederick Bolling as the "Great Captain below." In
1687 the French traveler Simon de la Loubère even found a trace
of Manicheism in this apparent dualism. If Hottentots displayed

a theological heresy, they might just as easily hold a demonic religion. Johan Schreyer thought he had found this demon in a deity by the name of *Tsiqua* that the Hottentots appeased with offerings. Although this being was not apparently regarded by the people as an evil spirit, Schreyer nevertheless thought that Tsiqua "may well be the Devil." He thus employed a particular Christian demonology distinguishing between God's religion and the Devil's superstitions, which would have a long history in the practice of comparative religion in southern Africa. "It may well be believed," Schreyer asserted, "that the Devil has his congregation among these unbelievers, and the more so in that many superstitious acts are to be seen among them."[16]

During the 1680s, as reports about Hottentot religion proliferated, the earlier clarity gained by the discovery of their lunar religion became lost in the competing claims of contradictory accounts. Four reports by French travelers in 1685 suggest these conflicting versions of the religion of the Hottentots. In his account, Father Gui Tachard combined distance and difference in a single rhetorical formula to suggest that people furthest from Europe were most different in matters of religion. "The most southernly point of Africa is not less distant from Europe," he observed, "than are the customs of the inhabitants different from ours, since these peoples are ignorant of the creation of the world, the Redemption of man, and the mystery of the most holy Trinity." Although they lacked revealed religion, the Hottentots nevertheless worshiped a God by means of ritual sacrifice. However confused their ideas about God were, they displayed knowledge of a deity in their ritual slaughter of cows and sheep, presenting flesh and milk as sacrificial offerings. In this first mention of sacrifice as a central component of Hottentot religion, Tachard shifted his account of their religious focus away from the wild, frenzied lunar dancing to the solemn sacrificial offering in gratitude to a beneficent deity. Accordingly, Tachard came closest among eighteenth-century travelers to identifying Hottentots as "noble savages." As he insisted, "Barbarism has not however so completely effaced all traces of humanity that no vestige of virtue remains." There was no reason to despise these barbarians, Tachard concluded, because they showed more charity and faithfulness in their relations with each other than was usual among Christians.

During the same year, however, a French report by François-Timoleon de Choisy, while accepting the redefinition of Hottentot religion as based on sacrifice, used this new discovery as evidence that "they have hardly any religion," which was close to having no religion. On his travels to Bantam, Batavia, Siam, and the Cape, Chevalier de Forbin reported about the Hottentots that "these tribes live without religion." Even the religion of the moon, which had been the central feature of Hottentot religion, was now being denied. As Chevalier de Chaumont reported in 1685, "These people have no religion." It was true, he conceded, that they observed certain ceremonies at full moon, "but these have no religious significance." In spite of Father Tachard's affirmation, therefore, other reports returned to the categorical dismissal of Hottentot religion, even denying the religious character of their all-night dances under the moon. Over the next fifteen years, such denials predominated in reports about Hottentot religion.[17]

No Religion, Priests, or Temples (1685–1700)

This return to denial on the part of European observers was anticipated by about ten years within the Cape Colony. In the midst of protracted wars of resistance, relations between settlers and Khoikhoi were increasingly defined on a battlefield. Although violent conflict had flared briefly during the first Khoikhoi-Dutch war in 1659, the open hostilities had lasted only a few months. The second war, however, raged between 1673 and 1677.[18] In addition to the endemic conflicts over cattle, land, and labor, therefore, intercultural relations in the frontier were shaped by armed combat. In that context, colonists were predisposed once again to dismiss the religious character of the Khoikhoi. On the other side of the battle line of the colonial frontier, the Khoikhoi were once again described as having no religion.

In 1676 Abraham van Riebeeck undertook an investigation of the religion of the Hottentots. "We talked somewhat with them," he reported, "principally to understand a little concerning their religion." These conversations in broken Dutch, however, disclosed that the Hottentots had no religion at all. According to Van Riebeeck, they knew nothing about God, the Devil, or the Bible of revealed religion. But they also lacked any characteristics of natural religion that might have been derived from reason or experience. As Van Riebeeck insisted, "no shape of the heavens, noise of thunder and lightning, wind or storm, rain or hail had ever been able to imprint [upon] them [the idea] that there was a

God."[19] Therefore, while commentators in the mid–1670s were still reporting in Europe about the lunar religion of the Hottentots, colonists on the front lines of armed conflict in the Cape were denying that they had any religion.

On the battlefield, this denial of religion was a significant maneuver, a strategy for dismissing any legitimate Khoikhoi claims to the land. Denying their religion was consistent with a military strategy that denied the humanity of an enemy. As the Cape Colony expanded, extending the frontier during the 1680s, denial became the dominant mode of accounting for the religion of the Hottentots not only in the Cape but also in Europe. Under the weight of these denials, the religious significance of their dances under the moon entirely disappeared. Based on his visit to the Cape in the 1680s, William Dampier admitted that their "nocturnal pastimes" under the moon looked "as if they had some Superstition about it." However, although they might involve superstition, these dances had nothing to do with religion. A report in 1689, by a certain Dr. Browne, maintained that "they worship nothing that the Dutch can perceive." The "great noise" they made under the moon could not be regarded as religion. In the 1690s John Ovington noted their dances under the moon but only cited the dances to prove that they "have lost all kind of Religious Devotion." In 1694 this denial of the religion of the moon was certified by Christoffel Langhansz, who contradicted all previous reports that they "reverence the moon." He acknowledged that Hottentots danced under the moon, but that activity held no religious significance, since "dancing is done only for their pleasure." Serving in the Cape as secretary to the Dutch East India Company's Council of Policy, Johannes Guillelmus de Grevenbroek in 1695 went so far as to assert that Hottentots despised the moon because they associated it with disease and disaster. This denial of the religion of the moon was further confirmed in 1698 by François Leguat, who suggested that Hottentot dances under the moon were not mysterious ceremonies, denoting a belief in a sovereign being, or the worship of the planet, but were simple demonstrations of joy. "In truth," he insisted, "they have no Religion."[20]

The denials issued between 1685 and 1700 had a slightly different character than the earlier denials. Before the establishment of the Dutch settlement, observers asserted that the Hottentots had no religion because they lacked religious beliefs. At the end of the seventeenth century, however, observers denied the existence of any Hottentot religion on the basis of their lack of any observable signs of religion, especially emphasizing the absence of idols, temples, or priesthoods. "Their Religion, if they have any, is wholly unknown to me," Dampier observed, "for they have no Temple nor Idol, or any place of Worship." According to John Ovington, the Hottentots, who had "sunk even below Idolatry, are destitute both of Priest and Temple." Nevertheless, their lack of any religious beliefs was still noted in these reports. In Ovington's account, nature had not impressed upon the minds of the Hottentots the basic doctrines of a natural religion. In fact, their natural environment had made life too easy for them. "Nature has so richly provided for their convenience in this Life," Ovington remarked, "that they have drown'd all sense of the God of it, and are grown quite careless of the next." In these terms, the Hottentots were depicted as being just as careless about the afterlife as they were lazy in life.[21]

This motif of the "lazy Hottentot" permeated the discourse of the colony. Colonial conflict with the Khoikhoi was not only over land but also over labor as settlers tried to obtain workers for their farms. Resistance to being coopted as laborers was interpreted by colonists as an endemic lack of industry. This assumption was so pervasive that Georg Meister, who had characterized Hottentot religion as moon worship in 1677, asserted ten years later that the absence of any religion among them was equivalent to their lack of literacy and industry. "Just as the Hottentots can neither read nor write, nor have any religion," Meister insisted, "so also most of the labour of the men is merely to laze and sleep." Since they were too lazy to work, according to this colonial ideology, the Hottentots were also too lazy to have any religion. "They wish to know nothing of God," Christoffel Langhansz complained in 1694. When informed about God, redemption, and the resurrection, they replied that the "Dutch work and toil but not the Hottentots, and at last both die and one is buried in the earth like the other." Reinscribing the colonial distinction between European industry and Hottentot laziness in his investigation of religion, Langhansz dismissed the Hottentots as atheists. He sealed his denial of their religion with complete dismissal by concluding, "let this be enough concerning the Hottentots."[22]

The denial of the religious character of the Hottentots, however, was not sufficient to assert European dominance on the expanding Cape frontier. Once again, denial of religion supported a more basic denial of the humanity of the Hottentots. "As to their religion, they have none," Langhansz insisted, "but live like the unreasoning brutes from day to day." Like animals, without reason, the Hottentots were characterized in the 1690s as "the very Reverse of Human kind," an inverted image of the European human beings asserting their claims to land, livestock, and labor within an expanding frontier. If Hottentots were not actually animals, it was only because they could be identified as some middle ground between the human and the bestial. "If there's any medium between a Rational Animal and a Beast," John Ovington asserted, "the *Hottontot* lays the fairest Claim to that Species." Whether as an absence, an inversion, or an approximation of the human, the Hottentots were consistently depicted through the 1690s, in the words of William Erle, as "a Brutish sort of People" because they were "void of Religion, & all manner of Civility."[23]

CHILDREN OF ABRAHAM

Khoikhoi resistance to the encroachments of the colony had largely been subdued by 1700. Indicating that relations had been normalized, the Dutch East India Company removed all legal restrictions that had prevented settlers from trading with the Khoikhoi. Within its new, expanded boundaries, the Cape Colony had succeeded in subjugating the Hottentots. Although they might still be regarded as bestial, the Hottentots under European domination appeared as tamed animals. Under these new conditions, the Hottentots again seemed to have a religion. Visiting the Cape in 1702, Luillier observed that the indigenous people of the country were "more like animals than men." Nevertheless, he found that they had a religion. "They worship the sun, prostrating themselves when it rises," Luillier reported, "and believe that they receive light and life only from it."

This recognition of the existence of a Hottentot religion, even though it was characterized as sun worship, rather than moon worship, recalled the tenor of reports that followed the initial establishment of a Dutch settlement at the Cape. In common with that period, observers investigated the religion of the Hottentots within the confines of relatively secure colonial borders. Significantly, their reports revived earlier assumptions about the religious significance of the moon. "They show reverence for the

New Moon," Abraham Bogaert reported in 1711. "Their greatest observance is that they come together on a hill at each new
moon," added Martin Wintergerst in a publication that appeared
the following year. Although the Hottentots lacked revealed religion, they showed, according to both of these witnesses, decisive
evidence of "natural" religion. Bogaert, following biblical principle, suggested that even the heathen, guided by the light of nature, could be found to observe religious law: "As regards their
religion, from close examination I have perceived that the saying
of the Apostle Paul is true of them, 'that the Heathen who know
not the Law, by nature do the things of the Law.' Since although
they have only a very confused knowledge of God, they nevertheless pray to His Majesty, and to His honour kill cows and sheep,
offering up with gratitude the flesh and milk of them, to show
their thankfulness to a Godhead which they believe grants them
rain, fine weather, and whatever they have need of."

By nature, therefore, the Hottentots had a religion involving a
belief in God, however confused, as well as prayer, sacrifice,
thankfulness, and love for one another that was as great as Christian love. Wintergerst concurred in this assessment, noting that
although they knew nothing of "special religion," the Hottentots
had nevertheless, "by nature," developed beliefs in a divine being
whom they called their Great Captain. They believed that they
would meet this Great Captain after death, when he returned.
Although they were "poor pagans," in Wintergerst's terms, the
Hottentots under colonial domination demonstrated virtues,
such as frugality, obedience, service, humility, and restraint, that
"put many of us Christians to shame, exceeding us in many respects." Not quite noble savages, the Hottentots had nevertheless
succeeded, under colonial rule, in acquiring virtues of submission
to higher authority that were consistent with "natural" religion.
Ironically, these "beasts" could now serve as models of virtue
even for Christian subjects of the Colony.[24]

Their political independence shattered, the Khoikhoi were
nearly destroyed in 1713 by the outbreak of a smallpox epidemic
that claimed almost the entire population. The extent of this
tragedy was deepened by the spread of a cattle disease that killed
most of their livestock the following year. Broken by these catas-
trophes, survivors were increasingly incorporated as labor into
the colony. In this context, a German visitor, Peter Kolb, who
spent eight years at the Cape, produced the most elaborate inventory to date of the religion of the Hottentots. With German spon-

sorship, Kolb came to the Cape in 1705 to make astronomical observations, but he proved incompetent in that assignment. After a time of unemployment, Kolb secured a post as interim secretary to the *landdrost* of Stellenbosch. According to his critics, Kolb spent his time smoking and drinking, having to resign his post and return to Germany in 1713 because he had gone blind. Kolb, however, claimed that he was doing research.

Regaining his eyesight, Peter Kolb published his monograph, *The Present State of the Cape of Good Hope,* in 1719. Translated from the original German into Dutch in 1727, English in 1731, French in 1742, and back into German in 1745, Kolb's work was widely read in Europe. It remained the most influential account of the religion of the Hottentots until the 1770s. Even in the 1930s, according to social anthropologist Isaac Schapera, "Kolb's account, notoriously inaccurate as it is in many respects, is by far the most detailed and useful." Detailed, it certainly was. But its usefulness as an analysis of Hottentot religion was most suited for representing a people under colonial subjugation. During the last quarter of the eighteenth century, when Khoikhoi once again mobilized armed resistance against the colony, Kolb's account of their religion would be dismissed as inaccurate, as well as useless, for the purpose of representing an enemy. Thus, the Hottentots acquired a religion in the early 1700s only to lose it again in all reports about their beliefs and customs at the end of the eighteenth century.[25]

Questions of Method

Peter Kolb has the distinction of being the first commentator to reflect on matters of method in the study of religion in southern Africa. As Kolb explained, his investigations into the religion of the Hottentots were guided by observation, interviews, and comparison. Insisting on the evidential authority of his own direct observation, Kolb rejected all previous literary accounts. "I threw away the Historical Rubbish I had gather'd upon Information," he submitted, "and made it a Rule, not to believe any Thing I did not see, of which a Sight could be had." On the basis of what he claimed to have personally witnessed, Kolb dismissed the received opinion in Europe that the Hottentots had no religion. Not only did they have a sense of God and religious practices, he noted, but "they are not so stupid, irrational and inhuman, as

Peter Kolb (From Kolb, *Naaukeurige en Uitvoerige Beschrijving*)

they have been represented among us." In support of these claims, Kolb promised, "I have Evidence enough."

His evidence, not just based on observation, was also drawn from conversations he claimed to have had with Hottentot informants. Interviews, however, involved their own methodological problems, since Hottentots, as Kolb argued, were notoriously secretive about the meaning of their religious practices. "They keep all their religious Opinions and Ceremonies," he noted, "as secret as they can from Europeans." When questioned about religion, they might remain silent or run away, but they also might amuse themselves by relating fictions to deceive or mock Europeans. Many errors in previous reports about Hottentot religion, Kolb revealed, had resulted from informants playing such tricks on European inquirers. How, then, could the truth be acquired? According to Kolb, accurate information could only be gained through a type of exchange. If asked to explain a custom, Hottentots would refuse. For a pipe of tobacco, or a dram of brandy, however, they would provide a complete account of its religious significance. As an important aspect of his method, Kolb revealed that many times he had "allur'd them in small Companies with Tobacco, Wine, Brandy, and other Things" to conduct interviews on religious matters. Getting to the truth about Hottentot religion, therefore, required entering into relations of exchange.[26]

In addition to these techniques of discovery, Kolb also proposed a self-consciously comparative method for the analysis of Hottentot religion. In the absence of written records, he argued, only comparison could reconstruct its history. "When Records are wanting, and Tradition is grown a blind Matter, concerning the Origin of a People, all that can be done in it, is to compare that Tradition, together with their Customs and Institutions, with the Histories, Institutions and Customs of other Nations, and to fix it, if Nothing shall hinder, where the Parity most appears."[27] Formulated in this way as a general principle, the comparative method could reveal the origin and development of the religious beliefs, practices, and institutions of the Hottentots. Taking oral tradition as his primary evidence, Kolb compared the religion of the Hottentots with what was known from written sources about other nations. Through this comparative exercise, he claimed to have discovered the historical roots of the religion of the Hottentots. Surprisingly, the Hottentots turned out to be children of Abraham, who had preserved, in distorted form, religious traditions that could be traced back to ancient Israel. Therefore, Kolb's comparative method revealed that the Hottentots were like Jews, with a religion derived from Abraham.

Kolb reported that the Hottentots preserved an oral tradition about their first parents, who had been sent by God, Tikquoa, to enter the country through a window or a door and to settle there with their cattle. These ancestors were named Nôh and Hingnôh. Could this tradition be a fragment of the biblical story of Noah, alluding to the great flood and the reentry of human beings in the world through the door or window of the ark? Earlier commentators might have assumed that the tale had been learned from the Dutch or other Europeans in the Cape. Using his comparative method, however, Kolb cited this tradition as evidence of an oral transmission stretching all the way back to the deluge. If the Hottentots preserved this memory of Noah and the great flood, they must have descended from Abraham. Further evidence of that descent was provided by their religious practices. "In their Customs and Institutions," Kolb argued, "they cannot be said to resemble any People besides the *Jews* and the Old *Troglodytes*."

Proposing a systematic comparison between the Hottentots and these two lines of descent from Abraham, Kolb first listed customs that the Hottentots held in common with Jews. Grounds for resemblance could be found in their sacrificial offerings, the regulation of their chief festivals by the new and full moon, avoidances between husbands and wives, the abstention from eating certain foods, especially swine's flesh, the circumcision of males, and the exclusion of women from full participation in religious ritual. However, for all these common features, the Hottentots lacked any memory of the Children of Israel, Moses, or the Law. Therefore, Kolb proposed, it was more likely that they had descended from the Troglodytes, children of Abraham by his wife, Chetura (Keturah; Gen. 25:1–4), who "not only observ'd all or most of the Customs in which the Hottentots agree with the Jews, but likewise many others, observ'd by the Hottentots at this Day." Basing his information about Troglodytes primarily on the authority of the ancient historian Diodorus Siculus, Kolb noted that both Troglodytes and Hottentots named children after their favorite animals, abandoned the aged, displayed swiftness in hunting, and practiced the same funeral ceremonies. On this comparative basis, therefore, Kolb concluded that it was probable that the Troglodytes were the ancient ancestors of the Hottentots of the Cape. Accordingly, their religion, agreeing with the customs of both the Jews and Troglodytes, could be traced back to the religion of Abraham.[28]

Inventory and Intervention

Since the Hottentots also preserved no memory of Abraham, Kolb left open the possibility that they had remained precisely as they presently were ever since the flood. Although Kolb clearly preferred his historical account of the Abrahamic origin of their religion, his proposed similarities between Hottentot and Jewish religion were still significant, even if they were divorced from a common biblical history. As a purely morphological comparison, the similarity between Hottentots and Jews remained salient for Kolb for two reasons.

First, these comparisons allowed him to recast the strange features of Hottentot religion in terms of the more familiar forms of Judaism. In drawing up his analysis of Hottentot religion, Kolb introduced for the first time the distinction between a supreme God—*Gounja, Gounja,* or *Gounja Ticquoa*—and a lesser God, known simply as *Gounja.* The former was the God of all dwelling beyond the moon, while the latter resided in the moon, acting as the visible representative of the invisible supreme God. Although the supreme God was not worshiped, the visible God in the moon was honored through dance. Like commentators before him, Kolb reported that "in Shouting, Screaming, Singing, Jumping, Stamping, Dancing, Prostration on the Ground, and an unintelligible Jargon, lie all their Formalities in the Worship of the Moon." However, rather than pagan moon worship, this celebration, Kolb insisted, resembled most closely the festivals of the Jews. Noting that this ritual "enter'd into the Divine Worship in Times as early as the Flood," Kolb informed his readers that "the Jews retain it, on certain Festivals, to this Day." In these terms, therefore, the religion of the Hottentots could be imagined, not as barbaric paganism, but as a variety of Judaism. Of course, this comparison also required a redefinition of Judaism as a religious tradition that resembled the practices of the Hottentots.[29]

Kolb used a similar strategy to compare certain beliefs and practices in Hottentot religion to Roman Catholicism. In discussing the significance of the mantis, an insect regarded by the Hottentots as "a benign deity," Kolb observed that any person the

Hottentot religion: The Moon and the Mantis (a) The Hottentots worship the Moon; (b) The Hottentots worship an insect. (From Kolb, *Caput bonae spei hodiernum*)

insect landed upon was "reverenc'd as a Saint and the Delight of the Deity ever after." At another point, Kolb observed that they paid "a Religious Veneration to their Saints and Men of Renown departed." Like Catholics, the Hottentots associated special places with the sanctified dead, where they revered the memory and petitioned the protection of their saints, even though they did not mark the places with tombs, statues, or inscriptions. In discussing Hottentot saints, therefore, a comparison with Catholic practice was implicit. While not as obvious or belabored as his comparisons with Judaism, this allusion to similar Catholic and Hottentot practice also served to reinvent both religions. If Hottentots were like Catholics, Catholics were also like Hottentots. At the time, there was no formal Jewish presence at the Cape. Catholics were excluded by law from public worship. Nevertheless, through Kolb's comparative method, both Jews and Catholics were re-created in the Cape as Hottentots.[30]

Therefore, by emphasizing, in particular, comparisons between Hottentots and Jews, Kolb, in an important sense, reinvented Judaism in Christian terms by relocating it in the Cape as an opposition to Christianity. Accordingly, a second reason that comparisons with Judaism remained relevant, even if no historical connection could be established, was the implication that the Hottentots, like the Jews, stubbornly resisted Christian conversion. Kolb provided an inventory of Hottentot religion that included the supreme God, the lesser God, the mantis, reverence for saints, belief in immortality, and the practice of dancing under the moon. Hottentot religion also included belief in an evil deity, *Touquoa*, and the witchcraft he taught. Kolb represented all these elements as comprising a comprehensive system. "I have now given the Whole System of the Hottentot Religion," he concluded, "every Tenet of which, tho' labouring with the wildest Absurdities, they embrace so heartily, and hold so dear." As an entire system, Kolb observed, this religion was an obstacle to Christian conversion. It could not be removed, reformed, or reasoned against. "Never certainly were there," Kolb complained, "in Matters of Religion, so obstinate and so infatuated a People." In evidence, he cited examples of failed conversions to Christianity. The governor of the Cape, Simon van der Stel, became legal guardian of a Hottentot, raising the child as a Christian, only to be told by his ward, "It is my Design to live and die in the Religion, Manners and Customs of my Ancestors." The convert of a German missionary had rejected Christianity and had tried to return "to his native Residence and Idolatries, when he was sent away to the Robben Island, where he died an Infidel." No people, Kolb concluded, were as stubborn in resisting Christianity as the Hottentots. None, that is, except one. Kolb concluded that the Hottentots were precisely as "Stiff as are the Jews." The religion of the Hottentots was like Judaism, therefore, because it could be perceived by Christians as resisting the advance of Christianity.[31]

Kolb extended this analysis of Jewish stubbornness to all Hottentot customs and, in broader terms, to the intractable force of customary behavior in general. He highlighted, for example, the Hottentot practice of an elder male urinating on people during initiations, weddings, and funerals. These rituals, referred to as *andersmaken*, or "difference-making" rites, supposedly required "a Stream of Urine" to flow onto the bodies of the participants. Each rite was marked by this *Pisplechtigheid* (Pissing Ceremony). "I took Abundance of Pains, and spent not a little Money," Kolb noted, "to come at the Meaning of the Pissing." The meaning of the Pissing Ceremony, he found, was its importance as a sign of honor and respect. After a burial, for example, old men urinated on all those in the funeral party to thank them for accompanying the deceased to the grave. In this ritual act, Kolb found a dramatic reversal of European custom. It inspired him to exclaim upon the strange force not only of Hottentot practice but of custom in general: "Strange! The different Notions different Nations entertain of the same Thing! The Force, the Witchcraft of Custom! To be piss'd upon in *Europe* is a Token of the highest Contempt: To be piss'd on in the *Hottentot* Countries is a Token of the highest Honour. Pissing is the Glory of all the *Hottentot* Ceremonies." In this account, therefore, the Hottentots appeared, not necessarily as the "Reverse of Human kind," but, more specifically, as the reverse of Europe. Since different nations held different notions, a note of cultural relativism entered Kolb's analysis. Nevertheless, this comparative perspective did not inhibit Kolb from trying to intervene and change Hottentot custom. "I took Abundance of Pains both to reason and to ridicule the *Hottentots* out of the Veneration for the Ceremony of Pissing," he revealed. Just as he took pains to discover its meaning, Kolb took pains to break the stubborn hold of custom that attached the Hottentots to the ritual. His efforts were in vain, however. "They hold the Custom so dear and venerable," Kolb concluded, "that they have hardly Patience to hear a Word against it." By concentrating on the Ceremony of Pissing in this way, as part of an inventory of Hottentot religion but also as a point of intervention in efforts to alter that religion, Kolb was not merely identifying ritual urination as a "filthy rite." Rather, he used the ceremony as a dramatic emblem for the stubborn, resistant force of custom, a force that was impervious to rational intervention.[32]

Peter Kolb reinvented the religion of the Hottentots within the new power relations of a secured colony at the Cape. Broken and contained, they had a religious system. Kolb advanced a comparative method through which that religion could be represented. The Hottentots might have had their magicians, who exercised supernatural power, but, Kolb observed, "I have often been look'd upon by the Hottentots as a Wizard my self." His Magic Lantern, Burning Glass, and other technological instruments might have baffled them. But his wizardry also extended to his power to represent the Hottentots to the world. As we have seen, he succeeded in reinventing their religion, for better or worse, as a variety of Judaism. At the same time, he also tried to rehabilitate their image in Europe. They might have been lazy and irrational, but "they make excellent Servants," Kolb maintained, "perhaps the faithfullest in the World." Under European mastery, the Hottentots were acknowledged not only as useful servants but also as people who had a religion. They might have had a "false" religion that was similar, in Kolb's terms, to Judaism or Roman Catholicism, which stood as an obstacle to Protestant Christianity. But at least they had a recognizable religious system. In the Cape, the religious system of the Hottentots discovered by Kolb continued to be recognized until European domination was again threatened. When open conflict resumed in the 1770s, the Hottentots, by all reports, once again ceased to have a religion.[33]

PERMANENT CHILDREN

Between 1740 and 1770, frontier relations seem to have been relatively peaceful, since the historical record contains fewer references to conflict. The impact of the colonists upon the Khoikhoi living beyond the colony's borders was fairly limited. However, in the 1770s this situation changed. As the European population of the colony grew, and the Cape became increasingly important as a naval station, the Dutch East India Company made greater demands for livestock. On the borders, the Dutch herders known as

Hottentot religion: The Pissing Ceremony: (a) Young males being received into the society of men; (b) The Hottentot marriage ceremony. (From Kolb, *Caput bonae spei hodiernum*)

trekboers engaged in renewed conflicts with the Khoikhoi over limited environmental resources. The expansion of the colony into new settlement areas and grazing lands was blocked by Khoikhoi to the northeast. In pushing its borders, the colony in 1774 reintroduced the military formation of the commando system. As a citizen militia, the commando system became an emblem, as historian Nigel Penn has noted, "for the structure of social, political, and economic domination which crystallised during the last three decades of the eighteenth century." Between 1774 and 1800, the commandos waged a war of extermination against the Hottentot herders and the Bushmen hunters and gathers in the Cape. Military expeditions wiped out Khoikhoi resistance, but they also captured and incorporated laborers. By 1800 Khoikhoi survivors had been reduced to the status of peons or serfs working on European farms or in the colony. After 1770, therefore, intercultural relations within the Cape frontier zone were once again shaped on a battlefield.[34]

When the British traveler John Barrow visited the Cape in 1797, he found the indigenous people not only subjugated but their numbers reduced and the survivors dispersed throughout the colony. In his travels through the region, Barrow found not "a single horde of independent Hottentots" and "perhaps not a score of individuals who were not actually in the service of the Dutch." By 1800 the colonial domination of the Khoikhoi was almost complete. Under these conditions, many turned to the Christian missions as a place of refuge. The Moravians, returning in 1792, and the London Missionary Society, beginning its work in 1799, established stations in the northern and eastern Cape that attracted displaced Khoikhoi. By the 1820s, according to most reports, the Hottentots had a religion. They were Christians.[35]

Since most survivors had adopted Christianity, little interest was shown by European observers during the first half of the nineteenth century in either affirming or denying the existence of any indigenous religion of the Hottentots. The question had become irrelevant. Before their destruction, however, the religion of the Hottentots remained a matter of concern. During the last three decades of the eighteenth century, in the midst of the frontier war of extermination against the Khoikhoi, reports about the Cape demonstrated this interest by insisting that the Hottentots lacked any trace of religious beliefs, practices, or institutions. On the battlefield, once again, the Hottentots had no religion.

New authoritative voices emerged at the end of the eighteenth century to certify that denial. A new generation of naturalists influenced, and in some cases trained, by the Swedish scientist Linnaeus (Carl Linné) came to explore the flora, fauna, and humans of the Cape. In the *Systema Naturae* introduced by Linnaeus in 1735, achieving final form in its tenth edition in 1759, natural science was a science of classification. Taxonomy organized all nature, including human nature. Linnaeus divided the species *Homo sapiens* into four basic types: *Americanus*, reddish, choleric, and erect; *Asiaticus*, sallow, melancholy, and stiff; *Afer*, black, phlegmatic, and relaxed; and *Europaeus*, white, sanguine, and muscular. Although Linnaeus also left room in this scheme for *Homo Ferus*, wild humans, his fourfold classification otherwise accounted for all human diversity in terms of basic differences in complexion, physiology, and disposition. For the study of religion, this Linnaean taxonomy provided a system for classifying the different moral orders in the world. According to Linnaeus, *Americanus* was governed by customs, *Asiaticus* by opinions, *Afer* by caprice, but only *Homo Europaeus* developed social relations regulated by rational law. Therefore, this taxonomy provided a new basis for dismissing the religious systems of the world as irrational custom, as unfounded opinion, or, in the case of Africans, as nothing more than accidental capriciousness.[36]

Conceptually, the Linnaean taxonomy was a scheme of global order. By the 1770s this approach to natural science had truly become a global enterprise. As Linnaeus observed in 1771, "My pupil Sparrman has just sailed for the Cape of Good Hope, and another of my pupils, Thunberg, is to accompany a Dutch embassy to Japan." Both of these students, visiting the Cape in the interest of fitting new species of plants and animals into the Linnaean taxonomy, also made observations about the local humans. In the service of classification, they reinforced an emerging colonial distinction between Hottentots and Bushmen. Earlier accounts did not always distinguish between herders and hunter-gatherers, employing the term *Hottentot* for both. Instead of viewing Bushmen as "Hottentots without cattle," however, the natural scientists identified them as a distinct race. By classifying them in this way, the scientists reinforced an emerging colonial discourse in which Bushmen were referred to as Chinese or "Chinese Hottentots," terms designating what colonists perceived as their absolute strangeness. Although distinguished as a separate people, Bushmen shared with Hottentots, according to all reports at the end of the eighteenth century, a common feature: they also lacked religion.[37]

Children of Nature

Anders Sparrman arrived at the Cape on his scientific mission in 1772. After accompanying Captain James Cook around the world on board the *Resolution*, Sparrman returned to the Cape in 1775 for an extended exploration of the interior. His *Voyage to the Cape*, published in 1786, documented his investigations. Although primarily concerned with natural history, Sparrman also reported on the religion of the indigenous people of the Cape. He distinguished between Bushmen and Hottentots by noting that the latter were "more civilized." Previously the lowest point on the scale of civilization, the Hottentots now had Bushmen below them. Nevertheless, both were in agreement on matters of religion. They were "not sensible of the existence of any being, who is the origin and ruler of all things." If questioned, Sparrman reported, they said they knew nothing about God and went so far as to excuse themselves from any discussion of religion by saying, "We are poor stupid creatures, and have never heard, neither are we able to understand, any thing of the matter." The natural scientist noted that they did have a belief in magic, which suggested evidence that they held a concept of "some evil being." However, Sparrman insisted, they did "not worship him or anything else." They seemed to have some notion of spirits and a belief in an afterlife, but these confused ideas did not constitute a religious system. Certainly, they had superstitions, acquired in childhood, but no religious ideas that had been "taken up on due deliberation and consequent conviction."

Claiming the authority of firsthand investigation, Sparrman contradicted earlier findings on Hottentot religion on two counts. He denied their supposed worship of the mantis and their worship of the moon. Although Kolb had insisted on these two points, Sparrman dismissed any religious significance in Hottentot attention to the mantis and the moon by comparing their practices to familiar European customs. Regarding their attention to the mantis, Sparrman concluded that "we have no more reason to look upon [it] as a kind of religious worship, than we have to consider in the same light, a certain superstitious notion prevalent among many of the more simple people in our own country, who imagine, that three sins will be forgiven them, if they set a cock-chafer on its legs again that has happened to have fallen upon its back." This comparison not only distinguished between religion and superstition, but also introduced a new comparative strategy by translating strange Hottentot customs into the more familiar terms of superstitions held by the "simple people" of European peasantry. Likewise, Hottentot interest in the moon held no religious significance. As they danced under the moon, Sparrman insisted, they had "no more thoughts of worshipping her than the Christian colonists, who are seen at the same time strolling in great numbers about the streets in Cape Town." Motivated by ignorance or pleasure, therefore, these practices, according to Sparrman, had nothing to do with religion. In the case of Hottentot magicians, however, Sparrman found not only ignorance but fraud. They were nothing more than designing imposters, since, as Sparrman concluded, "the artful conjurers themselves are most of them without either superstition or religion of any kind." Bringing the Hottentots into natural history, therefore, Anders Sparrman denied their religion not only by identifying it as superstition but also by explaining their customs as the result of the ignorance of peasants and the fraud of magicians.[38]

Another student of Linnaeus, the physician and botanist Carl Pehr Thunberg, spent a total of three years at the Cape during his travels between 1772 and 1778. Returning to Sweden, Thunberg distinguished himself as a professor of botany at Uppsala. In the four-volume accounts of his travels, published in 1793, Thunberg also touched on the question of Hottentot religion, but only long enough to confirm Sparrman's denials. Although they had some religious features, including notions about a Supreme Being, an evil spirit, and the immortality of the soul, Thunberg observed that they lacked a religious system because "they have no temples, pay no kind of worship to any divinity, and give themselves no thought about rewards or punishments after death." Furthermore, like Sparrman, Thunberg denied any religious significance in Hottentot practices directed toward the moon or mantis. Although they danced under the moon, Thunberg asserted, "it does not appear very probable that their rejoicing is thus any kind of religious ceremony, or that they worship the moon." Regarding the mantis, Thunberg insisted that he "never found that any worship was paid to it." Where Sparrman explained this lack of religion as the result of ignorance and fraud, however, Thunberg introduced a single explanation for the absence of religion among the Hottentots. They were lazy. Few animals, he asserted, were lazier than Hottentots. Too idle to work, the Hottentots, according to Thunberg, were also too lazy to have a religion. "In consequence of this extreme supineness," he concluded, "they have little or no religion." In Thunberg's account, therefore, colonial prejudice against "lazy Hottentots" became a scientific finding of natural history. Guided by Linnaean taxonomy, Thunberg expected Africans, in general, to be "phlegmatic" and "relaxed." Accordingly, in the Hottentots Thunberg found people so sluggish and idle that they did not have a religion.[39]

Sparrman and Thunberg implicitly contradicted Peter Kolb's claims about Hottentot religion. A third scientist, however, the French naturalist François Le Vaillant, who was in the Cape from 1781 to 1785, confronted the legacy of Kolb's work more directly. In conversation with Hottentots, Le Vaillant would recite passages from Kolb concerning their religion. In response, he reported, "they openly laughed in my face." Among the many fanciful features of Hottentot religion described by Kolb, the most ridiculous, according to Le Vaillant, was the Pissing Ceremony. Falsely attributed to the Hottentots, this ceremony, which supposedly invoked "the supernatural power of drenching from the urinary passage," was a product of the imagination of Kolb, the "fire-side traveller," who was too much under the influence of tall tales told by local white farmers. Although Kolb seemed to think he was rehabilitating the European image of the Hottentots, Le Vaillant maintained that Kolb had only succeeded in making them seem absurd. Kolb's fantasy had proliferated through every subsequent account. "I have never read any voyage to Africa," Le Vaillant complained, "in which the absurd dreams of Kolben have not been more or less introduced." In the process, an injustice had been done to the Hottentots. From a comparative perspective, Le Vaillant observed that European commentators passed over abhorrent customs in the Far East, holding Asians in greater esteem, while they reviled the Hottentots for similar practices. Reports from Tibet, for example, related that people obtained excrement from the great Lama to be worn in amulets or sprinkled on food. Tibetans, however, were not held in contempt by Europeans as the Hottentots were for their Pissing Ceremony. Not only false, therefore, Kolb's fantasy about the ritual use of urine had caused damage by reinforcing European prejudices against Hottentots.

Le Vaillant's solution to this problem, however, was not only to deny the existence of the Pissing Ceremony, but, more generally, to deny that Hottentots had any religious practices at all. No Hottentot priest could have served as master of ceremony at such a ritual, he argued, because they had no priests. Furthermore, their language lacked any word to express the notion of a priest. In this sense, therefore, Le Vaillant insisted that religion was absent. Not only living without religion, however, the Hottentots even lacked any form of superstition. In this surprising assertion, Le Vaillant introduced a redefinition of religion that would be contested by later commentators. "Where there is no religion nor worship," he maintained, "it is impossible there can be superstition." In this formulation, Le Vaillant held that superstition was an extension of religion. Rather than being religion's opposite, superstition was part of the fabric of religion. Since Hottentots had no religion, they could not be said to have superstitions. In these terms, therefore, they had nothing. In this way Le Vaillant hoped to rescue the Hottentots from European contempt and abuse. They could not be a superstitious people, as others had claimed, because they lacked the very basis of superstition, religion.[40]

Shipwrecked Children

The most detailed refutation of Kolb's invention of Hottentot religion appeared in 1787 in Otto Friedrich Mentzel's *A Geographical and Topographical Description of the Cape of Good Hope*. Like Kolb, Mentzel had been in the Cape for eight years. Between 1733 and 1740 he had served as a soldier for the Dutch East India Company, as a teacher, and as a clerk in the company's trading store. In January 1741, while at the harbor to see off a friend, Mentzel accidentally set sail for the Netherlands. He never returned to Africa. Although his visit had ended nearly fifty years earlier, Mentzel's published analysis of the religion of the Hottentots corresponds with the general trend of denial at the end of the eighteenth century. His polemic against Kolb was supported by the impression created over the intervening years that Kolb had written with the political motive of discrediting the government of the Cape Colony. Increasingly, Kolb was seen as an unreliable witness. In a posthumous publication in 1763, Father Nicholas de la Caillé had even insisted that Kolb was not a witness at all but had plagiarized, and embellished upon, a manuscript by the secretary of the local Council of Policy, J. G. de Grevenbroek. Mentzel repeated this allegation, observing that through Grevenbroek's manuscript Kolb had "acquired a rich collection of material, but bundled together higgledy-piggledy." In place of the untrustworthy Kolb, who had been extensively copied in subsequent reports, Mentzel offered an account of the Hottentots that he claimed was based on "true facts."[41]

The truth about Hottentot religion, according to Mentzel, was its absence. Kolb might have deduced their knowledge of a Supreme Being from their dances and festivals, but Mentzel insisted that he could "give a truthful assurance that they neither know nor want to know anything of God and religion." Since no religious terms existed in their language, he maintained, the Hottentots were incapable of formulating basic concepts of religion. On this point, however, Mentzel's reasoning seems a bit circular. He argued that the name for God, *Tikquoa*, could not be of Hottentot derivation because Hottentots lacked any innate idea of a divine being. Nevertheless, his denial of any concept of God among the Hottentots was only one aspect of a more general, comprehensive project of denial. Systematically, Mentzel sought to debunk every aspect of Hottentot religion that had been described by Kolb. Regarding their dances under the moon, Mentzel concluded that "one cannot possibly deduce any idea of Moon worship or veneration of the moon from the dance." Concerning the mantis, Mentzel insisted that any claim that "the Hottentots worship a certain insect as a god is absolutely false."

As for the Pissing Ceremony, which came in for special attention in Mentzel's account, it bore absolutely no religious significance. "Some writers see in this ceremony a religious act," Mentzel observed, "but it is nothing of the kind, being only a ceremony invented to provide something out of the common and festive, to attract a measure of attention. Similar festive acts are practised by all idolators and heathens which, in the absence of scientific knowledge, have been invented by their priests and Druids, to make hocus-pocus for the common people, and which have neither a mystical nor mythological nor an allegorical meaning." Accepting the existence of such a ceremony, Mentzel argued that it meant nothing. Since Hottentots supposedly lacked imagination or skill, they invented a ceremony that required minimal effort and expense. Using materials at hand, in this case urine, they performed a ceremony that was "invented by one of the old chieftains," Mentzel proposed, "merely for the sake of introducing a ceremony." While the ritual might have carried traces of its origin in chiefly power and priestcraft, it was nevertheless performed by Hottentots, not as a sign of honor or respect, as Kolb had held, but for absolutely no reason whatsoever.[42]

Lacking religion, Hottentots, according to Mentzel, were immersed in superstition, which was worse than unbelief because it required "something perceptible and dazzling," like the Pissing Ceremony. Along with all other "savage tribes," who lacked belief in God, or forms of worship, or even idols, the Hottentots lived in a world of superstition and fear of evil forces. Once again, therefore, this fundamental distinction between religion and superstition was reinscribed in an analysis of the Hottentots. Mentzel repeated most of the stereotypes about them: they were lazy, simple, and stupid. In the colonial context, their stupidity was most dramatically demonstrated, according to Mentzel, by their ignorance of the trade value of cattle. From such a "true fact," Mentzel generalized that Hottentots did not think. "They reflect on nothing because that requires thinking," he asserted, "and their greatest pleasure is to avoid thinking." If they did not think, how could they think about religion? Without reason, and without reasons for their actions, Hottentots were enveloped in a haze of superstition that bore no relation to religion.[43]

In refuting Kolb's construction of Hottentot religion, however, Mentzel also had to address Kolb's theory of the historical origin of the Hottentots as children of Abraham. While he acknowledged that the Hottentots must have had an ancestor, Mentzel insisted that it was futile to attempt to trace their descent. They could not have migrated from Asia, Mentzel held, because of the impassable distance and the intractable differences between Asians and these people of southern Africa. Neither could they had descended from the Jews. In support of this conclusion, Mentzel, like Kolb, employed a self-consciously comparative method. Where Kolb had found similarities, however, Mentzel insisted on differences between Hottentots and Jews that made their common descent impossible. In a point-by-point consideration of Kolb's comparisons, Mentzel advanced three types of refutation.

First, he identified absences. In spite of Kolb's claims, Mentzel found the Hottentots had no festivals calculated by changes of the moon because they had no festivals at all. Likewise, they maintained no dietary regulations that were similar in any respect to Jewish observations. In drawing these comparisons, therefore, Kolb had asserted common ground that simply did not exist. Second, Mentzel explained any similarities between Jews and Hottentots as the result of universal human behavior. Like

Jews, Hottentot men avoided their wives at certain times and excluded them from participation in public meetings. But then, Mentzel insisted, all nations did the same. In these comparisons, Kolb had merely identified universal human customs, rather than specific commonalities between Hottentots and Jews. Third, Mentzel reduced superficial similarities to more basic differences. The Hottentot practice of sacrifice, for example, was not an offering to God, or even gods, but an ordinary, common meal. Likewise, the excision of a testicle, as an initiation into manhood, was radically different than the Jewish practice of circumcision. In any event, Menzel argued, circumcision, when it was practiced by Hottentots or other people in Africa, was a custom of Muslim, not Jewish, origin. Reducing Kolb's comparison to incomparable absurdity, Mentzel observed that although Germans shared common features with Jews, such as the Sabbath and the Ten Commandments, no one could imagine that they were on that account descended from the Jews.[44]

Although Kolb had taken great pains to prove a shared descent, Mentzel concluded that there was absolutely no common ground between Hottentots and Jews. Sealing his argument, Mentzel reasserted the stereotype of the "filthy Hottentot," observing that "there is no greater contrast between day and night than between the cleanliness of the Jews of the Old Testament and the filthiness of the Hottentots." However, Mentzel carried this argument of the incompatibility between Hottentots and Jews further by declaring that the Hottentots were incomparable not only with Jews but with anyone else. "There is as little in their national customs as in their religious rites," he insisted, "that might be compared with any other peoples." In these terms, therefore, Hottentots were distinctive, a unique anomaly in human history. Their origin must have also been unique.

At this point, Mentzel introduced his own theory of the origin of the Hottentots. They were originally shipwrecked children. In support, he adduced evidence of their supposed childishness. Speaking a childish language, made up of clacking, cracking, and rattling sounds, they were like dirty children, crawling about in dung and filth, and like naughty children, taking pleasure in torturing animals at their sacrifices. Mentzel even invoked the child psychology of Von Justi to argue that Hottentots lived in a fantasy world, like children who "mix their own excrement with sand . . . and knead this into a paste with their small hands, pretending that these were tarts and pancakes." Lacking adult language, hygiene, maturity, or grasp of reality, the Hottentots had remained like children. Accordingly, Mentzel proposed, it was likely that they descended from children who had survived a shipwreck long ago off the Cape coast. Perhaps sailing from Carthage, Phoenicia, Tyre, Sidon, or ancient Israel, that ship sank, killing all adults but leaving the children, along with some livestock, to swim ashore. The local Hottentot story about entering the country through a window, which Kolb had seen as preserving a tradition about Noah and the flood, was invoked by Mentzel as evidence that the children had come ashore through a hole in the side of the sinking ship. Too young to have acquired adult language or standards of hygiene, these children grew up wild in the Cape to become the childish ancestors of a childish race. In summary, Mentzel proposed that "the Hottentots are descended from some children who came by accident to this part of the earth, grew up untaught and unguided, and in the course of several thousand years increased to many tribes, retaining all the while a childish and uncleanly mode of life."[45]

In Mentzel's shipwreck theory, therefore, Hottentots were not children of Abraham, preserving aspects of Jewish tradition, but permanent children without any religion at all. This genealogy of the Hottentots, as fanciful as it might have been, bore a practical implication in conflicts over land in southern Africa. Having arrived by accident, and never attaining adulthood, Hottentots had no rights in the Cape that had to be respected by Europeans. Denial of religion, therefore, was an aspect of a more general project of dismissing the legitimacy of any Hottentot entitlement to the land. Since they supposedly did not belong there in the first place, Hottentots could be removed with impunity. Although subsequent commentators did not embrace Mentzel's shipwreck theory, they did propose alternative explanations for the origin and migration of the Hottentots. Originating elsewhere, the Hottentots had no intrinsic claim to the land. They belonged in Asia, the Middle East, or North Africa, but not in the Cape. To the extent that it was drawn into supporting these theories of origin, comparative religion was complicit in the displacement of the Hottentots.

HOTTENTOT RELIGION

After 1800, with the destruction of independent Khoikhoi societies, little European interest was shown in their indigenous religion. Not until 1881, when the missionary ethnographer Theophilus Hahn published a book-length inventory, did any author undertake a study of Khoikhoi religion. For Hahn, however, the study of that religion had a retrospective, nostalgic quality, recollecting "sacred fragments and relics" of a broken people. For the most part, Hahn re-created Khoikhoi religion along the lines proposed by Peter Kolb. In addition to the moon, a supreme benevolent being, and a supreme malevolent being, Hahn emphasized the importance of the hero, Heitsi-eibib, whose graves throughout the Cape were marked by mounds of stones. Like those cairns, however, the religion of the Khoikhoi only remained as a fossilized remnant from the past. A similar concern for preserving the relics of disappearing people, a "dying out race," was found in the folklore collections of the philologist W. H. I. Bleek and his sister-in-law, Lucy Lloyd, at the end of the nineteenth century.

In the emergence of social anthropology in the 1920s, living Khoikhoi communities, such as the Nama, were themselves treated as fossils from the past. They preserved ancient beliefs about magic, water, or death. Nevertheless, even these living fossils survived in a predominantly Christian context. "All the Hottentot tribes have for a considerable time been more or less under the influence of missionaries," the social anthropologist Isaac Schapera observed in 1930. "As a result their traditional religion has fallen largely, if not completely, into decay, and the great majority of the people in fact now claim to be Christians." For the social anthropologist, however, the fact that Khoikhoi people in the twentieth century were Christian could be elided in providing an account of their religion. In Schapera's terms, Khoikhoi religion was not Christianity but the worship of the moon and other supernatural beings that had been described by Peter Kolb and verified by Theophilus Hahn. Perhaps this attempt to reconstruct a traditional Khoikhoi religion, uncontaminated by Christian influence, should be regarded as another form of denial. Ignoring the actual historical situation of Khoikhoi people, in which Christian missionaries had coopted their religious terms and many Khoikhoi had adopted Christianity, social anthropologists in the 1920s and 1930s invented a timeless tradition of Khoikhoi religion that could be preserved in the museum of a history of religions.[46]

In reviewing the "learned speculations" on the nature of Hottentot religion between 1600 and 1800, certain characteristic strategies of comparison have emerged. The first, and most persistent, of these strategies was denial. Beginning with the earliest reports about the Cape, and recurring over the next two centuries, European observers denied the existence of any Hottentot religion. Although often laden with Christian assumptions, these denials did not merely signify the absence of Christianity. Most commentators accepted the fact of religious diversity in the world. They acknowledged the existence of religions other than Christianity. However, when it came to the Cape, they made the remarkable discovery of a people without religion. As we have seen, the recurring denials of Hottentot religion can be correlated with expanding boundaries of a contested frontier. Reports about the Hottentots have demonstrated this "frontier hypothesis" of comparative religion: when a frontier opens, the enemy has no religion, but when the frontier closes, and hegemony has been established, a dominated, subjected people are discovered to have a religion that can be inventoried and analyzed. Hottentot religion was invented, denied, and reinvented in such a shifting frontier zone. Over a two-hundred-year period, the Hottentots, who lacked a religion between 1600 and 1654, acquired one after a European settlement had been established, only to lose it between 1685 and 1700 as the colony expanded and to regain it when new boundaries had been secured. But they lost it again in the 1770s as the colony grew to encompass the entire Cape region. As this correlation suggests, comparative religion during the seventeenth and eighteenth centuries was a science situated in the conflicts of the colonial frontier.

Not only denials but also other comparative strategies can be located on the frontier battlefields of the Cape. As we have seen, observers advanced two types of comparison, morphology and genealogy, in the analysis of Hottentot religion. In the work of Peter Kolb, both these strategies were evident, as Hottentots shared not only similar morphological forms with Judaism but also a common genealogical origin in the religion of ancient Israel. Other commentators, however, discovered different structures and historical origins to account for the religion of the Hottentots. A Christian, biblical frame of reference tended to be assumed. But other European notions about religion, including the universalism of Edward Herbert of Cherbury and the taxonomy of Linneaus, also surfaced in accounts of the Hottentots. From biblical theology to natural history, however, these theoretical concerns were not merely imposed upon the Cape by European theorists.

As Arjun Appadurai has remarked about anthropological theory, inventions of Hottentot religion depended upon a "complicated compound of local realities and the contingencies of metropolitan theory."[47] In the Cape, the local realities of conflict over land, labor, and political control provided the basic context in which theories of Hottentot religion were developed. Accordingly, comparative strategies were exercised as maneuvers on a battlefield. In the process, a body of knowledge about Hottentot religion accumulated that was entangled in the local power struggles of the Cape. Whether they were described as being stubborn as Jews or superstitious as Catholics—whether they were viewed as lunatic moon worshipers or ignorant, lazy, and filthy children—the Hottentots were credited with a religion that discredited them. Even when granted a religion, therefore, the Hottentots were denied.

During the eighteenth century, the colony had entrenched a single dominant regime over the religious life of the Cape. As John Barrow observed during his tour of 1797, Calvinism, as institutionalized in the Dutch Reformed Church, was the colony's sole established religion. Lutherans had been permitted to build a church in 1782, as long as it had no steeple or bell. Other Protestants, including Methodists and Moravians, were present in the colony but were not permitted to build churches. Roman Catholics were strictly forbidden from public worship, as were Muslims, who were forced to hold services in the stone quarries of Cape Town. Jews had no recognized presence. Although religious diversity was evident in the Cape, it was inhibited or outlawed by colonial policy.[48]

Nevertheless, comparative religion allowed religions of the world to proliferate in the Cape, if only in the imagination of comparativists. By tracking similarities with Catholic, Jewish, or Muslim practices, comparative religion found new ways to re-create those religious traditions in the Cape, reinventing them, however, in the guise of Hottentot religion. Although Catholic, Jewish, and Muslim traditions provided the most common referents for Protestant comparativists, Hinduism was also present in the stereotype of "idol worship," and even a glimmer of Buddhism appeared in the practice of designating the Bushmen as Chinese or "Chinese Hottentots." Jan Van Riebeeck compared them to the inhabitants of northern China; John Barrow thought they were related, through the Egyptians, to the Chinese. Eventually, the comparison between Bushmen and Buddhists became more explicit, as comparativists argued that Bushmen must have come from China because they, like Chinese Buddhists, practiced a religion involving cave art. As historian James McKay noted in 1911, "the Bushmen's assertion that their paintings were intended as embellishments of the caves, which were designed not as dwellings, but as places of worship, probably proves this custom to have been inherited from Buddhist ancestors in East Africa, who would seem to have been a mixture of Egyptian and Chinese." According to McKay, since the Bushmen worshiped their rock paintings like Buddhists, they must have been descendants of Buddhists. Control of the field of religion, therefore, was reinforced not only by the denial or exclusion of others but also by the proliferation of knowledge about the world of religions. In this comparative enterprise, the invention of Hottentot religion simultaneously reinvented the religions of the world.[49]

What was the truth about Hottentot religion? What was it really like? In the 1930s anthropologist Isaac Schapera tried to reconstruct the genuine forms of that religion by comparing the historical reports that we have considered with accounts from contemporary fieldwork. In the end, however, fieldwork merely lent an aura of authority to a representation of Hottentot religion that was similar to previous inventions. The same basic inventory was reproduced. If those previous accounts are suspect, then any representation of Hottentot religion based on them must also be suspect. As Jonathan Z. Smith has argued, the European notion of "religion" has been invented through a history of "imaginative acts of comparison and generalization."[50] Likewise, as this review of European accounts of Hottentot religion should suggest, specific religions have also been invented through similar imaginative acts.

As we have seen, the comparisons and generalizations through which Hottentot religion was invented were worked out on a battlefield. As a result, they remain contestable assertions. They do not provide solid evidence for establishing the truth about Hottentot religion. Rather, they demonstrate the fluctuation of comparative maneuvers on a contested frontier. Although Khoikhoi people have certainly had human experiences and expressions that could be designated as religious, their "religion" was thoroughly and completely a European invention, a product that was invented and reinvented by a frontier comparative religion. As powerful (and by no means innocent) inventions, European denials, discoveries, and constructions of Hottentot religion contributed to the dispossession and displacement of Khoisan people in the

Cape. By denials, European comparativists dismissed any indigenous entitlement to the land. In their discoveries of religion, however, European comparativists did not necessarily affirm Khoisan
humanity. Instead, they certified the containment of the Hottentots and Bushmen within secured colonial boundaries. Once they
were rendered harmless, the Khoisan were found to have a religion that could be museumized and preserved in the archive of
the comparative history of religions.

3

THE RELIGION OF
UNBELIEVERS

As one frontier closed with the establishment of European hegemony over Khoisan people, a second frontier opened against Xhosa-speaking people in the eastern Cape. During the "hundred years' war" from 1779 to 1878 on that frontier, comparative religion was once again conducted on a battlefield. As we should now expect, the practice of comparative religion there also began with denial. The Xhosa had no religion. Missionaries, travelers, settlers, and agents of the colonial government consistently reported that they had no religion. As a people, they were even designated by the term *Kafir*, which meant "unbeliever." O. F. Mentzel explained the term as a religious judgment, with ancient Chaldean roots, that had been incorporated in Jewish and Muslim discourse. Jews referred to those who denied God or who abandoned their religion as *Cofar*; Muslims identified people who were ignorant of the true God or rejected the religion of Islam as *Cofers* or *Caffers*. By the sixteenth century, the reports submitted by the Portuguese Dominican father Joao dos Santos, published in *Ethiopia Oriental* (1609), showed that European Christians were using the same term to designate people living on the Mozambique coast of southern Africa. Drawing together Jewish, Muslim, and Christian judgments, European observers characterized the indigenous people of southern Africa as unbelievers, as people, by definition, without religion.[1]

During the seventeenth century, the term *Cafres* was often applied to the Hottentots and Bushmen in the Cape. As Jodocus Hondius recorded in 1652, there were "no signs of Belief or Religion to be found among them, and its is for this reason they are called Cafres." By the end of the eighteenth century, however, the

term had been reserved for Nguni people in the eastern Cape and
Natal regions. As O. F. Mentzel insisted, these unbelievers were
even worse than the Khoikhoi. "In comparison with other wild
African nations, such as Kaffirs," Mentzel argued, "the Hottentots are far more moral, humane, just, honest and faithful." As
bad as the Hottentots were, therefore, wilder people lived beyond
the frontier. As the frontier opened, those people, the true unbelievers, had no religion. The unanimous European denial
of the existence of any Xhosa religion continued as long as the
Xhosa maintained political independence and mounted armed
resistance against colonial encroachment. After their national
destruction in 1857, the Xhosa suddenly had a religion, proving
that even unbelievers could acquire a religion under colonial subjugation.[2]

THE ANCHOR

In one of the earliest encounters on the eastern Cape frontier,
John Barrow tried to engage the Xhosa in conversations about religion. Sensitive to the difficulties inherent in his inquiry, Barrow
observed that "so different are the opinions and the feelings of
different nations concerning religion, and so difficult do the most
civilized people find it to express their notions clearly and consistently of the 'unknown God,' that little satisfactory information
can be collected on these points without a very familiar and extensive knowledge of the language of the people among whom
the inquiry is made." Communicating through a Khoikhoi interpreter, Barrow thought he could discern Xhosa beliefs in a supernatural power. This power was sometimes benevolent. It was the
creator of all things and the regulator of the movements of the
sun and moon. But it often brought evil through thunder and
lightning and premature death. In these notions, Barrow supposed, the Xhosa might have had some kind of religion.

While conversing on these topics, Barrow showed them his
watch. Astonished, the people shouted, "*Feegas!*" Barrow understood this exclamation to refer to some supernatural influence of
the dead over the living. Although the Xhosa were bewildered by
his watch, Barrow suspected that their reaction might indicate a
glimmer of religion. However, since the Xhosa had never "bewildered their imaginations" with metaphysical concepts about im-

mortality or future states of existence, their response might have merely been a superstitious fear of the dead. Undecided, Barrow abandoned his investigations into Xhosa religion. "As little information was likely to be gained on such abstruse points through the medium of a Hottentot interpreter," he concluded, "the conversation was turned to other subjects less embarrassing, and such as came more immediately before the senses."[3] At the beginning of the nineteenth century, other travelers, as well as missionaries and government officials, continued those investigations. They followed Barrow's advice by following their senses. Focusing their attention on a European artifact—not a watch, but an anchor that had been cast ashore off the Cape coast—they determined that the Xhosa had no religion.

Missionary, Traveler, and Government Agent

In 1800 the first representative of the London Missionary Society in southern Africa, the former soldier, farmer, linguist, and biblical scholar J. T. van der Kemp, reported about the situation in his mission field in the eastern Cape. In the context of a general survey of customs, population, government, language, history, and natural productions, Van der Kemp provided a preliminary assessment of the indigenous religion of the Xhosa-speaking people in the region. Van der Kemp had made a surprising discovery. He had found "no religion," an absence, an empty space in the intellectual register and cultural practices of Xhosa-speaking people. "If by religion we understand reverence of God, or the external action by which that reverence is expressed," Van der Kemp reported, "I never could perceive that they had any religion, nor any idea of the existence of God." Obviously, the Protestant missionary operated with a specific definition of religion that was influenced by certain Christian assumptions about the content of religious belief and the practice of religious worship. Based on his single standard for what counted as religion, Van der Kemp was able to deny the presence of any religion at all among the Xhosa-speaking people of the eastern Cape.

As evidence in justification of that denial, however, Van der Kemp pointed to the presence of certain "superstitions." He argued against Le Vaillant's assertion that there could be no superstition where there was no religion. If Le Vaillant had lived among these unbelievers, Van der Kemp insisted, he would have observed

Bowing to the Anchor. (From Taylor, *Scenes in Africa*)

that they were "extremely superstitious without religion." They combined "credulity and unbelief." For example, Van der Kemp noted that the people displayed a peculiar, superstitious awe before an anchor that had been deposited at the mouth of the Keiskamma River as the result of a shipwreck.

> There lays, near the mouth of the Keiskamma, an old anchor, belonging to a ship which was lost on the coast. Chachabee [Rharhabe, d. 1782], who governed this country (as far as I can find out) about the year 1780 ordered a piece of this anchor to be cut off; the Caffree, who was employed in this work, died soon after. The accident was enough for this people to take in their heads that the anchor had the power of punishing every one who should treat it with disrespect, and also some dominion over the sea. In order to reconcile it, it has been honoured with a peculiar name, and when a Caffree passes by, he salutes it.

People regarded the anchor, Van der Kemp reported, with a strange mixture of fear and respect, avoiding contact but saluting it when they passed. The missionary adduced this curious regard and inexplicable behavior before the anchor as conclusive evidence of a lack of genuine religion among the indigenous people in the eastern Cape. They might have superstitions, but they had no religion.[4]

A few years later, the missionary's observations were confirmed by the findings of a traveler, the German physician and botanist Martin Karl Heinrich Lichtenstein, who explored the same region between 1803 and 1806, a period that coincided with the brief Batavian rule in the Cape. In designating the Xhosa-speaking people of the eastern Cape, Lichtenstein, like Van der Kemp and other missionaries, travelers, and colonists had done before, duplicated the categorical denial of religion that was traceable back to the earliest Arab explorations of Africa. The indigenous people, Lichtenstein noted, had been designated by Muslim travelers and traders as "Cafer (Liar, Infidel)." Operating with their own standard for what counted as religion, Muslim explorers had discovered "no religion" among people in the eastern Cape. Repeating that earlier denial, Lichtenstein also found an absence of religion. Like Van der Kemp, the traveler measured the absence of religion by the presence of what he regarded as "superstition." Among the people of the eastern Cape, he insisted, "there is no appearance of any religious worship whatever." However, in the absence of religion, and as a result of that absence, the people were "addicted to the grossest superstition." They believed in magic, charms, oaths, curses, prognostics, piles of stones, and an anchor that had been washed ashore from a shipwreck off the Cape coast.

> At the mouth of the river Keissi, or Keisskamma, as it is called by the Hottentots, lies the anchor of a stranded ship. Chachábe [Rharhabe], the grandfather of the present king [Ngqika, 1778–1829], had a piece of it broken off, and it so happened that the person by whom this was done died soon after. The anchor was immediately considered as an enchanter, who had power over the sea, and was angry at the offense which had been given him; a name was in consequence conferred upon him, and he is saluted by it whenever any one passes the spot.

Invoking the anchor to illustrate the pervasive superstition among people in the eastern Cape, Lichtenstein concluded that their "superstition, their belief in magic or enchantment, and in omens and prognostics, is in proportion to their want of religious feelings." The anchor, therefore, stood as evidence of an absence of religion. Like the missionary before him, the traveler used the anchor at the mouth of the river to objectify and localize a more general conclusion, the denial of an indigenous African religion.[5]

This same anchor featured in the 1807 report about the life and

customs of the people of the eastern Cape submitted by the government's magistrate in the region, Ludwig Alberti. The magistrate had apparently been so impressed by the anchor that when
the Batavian Cape governor Jan Willem Janssens met in 1803 with
Chief Ngqika to conclude a treaty ending a recent devastating
war, he mentioned it prominently in the account of Xhosa customs he gave to the governor's party. Following the missionary
and the traveler, the agent of the colonial government also used
the anchor as evidence for an absence of religion among the
Xhosa. They had no God, no worship, and no religious ceremonies. "One sees other uncivilized races," Alberti observed, "who
worship the sun or other real or imaginary objects, thereby indicating that they surmise that they are the origin of the ordinary
or extraordinary occurrence of nature or owe their existence to a
particular all-embracing authority, from which to expect benefit
or detriment." In these terms, Alberti recognized a broader definition of religion, including, for example, solar worship within
the scope of what could count as religion. In the eastern Cape,
however, all these forms of religion were absent. Alberti complained in particular about the absence of a priesthood, noting
that in other nations useful information could easily be obtained
from local priests. Among these people such a source of information was entirely lacking. Therefore, the observer had to rely upon
direct observation of behavior, such as the strange practice of honoring an anchor. Their conduct before the anchor, however, was
evidence, not of religion, but of the pervasive hold of superstition.
"More superstitious customs," Alberti promised, "will appear in
sequence." Religion, however, would not appear in these earliest
accounts of the unbelievers in the eastern Cape provided by missionaries, travelers, or government agents.[6]

Land and Sea

On another frontier, therefore, another campaign of denial was
mounted against local religion in southern Africa. But why this
fascination with the anchor? It is tempting to speculate that observers were preoccupied with the apparent mystification of a European artifact as if it symbolized supernatural European power
in Africa. However, it is difficult to recover anything of the meaning or significance of this anchor for the Xhosa-speaking people
in the eastern Cape at the beginning of the nineteenth century.

If we knew its source, which might have been the wreck of a British ship, the *Grosvenor East Indiaman*, that sank in 1782 by the mouth of the Keiskamma River, we would still know very little about the anchor. There was considerable interest in this shipwreck in Britain. The London press expressed horror that the "ship was lost upon the coast of the Caffres, a country inhabited by the most barbarous and monstrous of the human species."[7] For the most part, however, survivors seem to have been received with kindness by local people. They were especially helped by a Muslim "Malayman" who spoke Dutch. Some remained and intermarried with the Xhosa. Knowing that the anchor was from this shipwreck, therefore, would at least remind us that the eastern Cape was not a region populated only by indigenous, Xhosa-speaking people living in primitive isolation. It was a plural, diverse social field, a network of cross-cultural social relations that also involved Khoisan, Muslims, and European settlers, as well as Christian missionaries, travelers, and agents of an expanding colonial government.

To understand Xhosa regard for this anchor, assuming that the reports by Van der Kemp, Lichtenstein, and Alberti are in any respect reliable, we would need to know much more about the local symbolic idioms in which it might have been perceived by Xhosa-speaking people. Hints and guesses might suggest tentative answers to the question of the anchor's local significance for the Xhosa. First, royal authority was asserted in a context of intense political turmoil in the eastern Cape region at the end of the eighteenth century. After 1775, at the death of the Xhosa paramount chief Phato, the polity divided into two factions, one of which was led by Rharhabe. Losing a struggle for dominance, Rharhabe had to accept a subservient position as tributary to a new Xhosa paramount. Following Rharhabe's death in 1782, his political faction was further divided as a result of rivalry between his son Ndlambe and his grandson Ngqika, who descended from another son. Defeating Ndlambe in battle in 1793, Ngqika centralized and broadened the territorial base of his political power. Nevertheless, his dominance remained unstable and contested. In this context, therefore, it is possible that Ngqika regarded the anchor as a specific symbolic assertion of his political power, signifying that he, rather than Ndlambe, controlled a symbol of royal authority that was directly associated with the previous king, Rharhabe.[8]

Second, Van der Kemp and Lichtenstein identified the anchor's

J. T. van der Kemp of the
London Missionary Society.
(Courtesy South African
Library, Cape Town)

Meeting between General J. W. Janssens and Chief Ngqika in 1803.
(Courtesy South African Library, Cape Town)

Chief Ngqika of the Rharabe Xhosa, ca. 1805. (Courtesy Cape
Archives Depot, ref. AG7531)

primary significance in its relation to an unnatural death. Missionaries and travelers frequently observed that Africans lacked any understanding of death by natural causation. As the missionary John Philip reported, "all the Kaffir tribes, have no idea of any man dying except from hunger, violence, or witchcraft. If a man die even at the age of ninety, if he do not die of hunger or by violence, his death is imputed to sorcery or to witchcraft." In these terms, the anchor was an element in a more general theory of the unnatural or supernatural causation of death. However, within its specific historical context, the anchor was located in a region that had in fact recently been transformed by European conquest and settlement, cattle and slave raiding, and persistent drought into a world of hunger, violence, and large-scale, unnatural death. During the 1790s, as one colonial official reported, "It has been noticed that their wealth of cattle is declining noticeably, for which reasons are to be found in their hard and damaging wars with the Christians . . . and in many bad years." Within the local symbolic idiom, witchcraft or sorcery were synonyms for violence, signifying the cause of harm to persons or property. In this respect, the acts of preserving, naming, and saluting the anchor might have signified some measure of ritualized control over the unnatural violence and death that had been unleashed in the eastern Cape. After all, one source of that unnatural violence and death could in fact be located as coming from the sea, from the European invaders and colonizers who, like the anchor, did not belong on the land.[9]

Third, this distinction between sea and land, a symbolic opposition that the anchor could easily have marked, was an important aspect of Ngqika's political vocabulary. In a report of his travels published in 1815, the missionary John Campbell, who cited the anchor as evidence that the Xhosa had "scarcely any religion" but were "very superstitious," alleged that Ngqika had ordered the killing of survivors from shipwrecks off the eastern Cape coast. According to Campbell, "When the Landdrost asked Gika [Ngqika], why the people had murdered those who were driven ashore upon his coast, he said they had no business in his country, but should have kept in their own, meaning the sea, for the Caffres thought they had risen up from the bottom of the sea, having seen the top mast first, then gradually more and more till they beheld the hull, which made them conclude they were natives of the water." Campbell quoted these remarks as evidence of African ignorance. However, Ngqika's insistence that European colonizers "had no business in his country, but should have kept in their own" must surely be read as a statement of political resistance to European presence on the land. Marking and mediating the symbolic opposition between sea and land, the anchor stood as a ritualized monument that asserted "dominion over the sea." By signifying power over the sea, the anchor reasserted political authority over the land that was being violently contested by those "natives of the water" who came from the sea.[10]

The potent symbolic opposition between sea and land was articulated elsewhere in southern Africa during the nineteenth century. For example, by the 1850s the opposition between sea and land had been integrated into a Zulu creation myth. According to one account of this myth, the creator, *uNkulunkulu*, made human beings white and black—one with clothing, the other without, one with guns, the other with spears—and assigned them to different spheres. "The white men may live in the midst of the water, in the sea," the creator said, "the black people shall live within this land."[11] In this story, the violent oppositions of the colonial context were encoded in the basic difference between land and sea. Like the anchor, this myth was a means for reflecting upon and clarifying the colonial situation. The symbolic opposition between land and sea did not represent an ancient, primordial myth; rather, it signified the battlefield of colonial conflict.

In many "peripheral" regions of the world, myths emerged under violent conditions of colonial oppression. Local, indigenous mythographers appropriated symbols from the nineteenth-century Christian missions, while also recasting older mythic themes, to fashion symbolic instruments for reflection upon and resistance to colonial domination. In this symbolic labor, indigenous mythographers acted as comparative religionists. At the beginning of the nineteenth century in southern Africa, while the missionary Van der Kemp was denying that Ngqika had a religion, the Xhosa chief was comparing the missionary to a familiar category in his own religious world, the diviner, a sacred specialist responsible for promoting healing, combating evil, and causing rain. In fact, soon after meeting the missionary, Ngqika purchased Van der Kemp's services, paying him the customary diviner's fee in cattle, for performing a rainmaking ritual. Gradually, however, this morphological comparison between missionary and diviner was replaced by a "hermeneutics of suspicion." Ngqika, like many other chiefs in the region, demythologized the missionary, seeing him, not as a diviner, but as the agent of advancing colonial commerce, conquest, and political administration. On these grounds, Ngqika agreed to accommodate a missionary within his territory, as a diplomat, rather than a diviner. He wanted "to have one who can write for him to the Governor and read his answers, but he has manifested much hostility to the precepts of the word of God."[12]

However, the work of comparative religion continued. For example, it was pursued under the political sovereignty of Ngqika's uncle and rival, Ndlambe, by the prophet and military leader Nxele. Between 1816 and 1819, Nxele refocused the violent oppositions of colonial conflict into a mythic dualism that posited two gods—the god of the whites, whom he called *Thixo* (transposing the Khoi, and later Xhosa, name for God used by the missionaries), and the god of the blacks, *Mdalidiphu*, the "Creator of the Deeps," who was the divine power residing in the land but holding dominion over the sea. According to Nxele's myth, whites had been punished for killing the son of their god by being cast into the sea. Although whites had come ashore in search for land, they would soon be forced back into the sea by the superior power of Mdalidiphu. As this apocalyptic scenario unfolded in colonial history, however, Nxele was forced to surrender shortly after an unsuccessful attack on Grahamstown in 1819. Imprisoned on Robben Island, off the Cape coast, Nxele drowned in the sea while attempting to escape. Although his primary role was prophet, Nxele also acted as a comparative religionist by developing a dual classification that distinguished between the religion of the land and the religion of the sea. By modulating the recurring symbolic opposition between land and sea, Nxele advanced a comparative religion in early-nineteenth-century southern Africa in which comparisons were worked out on a battlefield.[13]

Religion and Superstition

On the other side of the battle lines, Van der Kemp, Lichtenstein, and Alberti used the anchor to punctuate an opposition between superstition and religion. This opposition was commonplace in the comparative discourse of the frontier, as British missionaries and travelers also used it to dismiss the religion of white, Dutch-speaking farmers, observing with the traveler James Chapman that "the majority of Boers are superstitious." Lacking genuine religion, they were also idolaters. As British Naval officer Robert Percival observed, "money is the idol of the Dutch." In their reading of the anchor, therefore, missionaries, travelers, and colonial administrators submerged its political significance under a more general project of religious denial. Employing the fundamental distinction between religion and superstition, these observers discovered an absence of religion in the eastern Cape. That denial was picked up and perpetuated in Europe, appearing in 1858, for example, in James Gardner's standard compendium of religions, *Faiths of the World*. "From all that can be ascertained on the religion of the Kaffirs," Gardner concluded, "it seems that those of them who are still in their heathen state have no idea (1) of a Supreme Intelligent Ruler of the universe; (2) of a sabbath; (3) of a day of judgment; (4) of the guilt and pollution of sin; (5) of a Saviour to deliver them from the wrath to come." In Europe, as in southern Africa, therefore, comparative religion could be devoted to a strategic tracking of absences.[14]

Although this project of denial represented the mission field as an empty space for religious conversion, it also performed another important function by transposing into southern Africa a particular kind of Protestant comparative religion in Europe that had distinguished Roman Catholic "superstition" from genuine religion. Drawing upon a tradition of comparison that can be traced back to the end of the sixteenth century, when the Protestant theologian Richard Hooker first used the plural English term *religions* specifically to distinguish between Protestants and Roman Catholics, the missionary, traveler, and magistrate projected an ongoing Protestant polemic against Catholics onto African religion. In Europe, Protestant comparativists had often contrasted their own religion, specified simply as *religion*, with what they dismissed as "pagano-papism," a complex of what they regarded as Catholic superstition, magic, worship of the dead in the persons of saints, and worship of objects in the forms of icons, statues, or relics.

At the same time that the London Missionary Society (LMS) was opening its mission in southern Africa, the society was engaged in mission work on a second front in France against what the directors called "the pretensions of the Papacy" and "the abominations of Popery." In its "Report concerning the State of Religion in France," the directors of the LMS identified Roman Catholicism not only as a false religion but as superstition: "the superstitions of Popery." With the advance of Protestant religion,

they promised, "the day of infidelity and superstition is closing."
In the early nineteenth century, therefore, Protestant observers, whether missionaries, travelers, or government officials,
could easily transpose this basic comparative opposition between
genuine religion and superstition onto local African beliefs
and practices. Like Roman Catholicism, indigenous African
religion could be dismissed by these Protestant comparativists
as superstition, magic, worship of the dead, and worship of objects.[15]

For their part, Catholic missionaries occasionally returned the
denial. For example, Bishop Patrick Raymond Griffith observed
in 1838 that the Protestants might teach their converts to sing,
"but [they] teach them *no* religion."[16] Eventually, however, Catholic missionaries in southern Africa also learned to represent African religion as superstition, magic, and the worship of the dead
and objects. These resilient comparative categories that originated on the religious battlefield of Protestant anti-Catholic
polemics remained the primary terms under which African religion was regarded in comparative religion throughout the nineteenth and well into the twentieth century. Imagining it as suffused
with superstition and magic, rather than with genuine religious
thought or feeling, European comparativists represented African
religion as the worship of the dead, referring to the importance of
ritual veneration directed toward ancestors, and the worship
of objects, whether that worship was termed by European scholars
as *fetishism, animism,* or *totemism.* In this respect, the anchor
could stand as an emblem of African religion, representing both
a superstitious regard for the dead and for objects. Therefore,
rather than merely a denial of religion, Van der Kemp, Lichtenstein, and Alberti proposed an opposition between religion
and superstition that transferred the polemical comparative categories of a European religious battlefield onto a southern African
religious landscape.

These suggestions about the significance of the anchor are
nothing more than speculation. They represent only a preliminary attempt to reanchor the object in its historical, geographical,
and political context. What is certain, however, is that the missionary, traveler, and government agent appropriated the anchor
for their own purposes in a specific symbolic project. They used it
to mark a symbolic opposition between religion and superstition.
Accordingly, in their accounts, the anchor stood as a monument
to the lack of religion among this indigenous people of southern
Africa. Ironically, in the light of the history of European denials

of Khoikhoi religion, the Xhosa-speaking people of the eastern Cape were thought to be so devoid of religion that they had to borrow from the Hottentots. As Van der Kemp reported, a Xhosa word for God, *Thixo*, had been adopted from the Khoikhoi. The missionaries, in turn, had appropriated this word for their own evangelizing purposes as the name of God. Alberti reported that the Xhosa had to rely on the ritual expertise of Hottentot rainmakers. They had also adopted the Khoikhoi practice of building stone cairns by roadways or river crossings. The Xhosa were so superstitious, therefore, that they had to acquire beliefs and practices from people who had been characterized in European reports as the most superstitious in the world.[17]

Many implications could be drawn from this religious project of denial, a project that was extended all over southern Africa during the first half of the nineteenth century, as missionaries repeatedly reported home their remarkable discoveries of "no religion" among people in southern Africa. Most dramatically, perhaps, this assertion that the indigenous people of the region lacked religion negated their full humanity and thereby contributed to the colonial representation of southern Africa as an empty, open space for colonization. By midcentury, however, this denial could no longer be sustained. In the face of resistance to conversion and conquest, missionaries and agents of the colonial government increasingly realized that they were engaged in a contest of religions. As colonial agent Joseph Cox Warner observed in the 1850s, the Xhosa-speaking people in the eastern Cape had "a regular system of superstition which answers all the purposes of any other false religion." Still identified as superstition, the local, indigenous religion was nevertheless rescued from complete denial. Rather than appearing as "no religion," it could be engaged, like other religions, as a "false religion." That recognition, however, only came after the national destruction of the Xhosa people. Like the Khoikhoi, the Xhosa would be credited with a religion only after they had been subjected to colonial domination.[18]

MISSIONARY THEORIES OF RELIGION

While the distinction between religion and superstition provided the basic framework for their comparative religion, missionaries also advanced morphological and genealogical comparisons in their efforts to make sense out of Xhosa beliefs and practices. Missionary societies in Europe showed an interest in comparison. In 1831, for example, the Glasgow Missionary Society called upon its agents in southern Africa to investigate Xhosa customs with a view to comparing them with the customs of the Jews. The only response to this instruction was an "Essay on the Antiquity of Circumcision" submitted by William Ritchie Thomson. Nevertheless, morphological comparisons were common. Frequently, missionaries in southern Africa compared Xhosa superstition with basic religious forms or structures, such as the priesthoods, temples, or practices of idolatry found by their colleagues in India or other pagan lands. In the eastern Cape during the first half of the nineteenth century, most missionaries would have agreed with the observation of Andrew Steedman that the absence of religion represented an obstacle that was comparable to its presence in pagan religious systems. As Steedman explained, "Although the missionaries in this country are unopposed by those obstacles which present so formidable a barrier to the progress of Christianity in India and other parts of the world—since the natives of Cafferland can scarcely be said to have any religion at all, and have no priests, nor temples, nor any form of worship—there are, nevertheless, great difficulties to contend with, proceeding from their ignorance, and more especially from their deep-rooted superstitions." In this morphological analysis, Xhosa superstition, although not designated as religion, assumed the same structural position as the idolatrous forms of worship of India in posing an obstacle to Christianity.[19]

More often, however, missionaries on the eastern Cape frontier proposed temporal comparisons. They advanced theories of the progress or degeneration of the Xhosa from some primordial origin. While the missionary administrator John Philip suggested that Xhosa superstitions had developed from an original ignorance, most missionaries proposed that Xhosa beliefs and practices had degenerated from an ancient religion, even arguing that the Xhosa had descended from the ancient Near East. Through an analysis of language and customs, missionary comparative religion in the eastern Cape developed a genealogy for the Xhosa that suggested they were the Arabs of southern Africa.

Arriving in the Cape in 1819, the Reverend John Philip assumed direction of the expanding work of the London Missionary Society in southern Africa. A controversial figure known for defending Khoikhoi rights but also for advocating British inter-

ests, Philip supervised the mission society for thirty years from
its headquarters in Cape Town. Maintaining close contacts with
London, he published in 1828 a two-volume defense of mission
work, *Researches in South Africa*, which was designed, in part,
to promote the image of the mission in Britain. In Philip's terms,
the Christian mission was good not only for "natives" in foreign
lands, among whom it was "scattering the seeds of civilization,
social order and happiness," but also for "extending British interests, British influence, and British empire." At the same time,
Philip implicitly advanced a comparative religion. Missionaries,
he argued, had made a special contribution to scientific knowledge because of their expertise in foreign languages. Translation
had expanded knowledge. Missionary translations had made foreign literatures, such as the literature of the East, available to British readers. But translation had also required extensive knowledge on the part of missionaries since every field of knowledge,
"in science or literature, in the history of men or manners,"
was required to make successful translations. By expanding the
scope of knowledge, missionaries had been pioneers in comparison. "Every new translation of the Scriptures into a modern
language," Philip observed, "provokes comparison." Every act of
translation required comparisons between ancient and modern,
the familiar and the foreign, the known and the unknown.
"The effects of missions are not to be confined to what consti-
tutes their principal object," Philip advised. In addition to extending Christian civilization, the missions also performed a
scientific role through the work of translation and comparison.
In this regard, the mission was also engaged in comparative
religion.[20]

Progress and Degeneration

In surveying the indigenous religions of southern Africa, however,
John Philip, like other commentators of the period, found no belief in God among either Hottentots or "Caffers," although he did
note that the missionary John Brownlee had recently found that
the Xhosa held "some idea of a Supreme Being, whom they call
Uhlanga." Without a clear belief in God, however, Africans could
not be said to have a religion, even though they did have numerous superstitious beliefs and customs. In repeating this distinction between religion and superstition, Philip proposed more than

merely another denial of African religion. Instead, he outlined a theory of the origin of superstition. "The different superstitions in the world," Philip maintained, "have one common origin: they spring from confused ideas of an invisible agency." All superstitions, whether the "elegant" mythology of ancient Greece, or the "vulgar" notions of contemporary Africa, had the same source. "Everything in a state of ignorance, which is not known, and which is involved in mystery, is the object of superstitious veneration," Philip observed. More specifically, superstition was born out of an ignorance of secondary causes. When the actual causes of events were unknown, people substituted some invisible agency in their place. Hence, superstition arose, according to Philip, from a natural ignorance of natural causation. Without the benefit of revealed religion, and the scientific knowledge that Philip assumed came with it, superstition was "a natural growth of human nature in every climate, and in every soil." This original, natural ignorance, however, held the potential for progress. Beginning in ignorance, human beings could develop into religion. As the superstitions of ancient Greece had given way to Christianity, Philip promised, so would those of Africa. Although they started with superstition, Africans could progress to religion.[21]

In the meantime, the superstitions of Africans were only of interest to the extent that they provided a dramatic contrast to the religion of the mission. Philip had no intention of embarking on an inventory or analysis of the superstitions of different political groupings in southern Africa. "The aspects of superstition among savage or barbarous tribes are so various and so trifling, and the resemblance between them is so great," Philip asserted, "that on knowing the superstitions of one tribe, all is known that is worth relating." Accordingly, Philip's comparative religion distinguished only between an undifferentiated mass of superstition and what he regarded as genuine religion. If Africans were "not brought under the influence of pure Christianity," he concluded, "they must be left to fall under the influence of superstition or infidelity." By identifying the potential for moving from an original ignorance to revealed religion, however, Philip advanced a theory of progress.[22]

By contrast, other missionaries proposed that Xhosa-speaking people had once had a religion, perhaps even a revealed religion, but that they had subsequently lost it. Instead of progress from an original ignorance, therefore, these missionaries traced a trajectory of degradation. In 1829 Cowper Rose, who served for four years on the Cape frontier with the Royal Engineers, recalled that this theory of degradation had been proposed by a missionary in the region. The missionary told Rose that "the Kaffers are a people who had once a much greater degree of civilization than they now possess." As evidence, the missionary cited their superstitions, including their belief in witchcraft, their practice of circumcision, and their funerals. Rather than original ignorance, therefore, African superstition was the trace of a lost religion.[23]

The missionary in question was very likely the Wesleyan William Shaw. Entering the eastern Cape with the influx of British settlers in 1820, Shaw formulated a theory of African degradation in his earliest reports to the Wesleyan Missionary Society. Published as a book after his retirement to England in 1856, Shaw's researches in comparative religion were situated in the eastern Cape frontier conflicts of the first half of the nineteenth century. Like other missionaries in the region, Shaw found that the Xhosa were "not only without a knowledge of the *true God*, but without the knowledge of *any* God true or false." Restating the opposition between religion and superstition, he observed that "the Kaffir nations cannot properly be said to possess any RELIGION; but they practice a complicated system of SUPERSTITION." As Cowper Rose recalled, the missionary insisted that these superstitions should be understood as remnants from an earlier lost religion. According to William Shaw, "There can be little doubt that the remote ancestors of the Kaffirs professed some kind of religion; but, from the absence of any form of hieroglyphical or other kind of writing, tradition has merely served to preserve certain outward ceremonies, which have necessitated the perpetuation of a class of persons who are obviously the living representatives of an ancient Priesthood, that was accustomed to celebrate the rites of some old but unknown form of religion." In this formulation, the rainmakers and other diviners were unknowingly the successors of a former priesthood that had conducted the rituals of a forgotten religion. In the past, Shaw suggested, that ancient religion had sought the favor of God and blessedness in a future life. These religious concerns, however, had become submerged over time by interests in obtaining practical benefits and averting evil. As they were currently performed, he concluded, "these rites are superstitious rather than religious." Nevertheless, in the absence of hieroglyphics, or other written records, these superstitions could be read as traces of ancient history. Although forgotten by their degraded descendants, these remnants of superstition suggested to

William Shaw that the ancient ancestors of the Xhosa had once
had a religion.[24]

Xhosa Arabs

The theory of degradation from an earlier, higher religion frequently appeared in reports about Xhosa-speaking people in the
eastern Cape. Sometimes, that higher religion was identified as
Islam. John Barrow, for example, had found in their practice of
circumcision remains of "that grand feature of Islamism." Most
often, however, that origin was specified as a pre-Islamic Arab
descent that was shared by Muslims. "Were I to speculate upon
their origin," the missionary Stephen Kay reported in 1833, "I
would have little hesitation in giving it as my opinion, that they
are descended from some of the tribes of these wandering Arabs,
known by the name of Bedouins." In the 1840s John Appleyard
held that the Xhosa were of "Ishmaelitish descent," having the
same origin as the Muslims of Arabia. Based on five years' experience on the colonial frontier in the 1840s, Harriet Ward recounted
the biblical history of the patriarchs in some detail to situate the
Xhosa as descendants of Ishmael. Because not everyone was sufficiently familiar with the Pentateuch, she complained, there had
arisen "a confused idea that the Kaffir habits, customs, ceremonies, etc., are of Jewish origin, which they are not—but they are
decidedly patriarchal." Their roots could be traced back to Arabs
who had either "refused to admit the doctrines of Mahomet"
or had already begun their migrations south by the time of the
Prophet.

By 1853 the Reverend Francis Fleming, who served as chaplain
for the colonial army on the frontier, could identify the Xhosa
with the "wandering Arabs of the Desert." In support of this Arabian connection, Fleming cited "the few indistinct traces of religion, which are yet to be discernible among them." Although they
no longer believed in God, according to Fleming, the Xhosa had
maintained beliefs and practices, such as animal sacrifice and circumcision, that provided "strong corroboration to this conjec-
ture, which refers the origin of this people to Ishmael, the son of
Abraham by Hagar." They were, Fleming reinforced three years
later, "Ishmaelitish sons of Abraham." Ironically, therefore, the
Xhosa, who had been designated by the Arabic term for unbeliever in the religion of Islam, were now, according to this theory,

actually descendants from the same original stock as Muslim believers of Arabia.[25]

As these missionary theorists knew, Muslims were in fact living in the eastern Cape frontier. On the earliest mission to the region, J. T. van der Kemp had reported meeting a "Mahometan Hindoo" who had requested lessons from him in reading and writing Dutch. Indicating a widespread Muslim presence, tombs bearing Arabic inscriptions from the Qur'an were found in the region. Muslim festivals were popular local events. Harriet Ward recalled participating in a celebration of the end of Ramadan not only with Muslims but also with a Dutch farmer, a British soldier, and a group of Khoikhoi who all sang along with the chorus. There is even evidence to suggest some Xhosa interest in the religion of Islam. During his tour of duty in the eastern Cape, Lieutenant Colonel John Sutherland introduced his Muslim servant to Maqoma, the Xhosa chief and military leader. As Sutherland recalled,

> I told MAKOMA that a Mahommedan servant of mine, with a fine black beard, who happened to be giving us a glass of wine, would, as a term of reproach, call him a Kaffer, call me a Kaffer, and call all men Kaffers who did not believe in the God which he worshipped. MAKOMA was very solicitous to know where the God of the Mahommedans was to be found, and when I told him that he must ask SEYUD JAFFER, for that their God was not my God, he said that he would summon the servant to his resting place, and enter on the inquiry immediately.

European observers, therefore, were aware that Muslims were present in southern Africa, both in the established Muslim community in Cape Town and on the eastern Cape frontier. Occasionally, a comparison was drawn that highlighted a fundamental difference these observers perceived between the Cape Muslims, referred to as *Malays,* and the Xhosa on the frontier. As the British visitor Alfred Cole argued, the Muslims in Cape Town were more respectable than other people of color in southern Africa because their religion promoted cleanliness and temperance, the two virtues, he concluded, that were "the very ones in which the other coloured tribes are mainly deficient." For the most part, however, missionary comparativists showed a remarkable lack of interest in their Muslim contemporaries in southern Africa. If they thought about Islam at all, missionaries tended to imagine an Arab language, culture, and religion from which the Xhosa had supposedly descended.[26]

Although William Shaw had proposed that the Xhosa had lost an unknown ancient religion, these attempts to link them to Islam or to pre-Islamic Arabs specified their degradation as apostasy from a more familiar religion. In either case, however, emphasis on their current degradation was prominent in these reports. Barnabas Shaw, who had arrived in 1816 to establish the first Wesleyan mission stations in the region, insisted that the Xhosa were "deeply sunk in degradation and ignorance." Without any idea of a Supreme Being, according to Barnabas Shaw, they had even lost all recollection of the basic truths of "Natural Religion." This theory of degeneration was also popular in London during the first half of the nineteenth century. As Archbishop of Dublin Richard Whately put it as late as 1854, "All savages are degenerated remnants of more civilised races." On southern African frontiers, the theory of degeneration, which proposed that indigenous people had lost or forgotten an earlier religion, was part of the larger project of denial. Any traces of religion that might be found could still be used as evidence for denial because they represented broken fragments rather than a religious system. As the historian Robert Montgomery Martin noted in 1843, "no regular system of idolatry exists among them . . . [but] some scattered traces may even be found of the remains of religious institutions." Although the Xhosa might display degenerate traces, remnants, or fragments of a former religion, they had no religious system, not even a "regular system of idolatry."[27]

As we have seen, such total denial was a comparative strategy particularly suited for the conditions of a contested frontier. On the battlefield, the enemy had no religion. At the front lines of a contest of religions, Christian missionaries adopted this strategy of denial. However, denial was also a strategy that suited the interests of European settlers who during the 1820s and 1830s had increasingly established their presence, and their claims on land, in the eastern Cape. In addition to missionary accounts, therefore, the frontier also produced settler theories of religion.

SETTLER THEORIES OF RELIGION

In 1820 British settlers were placed on the contested frontier of the eastern Cape as a buffer between Xhosa and the colonial town of Grahamstown. Although the Xhosa had only recently been driven out of the area, these settlers imagined that they were staking their claims on vacant land. "Tribes of barbarians *had* dwelt in it," the Reverend Henry Dugmore remarked. "But they had gone before the British Settlers came." As one of the Methodist clergy accompanying those settlers, Dugmore indicated that the settlers had an interest in religion. In Dugmore's case, however, that interest did not extend to the black "barbarians" on the frontier. Rather, Dugmore was alarmed by what he saw as the descent of Dutch-speaking farmers and cattle herders into barbarism. According to Dugmore, the example of these frontier Boers proved "that families of a civilized race may go down fearfully in social condition, where the elevating influences of Christianity are superseded by those of Heathenism."[28] In order to counter the influences of heathenism, the clergy's first priority was to attend to the religious life of European settlers. As we have seen, however, a missionary such as William Shaw, who also accompanied these settlers, did display an interest in Xhosa religion, finding that they had degraded into barbarism long before the supposed degradation of the Boers under their heathen influence. Like the missionaries, British settlers developed this theme of degeneration as an explanatory device in their theories of religion.

In 1827 the settler Thomas Philipps, who, in many respects, was sympathetic to the Xhosa, remarked about their religion in terms that must have been commonplace among the British settlers. They were named, he noted, by "an Arabian word for infidel, or bad man." Although many settlers were convinced that the Xhosa had earned this epithet—*infidels*, because they lacked religion; *bad*, because they stole cattle—Philipps observed that they nevertheless had traces of religious heritage. "They have some Mahometan and Jewish rites," he stated. These traces, however, were mixed with idolatry, since they supposedly idolized two species of birds, the toucan and the black crane. Although he identified these religious elements, Thomas Philipps concluded on a note of denial by insisting that "with these and a few similar exceptions, they have no idea of worship."

Reports about the evil nature and infidelity of the Xhosa escalated in the context of the Fourth Frontier War, which broke out in 1835. Serving in that campaign, James Alexander noted that the Xhosa were thieves by nature. "The Kaffir amusements are various," he asserted. "The last and great amusement is *stealing cattle*." More than merely amusement, cattle theft was an almost religious devotion. "Their god is their cattle," the Reverend John

Appleyard noted, taking the settlers' side on this point, "and plunder is their prominent desire." However, although cattle was presumed to be their god, cattle stealing was not a religion, but the absence of religion. Ignoring the historical context in which cattle raiding had become a strategy of war on both sides of the frontier, James Alexander explained that Xhosa retaliation resulted from their lack of religion. "What is to be expected," he exclaimed, "from a people who know not God, and have no sense of obligation." Lacking any idea of a creator, or any belief in an afterlife of reward and punishment, the Xhosa, according to Alexander, had no sense of morality. Since they had no morality, British forces, for their part, could act against them without moral restraint.[29]

Christianizing, Civilizing

This denial of the religious and moral character of the Xhosa was clearly located as a strategy on the frontier battlefield. But it was also directed against the efforts of parliamentary liberals in London, who, with the support of some missionaries in southern Africa, were conducting investigations into the treatment of aborigines in British colonies. Not only committed to ending the slave trade, they were also concerned about the displacement of indigenous people from their land. British humanitarians, like Saxe Bannister, argued that it was "impossible to justify our present course of destroying every where those, whose only crime is, that they precede us in the possession of lands, which we desire to enjoy to their exclusion." On the eastern Cape frontier, however, settlers and colonists, who were asserting their claims to the land, complained that Parliament was being manipulated by self-serving missionaries. As James Alexander insisted, the entire world was being misled by a certain "religiopolitical party, [who] in their mad ambition for extending their sway over South Africa, have pretended [that Africans] were far more 'sinned against, than sinning.'" Caught in this conflict between British missionaries and settlers, as well as between London and the eastern Cape, colonial official Andries Stockenstrom reflected with some skepticism on the motives of all the interested European parties. Although all professed Christian commitment, Stockenstrom noted, for most "the question is not whether it is right or wrong, Christian or brutal, to plunder, massacre, and exterminate the

Irish Celt, the Red Indian, the Hottentot, the Kaffir, the Hindoo, the Burman, the Chinaman, and the Japanese, but the simple question is *'will it pay.'"*[30]

Under the direction of Thomas Fowell Buxton in 1834, the Parliamentary Select Committee on Aborigines had begun its hearings, drawing witnesses from the missionary and anti-slavery movements. After the committee published its findings in 1836–37, its work inspired the formation of organizations—the Aborigines' Protection Society in 1838 and the Society for the Extinction of the Slave Trade and for the Civilization of Africa in 1839—dedicated to ensuring better treatment for the "natives" in British colonial possessions. These initiatives in London further widened the rift between missionary and settler positions in southern Africa. Many missionaries saw the hearings of the Select Committee as an opportunity to gain support for their particular approach to the extension of "Christian civilization" in Africa. First Christianize, they urged; then civilization would necessarily follow. The missionaries presented Andrew Stoffell, a "converted Hottentot," who testified before the Select Committee that as a result of the mission "we are altogether better men." As evidence of that improvement, Stoffell submitted that Hottentots could now read and write, wear clothes, use a plow, learn trades, and "make all things except a watch and a coach." The mission had produced not only better men but also better women. As another example of missionary success, Stoffell noted with pride that as a result of the influence of Christianity an observer could not tell the difference between a Hottentot woman and an English woman when viewing them from behind. This material proof of Christian conversion, according to Andrew Stoffell, demonstrated the benefits of the missionary approach to civilization. "The Missionaries have done much good," he concluded; "they have tamed the Hottentots."[31]

The initiatives of Parliament and benevolent organizations for extending "Christian civilization" and protecting aboriginal people from its destructive byproducts were largely informed by the missionary project. To the extent that these interventions were influenced by missionaries, however, they were resented by British settlers on the colonial frontier. From the settler perspective, the missionaries had reversed the proper formula for "Christian civilization." First civilize, they argued, by breaking the political independence of the "natives" on the frontier; then Christian conversion would inevitably follow. On the military front, for example, Harry Smith, at the conclusion of the brutal 1835 war against the Xhosa, introduced a new religious policy. After containing Xhosa resistance, Smith undertook his own investigations into their religion, spending six hours a day, over several days, discussing Xhosa customs and traditions with a senior counselor of Chief Maqoma. Smith claimed to have discerned resemblances with the laws of Moses. Nevertheless, based on what he had learned from his informant, Smith intervened in Xhosa religious life not only by insisting on being called *Inkosi Inkulu*, "chief of chiefs," but also by outlawing the practices of witch detection, rainmaking, and female initiation. Through these measures, Smith assumed that he was doing better than the missionaries in advancing "Christian civilization." As a comparative religionist on the frontier, Harry Smith learned just enough about Xhosa religion to identify the precise points at which it could be destroyed.[32]

Armed Comparative Religion

Along similar lines, a settler theory of religion was developed by Robert Godlonton, editor of the *Graham's Town Journal*. As a prominent spokesman for the settlers, Godlonton attacked not only the Xhosa for their alleged plunder and murder, depredation and molestation, but also any "philanthropist" who might take their part in the frontier struggle. In his account, *A Narrative of the Irruption of the Kafir Hordes*, published in 1835, Godlonton formulated the position of the settlers on the religious beliefs and practices of the Xhosa. "They have no system of religion, nor form of worship," he asserted, "and scarcely any idea of a supreme being." Qualifying this denial, Godlonton admitted that remote tribes preserved a notion of a deity in the name *umDali*, the creator, to whom they made sacrificial offerings for rain. Furthermore, they seemed to have some indistinct notion about the immortality of the soul that was evident in their sacrifices for the departed. Nevertheless, Godlonton insisted, "On all these subjects the mind of a Kafir is deplorably dark; all they can say is, that it is, and has been, from time immemorial, their custom; and that which their forefathers have done, they must also do." Lacking religion, "like all barbarous people," Godlonton concluded, "the Kafirs are lamentably superstitious."[33]

However, as a comparativist religionist, Godlonton claimed to know Xhosa religion better than the Xhosa. Their superstitions had not been performed unchanged from time immemorial, as the Xhosa claimed, but had degenerated from the beliefs and practices of an earlier, more noble religion. Godlonton insisted that "these tribes, whatever their origin, have greatly degenerated from the manners and customs of their forefathers." Without written records, Godlonton's reconstruction of that ancient religion had to be guided by analogy and inference. It was possible, he maintained, to infer from their language a foreign origin. The Xhosa language, Godlonton held, displayed "traces of its eastern origin in the frequent occurrence of words which are plainly of Hebrew or Arabic extraction." Agreeing with John Barrow on this point, Godlonton traced the Xhosa back to a remote home in Arabia. Over centuries of migration, he argued, their original language, sharing common features with Hebrew and Arabic, had degenerated under the influence of the African dialects they encountered on their way to southern Africa. This reconstruction of Xhosa history through linguistic analysis was common on the eastern Cape frontier. For example, Henry Calderwood, the former missionary turned government official, introduced a variation into the analysis of the Xhosa language that had the same effect as Godlonton's argument. Instead of identifying foreign words, Calderwood focused on linguistic structure. Although Xhosa was, according to Calderwood, a "barbarous" language, attention to the "philosophy of the language"—its construction, completeness, and conformity to definite rules—seemed "to indicate a higher and more civilised origin than the present condition of this people would lead us to suspect." Like Godlonton, Calderwood concluded from this linguistic analysis that "their forefathers have been intruders into the present home of this people." Therefore, on linguistic evidence, the Xhosa supposedly did not belong in southern Africa.[34]

If a foreign origin could be inferred from their language, Godlonton argued, then an original religion could be deduced from their customs. Using a similar comparative method, he noted that "many persons suppose that they can discover in many of their ceremonies an affinity to those established by the ancient Jews." Circumcision, for example, had often been cited as a custom inherited from Jewish or Islamic practice. Instead of tracing a genealogy back to a known religion, however, Godlonton proposed that Xhosa customs could provide evidence for reconstructing something of the character of an earlier, unknown religion. Godlonton provided three illustrations of his comparative method. First, he suggested that the ceremonial clothing worn during male initiation was evidence of an earlier mode of dress worn by everyone under the influence of their earlier religion. Assuming that, like European Christians, the Xhosa once wore clothing, Godlonton inferred that "the barbarous state of nudity in which they are found at the present day,—and which indicates the very lowest grade of savage life—is evidently an innovation upon former custom." Second, he proposed that incest avoidance, a healthy feature of the earlier religion, had degenerated into more elaborate and extreme avoidances of certain kinds of association between males and females. As a result, an ancient praiseworthy custom had "been corrupted by the lapse of time so as to deaden the most sacred affections of the human mind, and to mar the most pure and amiable associations—that of social family intercourse." Third, he maintained that Xhosa hospitality, which was so incongruous with the settler image of them as ruthless barbarians, was a remnant of an earlier religious life from which they had degenerated. In all these cases, Godlonton found "relics of customs which clearly indicate a much higher state of morals, and far greater advancement in civilization than that which is now perceived or found among them." These relics of a better past, however, were allegedly mixed with disgusting vices, appalling cruelties, and "the most barbarous rites and practices." As Godlonton concluded, comparison of the contemporary Xhosa with their lost past only made their current "moral darkness" all the more apparent.[35]

According to Godlonton's settler theory of religion, the customs of the Xhosa were not only degenerate but also dangerous. In particular, their customs were conducive to raiding colonial cattle. The practice of circumcision was not merely a rite of initiation into adulthood. It constituted a military force committed to cattle raiding that comprised all adult males. Their gendered division of labor, in which women were responsible for agriculture while men tended to cattle, politics, and ritual, freed men from labor to devote their full time to fighting and raiding cattle. On the colonial frontier, therefore, Godlonton interpreted the "cattle complex" of Xhosa society as a direct threat to settler interests. Although missionaries had spent decades trying to convert the Xhosa, little had been accomplished. However, Godlonton observed, "Pagan superstitions and national customs are not to be overturned or subverted in a day." They could only be changed, not by Christian missions, but by a sustained exercise of military force on the frontier.[36]

Another settler of the same generation, John Mitford Bowker, agreed with this analysis. Having served from 1835 to 1839 as resident agent among the Mfengu, a disparate gathering of refugees who had attached themselves to the colonial government, Bowker became a prominent spokesman for settler interests during the 1840s. Bowker offered the fate of the Mfengu as a model for the advance of "Christian civilization" in southern Africa. In a letter to Colonial Governor Benjamin D'Urban in 1837, Bowker observed that unconquered nations value their own customs and despise those of other nations. Once a nation was conquered, however, the hold of ancestral custom vanished. The destruction of the Mfengu had broken their national pride, prejudices, and customs. "They are a conquered people," Bowker concluded, "and their spirit as an independent nation . . . is gone, and a desire to adopt our manners and customs is daily developing itself." According to Bowker, therefore, conquest was the only formula for advancing "Christian civilization" in southern Africa. Throughout the 1840s he attacked the Aborigines Protection Society, the anti-slavery movement, and other philanthropic institutions as "things of naught." The Christian mission, in particular, had been "*a perfect failure.*" However, a "firm and enlightened Government on the Kafir frontier," Bowker insisted, "would speedily have more effect in civilizing and Christianizing the Kafirs."

Implicit in Bowker's analysis of the colonial situation was a theory of religion. All over the world, he maintained, people aspired to imitate their superiors in matters of custom and religion. If it really believed its Christianity to be a superior way of life, the British government, as Bowker wrote in an open letter to its secretary, had a responsibility to teach "savage nations," by means of conquest, "to fear and respect, to *stand in* awe of a nation whose manners and customs, whose religion, it is beneficial and desirable for them to adopt." If they could not be conquered and converted, then the Xhosa would have to be destroyed, since, according to Bowker in 1845, "the history of colonization is the record of the dark man's disappearance."[37]

Settler theories of religion, therefore, implied an armed comparative religion, with comparisons backed up by force or the threat of force. Behind the theory that Xhosa superstitions were based on fear, awe, or terror, and derived from distant Arabia, stood British troops who were deployed on the frontier to terrorize and displace the Xhosa. On the other side of the battle lines, Xhosa comparativists were also trying to analyze the different religions engaged in the colonial conflict. Although their voices were submerged under the reports of missionaries and settlers, they occasionally surfaced to cast a different critical perspective on the assumptions of European comparative religion on the frontier. In response to the mass killing, destruction, and displacement that had been inflicted on them by the troops of Lieutenant Colonel Henry Sommerset, many Xhosa people apparently concluded that the Europeans had more than one religion. "How many are these gospels that you preach?" they wondered. "We ask because Somerset came and said 'stop doing evil,' and yet he kills people every day." For a similar reason, others asked, "Why do not the missionaries first go to their own countrymen and convert them first?" In contrast to missionary and settler theories of religion, Xhosa comparativists articulated their own critical analysis of the Christian mission. After a church service in Grahamstown in the 1840s, a Xhosa man stood to question the minister: "How strange that the word of your One God should be allowed to weigh against the will and inclination of the whole world! Your cause is hardly a good one, when hundreds and millions are opposed in deed and opinion to One!"[38]

This critical perspective was echoed in London in the mid-1840s by the Aborigines' Protection Society, which observed that in Africa not even the slave trade had been "so destructive of the aboriginal population of the country as European civilisation." British settlers in the eastern Cape were outraged by such observations. However, they were consoled by realizing that self-critique was not the official policy of the British government. By 1853, in Earl Grey's account, the settler perspective on religion had been internalized in British foreign policy. If the "natives" remained "uncivilized and unimproved, adhering to the barbarous customs of their ancestors," Earl Grey warned, they would only "prove an intolerable nuisance to European Settlers." In Grey's admonition, therefore, the Foreign Office repeated the basic principles of a settler comparative religion that had found Xhosa beliefs and practices both degenerate and dangerous on a contested frontier.[39]

RELIGIOUS SYSTEM

European commentators persisted in denying the existence of a Xhosa religious system. Other indigeneous people, from North

America to West Africa, might have religious systems, but the Xhosa had no religion. "The Kafirs can scarcely be said to have any religion at all," Alfred Cole maintained in 1852. "The North American Indian has his Great Spirit; the Negro his fetish; the Hottentot his Grasshopper; but the Kafir has literally no idea of a Supreme Being or a future state." Without religion, Cole concluded, the Xhosa were subject to "the absurdest superstitions."[40] At the beginning of the 1850s, therefore, observers continued to mark the absence of Xhosa religion by the presence of superstition. This judgment changed during that decade, however, with the military defeat and national destruction of the Xhosa.

The colonial military campaign against the Xhosa intensified during the frontier war of 1850 to 1853. As resistance was mounted against colonial encroachments by the prophet and war leader Mlanjeni, it was crushed by the total warfare waged by colonial forces. Unlike Xhosa warfare, British military strategy was targeted not only at taking cattle but also at killing men, women, and children, destroying crops, and displacing the survivors from the region. Following their defeat, many Xhosa turned to the millenarian promise of redemption contained in Nongqawuse's vision of the imminent return of the ancestors, who would bring cattle and restore the land to the people. In preparation for that redemptive return, people were exhorted to sacrifice all their cattle. Between April 1856 and May 1857, the majority of Xhosa homesteads sacrificed herds and refrained from planting crops. When the prophecy failed, they were left destitute. Over forty thousand people died, and as many were incorporated into the colony as wage laborers. After decades of resistance, Xhosa political independence was destroyed through an event that appeared to the colonists as an act of national suicide. In the development of frontier comparative religion, however, the Cattle-Killing emerged as the single most important event of the nineteenth century. Before the Cattle-Killing, the Xhosa, according to all reports, had no religion. After the ensuing destruction, as their independence was largely shattered, the Xhosa were finally recognized as having a religion.[41]

In 1858 government agent Henry Calderwood published his observations about the Xhosa, describing on the basis of his years of experience on the frontier "their character, mental, moral, and religious, and their capability of improvement." In his account, the Cattle-Killing featured as a decisive turning point in frontier history. He maintained that the Xhosa had acted under a superstition that had been devised and employed by their leaders with the ultimate objective of destroying the white colonists. In this settler interpretation, the Cattle-Killing movement had been designed to deprive the Xhosa of resources so they would be driven by desperation to attack white settlements. At the same time, however, Calderwood proposed that the Cattle-Killing had actually been a divine visitation on the frontier. "It really seemed as though God had given them up to a strange delusion," he observed, "that they might subdue themselves." Subdued by their own hands, with, however, some help from the government, which had exploited the situation to enforce its control over the frontier, the Xhosa had finally come under colonial domination.

In that new context, Henry Calderwood was prepared to recognize that the Xhosa in fact had a religion. Repeating the etymology of *Caffre*, or *Kafir*, Calderwood noted, as so many commentators had before him, that it was a term employed by followers of Muhammad to indicate unbelievers in the religion of the Qur'an. "I was long under the impression that the Caffres were literally infidels, having no religious ideas whatever," he admitted, "but this is not strictly correct." There were indications, he now found, "even in the dark Caffre mind, of vague impressions of an unseen power and state." Although many authors had made similar observations previously, citing these "vague impressions" as evidence of superstition, in 1858 Calderwood, indicating a change in his own mind, designated them as religion.[42]

The Discovery of Religion

During the same year, another government official, the resident agent among the Thembu, Joseph Cox Warner, was the first person on the eastern Cape frontier to use the term *religion* for a Xhosa *system* of beliefs and practices. This recognition coincided with the implementation of the "Village System" designed by the governor of the Cape Colony, Sir George Grey. In the Grey system, the eastern Cape region was divided into magisterial districts for the purposes of colonial administration, military containment, law enforcement, tax collection, and surveillance. Although Grey proclaimed the introduction of this magisterial system before the first Parliament of the Cape Colony in 1855, it was not enforced until after the devastation of the Cattle-Killing. In 1858 the system was extended throughout Xhosa territory. Under Grey's authority, the chief commissioner, Colonel John Maclean, administered the system through a network of magistrates who usurped the authority of local chiefs by ruling directly in liaison with appointed Xhosa headmen. In the interest of the efficient management of the system, Maclean compiled a detailed government manual on the region, *A Compendium of Kafir Laws and Customs*. He solicited notes on Xhosa beliefs and practices from the magistrate Joseph Cox Warner for inclusion in that report. Significantly, with the introduction of a comprehensive colonial administrative system, Warner found that the Xhosa had an indigenous religious system.[43]

Originally a missionary, Warner had determined by 1850 that he was "utterly unfit for so holy an office." Under the magisterial system, he administered the "Tambookie location" that had been established in 1852 for displaced and impoverished Xhosa-speaking Thembu. There he served as "Government Agent, with supreme control over all." In 1858 Warner was adamant that the Xhosa had a "regular system of superstition" that, however false it might be, had to be recognized as a religious system. In his report on that system, Warner produced an account of "the principal customs and rites connected with, what I choose to call, the *Religion* of the Kafir tribes" (emphasis in original). Warner provided a remarkably detailed inventory of Xhosa religion, describing beliefs in ancestors, the initiation of diviners, rituals for the detection of witches, healing and rainmaking practices, male and female initiation, funerals and mourning, and sacrifices for strengthening and protecting the homestead, chiefdom, and country. For all this detailed description, however, Warner's most remarkable contribution was his insistence that all these elements comprised a comprehensive religious system.[44]

Warner was aware that his use of the term *religion* was a dramatic departure from previous convention. In fact, he argued that the failure to recognize the beliefs and practices of the Xhosa as a comprehensive religious system had frustrated the designs of the mission to convert and the government to control the Xhosa people on the eastern Cape frontier. Failing to recognize that the Xhosa had a religious system, many missionaries, for example, had assumed that the people simply held isolated and unconnected superstitions that might be entertained by any ignorant or weak-minded person. As a result, missionaries made the mistake of thinking they dealt only "with *ordinary* darkness and corruption of the human heart, and that opposition to its spirituality which is common to all our race" (emphasis in original). How-

Joseph Cox Warner, at center of picture, presenting the Thembu to
Prince Alfred in 1860. (From Solomon, *The Progress of Prince Alfred*)

ever, Warner insisted, in addition to this ordinary opposition, the
Xhosa had an extraordinary system of superstition, or religion,
that permeated their lives and presented a resistant force to the
religion of the mission. Therefore, the Xhosa had to be recognized
as firm believers in their religious system, rather than as infidels
without religion, if they were to be effectively converted and controlled.[45]

Warner advanced his new inventory and analysis of Xhosa religion motivated by a political agenda inherited from earlier settler
theories of religion. As the colonial mission and government
cooperated in the extension of "Christian civilization," however, both had to recognize that religion and politics were also in-
tertwined in the system of the Xhosa. While priests supported
chiefs, and chiefs supported an established priesthood, religion
and politics were interwoven in "one vast system of paganism."
This interpenetration between religion and politics had to be
appreciated, however, not only to gain a clearer understanding of
Xhosa life, but also for more successful intervention. "The political and religious governments of the Kafir tribes are so intimately
connected," Warner observed, "that the one cannot be overturned
without the other." As an extraordinary obstacle to the advance
of Christianity, their religious system had to be subverted. Since
it pervaded the fabric of their political life, however, that religion
could only be overturned if the colonial government managed to
"break them up as tribes, and destroy their political existence."

Following their destruction, Warner promised, Christian civilization would spread quickly among the Xhosa in the eastern Cape.[46]

By calling for the destruction of Xhosa independence, therefore, Warner's comparative religion clearly served the interests of local colonial domination. But he also introduced a new comparative framework that was international in scope. As an obstacle to Christian missions, Warner compared the religious system of the Xhosa to the religions of India and other "idolatrous nations" that had to be overturned before Christian conversion could occur. To some extent, Warner maintained a biblical frame of reference for comparison. He observed, for example, that pagan religions were under "satanic influence" because "the idolatrous and heathen nations of the earth are declared, in the inspired volume, to be in a peculiar manner under the influence and power of the devil." Independent of biblical reference, however, Warner cautioned against mixing different religious systems. Because of the systematic character of religion, the old had to be entirely replaced by the new. Otherwise, he warned, if the Xhosa, just as the Hindus, were not first convinced of the falsehood of their religious system, Christianity could only be built on "the rotten foundation of their pagan superstition, as the Roman Catholic Missionaries have done in some parts of the world." Adopting an international perspective that placed southern Africa between India and the Americas, Warner proposed a comparative religion that was also a comparative theory of missions. Unless religions were recognized as comprehensive systems, they could not effectively be destroyed and replaced by the mission. Failing this recognition, Roman Catholic missions in America, according to Warner, had produced syncretistic mixtures that were more pagan than Christian in their religious character.[47]

The Discovery of Functionalism

In addition to his political and missionary agenda, however, Joseph Cox Warner also introduced a new functional analysis into his discussion of Xhosa religion. Although this religion appeared unlike other religions in many respects, Warner suggested that it served the same psychological and social functions as any other religious system. Throughout his discussion, Warner tried to identify the purposes of Xhosa religious beliefs and practices.

Consistently, their purposes were their functions. Although the Xhosa lacked visible symbols to represent the "imaginary beings" they feared and propitiated, they had, Warner argued, "that which exactly answers the same purpose." According to Warner, their religious system, like other religions, fulfilled its primary function by providing psychological comfort. In general terms, Warner maintained that the human mind "demands something of a supernatural nature on which to rest, and in which to trust." The religious system of the Xhosa, he argued, fulfilled that psychological need.[48]

In addition to this psychological function, Warner also identified a second purpose of religion in the maintenance of social order. By stressing the interrelation between religion and politics, he had already established that Xhosa religion had a social function. Again drawing a comparison with India, however, Warner further suggested that Xhosa religion served the purpose of maintaining a social order like the traditional Hindu caste system. In performing the rituals of their religious system, people maintained their place in Xhosa society. Any person who failed to perform them, however, would *"lose caste"* (emphasis in original). In fulfilling these basic psychological and social functions, therefore, the religious system of the Xhosa operated like any other religion.[49]

Although he situated his analysis on the colonial frontier, Warner also introduced a new note of universalism into the study of religion. Because psychological comfort and social order were universal human needs, religion, which functioned to satisfy those needs, was also a universal human phenomenon. In this functional analysis, therefore, Warner identified the Xhosa religious system as a specific instance of the human phenomenon of religion. As Warner maintained, Xhosa beliefs in the existence of invisible beings, and practices for propitiating them, were features of religion "common to the whole human race." Although all religions shared these features, the Xhosa system, supposedly without a clearly defined supreme deity, identified the invisible beings to be propitiated as "ghosts of the dead." Since Xhosa priests drew their power from these ghosts, Warner argued, they should strictly speaking be designated as "necromancers." With this specification, therefore, the Xhosa had developed a distinctive type of religious system that Warner was prepared to recognize among all the other "tribes" of southern Africa. However, he suggested that this pagan system was found "in its most perfect and systematic form among the Fingo [Mfengu] tribes." Ironically, this political grouping of refugees, comprising people most displaced by frontier warfare, was credited by Warner with the most perfectly developed religious system. The Mfengu, however, had been under colonial control for years. Only after the Cattle-Killing, as suggested by Calderwood's change of mind and Warner's detailed inventory, had the Xhosa been sufficiently dominated to be credited with having a religion. However, they were still not as completely controlled as the Mfengu, who supposedly had a perfect and systematic religion. In Warner's terms, vestiges of the Xhosa's independent political existence remained and still had to be destroyed. Nevertheless, until converted to Christianity, the Xhosa would continue to have a recognizable religious system, as Warner explained, "which answers all the purposes of any other false religion."[50]

For the most part, subsequent commentators followed Warner's construction of a Xhosa religious system, especially in identifying its distinctive feature, if not as necromancy, then at least as the worship of "ghosts of the dead." In *The Past and Future of the Kaffir Races*, published in 1866, the Wesleyan William C. Holden followed Warner in concluding that the Xhosa devoted their ultimate attention to "the ghosts of the departed; but they attribute to these all the powers ordinarily ascribed to Deity." Likewise, Holden determined that the Cattle-Killing had provided overwhelming testimony to "the existence and wide-spread influence of this Satanic system." The destruction brought about by the Cattle-Killing, therefore, caused European observers to acknowledge that, for better or worse, the Xhosa had a religious system. It was not idol or fetish worship, as the Reverend Thornley Smith observed, but consisted in "the worship of their ancestors." Recognizing it as a particular kind of pagan religious system, many concluded, as the German missionary Albert Kropf put it, that "the cult of the Kaffir is not God worship, but ancestor worship."[51]

Subsequent observers also showed an interest in placing the Xhosa religious system in a wider comparative framework. Government officials tried to place that religious system in a broader international perspective. In a memorandum submitted in 1875 by Secretary of Native Affairs Charles Brownlee, the religious system of the Xhosa, with its belief in and propitiation of the spirits of the ancestors, was located at the midpoint on a spectrum of paganism between the "refined" immorality of pagan India and

the "debased" immorality of pagan tribes on the west coast of
Africa. In this scheme, Xhosa "ancestor worship" could be located between two extreme images of paganism: the "idol worship" of India and the "fetish worship" of the West Coast of Africa. As the colonial government sought to put Xhosa religion in
an international perspective, missionaries also found new ways to
represent the religious system of the Xhosa in terms of a world-
wide Christian comparative religion. In an 1880 pamphlet on the
work of the London Missionary Society, its agent in the Cape,
William Thompson, proposed that "it might be said that in Asia
Satan's seat is, for there is the birth-place of Brahmanism, of Buddhism, and of Confucianism; and there the followers of the man
of Mecca have their chief home." However, missionaries did not
have to journey to the East to find fully developed religious systems under "satanic influence." In Africa, "there are Brahmins,"
Thompson asserted, appearing in local guise as African rainmakers and doctors. In these formulations, Xhosa religion appeared,
as Warner had insisted, not as a collection of superstitions, but as
an integrated religious system like any other non-Christian religion. As such, government and mission comparativists could
place it in a comparative framework with all the other religions
of the world. They did not have to like it and might still work to
suppress it, but they at least had to recognize that the unbelievers
had a religion.[52]

THE RELIGION OF UNBELIEVERS

In the Cape, as we have seen, comparative religion was practiced
on the frontier battlefield. But it was also practiced in the Cape
Parliament. While Joseph Cox Warner was submitting his report
on the religious system of the Xhosa, a Select Committee of the
House of Assembly was conducting hearings on the use of public
tax revenues for the support of religion. Three years earlier, the
liberal politician Saul Solomon had introduced a "Voluntary Bill"
that proposed to discontinue the use of public funds to support
Christian ministers and churches. Although the bill was not
passed into law until 1875, it generated considerable public controversy about the relation between religion and the state. The
hearings conducted during 1857 and 1858 provided an occasion
for representatives of Christian churches to present their particu-

lar approach to comparative religion in a public forum. Certainly, evidence was also heard from Muslim and Jewish leaders, who argued that the current system of public support for certain Christian churches should either be broadened to include other faiths or entirely eliminated. However, as they resisted the proposed loss of public funds, Protestant ministers received the most attention from the Select Committee. In opposing the measure, these Christian spokesmen had to formulate arguments to justify the government's support of certain forms of religion at the exclusion of others. From their perspective, they were outlining a Christian comparative religion that could form the basis of government policy.

In evidence before the committee, the primary comparative principle proposed by Christian ministers was the distinction between true and false religions. The Reverend Gorrie of the Free Mission Chapel in Cape Town stated this principle bluntly: "there are many sects who do not hold the truth." On that principle, however, the Reverend Gorrie specifically identified the Roman Catholic Church and Mormons as sects that should not receive public funds. On a similar basis, the Reverend Moister added Unitarians to the list of sects that should be excluded from receiving state funds, while observing that it went without saying that Jews and Muslims should not be supported because "the very foundation of the British throne [was] based upon religious principles totally at variance with the sects named." If non-Christian religions were supported by tax revenues, as the London Missionary Society (LMS) representative William Thompson declared, "The government ought to take the taxes and appropriate them to the Emperor of China, or the Temple of the Juggernaut;—but I hold that it would be a breach of trust on the part of the government, if it devoted taxes for such objects." In this missionary comparative religion, therefore, "other" religions included the sects of Jews and Muslims, as well as the Hindus of India, and the Buddhists of China, but also Unitarians, Mormons, and Roman Catholics. Reinforcing the Protestant missionary classification of Roman Catholicism as a non-Christian religion, the Reverend Morgan observed that "the church which is supported in France is not one of those churches which I have included in my definition of a Christian Church. It is a Roman Catholic Church." As a non-Christian sect, he argued, Roman Catholicism should be excluded from public support.

In response to this evidence, members of the Select Committee tried to suggest a different basis for comparative religion in the principle of government neutrality. Like Protestants, adherents of other religions, including Jews, Muslims, and Catholics, paid taxes and could be elected to Parliament. They were free of any other civil disability, except for this exclusion from receiving financial support from public tax revenues. Members of the committee occasionally tried to shift the relevant basis of comparison from the truth to the usefulness of religion. In terms of governance, one religion might be as useful as any other if it contributed to maintaining peace and public order. However, as Justice Munnik challenged the ministers, "you wish the legislature of a Christian government to decide upon the comparative usefulness of the different sects of religion." Holding their ground, the Protestant ministers insisted that the only useful religion was a true one, which, from their perspective, was their own particular variety of Protestant faith.[53]

As we have seen, this Protestant assumption about the truth of their own religion and the falsehood of "other" religions established the dominant terms for frontier comparative religion during the first half of the nineteenth century in the eastern Cape. It was a premodern approach to the comparison of religions that denied and demonized religious diversity. Nevertheless, on the frontier battlefield this comparative religion not only denied but also produced knowledge about other religions. Like the invention of Khoisan religion over the preceding two centuries, the knowledge produced about Xhosa religion could be situated as strategic maneuvers along a contested frontier. Consistently, these maneuvers represented Africans as being out of touch with the real world. In the earliest reports their religion was denied not only because they seemed to lack familiar Protestant beliefs and practices but also because they seemed confused by European artifacts. Apparently bewildered by a watch, in awe of an anchor, and baffled by wagons, guns, and books, the indigenous people of the eastern Cape displayed conduct that European observers found remarkable. Their reactions suggested that they were unable to properly evaluate objects. If they could not evaluate objects, how could they know anything about religion? Accordingly, early-nineteenth-century judgments about their "superstition" were alleged not only on the basis of their beliefs and practices regarding spirits but also because they supposedly failed to understand objects.

After the anchor disappeared from reports about Xhosa customs in the 1820s, its place was taken by another object, the cairn. Piles of stones, to which travelers added a rock or stick when they passed, could be found throughout the country. European observers were fascinated by these cairns. They compared them to the cairns found in Britain, especially in Wales and Scotland. Significantly, however, they did not conclude from this morphological comparison that the indigenous people of the eastern Cape had descended from the British, as they had deduced an Arabic or Semitic origin for the custom of circumcision. Instead, as already noted, they deduced that the custom had been adopted from the Khoikhoi, suggesting that the Xhosa were so culturally impoverished that they had to borrow customs from the most deprived people in the world. But why did the people observe this custom? European observers demanded an explanation. Was it for good luck, or to make a wish, or to ensure a safe journey? These seemed reasonable explanations, identifying the possible purposes for this curious custom as instrumental acts. If done for any of these reasons, adding a stone to a cairn would be understandable as an act intended to achieve some useful or desired end. In almost every report, however, European observers expressed frustration that no Xhosa person could give a reason for the custom. They simply did it. They did not know why. They were "ignorant of the reason of this custom."[54] Accordingly, these piles of stones stood as monuments, in European reports about the Xhosa, to an endemic African inability to reason. Such frontier observations formed the building blocks of the stereotype of primitive mentality in European comparative religion.

The eastern Cape frontier was a fertile field for theories of religion. As we have seen, frontier comparativists engaged in more than a project of denial. They also proposed historical explanations to account for Xhosa religion. Did the Xhosa persist in the original state of human ignorance from which all superstitions of the world had developed? Or were the Xhosa remnants of some ancient religion from which they had degenerated? On the frontier, most European theorists preferred a theory of degeneration, especially if they could trace the higher origin of the Xhosa to a part of the world as remote as Arabia. If they originally belonged in the Middle East, the Xhosa did not belong in southern Africa— that is, not any more than the European settlers did. In this interpretation the Xhosa were further displaced, if only conceptually, by a frontier comparative religion. Beyond their immediate strategic advantage in discounting or displacing the Xhosa, these theories of religion anticipated later developments in the study of religion. With increasing sophistication, comparativists in the second half of the nineteenth century developed theories of religion based upon positing either original ignorance or historical diffusion. Religion, they held, evolved from a primordial ignorance of natural causation. Religions migrated from ancient cultural centers. In embryonic fashion, these comparative strategies were already being worked out before the 1850s on the eastern Cape frontier.

In addition to the seeds of evolutionary and diffusionist theories of religion, a nascent functional theory of religion appeared in the work of Joseph Cox Warner. Once Xhosa beliefs and practices were granted the status of religion, they could be explained as an integrated system. In ways that anticipated structural-functional analysis, Warner reduced the religious system of the Xhosa to basic psychological and social needs. Although a "false religion," in Warner's terms, the religious system of the Xhosa, like every other religion, provided psychological comfort. In social terms, it functioned to maintain order in human relations. Although undeveloped, Warner's observations about the purposes of Xhosa religion clearly anticipated later developments in the social-scientific study of religion. In that respect, Warner might be regarded as a pioneer of functionalism. But his historical situation on the eastern Cape frontier might also suggest a cautionary insight into functionalism's heritage. Warner's explanatory strategies—psychological needs, social order—were proposed to account for a religion that was not only false but also subjected to colonial domination. Recently, the structural-functionalists of the 1920s and 1930s have been accused of complicity in the British imperial policy of indirect rule. However, if Joseph Cox Warner can be regarded as their progenitor, that implication of functional analysis in political domination can be seen to have been present from its inception.

In these ways, comparative strategies on the eastern Cape frontier produced knowledge about religion, its definition, description, and analysis. But this frontier comparative religion also produced and reproduced knowledge about the religions of the world. In particular, as we have seen, Roman Catholicism was reproduced in southern Africa as African religion by Protestant comparativists who condemned the superstition, magic, worship of the dead, and worship of objects that they supposed both held in common. Initially, both were designated as superstition rather than religion. By 1858, however, Protestant comparativists had granted both the status of non-Christian religions, a dubious status if it meant, as the ministers giving evidence to the Parliamentary Select Committee understood it, that non-Christian religions were religions that should be suppressed by the state. In any event, a frontier comparative religion in the eastern Cape generated knowledge about a world of religions that included Christians, Jews, and Muslims as descendants of Abraham; Hindus and Buddhists as foreign idolaters; and, eventually, even an indigenous African religion that was practiced by people who, by definition, had been designated as unbelievers.

In this emerging global comparative religion, the term *worship* provided the genus within which the species of religion could be differentiated. The children of Abraham, whether Christian, Jewish, or Muslim, worshiped God, to better or worse effect. Accordingly, their religions were implicitly classified as religions of "God worship." Looking to the East, comparativists stereotyped Hindus and Buddhists as pagan idolaters. They were classified as practicing religions of "idol worship." If Africans had no clear idea of a Supreme Being, as nearly all European reports contended, and had no idols or other visible representations, how could they be classified? As neither God nor idol worshipers, Africans were classified by the acts of respect and veneration they demonstrated for their ancestors. In this classification system, Xhosa religion, like other indigenous religions in southern Africa, emerged as a special type of religion: "ancestor worship."

4

THE UNKNOWN GOD

ON NEW YEAR'S DAY 1901, magistrate and linguist James Stuart pursued his ongoing research into Zulu customs by conducting morning and afternoon conversations with three Zulu elders in his room at the Royal Hotel in Ladysmith. In the midst of the South African War (1899–1902), Stuart sought to recover a vanishing era of Zulu history. One of his conversation partners, Lazarus Mxaba, provided a distinctive reading of that history. Mxaba had been born in 1839, the very year, he noted, that Mpande had entered into an alliance with Boer forces to depose the Zulu king Dingane. Although Mpande had succeeded in establishing himself as Zulu king, he had, according to Mxaba, introduced a foreign element that severed the rope that ran through the life of his people from generation to generation. By joining forces with the Boers, Mpande had broken the traditional continuity of a Zulu way of life. "By doing so," Mxaba recalled, "he put an end to native methods of living."[1] As an amateur ethnographer, James Stuart attempted to record native customs that he thought were rapidly disappearing at the beginning of the twentieth century. From Lazarus Mxaba's perspective, however, traditional customs had long ago been destroyed. Sixty years earlier, he suggested, an independent Zulu history had already come to an end.

Mxaba recalled that he had grown up in a world under foreign domination. After the annexation of Natal to Great Britain in 1843, the Locations Commission of 1847 established the "location system" that brought the nearly one hundred thousand Africans living in Natal under the jurisdiction of the colonial secretary for native affairs, Theophilus Shepstone. From that point, as Shepstone declared, "The Native's own laws are superseded [and] the Government of their chiefs is at an end." Mxaba found employment as one of Shepstone's messengers, working as a civil servant in the administration of the African location system of

Natal. Although Africans within Natal were under direct colonial control from the 1840s, those in the outlying territory of Zululand lived under the influence of the colony. Mxaba had accompanied Shepstone on his official visits to the recognized rulers of Zululand, Mpande, who reigned until 1872, and then Cetshwayo, whom Shepstone had ceremoniously proclaimed as Mpande's successor as early as 1861. Following a border dispute between Zululand and the recently annexed Boer republic in the Transvaal, British troops invaded Cetshwayo's territory in 1879. Defeated at the Battle of Isandlwana, the British recovered to destroy the Zulu capital of Ulundi and capture Cetshwayo. Outraged at his treatment by the British, Cetshwayo exclaimed from exile in Cape Town, "How is it that they crown me in the morning and dethrone me in the afternoon?" Although 1879 marked the dramatic destruction of the Zulu kingdom, Cetshwayo's observation that he had been crowned by the British acknowledged the earlier colonial control of his domain.[2]

After defeating Cetshwayo, Natal governor Sir Garnet Wolseley partitioned Zululand into thirteen districts under the magisterial authority of chiefs who were loyal to the colony, thereby certifying the colonial authority over the region. Lazarus Mxaba accompanied the deposed Zulu king on a visit to Britain in 1882, as Cetshwayo pleaded his case before Queen Victoria. That meeting achieved nothing, however, because Britain formally annexed Zululand in 1887, establishing the Governor of Natal as the "Supreme Chief" over all the Zulu. On New Year's Day 1901, as Mxaba helped Stuart reconstruct Zulu history, Mxaba looked back to a lost, ancient history. He recalled a history that had ended, however, not with the annexation of Zululand in 1887, nor the defeat of Cetshwayo in 1879, nor the annexation of Natal in 1843, but at the date of his own birth in 1839.

As James Stuart noted, Lazarus Mxaba was a Zulu philosopher with a keen interest in comparative religion. In their New Year's conversations, Mxaba referred explicitly to the precedents of ancient Israel and Greece to reconstruct an ancient history of Zulu religion. On the one hand, Mxaba observed that many Zulu customs were held in common with Jews. Both the Zulu and ancient Jews slit their earlobes, burned incense in ritual, spread chyme on graves, and burned the bones and divided the meat of sacrificial animals in similar ways. Mxaba cited these commonalities as evidence of a prior historical contact between the Zulu and Jews. Granting those common features, Stuart nevertheless wondered how the Zulu could have been descendants of the lost tribes of

Israel since they had apparently forgotten any belief in God. In response, Mxaba reminded Stuart that some of the ancient Israelites themselves had taken to worshiping a golden calf. "If *they*, in a few years, could forget their God," Mxaba argued, "is it not easy to believe that, after the lapse of many centuries, the [Zulu] lost tribes might have fallen away from their original belief?" (emphasis in original). As Stuart realized, Mxaba and his colleagues were convinced that their lineage could be traced back to the lost tribes of Israel. In response, Stuart remarked that there were people in England who believed that the British were descended from the same lost tribes. As we recall, British colonists in North America had argued that American Indians had descended from the lost tribes. During the nineteenth century, British Israelites, inspired by the the work of Richard Brothers and John Wilson, were convinced that the lost tribes had settled in Britain. However, when Mxaba asked him to elaborate on the correspondence between English and Jewish customs, Stuart was at a loss. While Mxaba could list numerous customs held in common by Jews and the Zulu, Stuart could not produce a similar inventory for the British.

Having established this relation between the Zulu and Jews, Mxaba proceeded to invoke the example of ancient Greece, reminding Stuart of "the Athenians who erected an altar to the unknown God, who bear some sort of analogy with the Zulu who have forgotten their God." In the example of ancient Greece, Mxaba found a prophecy that applied to the Zulu: They would wander the world, forgetting their home, their mother tongue, and their original religion. They would forget their God. Under the influence of the Christian mission, however, they would remember. According to Mxaba, therefore, comparative religion provided resources for reconstructing the ancient history of the Zulu. They were lost children of Israel. But their future was also foretold. Mxaba proposed that the Zulu would be redeemed when they remembered and restored the worship of their ancient unknown God.[3]

ZULU RELIGION

Like other southern Africans, the Zulu were subject to denials of their religion. Survivors of the shipwreck of the *Stavenisee*, as reported by Simon van der Stel to the Netherlands in 1689, had discovered an absence of religion among people in the eastern coastal region. "During the two years and eleven months which they passed amongst that people," the Cape governor recorded, "they were unable to discover amongst them the slightest trace of religion." Sustained European reports about the Zulu, however, emerged only in the 1820s in the context of the political disruption of African societies that came to be known as the *mfecane,* "the wars and disturbances which accompanied the rise of the Zulu." The aggressive state building of the Zulu chief, Shaka, combined with interventions by European traders, land speculators, and slave raiders, displaced most of the people of the region. The European testimony on this frontier has been found to be suspect. Reports from the frontier emphasized the importance of the Zulu. However, that emphasis was not merely a response to the rise of a recently obscure clan to political power under the leadership of Shaka. British propagandists portrayed the Zulu king as the legitimate, but tyrannical, authority in the region for purposes of establishing diplomatic relations, trade agreements, and treaties, even if faked, that ceded land for European settlement. Traders operating from the European settlement at Port Natal had an interest in reporting that the region had been recently cleared of its African population by the tyrant Shaka because they were trying to establish claims to large tracts of land at a time when the Cape government was attempting to prevent further acquisition of territory. Along with their financiers in Cape Town, they promoted British annexation of Natal by depicting Shaka as a dangerous monster. These two themes—the vacant, depopulated land and the dominance of the Zulu nation under the tyrant Shaka—whether exaggerated or fabricated, persisted in the earliest European reports from Natal.[4]

On the contested frontier of the 1820s and 1830s, European investigations into the indigenous religion of southeastern Africa were consistent with these two themes. Out of all the political groupings in the region, they singled out the Zulu as the most representative. Accordingly, the beliefs and practices of the region came to be measured against an assumed Zulu standard. Differences in religion, whether found in remote groups that had been less affected by colonial influence or among refugees displaced by recent conflicts and colonial incursions, were regarded as signs of deviance from a Zulu norm. Although European commentators began with denial, as they had begun their investigations into African religion on the eastern Cape frontier, they proceeded very quickly to invent a standardized Zulu religion.

In the earliest account of Zulu religion, based on a visit in the 1820s, the traveler Nathaniel Isaacs made the same distinction between religion and superstition that had appeared in comparative religion in the eastern Cape at the beginning of the nineteenth century. Isaacs denied the existence of any religion among the Zulu. "Religion," he stated bluntly, "They have none." Lacking any concept of a deity, the immortality of the soul, or the mystery of creation, Isaac reported, "they ignorantly conceive themselves to spring from reeds." Because they were without religion, Isaacs concluded that the Zulu were "unquestionably the most superstitious creatures on the face of the earth." They were obsessed with sorcery, which Isaacs identified as the "prevailing superstition among the African tribes."

However, Isaacs found that the Zulu did have a recognizable political institution, kingship. Isaacs, like subsequent commentators, emphasized the centralized political authority held by the Zulu king. Underscoring the authenticity of his report on Zulu society, Isaacs recounted his personal audience with the Zulu king Shaka. "When we first held a conversation with him on the subject of the existence of a Supreme Being," Isaacs recalled, Shaka "at once evinced he had no idea of a deity, and that his people were equally ignorant on this subject. . . . He had no idea of religion, no symbol by which anything like a knowledge of a Supreme Being could be conveyed. The grossest state of ignorance on this sublime subject pervaded him." According to Isaacs, Shaka was so intrigued by the new Christian religion and its God that he requested that doctors and missionaries should be sent to his people to teach them its most potent secret, literacy. Based on these signs of religion and writing, Shaka reportedly observed "that he had discovered [Europeans] were a superior race." In Nathaniel Isaac's account, therefore, Shaka appeared not only as an African king but also as a foil for European interests in the region. Because he lacked religion and supposedly acknowledged that absence, Shaka represented the potential for new European interventions in the Zulu territory.[5]

Forgetting and Remembering

In 1828 Shaka was assassinated by a conspiracy supporting Dingane as a claimant to the throne. In the 1830s Captain Allen Gardiner embarked on a mission to establish diplomatic relations with the new Zulu king. After retiring from the Royal Navy in 1826, Gardiner undertook freelance missionary work, first in Natal and then in New Guinea and Tierra del Fuego, where he and his entire crew died of starvation in 1851. During his travels through Natal in 1835, Gardiner took every opportunity to preach his Christian gospel. At the same time, he inquired into the nature of African religion. Looking for a single, homogeneous religion shared by all Zulu-speaking people, Gardiner instead found a diversity of religious ideas among people recently displaced by war. Gardiner conducted his investigations among three groups of informants. He spoke with Zulu living across the Thukela River who had been in close contact with Port Natal, with the more remote Ngwane to the north, and with the Mfengu refugees to the south. In each case, Gardiner discovered different responses to his questions about African beliefs in a Supreme Being.

Gardiner's first inquiries into religion were conducted with a group of Zulu prisoners who were being taken from Port Natal to Dingane's kraal. Having fled Zulu territory to avoid serving the king, these prisoners were being returned under sentence of death. In searching for the unknown God of the Zulu, Gardiner discovered in his conversations with these prisoners, who had recently been among white colonists in Port Natal, that they had always known about a heavenly chief, that "they have always had some indistinct idea of a Supreme Being." As a prisoner by the name of Nonha put it, "We always believed that there was an Incosi-pezûla (a great chief above), who, before there was a world, came down and made it; he made men; and we knew also that there were white men." Their recollections of this Supreme Being were still vivid.

When he arrived at the Zulu settlement of Nodunga in the Clomanthleen district, however, Gardiner found that Zulu recollections of the Supreme Being were disappearing. They had heard of "Incosi pezûla," he found, but knew nothing about this "Great Chief." Concerning a knowledge of God, these Zulu displayed a marked degradation. "We seem to have arrived here," Gardiner proposed, "at a period when the traditionary knowledge of a Supreme Being is rapidly passing into oblivion." Besides this disappearing knowledge, they only vaguely recalled that their forefathers had believed in two beings of great power, "Villenangi," the "First Appearer," and "Koolukoolwani," who had visited the earth to separate the sexes and colors of human beings. However, Gardiner discovered that even these traditions were not generally remembered. Accordingly, he found that the Zulu had a recollection of a Supreme Being that was neither continuous with the past, since it was not his informants but their forefathers who believed these things, nor uniform in the present, since, as Gardiner reported, the "generality of the people are ignorant even of this scanty tradition."[6]

Although the prisoners taken from Port Natal supposedly had always known about a Supreme Being, the Zulu who had settled beyond the colonial border apparently had forgotten. Zulu religion, therefore, was a history of memory and forgetting. Beginning with an indistinct belief in a Supreme Being, a belief that was remembered by some but forgotten by most in the course of the degradation of the Zulu people, belief in God was being recovered under colonial influence. Gardiner asserted that "since their recent intercourse with Europeans, the vague idea of a Supreme Being has again become general." It is possible, as the traveler Adolphe Delegorgue maintained in 1847, that the notion of a heavenly chief, *Inkosi pezûlu,* had been introduced to the Zulu in 1824 by Lieutenant Francis Farewell. By 1835, according to Gardiner, this concept of God was most familiar to Zulu-speaking people in direct contact with Port Natal. They remembered. Ironically, however, according to the first missionary to the Zulu, the Reverend Francis Owen, they had already forgotten again when he began his work two years later in 1837. Proclaiming the "chief above" at Dingane's court, Owen was met with incomprehension. People asked, "Is there one? Can he see us if he is in the air? He must be a good climber?" As Owen reported, the people "did not know I was speaking of God, they thought I was talking of King George." When Owen described God as the supreme chief, Dingane apparently asked, "Was God among the English Kings?" Instead of leading to the recollection of a forgotten God, therefore, this European intercourse only seemed to result in confusion.[7]

By contrast to the Zulu on the colonial border, the Ngwane in the north under Chief Sobhuza of the Dhlamini clan, which would eventually emerge as the Swazi nation, lacked any trace of religion. They had never seen a white person. To underscore this point, Gardiner reported that they were terrified by his horses, guns, and matches when they met. He observed that they practiced certain rituals, such as a festival of first fruits and circumcision, but they had no knowledge whatsoever of a Supreme Being. "On the subject of religion they were in total darkness," Gardiner reported; "every tradition had worn out." In these terms, the

Ngwane had entirely forgotten their unknown God, but had not yet had sufficient interaction with the colony to recall it. According to Gardiner, the Ngwane "presented the awful spectacle of immortal beings without the knowledge or acknowledgement of a Creator." He characterized their religious life by absences. They lacked not only a God but also any knowledge of an evil spirit, the immortality of the soul, or a day of judgment. Beyond colonial influence or control, the Ngwane were an empty space. "What a blank is the life of man," Gardiner declared, "without a knowledge of God!"

Finally, Gardiner investigated the religion of Mfengu refugees to the south. Although Gardiner found that "on the subject of religion they are equally as dark as their neighbours the Zoolus," the Mfengu were not as ignorant on the subject as were the Ngwane. "They acknowledged, indeed, a traditionary account of a Supreme Being, whom they called Oukoolukoolu (literally the Great-Great), but knew nothing further respecting him, than that he originally issued from the reeds, created men and cattle, and taught them the use of the assegai." Although they performed sacrifices to their ancestral spirits, the Mfengu had also, according to Gardiner, retained a distorted memory of God. However, Gardiner found that they gave as little credence to stories about "Oukoolukoolu" as they did to the tales of their forefathers about Europeans. Having interacted with Europeans for years, the Mfengu were able to laugh about the stories of their first impressions that white people had fallen from the skies, or had appeared as monsters with only one arm, leg, and eye, or had shot lead from their mouths. If their forefathers could be mistaken about Europeans, they could also have been wrong about the Great-Great One.[8]

In these earliest reports about the Zulu, the denial announced by Nathaniel Isaacs was quickly replaced by Gardiner's discovery of traces of religion. After the British annexation of Natal, Zulu-speaking people under colonial influence or control were consistently credited with a religion. Following Gardiner, subsequent commentators imagined a religious history of the Zulu in three stages. First, the Zulu had an earlier knowledge of God, a knowledge going back centuries, rather than only to the first formal European contact in 1824. Second, under the impact of recent warfare, the Zulu had forgotten whatever knowledge of God they had previously held. Third, however, the Zulu were being assisted in the recovery of their unknown God through interaction with

Europeans. This imaginary history of Zulu religion was eventually supplemented by a morphological comparison that became commonplace in both European and Zulu reflections about Zulu religious heritage. By the 1850s commentators on Zulu religion had determined that it bore a striking resemblance to a more familiar religion. Whatever its historical roots, Zulu religion was recognizable as the same type of religion that had been practiced in ancient Israel.

Zulu Jews

Britain annexed Natal in 1843. Between 1849 and 1851 several thousand British settlers were moved into the region. In justifying settlement, a government commission of inquiry found that British immigrants were entitled to the land because the original inhabitants had gone, and those that remained had no right to the land because their political independence had been destroyed. If their political independence had not already been broken by the depredations of Shaka, it was formally ended in 1850 when the lieutenant-governor of Natal was proclaimed as the "Supreme Chief of the Native Population." As the commission of inquiry found, "The Natal tribes then ceased to have any separate national existence."[9]

Under the location system administered by Theophilus Shepstone, the Zulu lost political autonomy but gained the recognition by European commentators that they had an indigenous religious system. Subjected to colonial domination and control, the Zulu achieved that status of "religion" at an earlier date than the Xhosa on the eastern Cape frontier. They were also credited with what colonists regarded as a somewhat better, higher religion. On the eastern Cape frontier, Xhosa-speaking people had been designated by Europeans as Arabs or "Ishmaelitish sons of Abraham." In Natal and Zululand, European comparativists exercised a similar comparative strategy to account for Zulu religion. They identified the Zulu, however, not as Arabs, but as Jews. Contained and controlled under colonial administration, the Zulu had a religion. But they had a religion that distinguished them from the Xhosa who were still resisting colonial domination on the eastern Cape frontier. In evidence before the Natal Native Affairs Commission during 1852 and 1853, European experts on the Zulu repeatedly reinforced this comparison with Jews. Unlike the Africans on the eastern Cape frontier, who were depicted as wild, nomadic Arabs, the Zulu were represented as people living a relatively stable life like ancient Israelites. Perhaps a certain degree of prejudice against Islam and Arabs was implied in this comparison. But the crucial factor in this identification of the Zulu as ancient Israelites seemed to lie in the assumption that Jews could be contained, and perhaps even ghettoized, under a system of Christian rule. The Zulu in Natal had been contained by annexation and the location system. In that context, they were found to have a religious system. Consistently, the Zulu were depicted as the Jews of Natal.

Before the Native Affairs Commission, the magistrate of Pafana location, G. R. Peppercorne, emphasized the moral qualities of the Zulu living in Natal. They displayed the virtues of good subjects, including respect for authority, hospitality, honesty, and manners. Although they had not adopted Christianity, the Zulu nevertheless had a kind of recognizable religious life that could be distinguished from other religions. It was not the "debasing idolatry" of Asia, nor was it the "superstitious rites" practiced on the west coast of Africa. Furthermore, Peppercorne tried to distinguish the Zulu from Xhosa-speaking people on the eastern Cape frontier with respect to the question of superstition. The religion of the Xhosa had been denied under that designation, as European commentators had assumed that they lacked religion precisely because they displayed superstition. By contrast, Peppercorne insisted that the Zulu under his jurisdiction in Natal did not practice witchcraft, conjuration, or any other of the "superstitious rites" that were performed by "the Frontier Kafirs, who may have derived some additional superstition from the Western tribes, founded on charms, incantations, etc." According to Peppercorne, the Zulu had not been corrupted by the superstitions of West Africa. Avoiding both idolatry and superstition, the Zulu practiced a type of religion found in ancient Israel. "A general type of the customs and laws of the Ama-zulu," Peppercorne reported, "may be found in the early history of the Hebrews, until they became a nation under a settled monarchy."[10]

Zulu life, therefore, was organized on an ancient Israelite pattern. Ironically, given the importance of their king in European relations with the Zulu, Peppercorne characterized that pattern as premonarchic. Nevertheless, its basic forms had appeared in ancient Israel. Europeans who wanted to learn about Zulu religion, Peppercorne suggested, only had to read the Hebrew Bible.

For example, Zulu polygamy could be found in the narratives of biblical patriarchs; their marriage customs were outlined in the Book of Ruth; and their attitudes toward labor could be understood by reading the story of Jacob and Laban in Genesis. In Peppercorne's testimony, therefore, the Zulu had a recognizable religious life that made them, unlike the Xhosa on the eastern Cape frontier, more understandable. Relevant knowledge about their religious system was readily available not only by direct observation but also by comparison with the Old Testament. Since their religious system could be so easily known, the Zulu appeared to be more suitable subjects for colonial control than the Xhosa, who lived without religion on the eastern Cape frontier.

This comparison between the Zulu and Jews was reinforced by the evidence of Henry Francis Fynn, who had certified his expertise on the subject by establishing his own Zulu fiefdom in the 1820s. With over two thousand subjects and extensive wealth in land and cattle, Fynn had lived closely with Zulu-speaking people for decades, serving as both chief and magistrate. Drawing on those years of experience, he concluded that the Zulu lacked any clear idea of God before contact with Europeans. Rather than belief in God, their religion had been based upon a notion of survival after death and the importance of ancestors. "The opinion held by the most intelligent natives, during the reign of Chaka," Fynn reported, "was that at death they would enter a world of spirits, occupying in it the same position they had held in this; the last departed spirit of a person who had held the highest rank in a family becoming its ruling spirit." If the family prospered, they said that their ruling spirit was lying on his back. During bad times, they said he was lying on his face. But these expressions, Fynn insisted, were used in a figurative sense to represent the favor or disfavor shown by an ancestral spirit. Thus, Fynn found, attention to ancestors was the core of Zulu religion.

Nevertheless, with only a confused idea of a deity, the Zulu, Fynn concluded, displayed a remarkable similarity to the religion of the Jews. "I was surprised to find a considerable resemblance," Fynn recalled, "between many of the [Zulu] customs and those of the Jews." He produced an inventory of the most striking similarities: "War offerings; Sin offerings; Propitiatory offerings; Festival of first fruits; The proportion of the sacrifice given to the Isanusi (or witch doctor, as he is termed by Europeans); Periods of uncleanness, on the decease of relatives and touching the dead; Circumcision; Rules regarding chastity; Rejection of swine's flesh."

In this list of common customs, Fynn proposed a morphological comparison between the religious life of the Zulu and that of ancient Israel. But those similar religious forms also contained hints of a forgotten history. Since, as Fynn remarked, the Zulu were unacquainted with their own history, comparison provided a basis for suggesting their historical origin. Because of "the nature of semblance of many of their customs to those of the ancient Jews, as prescribed under the Levitical priesthood," Fynn concluded, "I am led to form the opinion that the [Zulu] tribes have been very superior to what they are at the present time." If they had not originated in ancient Israel, then the Zulu at least displayed traces of a higher origin that was similar to the ancient religion of the Jews. This equation of Zulu and Jews would have a dramatic impact on the development of comparative religion in Natal.[11]

Ancestors and Snakes

In the 1850s and 1860s, standard accounts of Zulu religion depicted it as ancestor worship. In this respect, the import of the Xhosa Cattle-Killing was also evident in Natal. In a popular book about the Zulu, *The Kafirs of Natal and the Zulu Country*, published in 1857, Joseph Shooter devoted considerable attention to recounting a history of Xhosa prophets that began in the 1820s with Nxele and concluded with the devastation of the Cattle-Killing. That event, according to Shooter, marked the end of the Xhosa, proving "how are the mighty fallen." Although the Xhosa had apparently been destroyed, the Zulu survived, persisting, however, within an expanding colonial domain.

Drawing extensively on earlier accounts, Shooter's summary of Zulu religion incorporated the implicit judgments that the Zulu had forgotten their God and had degenerated from some higher origin. According to Shooter, Africans of Natal and Zululand had preserved traditions of a divine being under the titles the *Great-Great* or the *First Appearer*. Instead of distinguishing between them, however, as Gardiner had done, Shooter identified *uNkulunkulu* and *umVelinqangi* as two names for the same God. Nevertheless, he followed Gardiner in finding that this tradition was not universally known among Zulu-speaking people. "War, change, and the worship of false deities," Shooter argued, "have gradually darkened their minds, and obscured their remembrance of the true God." In the north, the remote Ngwane apparently knew nothing about uNkulunkulu, while in Natal one tribe still worshiped the Great-Great, "though its recollection of him is very dim." Forgetting their God, the Zulu had allegedly turned to false deities, worshiping their own ancestors as if the ancestors were their only gods. The spirits of their ancestors, according to Shooter, had been "elevated in fact to the rank of deities, and (except where the Great-Great is worshipped concurrently with them) they are the only objects of . . . adoration." The only thing that saved the Zulu from being nothing more than ancestor worshipers, Shooter concluded, was their vague recollection of uNkulunkulu, the Great-Great One, the Supreme Being that a few remembered, but most had forgotten during the disruptions of African wars and the establishment of the colony in Natal.

As the ancestors were elevated, Shooter suggested, the Zulu had degenerated. The Zulu performed ritual sacrifices, which, like those of ancient Israel, were designed to avert evil, procure blessings, or give thanks. However, as they came to be directed toward ancestors, Zulu sacrificial practices had become so degraded that the "original idea of a sacrifice appears to have degenerated into that of a present of food." Frequently, the sacrificial offering of food seemed to be presented to snakes because, as Shooter observed, ancestral "spirits are believed to revisit the earth and appear to their descendants in the form of certain serpents." This ritual regard for snakes fascinated European commentators on Zulu religion. Gardiner saw it as evidence of Zulu belief in the transmigration of souls, while William Holden went so far as to conclude that the Zulu were "serpent-worshippers." In either case, ancestral rituals appeared as proof of Zulu degeneration from an earlier religion that had been based on the worship of a Supreme Being. From that ancient faith, the Zulu, according to Joseph Shooter, had devolved a religion based upon the worship of the dead.[12]

In 1857, however, Shooter was already out of step with new developments in comparative religion initiated by the arrival two years earlier of three European immigrants, John William Colenso, Wilhelm Hendrik Immanuel Bleek, and Henry Callaway. While Shooter recollected and reproduced the earlier reports of travelers, missionaries, and magistrates, these three immigrants to Natal drew upon new developments in a wide range of European academic disciplines to reopen investigations into the nature of Zulu religion. Colenso drew upon new methods in biblical criticism, Bleek mastered the discipline of comparative philology, and Callaway was conversant with recent European innovations in the comparative study of religion, folklore, and anthropology. More than any other nineteenth-century commentators, these three received an audience in Europe. They became international authorities. Remarkably, however, in spite of the new European methods of investigation they employed, Colenso, Bleek, and Callaway became entangled in the local conflicts of the region. In many respects, they also reproduced the basic concerns and interpretive strategies of a frontier comparative religion.

JOHN WILLIAM COLENSO

Born in Cornwall in 1814, John William Colenso studied mathematics at St. John's College, Cambridge. Beginning in the 1840s, Colenso published a series of widely used mathematics textbooks. However, an abiding interest in theology, biblical criticism, and mission work shaped the course of his life. Serving from 1846 to 1853 as Rector of Forncett St. Mary's, near Norwich, Colenso acted as local secretary of the Society for the Propagation of the Gospel and edited two of the society's journals, *The Church in the Colonies* (1844–51) and *The Monthly Record* (1852–53). In 1853 he was ordained as Bishop of Natal. Undertaking a ten-week visitation of his new diocese the following year, Colenso investigated indigenous religion with the aim of identifying Zulu beliefs in a Supreme Being. In his search for the unknown God of the Zulu, Colenso discovered the God-names *uNkulunkulu* and *umVelinqangi*. Convinced that he had found the Zulu God under these titles, he advocated adopting the term *uNkulunkulu* as the name of God for the purposes of the Christian mission in the region. Although this proposal was controversial, Colenso justified the appropriation of a Zulu name for God in terms of a general theory of comparative religion. Distinguishing between a universal natural religion and the special revealed religion of Christian faith, Colenso argued that Zulu God-names should be understood as the local terms of a universal natural religion. By appropriating a Zulu name for God, Colenso believed he was converting elements of that indigenous natural religion into the service of Christian revelation.

Colenso's understanding of the purpose of the Christian mis-

John William Colenso. (Courtesy South African Library, Cape Town)

sion was largely influenced by his association, beginning in 1843, with the theologian Frederick Denison Maurice, one of the founders of "Christian Socialism." On theological grounds, Maurice argued for a kind of Christian universalism, recognizing seeds of religious truth in non-Christian religions. Maurice placed great value on the missionary movement as an opportunity, not only for extending the Christian gospel, but also for expanding European knowledge of the religions of the world. Maurice observed that missionaries would "recognize not only a conscience and a light among the heathen, [but they would also] see the materials out of which the divine universe has been created." However, Maurice also proposed a mission that met the needs of an expanding British colonialism. He insisted on a cooperation between colonization and conversion in which Britain should "bring no people within the circle of her government whom she did not bring within the circle of her light."[13]

In a series of lectures, published as *The Religions of the World and Their Relations to Christianity*, Maurice outlined his approach to comparative religion. Indicating the colonial imperative behind that field of study, Maurice argued for greater sensitivity to other religions precisely because Britain was currently "engaged in trading with other countries, or in conquering them, or in keeping possession of them." Maurice noted that a dramatic change had recently occurred in European attitudes toward "Religious Systems" around the world. During the eighteenth century, most theorists assumed that religions were inventions of lawgivers and priests designed solely to reinforce their privileged political power. However, following the political revolutions of 1776 in North America and 1787 in France, which in principle separated church from state, theorists began to realize that religious systems had to involve something more than merely politics. For Maurice, that something was the quality of faith in human hearts, a faith that might be cultivated by the many different religions in spite of apparent differences in doctrine or practice. Therefore, Maurice argued that political changes at home, as well as the extension of political rule abroad, required new attention to the role of faith in the religions of the world.

Maurice was aware that one possible response to this changing global situation was the classification of the religions of the world. Like comparative anatomy, or the emerging discipline of comparative philology, comparative religion could be a science of classification. Preferring dialogue, however, Maurice resisted this attempt to classify religions. "A man will not really be intelligible to you," he held, "if, instead of listening to him and sympathising with him, you determine to classify him." Nevertheless, Maurice did propose an implicit classification of world religions. Setting aside ancient religions, such as the Egyptian, Greek, Roman, Persian, and Gothic religions, as "defunct" systems, Maurice devoted most of his attention to religions practiced by people under British colonial rule, identifying Islam, Hinduism, and Buddhism as three "other" religions in the world that deserved sensitive study. Although Islam had long been familiar, Hinduism and Buddhism had only recently emerged in the European imagination in the 1820s. In Maurice's treatment, they joined Islam to form the major non-Christian religions. Although differing from Christian revelation in matters of belief and practice, these three religions nevertheless cultivated qualities of faith that Maurice felt had to be respected.

However, two omissions featured in Maurice's depiction of the religions of the world. First, Maurice had difficulty in accommodating Judaism into his classification of religions, perhaps because he felt that it was a religion that should have become in the course of history a "defunct" system. Maurice left the consideration of Judaism until late in his lecture series. In treating Judaism, however, he only remarked that it was the religion nearest to Christian revelation, but at the same time most distant, because "systems, rabbinical and philosophical, may choke that belief; money-getting habits may almost extinguish it." In this anti-Jewish polemic, Maurice displayed an ambivalence toward Judaism that was inconsistent with his appeals for a greater sympathetic understanding of non-Christian religions. Second, Maurice omitted any consideration of indigenous nonliterate religions in the regions of the world under colonial domination. No category of "primitive" or "savage" religion appeared in his discussion of the religions of the world. To a certain extent, Colenso simultaneously addressed both of these problems in Maurice's comparative religion—its ambivalence toward Jews, its omission of nonliterate religion—by undertaking a sensitive study of the traditional religious beliefs and practices of the Zulu, the Jews of Natal.[14]

Colenso's uNkulunkulu

Before his first visit to Natal, John William Colenso had become familiar with the basic regional distinction between "Hottentots" and "Kafirs." In an 1853 article he noted that they both originated in the north. The "Hottentots," he observed, could be traced back to the Copts of Egypt, while the "Kafirs" were thought to be of Arab descent. After visiting his new diocese, however, Colenso showed an interest in further distinguishing the Zulu from the other Africans on the eastern Cape frontier. Although he granted that Xhosa-speaking people might have been wild heathens or atheists, Colenso insisted that the Zulu believed in God.

> Like other Kafirs, the Zulus, in their wild, savage state, are excit-
> able and fierce, and debased with the vices and superstitions of
> heathenism. . . . Like other Kafirs, also, the Zulu have no idols, and
> it has been a common charge against them, as against the whole of
> the Kafir race, that they have no God. I know not what may be
> the case with the frontier Kafirs: but the Zulus have certainly two
> distinct names in their own tongue for the Supreme Being, and very
> expressive names, namely un-Kulunkulu, the Great-Great One =
> the Almighty; and un-Velinqange, the First Out-Comer, = the First
> Essence of Existence.

Colenso's conclusion about the Zulu God was presented as the result of extensive conversations with Zulu-speaking people in Natal and Zululand. Accompanied by Theophilus Shepstone, Colenso conducted his interviews at both Christian mission stations and African homesteads throughout the region. Attempting to factor out Christian influences, Colenso sought to identify among the Zulu "the impressions of natural religion which they still retain." He discovered a belief in God—the Almighty, the first Essence—that allowed him to attribute a natural religion to the Zulu. Furthermore, Colenso argued that their natural religion actually approximated revelation, since the two names they employed for God captured "the very ideas contained in the Hebrew words Elohim and Jehovah." Just as ancient Israel had two names for the same God, Colenso insisted, so did the Zulu.[15]

In the course of his inquiries, however, Colenso encountered some confusion, particularly at mission stations, regarding the Zulu name for God. Following the example set by J. T. van der Kemp at the beginning of the century, missionaries in the eastern Cape and Natal generally had adopted the word *uThixo* for the Christian God. Despite its Khoikhoi roots, *uThixo* had been easily assimilated into the Xhosa Christian vocabulary. However, at the Edendale mission in Natal, under the direction of the resident Wesleyan missionary James Allison, Colenso discovered that there had been resistance among Zulu-speaking Christians to the importation of this term. Zulu Christians found the term *uThixo* meaningless because they thought that it referred to a species of insect, the mantis, which was known as the "Hottentot's God." Instead, they proposed that the Christian God could better be translated by the Zulu term *iThongo*, which they glossed as "a Power of Universal Influence—a Being under whom all around were placed." In proposing the adoption of this term, they cited the advantage that it would be understood by all Africans from the eastern Cape frontier to the north of Natal. However, by suggesting the word *iThongo*, these converts translated the Christian God into a term traditionally used to designate an ancestral spirit. Finding this connotation unacceptable, James Allison rejected both *uThixo* and *iThongo* by coining the term *uYehova*. For similar reasons, other missionaries introduced the term *uDio*. Rejecting such neologisms, whether of Zulu-Hebraic or Zulu-Latin derivation, Colenso persisted in searching for the indigenous unknown God of the Zulu.

After leaving Edendale, Colenso and Shepstone journeyed to the kraal of Pakade, where they interviewed people that Colenso described as examples of "native barbarism in its purest form." The people of Pakade were supposedly untouched by the mission, even though some apparently knew the Lord's Prayer and had heard of the uThixo of the Christians. Nevertheless, Colenso identified them as "complete heathens." Accordingly, they provided the most authentic and compelling evidence for an indigenous Zulu concept of a Supreme Being. People at Pakade's kraal distinguished between ancestral spirits and uNkulunkulu, the creator. In Colenso's account, they said that "amaTongo and amaDhlozi were certainly not the same as uNkulunkulu: for they could not be till man was created; in short, they were departed spirits, but uNkulunkulu made all things." Based on these conversations, Colenso concluded that the Zulu "did know of umkulunkulu by their own traditions—that He was the same as unVelinqange, the First Out-comer."

However, these Zulu had allegedly forgotten the significance of their own terms for the Supreme Being. Therefore, Colenso requested Shepstone to inform Pakade's people that he had been sent to tell them more about their own God, uNkulunkulu. The Christian mission would remind them of the true meaning of their own religious vocabulary. For his part, Pakade listened with interest, observing that since uNkulunkulu was worshiped in England, there must be more common ground between them than he had realized. He was happy to listen to their interpretation of uNkulunkulu. However, when Colenso and Shepstone finished their theological lectures, the chief demonstrated his more immediate concern in the political and military relations of the region. European teachings about uNkulunkulu might be interesting, but, Pakade asked, "How do you make *gunpowder?"* (emphasis in original).[16]

On the Natal frontier, therefore, God-names proliferated in the context of colonial conflict. As Bishop of Natal, Colenso endeavored to standardize the name of God that would be used in Christian missions among the Zulu. Out of the many contradictory oral traditions that were related in the region, different terms for a Supreme Being contended: *uThixo, iThongo, uYehova, uDio, uLungileyo, umPezulu, Inkozi pezulu, uNkulunkulu,* and *umVelinqangi.* There was no consensus or clarity on the question. Whether at mission stations or at African homesteads, Colenso found disagreement among people over whether or not uNkulunkulu was the same as the ancestral spirits. Nevertheless, out of all the possibilities, Colenso suppressed those disagreements and identified *uNkulunkulu* and *umVelinqangi* as the normative terms for a Supreme Being of the Zulu. In deciding on these two terms, Colenso was convinced that he had identified two names for the same unknown Zulu God. Recent developments in biblical criticism helped Colenso arrive at that conclusion. Like the priestly editors who had woven together Yahwist and Elohist traditions to form the Pentateuch, Colenso could construct a Zulu religion that was based on a single Supreme Being. In Colenso's reading, uNkulunkulu, the Almighty, was the Zulu Yahweh, the dynamic creator of the world; umVelinqangi, the more abstract first essence of existence, was the Zulu Elohim. As in ancient Israel, Colenso found a Zulu religious vocabulary with two names that signified two aspects of the same God.

If textual criticism of the Bible informed Colenso's construction of Zulu religion, the reverse was also the case, as his reading of the Bible was apparently affected by his attempts to translate it into Zulu idiom. Taking this context seriously, Colenso tried to confront the factual and moral dimensions of the biblical text in conversation with Zulu converts. In the process of translation, comparative questions arose: How did the Bible sound to the Zulu? How did it compare with indigenous Zulu religion? From a Zulu religious perspective, was the Bible true? Was it moral? As a result of such questions, Colenso rewrote the Bible, not only into the Zulu language, but also into a comparative religion that included Zulu religion among the religions of the world.

Biblical Criticism

On the 1854 tour of his diocese, Colenso was accompanied, not only by the colonial administrator Theophilus Shepstone, but also by the Zulu convert William Ngidi. Over the next fifteen years, Ngidi assisted Colenso in his mission work at Bishopstowe. For Zulu converts, Bishopstowe was a "place of light," a center for learning, not only about Christianity, but also about their new place in the colonial world. As Ngidi recalled, Colenso employed as his basic texts a copy of Genesis, a prayer book, and a book about Christopher Columbus. In addition to his employment as a catechist, Ngidi helped Colenso with his Zulu translation of the Bible. According to Colenso, that collaboration forced the missionary to confront his own sacred text in a new light, leading him to embark upon a monumental biblical commentary, *The Pentateuch and Joshua Critically Examined*, which by 1879 had run to seven volumes. In his preface to the first volume in 1862, Colenso recalled that William Ngidi's skepticism had forced him to reconsider the historical accuracy of the biblical account. As Colenso recounted this incident: "While translating the story of the Flood, I have had a simple-minded, but intelligent native, —one with the docility of a child, but the reasoning powers of mature age,—look up, and ask, "Is all that true? Do you really believe that all this happened thus?"[17]

Recent findings of critical biblical scholarship, the science of geology, and even simple mathematical calculations, such as Colenso's estimate of the extraordinary number of sheep that would have been required to feed Noah's family on the ark, could all be invoked to discredit the historical accuracy of the biblical story. However, although he certainly drew upon these scientific resources in his commentary, Colenso depicted his entire enterprise of biblical criticism as a response to a crisis in his mission. If even "simple-minded" Zulu questioned the historical accuracy of the Bible, how could the Christian mission propagate it as unquestionable truth? The mission required not only a rewriting of the sacred text into the Zulu language but also a rereading of the Bible in the Zulu context.

William Ngidi. (From Colenso, *Diocese of Natal*)

Colenso tried to resolve this crisis in terms of a comparative religion that was based upon two interpretive principles. First, since the Zulu were the Jews of Natal, they represented a template against which the historical accounts of ancient Israel could be measured. As we have seen, the groundwork for this comparison between the Zulu and ancient Israelites had already been firmly laid. Building upon that foundation, Colenso asserted that their similar ways of life provided a basis for comparison. The Zulu "mode of life and habits, and even the nature of their country," Colenso maintained, "so nearly correspond to those of the ancient Israelites, that the very same scenes are brought continually, as it were, before their eyes, and vividly realised in a practical point of view." In these terms, the Zulu represented a living museum of ancient Israel. Colenso beheld biblical scenes in Africa. He observed a pastoral lifestyle, patriarchal households, animal sacrifices, seasonal festivals, and other features of Zulu life that seemed to memorialize in the present an ancient Israelite past. The Zulu perpetuated a cycle of religious life that was just like ancient Israel. "The Zulu keeps his annual Feasts, and observes the New Moons," Colenso observed, "as the old Hebrews did." They followed the ritual calendar of the Hebrew Bible. "The very Zulus have their festivals at the beginning of the Southern Spring and at the end of our Autumn, corresponding to the 'feast of the first fruits,' and the 'feast of ingathering' of the ancient Hebrews." Therefore, Colenso's immediate access to these ancient Jews of Natal lent a new kind of authority to his critique of biblical history. By comparing the Zulu and ancient Israelites, Colenso could claim to have had firsthand experience of ancient Israel.[18]

Arguably, this new authority was merely a rhetorical device that framed his biblical criticism. For example, in analyzing ritual sacrifice, Colenso based his critique, not on the evidence of his own experience of Zulu sacrifices, but on the mathematical improbability of the biblical account. Nevertheless, Colenso had witnessed Zulu sacrifices, and if they were in fact performed just like those in ancient Israel, they provided a new practical test for assessing the historical accuracy of the Bible. Revealing new contours of the religion of ancient Israel in the mirror of the "primitive," a comparative strategy that would eventually be developed by William Robertson Smith in his *Lectures of the Religion of the Semites,* Colenso proposed a new way of reading the Bible. Although the Bible had been used, and would continue to be used, to judge Africans, Colenso reversed this procedure by rereading the Bible in terms of the patterns and rhythms of African life.

While the equation of Jews with the Zulu represented Colenso's first comparative premise, his second identified the Zulu as evidence of universal religion. According to Colenso, William Ngidi questioned not only the truth of the Bible but also its morality. Reading a passage in the Book of Exodus that referred to slaves as "money" (Exodus 21:20–21), Ngidi was shocked by the apparent disregard for the humanity of the enslaved. As Colenso recalled: "I shall never forget the revulsion of feeling, with which a very intelligent Christian native, with whose help I was translating these last words into Zulu, first heard them as words said to be uttered by the same great and gracious Being, whom I was teaching him to trust in and adore. His whole soul revolted against the notion. . . . My own heart and conscience at the time fully

sympathised with his." Ngidi also questioned the morality of
biblical warnings of eternal damnation, inspiring Colenso's rejection of that Christian doctrine. Colenso cited Ngidi's objections as
evidence of a natural moral sensibility against which the biblical
text could be measured. In this comparative strategy, the Zulu
stood not only for ancient Israelites but also for a universal religion based on belief in a God of love. The divine spirit, Colenso
held, had inspired the most sublime passages of the Bible, particularly those that referred to a supreme and loving creator. However, that same spirit had also inspired other religions. As Colenso argued, "the same Divine Spirit, we must surely believe,
taught the Hindoo Philosopher to say, 'He thought, I will make
worlds, and they were there,' and taught also the Zulu first to say,
though, as it were, with childish lips, 'Unkulunkulu—the Great-
Great-One—made all things, made all men." Therefore, Colenso
found that Hindus and the Zulu, among others, had received the
same inspired revelation of a universal religion that appeared in
the most authentic moments of the biblical tradition. The Zulu,
therefore, provided evidence not only for reconstructing the religion of ancient Israel but also for imagining a universal religion.[19]

By replicating ancient Israel, the Zulu provided a measure
against which the scientific or historical accuracy of the Bible
could be tested. In addition to this specific comparison, the Zulu
also represented evidence of a more general religion that had appeared in sacred texts and traditions throughout the world. Relying heavily on previous commentaries, Colenso filled the pages
of his own text with comparative references to beliefs and practices of other religions, observing parallels with ancient Egyptian,
Persian, Indian, and Chinese religions, and concluded the fourth
volume of *The Pentateuch* with a review of wisdom to be found
in all the religions of the world. His comparative enterprise was
subjected to criticism in Britain. Matthew Arnold, for example,
criticized Colenso for taking apart the Bible mathematically and
then comforting the reader with "a fragment of Cicero, a revelation to the Sikh Gooroos, and an invocation of [the Hindu deity]
Ram."[20] However, Colenso pursued this effort to place the Bible
in a larger, universal comparative context, an interest that represented one important, but often overlooked, current in early-
nineteenth-century biblical scholarship.

Unlike his predecessors in Germany or Britain, however, Colenso ultimately grounded his critical and comparative work in an
African context by claiming that his "Zulu philosopher," William

Ngidi, had provided the rationale for the entire project. Like all Zulu, Ngidi was used by Colenso to represent both the particular religion of an ancient Israelite past and the universal religion of humanity. For this universalism, Colenso was accused of heresy and tried by the Anglican church. In 1862 he returned to London to defend his case. When the first volume of his commentary was published that year, it sold ten thousand copies in six days. Although finally exonerated by the Church of England, Colenso maintained a notoriety in Britain. He was even mocked in a popular verse that satirized his relationship with Ngidi:

> A bishop there was of Natal,
> Who took a Zulu for a pal,
> Said the Kafir 'Look 'ere,
> Aint the Pentateuch queer?
> And converted the Lord of Natal.

For his part, in 1869 William Ngidi drew his own comparison between the practice of polygyny among the Zulu and the patriarchs of the Hebrew Bible. Based on that comparison, he decided to marry a second wife. Although he also noted that a man with only one wife was nothing but a "poor fellow," Ngidi and other African converts read of polygyny in the biblical account of the patriarchs. When Colenso tried to prevent the union, Ngidi left Bishopstowe to start his own mission at Umsinga, proclaiming a Christian gospel that allowed for the retention of African customs. When little interest was shown in his new mission, however, Ngidi renounced Christianity and moved to a remote region of Zululand.[21]

John William Colenso's career as biblical critic, his travails as bishop, and his efforts to defend Zulu rights within the British empire have all been documented. As a comparative religionist, however, Colenso made a significant contribution. He initiated a series of transpositions that had far-reaching effect on the study of religion. By identifying ancient Jews with the Zulu, Colenso perpetuated a frontier comparison that was common in the colony of Natal. However, by simultaneously locating among the Zulu the basic elements of an original, revealed religion, Colenso anticipated a new comparative strategy by which the universal history of religion could be reconstructed, not from records found in the Hebrew Bible, but by evidence drawn from reports about the Zulu.

WILHELM HEINRICH IMMANUEL BLEEK

In the early nineteenth century, biblical scholars still saw the Old Testament as an account of universal human history. They could turn to the Bible, as the historian Henry Hart Milman noted in 1829, for "the remarkable picture which it presents of the gradual development of human society; the ancestors of the Jews and the Jews themselves pass through every stage of comparative civilization."[22] As the Zulu were identified with Jews during the 1850s in Natal, however, they took the place of Jews in presenting a picture of the origin and development of human society. The ancestors of the Zulu, and the Zulu themselves, represented the earliest stages in the advance of comparative civilization. This further development of the frontier comparison between Jews and the Zulu was central to the early researches in Natal undertaken by the German philologist W. H. I. Bleek. Arriving with Colenso in 1855, Bleek collected materials on Zulu myths and legends. His expressed purpose was to discover evidence of human prehistory. In searching for traces of the original human ancestors, therefore, Bleek did not look to Adam, ancient Israel, or the history of the Jews. He looked to the Zulu. As a result, Bleek replaced Jews with the Zulu—the Jews of Natal—in working out a theory of the origin and development of religion.

Son of a prominent biblical scholar, Bleek studied theology at Berlin, theology and philology at Bonn, and proceeded from studies in Egyptian and Hebrew to the study of African language. His doctoral thesis, submitted in 1851, was a comparative study of Hottentot grammar. Bleek made the acquaintance of Colenso through a mutual friend, the theologian F. D. Maurice, and came to Natal in 1855 as Colenso's translator and linguist. Like Colenso, Bleek must have been influenced by Maurice's sympathetic approach to world religions. In his personal religious convictions, Bleek seems to have been something of a universalist, explaining in 1864 that as "one who is sincere in striving, in his little way, to come nearer to the truth," he had been able "to win the confidence of person's holding the most different religious convictions."[23] Nevertheless, Bleek's search for the truth about religion was conducted less through theology than through the science of philology. With F. Max Müller, who was establishing himself in the field of comparative philology at Oxford when Bleek arrived in Natal, Bleek had benefited from the guidance and patronage of Baron Christian von Bunsen. The Prussian diplomat and scholar had directed both to the study of language as the key that promised to unlock the secret history of religion. As a result of Bunsen's influence, Bleek devoted his life to pursuing a comparative religion in southern Africa that was based on philology.

As a distinguished Egyptologist, Bunsen had set out in his *Outline of a Philosophy of Universal History*, published in 1854, "to discover and define the principles of progress and to apply these general principles to Language and Religion as the two Universal and primitive manifestations of the human mind upon which all subsequent social and national development is based." The great "scaffolding for the primeval history of religion," Bunsen held, was provided by the "genealogical tree of the families of mankind." More specifically, the genealogy of mankind was defined by three language groups—Japhetic, Chametic, Semitic—into which all human beings could be classified. From this classification, however, Bunsen drew historical conclusions. According to Müller, Bunsen's great discovery was that human beings in Africa had degenerated gradually from an original Asiatic stock. Although aspiring to provide a universal history, Baron von Bunsen, according to Müller, had outlined a history of Africa.

Bleek agreed with this assessment of Bunsen's importance. He noted in 1855 that it was "mainly owing to the noble exertions of Bunsen, that interest in African ethnological and philological research has so greatly increased within the last ten years." Bleek also supported Bunsen's historical discovery, arguing in his doctoral dissertation that the Cape Hottentots could be traced back to a North African origin because of the similarities in grammatical structure between the Khoikhoi and the Coptic, Berber, and Galla languages. Arriving in Natal, Bleek anticipated further dramatic discoveries in the study of African language and religion. In November 1855 he wrote to Donald Moodie, compiler of the Cape Records, to suggest that African studies promised to play the same kind of intellectual role that Oriental studies had played in the early nineteenth century. While F. Max Müller was exploring the Indo-European as an ancient origin of human civilization, therefore, W. H. I. Bleek intended to discover traces of the original human language and religion in Africa.[24]

In Search of the Original

In order to discover the original form of religion in Africa, however, Bleek had to reverse the colonial perception that Africans

W. H. I. Bleek. (Courtesy South African Library, Cape Town)

had degenerated from some prior religion. If African religion had devolved from ancient Israel, Judaism, Islam, or some other "higher" religion, then it could not represent an original in its own right. Accordingly, Bleek insisted that African religion should be understood, not as degeneration, but as preservation. It had not degenerated from some other religion but had preserved and perpetuated its own origin. In 1854 Bleek asserted that the indigenous people of southern Africa had managed to maintain the earliest forms of African religion. "I believe that the most ancient types of African life have been best preserved there," Bleek claimed, "in respect to language as well as to religion, manners and customs." As a result, Bleek proposed that the "Hottentots" and "Kafirs" would reveal the underlying principles of language and religion that held for the entire continent of Africa. Three years later, however, Bleek was convinced by his Zulu researches that he had discovered the original religion—not merely of Africa but of all humanity. In an 1857 article published in the *Cape Monthly Magazine,* Bleek asserted, "It is indeed true that the Kafir tribes, and perhaps chiefly among them the Zulus, have, of all African nations of their kindred, preserved in general the most primitive and original state of language, manners, customs, etc." According to Bleek, the Zulu were less advanced than the Sotho-Tswana or other African tribes of their race. Therefore, they had adhered more faithfully to their primitive origin. That primitive and original religion of the Zulu, Bleek insisted, was evidence of the origin of humanity.[25]

In the course of researches conducted between 1855 and 1856, Bleek collected Zulu oral traditions. Published in 1857 as *Zulu Legends,* this compendium was understood by Bleek to be more than merely an account of contemporary Zulu myths and ritual practices. Rather, Bleek understood his collection as an archeological excavation of human prehistory. While collecting this material, Bleek reflected in his diary upon "how essential is a comparison of the branches of human-kind spread over Africa, to an investigation of the earlier developments of our race." In Bleek's terms, the Zulu had preserved not only their own origin but the origin of humanity. Writing to his parents in the midst of these researches, Bleek revealed that his interest in Zulu religion served his broader concern in reconstructing the origin and development of human religion more generally. The "religion of the kaffer is naturally a very special and important, as also an interesting part of my studies," Bleek noted, "and I hope to be able to report some valuable facts which are also of importance to the history of religion."[26]

In presenting his findings on Zulu religion, Bleek employed the significant rhetorical strategy of organizing the oral traditions he had collected into the format of numbered chapters and verses. Like the Bible, Bleek's chapters, or *Imhlamvu,* constituted the sacred literature of the Zulu. While Colenso reread the Old Testament under Zulu influence, Bleek turned the oral testimony he had gathered in Natal into the chapters and verses of a Zulu Bible. In a letter written in 1856, Bleek observed that the original form of Zulu religion was found in their regard for ancestors. "They are extremely religious," he wrote, "but their religion consists of veneration for the spirits of their ancestors, in particular the souls of their departed chiefs." Ancestor worship was the primordial religion of the Zulu. At the same time, however, Bleek hinted at the contemporary importance of Zulu ancestors. They were effective as a means for dismissing the presence of Europeans, even a European scholar, within the idiom of traditional religion. Bleek wrote that he often asked his Zulu assistant, a conservative religious person, "What are you saying?" Instead of answering, however, the Zulu assistant dismissed Bleek. "I am not speaking to you," he would say, "I am praising the Amahlozi [ancestors]." Although the ancestors must have assumed new importance in the colonial context as a force that might counteract the European impact in southern Africa, Bleek was convinced that the Zulu ancestral religion he observed in Natal represented a primitive and original form of religious life. Consistently, Bleek held that "ancestor-worship [is] a form of religion which must be reckoned among the most ancient."[27]

In spite of this preeminence of ancestors in Zulu belief and practice, Bleek began his redaction of Zulu sacred literature with the "unknown God." Like Colenso, Bleek found that the Zulu term *uNkulunkulu* most closely approximated the Christian notion of God. Bleek established the authenticity of this term, however, not through theological speculation, but by means of the science of comparative philology. "That it is not of modern date and recently introduced among them," he found, "is clear from a comparison with the traditions of some of the kindred nations of Africa, who though separate for many centuries, and living now as far distant as Damaraland, Zanzibar and even Sierre Leone, have substantially the same name for God." Although Bleek observed no worship of uNkulunkulu, since Zulu ritual was directed toward ancestors, he nevertheless concluded that Zulu people believed in a god that was above and superior to ancestral spirits. The unknown God was preserved, not in worship, but in the Zulu language, which, in its supposedly conservative character, had deviated only slightly from what Bleek determined was the original African name of God, *Mukulunka*. Again, Bleek found not degeneration but the perpetuation of an original form of African religion among the Zulu.[28]

Certainly, Bleek's search for an original and permanent Zulu religion obscured the kind of cultural work that religion could accomplish through the contemporary reworking of traditional mythic material. In collecting Zulu legends, Bleek might have thought that he was gathering data on one of the earliest, most primitive stages of religion. But what he in fact collected was evidence of a certain kind of mid-nineteenth-century religious and cultural work. For example, after recording a traditional Zulu myth about the origin of death, Bleek related a myth about the creation of human beings by uNkulunkulu, "the Great-great one." According to this myth, uNkulunkulu emerged from beneath the ground to create humans, male and female. But he also created black people and white people. He said: "The white men [*abe-lungu*] may live in the midst of the water, in the sea. He gave them clothing. . . . the black people [*aba-ntu*] shall live within this land. . . . the white men shall carry guns. . . . the [black] men shall carry spears."[29] In this account we find myth operating as comparative cultural work. This myth manipulated certain oppositions that might have been perceived as natural, such as life and death, up and down, or male and female. However, in the version recorded by Bleek, the myth also manipulated contemporary, historical oppositions that defined the modern world of Zulu religion in the middle of the nineteenth century. It was structured in terms of the oppositions represented by white and black, sea and land, and the violent confrontation of spears against guns. Although Bleek recorded this creation myth as evidence of a primordial Zulu religion, it was obviously a creative improvisation on colonial conflict. Whatever the term *uNkulunkulu* might have meant previously, the "unknown God" featured most prominently in Zulu efforts to make sense out of the colonial situation.

Recording this mythic account of uNkulunkulu, Bleek nevertheless determined that the fundamental character of Zulu religion was ancestor worship. Although uNkulunkulu appeared in myth, he was not worshiped. The heart of Zulu religion was ancestral ritual. Therefore, if the Zulu had in fact preserved their own origin, they stood as living fossils of the original ancestor religion of humanity. At the same time, however, a second and parallel original could also be discerned in southern Africa. Besides the Zulu, Bleek found that the Hottentots and Bushmen also represented the primitive, original condition of language and religion. In the same article in the *Cape Monthly Magazine* in which he had identified the Zulu as the "most primitive and original," Bleek asserted that the Hottentots and Bushmen also represented a human origin.

> Since the Hottentots and Bushmen have in general retained, most faithfully, the primitive and original state of their race, in customs, manners, language, etc., a study of their peculiarities must be regarded as eminently important, nay, indispensable for attaining a knowledge of the prehistorical condition and unrecorded history of their kindred nations; and as these comprise, in many cases, some of the most advanced and civilized nations, should we not be entitled to infer that such researches, if once properly made, will prove of great interest for the history of mankind in general?

Like the Zulu, the Hottentots and Bushmen provided evidence for reconstructing human prehistory. Sixteen years later, when Bleek had devoted the remaining years of his life to recording Bushman traditions, he would still observe that they represented a point of human origin that would "throw an unexpected light upon the primitive stages of the mental life of nations of our own near kindred." Once again, therefore, not the Jews but the indigenous people of southern Africa represented the primordial ancestors of humanity.[30]

In the Zulu and Hottentots, however, southern African evidence suggested a dual origin for human religion. While Zulu evidence could be used to establish ancestor worship as the most ancient form of religion, research among the Hottentots had found an absence of ancestor worship. Rather than venerating their glorified dead, Hottentots appeared to worship the moon. Basing his earliest conclusions about Hottentot religion on the work of Peter Kolb, Bleek determined that a second, parallel origin for religion could be found in sidereal worship. According to Bleek, this form of religion, which was based on the worship of heavenly bodies, was the most ancient form of "heathen" religion practiced throughout western and northern Africa. From that Af-

rican origin, sidereal worship had developed into the more elaborate religious mythologies of ancient Arabia, Babylonia, India,
Greece, and Europe. In Bleek's analysis, therefore, ancestor worship and sidereal worship were two mutually exclusive types of
original religion. Significantly, their mutual exclusion could be
established in southern Africa. Just as the Hottentots lacked
ancestor worship, sidereal worship was entirely absent among the
Zulu and other African groups that Bleek designated as *Kafirs*.
The conventional frontier distinction between two types of indigenous people in southern Africa, therefore, provided Bleek with a
comparative key to unlock the mystery of the origin of religion.
In the beginning, Bleek implied, humanity had split into Hottentots and Kafirs and had developed religions that were based either
on the worship of the moon or the worship of the dead.

Philology of Religion

Drawing on the science of comparative philology, Bleek offered
two explanations for the perceived difference between Hottentot
sidereal worship and Kafir ancestor worship. In both cases he conducted comparisons that depended upon an analysis of language.
First, Bleek proposed an explanation based upon historical diffusion. He explained the difference between Hottentots and Kafirs
as a result of Hottentot migrations from North Africa. Since Hottentot language differed dramatically from Kafir language, while
sharing a common grammatical structure with the Egyptian,
Coptic, and Semitic languages of North Africa, the Hottentot and
North African were necessarily derived from the same historical
origin. As Bleek argued, "It has been shown that as the Hottentots, in appearance, manners, and customs differ from the Kafirs,
so also the structure of the language is unlike that of the Kafir
language, but so evidently similar to most North African languages that there does not remain the slightest doubt that it is of
common descent with them." In establishing this common descent on philological grounds, Bleek proposed a theory of historical diffusion that linked northern and southern Africa. As we
have seen, Bleek was not the first to make this connection. It
was a common strategy in frontier comparative religion to trace
Hottentot origins back to North Africa, Arabia, or Asia. However,
Bleek introduced a new approach to the analysis of religion in
southern Africa by insisting upon a distinction between histori-

cal and structural origins. In historical terms, Bleek assumed, Hottentot language and religion originated in North Africa and eventually migrated down the continent to the Cape. However, since they had supposedly preserved the most ancient linguistic and religious structures of their homeland, the Hottentots actually represented the point of origin from which all the languages of northern Africa had eventually developed. In terms of structure, therefore, the Hottentots represented, not the descendants, but the original ancestors of the Egyptian, Coptic, and Semitic languages of northern Africa.[31]

Building on this analysis of linguistic structure, Bleek proposed a second explanation for the difference between Hottentot and Kafir religion in his analysis of comparative morphology. Bleek's logic for comparative religion assumed that religion, like language, was a system. Both could be reduced to underlying structures. In the comparison of religious and linguistic structures, Bleek was convinced that religious systems ultimately could be reduced to different forms of language. He recognized that the "idea that mythological notions, or the outward forms of religious beliefs, are primarily dependent upon the manner of speech, is now generally allowed to be one of the most fertile and efficient for understanding rightly the natural history of religion and mythology." Here Bleek agreed with F. Max Müller that language was the key to the scientific study of religion. According to Müller, myth had originated through a primitive confusion about grammatical gender. In that primordial confusion, or "disease of language," nouns that were grammatically gendered into masculine and feminine classes were imaginatively transposed into mythological personifications. Male and female nouns were thereby transformed into gods and goddesses. Following Müller's theory of the origin of myth, Bleek argued that the structure of a language determined the basic patterns of religious and mythological thought. But he also proposed that all languages, and therefore all religions, were derived from two basic structural types that appeared in the gendered and nongendered families of human languages.[32]

Bleek concluded that languages that did not classify nouns by gender (which he called prefix-pronominal languages, a class that corresponded roughly to what Müller called Turanian languages) did not support the development of myth. By contrast, languages that did classify nouns by gender (which Bleek called sex-denoting languages) led to the production of mythological person-

ifications of nature. This broad family of sex-denoting languages
included Indo-European and Semitic languages. In southern Africa, this sex-denoting language family was represented by the Hottentots, who had, as a result, developed an elaborate mythology
based on the personification of heavenly bodies. Speaking a language in which noun classes were unrelated to biological gender,
"Kafirs" lacked such a mythology. Rather, since their language
provided no structural basis to support the mythological personification of the sun, moon, or stars, they had developed an alternative form of religion in ancestor worship. As Bleek explained,
"The primary cause of ancestor worship of the one race (Kafirs,
Negroes, and Polynesians) and the sidereal worship (or religions
originating in the veneration of heavenly bodies) of the other
(Hottentots, North African, Semitic, and Aryan) is supplied by
their very forms of language. . . . Sex denoting languages . . . have
higher poetic conception . . . forming the origin of mythological
legends. . . . This faculty is not developed in the Kafir mind."[33]
According to Bleek, therefore, two different linguistic structures
had produced the two most basic forms of religion. Prefix-
pronominal languages, which tended to set aside beings endowed
with speech as a particular grammatical class of nouns, produced
a religion that was based on reverence for the spirits of the dead.
Sex-denoting languages, however, with their gendered classes of
nouns, had produced a type of religion that was based on the pos-
tulation and worship of personified spirits of nature.

    Through comparative morphology, Bleek reduced differences in
religion to underlying linguistic structures. At the same time,
Bleek's philological analysis was consistent with developments in
other nineteenth-century comparative sciences, such as comparative botany, zoology, or anatomy, that were arranging morphological structures into evolutionary sequences. In that respect, Bleek
found that African language and religion represented not only basic structures but also fossilized remnants from earlier stages of
human evolution. Arguably, Bleek brought to this study a rare
sensitivity to the living dynamics of those fossils of human origins. For example, while his European contemporaries in comparative anatomy were assembling collections of bones and skulls
from all over the world, Bleek wrote home that he would be unable to make a contribution. "I doubt very much," Bleek wrote in
response to one request, "if I shall be able to obtain the skull and
pelvis of a kaffer. I presume the kaffers would not like the idea,
neither would they allow a corpse to be dissected." Similarly, in

his philological work, Bleek emphasized the need to study spoken languages. He chided F. Max Müller for relying only upon written sources in developing his theories, even comparing Müller at one point to a "zoologist who, e.g., only knows whole animal groups from the descriptions which are more or less incomplete and incorrect, without having studied the animals himself." Although he felt somewhat isolated from European developments in comparative philology, Bleek could nevertheless claim a different kind of authority that was based on his immediate contact with living people, languages, and religions in southern Africa.[34]

Although he relied on the authority of local fieldwork, Bleek did assume that he was collecting evidence in support of a universal theory of the evolution of religion. Retracing that evolutionary sequence, Bleek found that modern European theology had its origin, not in Jewish or Christian sacred texts, but in the ancient sex-denoting languages that had "filled the sky with gods." Modern ideas of God had evolved out of the kind of worship of the heavens practiced by the Khoikhoi. The mythological personifications of sidereal worship, however, had overlaid the earlier ancestor worship that had been supported by prefix-pronominal languages. In the course of human history, the religion of the heavens had generally displaced the religion of the ancestral underworld. But elements of an earlier ancestor worship nevertheless persisted in the concept of personal immortality, in hero worship, and even in the Christian theological doctrine of atonement, which Bleek conjectured had developed from a religious intuition that was first evident in the ritual propitiation of ancestral spirits.[35] While modern Christians looked to the heavens for their God, therefore, they unknowingly stood on the religious ground that had been established in ancient prehistory by the type of ancestor ritual practiced by Zulu-speaking people in southern Africa. Once again, in his philology of religion, Bleek concluded that the Zulu were the primordial ancestors of humanity. Zulu ancestor worship was the original ancestor of modern religion. The European present, therefore, depended upon a Zulu past. The evolution of religion could be traced from Zulu ancestor worship, through Khoikhoi sidereal worship, to the heavenly God of European Christianity. Remarkably the divisions of the colonial situation in southern Africa disclosed the evolution of the religion of all humanity.

In the course of human evolution, which corresponded to the progress of European colonization, Bleek expected that the distinctive, original forms of religion found in Khoikhoi sidereal worship and Zulu ancestor worship were bound to disappear. Indeed, like most of his European contemporaries, Bleek assumed that the disappearance of these forms of life would actually benefit the "uncivilized" people who practiced them. "We may with truth say that any well-conducted colonization by a civilized nation is a benefit for uncivilized tribes," Bleek observed in 1857, "even if it should (as most generally is doubtless the case) destroy their nationality and incorporate them individually into the body of the dominant race."[36] With the prospect of their imminent destruction, Bleek was motivated by a certain urgency in his collection of the language, myth, and religion of the indigenous people of southern Africa. After 1857, when he moved to Cape Town to serve as librarian for the colonial governor, Sir George Grey, Bleek embarked upon a similar reclamation project for the Bushmen, that "dying out race," which preoccupied him for the rest of his life. Although the indigenous languages and religions of southern Africa were destined for destruction, Bleek imagined that they would live on, not only in his texts but also in the process of human evolution that retained traces of its own origin, an origin that was most faithfully displayed in the languages and religions of the indigenous people of southern Africa.

HENRY CALLAWAY

The missionary Henry Callaway, who arrived in Natal with Colenso and Bleek, also embarked upon Zulu researches. His publications in this field eventually made him the leading nineteenth-century authority in the world on Zulu religion. Based upon his collections of oral tradition, Callaway's two major publications— *Nursery Tales, Traditions, and Histories of the Zulus* (1866–68) and *The Religious System of the Amazulu* (1868–70)—became the definitive statement on Zulu religious beliefs and practices for European anthropology, folklore, and comparative religion. European theorists, such as F. Max Müller, John Lubbock, Herbert Spencer, Edward B. Tylor, Andrew Lang, and James Frazer, depended heavily upon Callaway's texts not only to understand Zulu religion but also for evidence in building their own general theories of the origin and nature of religion.

However, Henry Callaway's account of a Zulu religious system was entangled in the local conditions of the colonial frontier on at least three counts. First, Callaway framed his research agenda in terms of what he saw as the needs of the Christian mission. In this regard, he conducted his research on the Zulu "unknown God" in the context of a theological polemic against Bishop Colenso. On theological grounds, Callaway argued that Colenso's adoption of the God-name *uNkulunkulu* was inappropriate for a frontier mission that had to distinguish itself from a surrounding heathendom. Accordingly, Callaway discovered, against the findings of Colenso and Bleek, that the term *uNkulunkulu* was understood by the Zulu, not as God, but as the first ancestor.

Second, Callaway collected evidence for this conclusion primarily from informants who had sought refuge at his mission station in Springvale. Like the residents of other Christian missions, these informants were social outcasts or refugees from African communities.[37] Furthermore, since they came from different regions that ranged from the remote northern Zulu territory to the eastern Cape, Callaway's informants had undergone different experiences of the expanding colonial frontier. As a result, instead of holding a single, coherent Zulu religious system, Callaway's informants asserted a spectrum of religious positions that can be correlated with varying degrees of colonial contact.

Finally, the bulk of Callaway's authoritative account of Zulu religion in the *The Religious System* was authored, not by the missionary ethnographer, but by the Zulu convert Mpengula Mbande. Although Callaway transcribed and edited the volume, providing footnotes and occasional commentary, the majority of the text appeared in the words of Mbande, reflecting, at many points, his own ambiguous position on the colonial frontier as a recent Christian convert. With one foot on either side of the frontier battle line that divided the colonial mission from African society, Mpengula Mbande's ambivalent personal position defined the dominant perspective on Zulu religion that emerged in Henry Callaway's *Religious System of the Amazulu*.

Callaway's uNkulunkulu

Born in 1817, Henry Callaway studied medicine between 1840 and 1844. He was admitted to the Royal College of Surgeons in 1842 and the Royal College of Physicians in 1853, and received his M.D. at Aberdeen in 1853. From the age of seventeen, Cal-

Henry Callaway. (From Benham, *Henry Callaway*)

laway had been a committed Quaker, even publishing a book, *Immediate Revelation*, on the "inner light" in 1841. In 1853, however, inspired by reading the work of F. D. Maurice, Callaway left the Society of Friends, gave up his medical practice, and offered his services to Colenso's mission to Natal. At Callaway's ordination at the cathedral church of Norwich on 13 August 1854, Colenso delivered a sermon that celebrated England's divine calling to surround the world with its colonial power so that "the lands, which our warriors have conquered, become the fair possessions of the Prince of Peace." Significantly, in the light of their subsequent controversies over the Zulu God-name, Colenso suggested at Callaway's ordination that this cooperation between colonial conquest and Christian mission was necessary "in order that God's name may be glorified."

After arriving in Natal in 1855, Callaway spent his first three years in Pietermaritzburg. During that time he formulated conclusions about Zulu religion. Callaway observed that the Zulu believed in spirits and the transmigration of souls into the bodies of animals, especially into a certain species of snake. Regarding any belief in a Supreme Being, however, he noted that the Zulu "also believe in a god; but I am not as yet quite clear as to what their precise notions are, or whether the belief is universal or even general among them." In 1858, wanting to pursue both his mission work and his research on Zulu religion far away from the corrupting influences of the colony, Callaway founded the Springvale mission station in southwestern Natal. There he began a more disciplined collection of oral evidence on the question of the Zulu "unknown God."[38]

Even before establishing himself at Springvale, however, Callaway had arrived at the conclusion that Colenso was wrong about the term *uNkulunkulu*. In March 1856 he had proposed three theological objections to Colenso's introduction of uNkulunkulu into the Zulu prayer book. First, since uNkulunkulu was a proper name, it was unsuitable for representing a Christian concept of divinity as *Deus* or *Gott*. The Christian mission, Callaway suggested, might as well use the proper names Jupiter, Mercury, or Woden to represent divinity. The proper name uNkulunkulu was similarly inappropriate for the Christian mission. Second, Callaway referred to the Old Testament precedent in which the ancient Israelites had been forbidden to adopt the names of heathen gods. By introducing a heathen god-name into its worship, the mission risked violating biblical prohibitions against serving foreign gods. Third, recognizing that the Apostle Paul had used the Greek term *theos*, Callaway insisted that the crucial point was that Paul had used a generic term for divinity for Jehovah, rather than using the name of any pagan Greek god. Repeating his point, Callaway insisted that since the God of the first-century Christian mission was not called by the name Zeus, the God of the nineteenth-century Zulu mission could not be called uNkulunkulu.[39]

Did the Zulu have a generic term, like *theos*, for divinity? Calla-

way thought they did not. In conducting his research at Springvale, he replaced theological with ethnographical arguments
against the use of uNkulunkulu in Christian worship. He questioned informants about their ideas of divinity. His ethnographic
findings only confirmed his theological opposition to the use of
the term *uNkulunkulu* for the Christian God. If it was bad to use
a heathen god-name for the Christian God, Callaway found that
it was even worse to adopt a name that actually did not refer to a
god at all. As Callaway argued, the term *uNkulunkulu* was generally understood by the Zulu to refer, not to a god, but to the first
ancestor. Since he was imagined as the progenitor of humanity, or
of a particular tribe, uNkulunkulu could not be the "unknown
God" of the Zulu.

As Callaway pursued his research during the 1860s, his argument about uNkulunkulu created some controversy among his
colleagues. In 1862, for example, Callaway responded to a challenge from W. H. I. Bleek by insisting that he alone had penetrated the total system of Zulu religion. Instead of singling out
one element of that system, uNkulunkulu, and then misinter-
preting it as if it were a Zulu god, Callaway claimed to have captured the genuine spirit of the Zulu religious system. As he wrote
to Bleek:

> It is not I who reject the tradition of the natives, my dear friend; it
> is you who reject all but one, and let aside nine-tenths of that by
> an arbitrary dictum. It is not I who do not enter into their spirit; it
> is you, who have failed to comprehend it, because you have inter-
> preted not as they ever do or could, but by the light received from
> Christian Theology, and so have supposed the heathen to be that
> which you yourself believe; and which by a few ingenious twistings
> of their sayings, a few suppressions and a few additions, may be
> extracted from them.

On the same day, Callaway wrote to Bishop Gray in Cape Town,
claiming not only that he had entered the Zulu religious system
more deeply than any other European observer but that he had
"entered far deeper, than the natives themselves could penetrate."
Knowing Zulu religion better than the Zulu, Callaway was able
to assert authoritatively that Zulu notions about uNkulunkulu
had nothing to do with religious faith in a deity. Zulu regarded
tales about uNkulunkulu as Europeans regarded fables, ghost stories, or idle gossip. Callaway insisted that the Zulu "have no reli-

gious convictions about [uNkulunkulu] whatever," because all of their "faith and religious convictions are devoted to . . . the Amatongo [ancestors]." Having developed a religious system based on ancestor worship, therefore, the Zulu had no "unknown God," as Colenso had insisted, that could be appropriated by the Christian mission.[40]

In the midst of prosecuting Colenso for heresy, Bishop Gray must have welcomed Callaway's implication that Colenso had been wrong not only about Christian faith but also about the character of Zulu religion. On two other issues, Colenso's principled tolerance of polygamy and his adoption of a comparative method in biblical criticism, Callaway also assumed an opposing position in the 1860s. As in the case of William Ngidi, Colenso tried to prevent Christian converts from entering into a second marriage. However, he argued for tolerance in the case of converts who were already in polygamous marriages. In a sermon published in 1862, Callaway insisted that polygamy was in every instance a bar to membership in the Christian church. Regarding biblical criticism, Callaway published a sermon in 1866 that reduced its emerging comparative method to caricature. Callaway accused the "Higher Criticism" of destroying the unique sacred history of the Bible. According to Callaway, this comparative biblical criticism claimed that the ancient Israelites originally had "no national deity." In the beginning, they worshiped a stone. Gradually, the Israelites adopted religious beliefs from other nations, worshiping the gods of Egypt or Canaan. In developing their religious ideas, the ancient Israelites had taken their stories about the creation of the universe and the fall of humanity from the myths of Persia. In this comparative biblical criticism, Callaway complained, the nature of ancient Jewish religion was found, not in the Bible, but at Mecca, while the central Christian doctrine of the incarnation was derived from Hindu myths of Vishnu. These comparisons, Callaway asserted, had distorted both biblical revelation and the distinctive historical character of the religion of ancient Israel.[41]

While Callaway adamantly rejected the application of comparative method to the Bible, he nevertheless applied a similar method to the study of Zulu religion. Finding that the Zulu had "no national deity," Callaway proceeded to compare their beliefs and practices to the religions of the world. In asserting that the Zulu thought uNkulunkulu was the "first man," Callaway invoked the comparative example of the Hindu avatar Krishna, "the most ancient person." If the Zulu thought that uNkulunkulu broke off (*dabuka*) from the "source of being" (*Uhlanga*), then Callaway could cite a comparable instance from Hindu myth in which the original human being was "produced by a division (*ukudabuka*) of the substance of Brahma."[42] By drawing such comparisons, however, Callaway had no intention of suggesting that Zulu religion was historically derived from Hinduism. Rather, he invoked comparisons as precedents that lent support to his general reconstruction of the religious system of the Zulu. Comparisons were warrants that guaranteed the coherence and viability of the structure of that system. If it seemed unlikely that anyone, let alone the Zulu, could hold such a myth, Callaway's comparisons made it seem more likely. Comparison, in this sense, reinforced the credibility of the overall structure of Callaway's depiction of the Zulu religious system. His reconstruction of a Zulu religious system was thereby made to appear more realistic by comparison with other religious systems.

While he compared the structures of religious systems, Callaway imagined the history of Zulu religion by resorting to the frontier theory of degeneration that had been such a prominent feature of missionary and settler theories of the indigenous religions of southern Africa. Where Bleek saw Zulu ancestor worship as a point of origin for a process of evolution, Callaway saw contemporary Zulu religion only as the end result of a "gradual deterioration of the religious opinions of the people." All that could be observed in the present was "the feeble representative of some old system." The Zulu, Callaway assumed, had "degenerated from a much higher position intellectually and morally than they now hold." Echoing theories that had been popular on the eastern Cape frontier, Callaway argued that Zulu diviners were "probably the descendants of some old *priesthood*, and retaining all the evil influence and cruel tyranny of priestcraft over the minds of the people."[43]

Eventually, Callaway formulated a three-stage history of Zulu religion that revived the theory of Allen Gardiner and other frontier devolutionists. First, Callaway proposed, the Zulu must have originally believed in a Father in Heaven, a Heavenly Lord, or a Divine Creator. But that primitive belief had been obscured by ignorance and the "tyranny of priestcraft" that had supported the emergence of ancestor worship. Second, therefore, subject to their own ignorance and under the influence of devious priests, the

Zulu had confused the Divine Creator with the first man. As a result, they had forgotten all about God. In their degenerate religious vocabulary, *uNkulunkulu* referred only to their first ancestor. Otherwise, they had no indigenous memory of God. Third, and finally, the Zulu were being reminded of their original belief in God by the advent of the Christian mission. If they were to remember God, however, they had to forget uNkulunkulu, their original ancestor.

On both structural and historical grounds, therefore, Callaway insisted that the mission could not adopt *uNkulunkulu* as the name of God without entangling Christianity in Zulu ancestor worship. Colenso remained unconvinced. As he wrote Bleek in 1868, "I am satisfied that Callaway is all wrong about Unkulunkulu. He has got a 'bee in his bonnet' on that subject, and runs wild after Unpengula [Mpengula Mbande] his catechist." According to Colenso, Callaway had been misled by his principal informant. After receiving a copy of Callaway's *Religious System*, Colenso reviewed its findings with one of his own informants, including a son of the Zulu king Mpande, and was reassured that Callaway was "entirely wrong about uNkulunkulu . . . and in fact in all ideas on this particular subject."[44]

If his catechist was not the cause of Callaway's errors, Mpengula Mbande was at least the source of most of his primary data about Zulu religious beliefs and practices. In the *Religious System of the Amazulu*, a large portion of the first section on uNnkulunkulu was information either directly provided or indirectly collected by Mbande; the other three sections, on ancestors, divination, and magic, were almost entirely dictated and signed by Mbande. Callaway described Mbande simply as "an educated, intelligent, Christian native." As such, Mbande became a hero of popular missionary literature. Like William Ngidi, however, Mpengula Mbande was also characterized by European commentators as a "Zulu philosopher." His depiction of Zulu thought and religion was taken as authentic. As Thomas B. Jenkinson observed, "The account given by the late Native Deacon Umpengula of the state of the native mind on the subject of their ancestor worship and degraded state, is very good." As a Christian, a philosopher, and a comparative religionist, Mbande placed his distinctive mark on the formulation of a traditional Zulu religious system. Arguably, however, in working out his own ambivalent relationship with both the Christian mission and his African religious heritage, Mbande actually produced, not an ethnographic account, but a theological critique of traditional Zulu religion.[45]

The Frontier Religious System
of the amaZulu

Born into a "chiefly family" south of Natal in an area that would become known as Griqualand East, Mpengula Mbande found his way in the early 1850s to the mission station of Ludwig Döhne near Pietermaritzburg. A violent family conflict apparently forced Mbande to take refuge in the mission, since his move to Natal coincided with the outlawing of his brother for patricide. After Ludwig Döhne left Natal in 1857, Mbande and his wife Mary joined Callaway at his new mission station at Springvale. Prospering as a maize farmer, Mbande also assumed responsibilities as catechist, Sunday-school teacher, and, after 1871, deacon at Callaway's mission. Eventually, he was joined by two brothers, one who had been trained as a traditional healer, the other who developed the symptoms of the diviner's calling. As a sacred specialist in the new Christian religion, however, Mbande was able to exercise new sacred power not only as a priest but also in his sustained critique of the old Zulu religion that he conducted in collaboration with Henry Callaway.

The first section of *The Religious System of the Amazulu* contained conflicting testimony from a disparate collection of informants whose statements about uNkulunkulu reflected very different religious understandings. Evidence collected in *The Religious System*, therefore, did not represent a single, coherent Zulu religious system. Rather, the voices in the text hinted at theological debates and arguments, as well as confusions and contradictions, that were situated on the colonial frontier. Although not systematized as such in Callaway's presentation, these reports can be organized in terms of a range of coherent and, perhaps, representative religious positions.

1. *umVelinqangi is the Creator:* This assertion was attributed to Ufulatela Sitole, who grew up on a Dutch mission station. Before the missionaries arrived, Sitole claimed, the Zulu knew of umVelinqangi as the divine creator who had brought forth human beings from a bed of reeds, but they did not know his name. Therefore, instead of worshiping the creator, they worshiped snakes. In giving

this account, Sitole, displaying resentment against the Dutch, claimed that they refused to tell Africans about the creator because they said that black people were like dogs, lacking a spirit, and would therefore burn in hell.[46]

2. *umVelinqangi is the Creator; uNkulunkulu refers to the first parents of humanity:* This solution to the relation between umVel-inqangi and uNkulunkulu was proposed by Unsukozonke Memela. It was the only time in *The Religious System* that any attempt was made to reconcile the two god-names identified by Colenso as equivalent to the Hebrew names for God, Elohim and Jehovah.[47]

3. *uNkulunkulu is the Creator:* The strongest, clearest statement of this position was provided by Mpengula Mbande, although he also suggested that this understanding of uNkulunkulu was a recent innovation. However, the identification of uNkulunkulu as creator was also made by Umfezi, a man living near Springvale, who added that uNkulunkulu received no worship since the Zulu prayed to "their own people." Another Springvale local, an old woman, was caught in a contradiction when one day she said that uNkulunkulu was above and the next day she said below. When Mbande went out to take her statement, she tried to resolve the confusion by declaring, "Truly uNkulunkulu is he who is in heaven." However, her understanding of uNkulunkulu's role as creator was only further confused when she followed this declaration by asserting, "And the white men, they are the lords who made all things." Significantly, this confusion about the location of uNku-lunkulu replicated Xhosa debates of the 1820s between the prophets Nxele and Ntsikana. As an old Xhosa by the name of Ulangeni related those debates to Callaway and Mbande, Ntsikana had located God in the heavens, while Nxele had insisted that the God of the land dwelt underground. Therefore, a similar question about the ultimate location of sacred power was apparently raised around the Springvale mission station.[48]

4. *uNkulunkulu is both Creator and the first parent of humanity:* This position was attributed to two anonymous strangers who happened to overhear Mbande and Callaway discussing uNkulun-kulu. They provided an account of the original bed of reeds, the emergence of uNkulunkulu, and uNkulunkulu's generation of human beings.[49]

5. *uNkulunkulu is the first ancestor of humanity:* In editing *The Religious System*, Callaway gave precedence to this position, placing in the opening pages of the volume Uguaise Mdunga's report that uNkulunkulu was the first man and original parent of human-

ity. Significantly, Callaway identified this particular informant as "an Ilala." By the 1860s European commentators generally assumed that the amaLala were a separate tribal group in Natal. In the 1820s, however, amaLala was a class designation, even a term of derision and abuse, referring to lower-class people who "sleep (*lala*) with their fingers up their anuses." As an informant told James Stuart, conquering Zulu "called us amaLala, just as you Europeans call us *amakafula* ["Kaffirs"], for people that defeat others insult them."[50]

These conquered and dispersed people were Callaway's main informants resident in and around Springvale. In *The Religious System*, the interpretation of uNkulunkulu as the first ancestor of all humanity was expressed by "detribalized" amaLala. Uguaise Mdunga was corroborated on this point by the account provided by Unolala Zondi, who qualified his report, however, by saying that it was based on stories he remembered hearing when he was a child. The only other informant to take this position was an old man by the name of Ubebe, an amaNtanja whose people had been destroyed and scattered by Shaka. When questioned by Callaway and Mbande, Ubebe, who lived near a Roman Catholic mission station fifteen miles from Springvale, held that uNkulunkulu was the ancestor of all humanity. According to Ubebe, uNkulunkulu was nothing more than the first ancestor, but also nothing less, since other political groupings, unlike the shattered and dispersed amaLala and the amaNtanja, were claiming that the term *uNkulunkulu* referred specifically and exclusively to the first ancestor of their particular "tribal" lineage. As a variation on this position, a refugee from Zululand proposed that both the terms *uNkulunkulu* and *umVelinqangi* should be understood as the ancestor of all humanity. From these reports, it might be assumed the interpretation of uNkulunkulu as the ancestor of all human beings depended upon informants who had suffered severe social dislocation. Torn from previous "tribal" allegiances, they identified uNkulunkulu as the original ancestor of all "tribes" in the world.[51]

6. *uNkulunkulu refers to both the first man and to tribal ancestors:* One informant, Ungqeto Wakwatshange, seemed to recognize this tension between the universal and particular in the significance of uNkulunkulu. He distinguished between the uNkulunkulu who emerged from the original bed of reeds and the uNkulunkulu who represented the generation of ancestors preceding his own great-great-grandfather. In these terms, all humanity had an uNkulunkulu; but each family also had its specific, genealogical uNkulunkulu.[52]

7. *uNkulunkulu refers to only a "tribal" ancestor:* In terms of sheer number of informants, this position was most frequently represented in *The Religious System.* Significantly, however, the informants who asserted that uNkulunkulu was only the first ancestor of their particular political grouping came from regions of the country that were furthest from the mission station and from the advance of colonial control. An informant by the name of Ukoto, who was identified as an old Zulu of the Isilangeni, a tribe directly related to Shaka, reported that uNkulunkulu stood at the beginning of the genealogy of his own tribal ancestors. In agreement, a refugee from Zululand held that uNkulunkulu was the ancestor of the Zulu. However, this understanding of the term *uNkulunkulu* as original "tribal" ancestor was also claimed by informants from other political groupings. As Uludonga, identified as an Ngwane, put it, "All nations have their own Unkulunkulu." Ushuguiwane Zimase reported that he knew of only the uNkulunkulu of his own tribe, not of all human beings. Likewise, a group of Bhaca informants held that uNkulunkulu was their first ancestor. Finally, four Dhlamini informants identified uNkulunkulu as only their "tribal" ancestor. When asked about uNkulunkulu, they related specific details of their own ancestral genealogy but claimed to know nothing about an uNkulunkulu of all humanity.[53]

Therefore, if interpretations of uNkulunkulu as creator or ancestor of all humans depended upon reports from socially dislocated informants, this understanding of uNkulunkulu as genealogical ancestor was grounded in more or less intact political groupings on the colonial frontier. When that political independence was broken, it seemed that they had two options: they could turn to an ancestor of all human beings or to the God of the mission.

This range of Zulu interpretations of uNkulunkulu was compressed in *The Religious System of the Amazulu.* However, it can be inflated and correlated with the dynamics of an advancing colonial frontier. While their indigenous political groupings remained intact, Zulu-speaking people could refer to uNkulunkulu as their own "tribal" ancestor. In Callaway's account, the remote Dhlamini maintained precisely such a localized understanding of uNkulunkulu as the progenitor of their own particular polity. Once their political independence was broken, however, Zulu-speaking people had to reinterpret their indigenous religious resources within the new colonial context. One option was to rede-

fine uNkulunkulu as the original ancestor of all people. The ama-
Lala, and other dislocated people, seem to have initiated such a
universal reinterpretation of uNkulunkulu. However, under the
same conditions of colonial disruption, and the rapidly expanding
scope of socioeconomic relations and exchanges, Zulu-speaking
people could reinterpret uNkulunkulu as a Supreme Being that
overarched the entire world.

As anthropologist Robin Horton proposed, the emergence of
African Supreme Beings to prominence in the nineteenth century
should be understood as a response to the conceptual dilemma
posed by the increased scale of intercultural social relations. In
that expanding social context, African spiritual resources could
no longer be only local but had to encompass a broader range
of cross-cultural contacts and conflicts. African "high gods" addressed that new situation. Accordingly, they increased in importance during the nineteenth century. They were reinterpreted to
address a more global situation. Coincidentally, perhaps, Christian and Muslim "high gods" presented a similar solution to this
new social situation by representing Supreme Beings that overarched the entire social world.[54]

On a different frontier among Sotho-Tswana in the northern
Cape, the missionary Robert Moffat reported that an African
sacred specialist proposed a local compromise with the universal demands of the mission. According to Moffat, the *ngaka*
suggested that his God dwelt in the north, while the God of the
mission belonged in the Cape. As Moffat reported, however, the
argument was concluded as the Sotho-Tswana sacred specialist
"looked rather stupid when I informed him that my God ruled
over all the earth."[55] The frontier, therefore, was an arena for such
contests over local and global solutions to the meaning of sacred
power.

As Callaway's collection demonstrates, the conflict between
local and global interpretations of religion was not merely conducted between European missionaries and Africans. Clearly,
Zulu-speaking people were engaged in ongoing internal debates
about the meaning and significance of their indigenous religious
vocabulary. They showed an interest in making subtle distinctions among different aspects of divinity. But they also adopted
different, conflicting positions in a contemporary religious controversy. Instead of a single, coherent religious system, therefore,
Callaway in fact recorded a religious argument among various
Zulu-speaking people who had recently experienced, in different

degrees, the disruptions of colonial conquest. As a Zulu transla-tor, interpreter, and commentator on that argument, Mpengula Mbande assumed a prominent role in shaping the critical perspec-tive on Zulu religion that appeared in *The Religious System of the Amazulu*. As a comparative religionist in his own right, Mbande advanced his own solution to the problem of the Zulu "un-known God."

Mbande's uNkulunkulu

While Callaway relied upon a three-stage theory of degeneration to make sense out of the diversity of Zulu religious beliefs on the frontier, Mpengula Mbande developed his own theological ratio-nale to derive religious significance out of the conflicts of the colonial situation. As a Christian theologian, Mbande held, agree-ing on this point with Colenso, that uNkulunkulu should be identified with umVelinqangi. "For my part," Mbande observed, "I say they speak truly who say that Unkulunkulu is named Umvelinqangi." According to Mbande, both terms referred to the "unknown God" of the Zulu. However, that god was not fully acknowledged before the Christian mission since, "as regards worship," Mbande noted, "they speak truly who say, he was not worshipped." Echoing the biblical formula of Joshua 24, Mbande observed that no one ever said, "For my part I am of the house of uNkulunkulu." Furthermore, Mbande revealed that uNkulun-kulu had previously been understood by the Zulu as the first man, an understanding that bore no relation to the recent "ac-count of uNkulunkulu we now see in books." Nevertheless, he insisted, the Zulu knew about God before Europeans arrived to introduce the Christian mission. They knew about the Lord of Heaven because whenever the sky thundered, they used to say, "The king is playing." As Mbande explained to Callaway, "This is why I say, that the Lord of whom we hear through you, we had already heard of before you came." However, because they did not worship the Lord of Heaven, Mbande had to conclude that the Zulu knew, but did not know, the truth before the Christian mis-sion. Although he affirmed a pre-Christian Zulu apprehension of religious truth, Mbande devoted most of his interpretation to a scathing critique of Zulu religion.

According to Mbande, whatever black men said about religion "has no point; it is altogether blunt. For there is not one among black men, not even the chiefs themselves, who can so interpret such accounts as thus about Unkulunkulu as to bring out the truth." Blacks suffered not only from ignorance but also from wickedness, greed, and drunkenness. Enveloped in this intellectual and moral darkness, they did not know the truth about uNkulunkulu. Nor did they know the truth about their own ancestors. "As regards the *Amadhlozi*," Mbande insisted, "we do not possess the truth. We worship men, who, when they too were departing from the world, did not wish to depart, but were very unwilling to depart, worrying us excessively, telling us to go and seek doctors for them, and that we wished them to die." In Mbande's critique, the Zulu had been mistaken in worshiping their own ancestors. Instead, they should have worshiped the heavenly Lord that Mbande equated with the terms *uNkulunkulu* and *umVelinqangi*, as well as with the source of all life, *Uhlanga*, and even with the collective term for all ancestors, *Itongo*. Since these terms held different significance in the traditional religious vocabulary, Mbande's interpretation suggested that the Christian mission had taught the Zulu the genuine meaning of their own religion.

In one of his most important contributions to *The Religious System of the Amazulu*, Mpengula Mbande related the "account which black men give white men of their origin." According to this creation myth, black men emerged first from the *Uhlanga*, the place of the origin of all nations, coming out, however, with only a few things. They emerged with some cattle, corn, spears, and picks for digging the earth. Arrogantly, with their few possessions, the black men thought that they possessed all things. When the white men emerged, however, they came out with ox-drawn wagons bearing abundant goods and were able to traverse great distances. By displaying this new, unexpected use for cattle, the whites demonstrated a superior wisdom that had been drawn from the *Uhlanga*. In relation to the power and possessions of white men, black men recognized that they were defenseless. As Mbande explained:

> We saw that, in fact, we black men came out without a single thing;
> we came out naked; we left every thing behind, because we came
> out first. But as for the white men, we saw that they scraped out
> the last bit of wisdom; for there is every thing, which is too much
> for us, they know; they know all things which we do not know; we

saw that we came out in a hurry; but they waited for all things, that they might not leave any behind. So in truth they came out with them. Therefore, we honour them, saying, "It is they who came out possessed of all things from the great Spirit [*Itongo*]; it is they who came out possessed of all goodness; we came out possessed with the folly of utter ignorance." Now it is as if they were becoming our fathers, for they come to us possessed of all things. Now they tell us all things, which we too might have known had we waited; it is because we did not wait that we are now children in comparison with them.

Therefore, Mpengula Mbande concluded, Europeans had not achieved victory over Africans by their superior force of arms. Rather, their wisdom and works had conquered. According to Mbande, European colonizers had been "victorious by sitting still." They had not required military force. The knowledge, capabilities, and wealth that whites had drawn from the *Uhlanga* were sufficient to overpower the black people, who reflected among themselves, as Mbande reported, that "these men who can do such things, it is not proper that we should think of contending with them, as if because their works conquer us, they would conquer us by weapons." In this mythic account, therefore, Mbande recorded an indigenous religious rationale for submission to the colonial government and its Christian mission. Obviously, this myth was not some primordial Zulu cosmogony. It was a critical reflection on the contemporary Zulu colonial situation. In Mbande's account, this story was the relevant creation myth in the living religious system of the Zulu. Blacks had emerged too soon from uNkulunkulu with nothing, but "the white men came out from a great Itongo with what is perfect." Another informant, a Zulu by the name of Usithlanu, placed a somewhat different interpretation on the same myth by telling Callaway that "You white men remained behind with *our* great Itongo" (emphasis added). In this subtle retelling of the myth, whites had acquired things that actually belonged to Africans because their wisdom, wealth, and weapons had been derived from the great creative spirit of the Zulu. In either case, however, the Zulu religious system revealed its most dynamic, creative character, not in trying to recover a forgotten past, but in these struggles to make sense out of the violent oppositions of a colonial present.[56]

THE UNKNOWN GOD

In 1873 Henry Callaway left Springvale to assume his new office as Bishop of St. John's, Kaffraria. Advocating strong colonial rule, Callaway called for the deployment of British troops against the Zulu monarchy and for the annexation of the Transkei. Unlike Mbande, Callaway was not convinced that whites would be "victorious by sitting still." Nevertheless, while among the Xhosa of the Transkei, Callaway pursued his research into the question of the "unknown God." Ironically, among Xhosa-speaking people who had been consistently characterized as atheists, Callaway claimed to have found the clearest evidence of an African theology. He discovered that an ancient Xhosa name for God, *Ukqamata*, had been preserved by Africans on the frontier. "It is a name almost totally unknown to white men, and entirely so to white missionaries," Callaway reported. "What the natives said of this Being was more remarkable, more like 'theology', than anything I have met with." His informants insisted that *Qamata* was the original name by which God was known among the Xhosa long before the arrival of the missionaries. As one informant put it, "there is no God who has just come to us. Let no man say the God which is, is the God of the English." Therefore, as in Natal, African theologians in the Transkei were recovering their precolonial unknown God.[57]

Independent African initiatives, inside as well as outside the mission, were also working out an indigenous comparative religion. As we have seen, the archive of conversations conducted by James Stuart provide a valuable record of some of the concerns of a nineteenth-century Zulu comparative religion. By 1900 the comparison between the Zulu and Jews had been thoroughly internalized in Zulu reflections upon their own religious heritage. John Kumalo described how he had gone to Pietermaritzburg in the 1850s because he wanted "to work in order to learn, as well as to find out about Nkulunkulu." A frequent visitor to Colenso's Bishopstowe mission, Kumalo learned to read and write. But he also learned that Bishop Colenso thought that Zulu people were descendants of the Jews. As Kumalo recalled, the bishop pointed to similar religious practices, such as circumcision, the strict proscription of adultery, the sacrificial offering of incense (*impepo*), and even the ritual role of snakes, which echoed the serpent set up by the Israelites in the wilderness, as evidence for a Zulu origin in ancient Israel. Half a century later, Kumalo and his colleagues were able to expand this list of analogous customs. They identified the ritual practices of setting up piles of stones, performing penance and purification rites, and the distinctive methods of killing, dividing, or burning the bones of sacrificial animals as all derived from the ancient Jews. From this evidence, Kumalo concluded, "the Zulu people in effect follow the law of Moses; their laws and customs to a great extent are very similar to those of the Jews." Lazarus Mxaba was even more emphatic that these analogous customs provided proof of Zulu descent from Jews. Five years later in 1905, another of Stuart's conversation partners, Dinya, reinforced this claim on Jewish ancestry. "We are anxious to find out where we came from," Dinya observed. "These Jewish customs of ours are evidence that we came from the north, for this evidence was in existence before we came in contact with the Europeans." For these Zulu comparativists, therefore, establishing the relation between the Zulu and Jews was important because it provided validation—not only with reference to a recognized, biblical religion but also through the imaginative construction of a precolonial ancient history.[58]

Like Zulu comparativists in Africa, British comparativists in Europe were also interested in the relationship between Judaism and indigenous religions. During the sixteenth and seventeenth centuries, comparisons between Africans and Jews were common in European anthropological thought. As historian Frank Manuel has shown, the "long history of Christianity's wrangling with Judaism has been marked by sharp and momentous discontinuities." One discontinuity in that long history, the eighteenth-century reevaluation of ancient Judaism, played a significant role in the emergence of European comparative religion. In the eighteenth century, English deists, following Herbert of Cherbury, justified their interest in the doctrines of other religions by arguing that monotheism had not been unique to ancient Judaism. Instead of depending upon a special revelation to the Jews, theism appeared as a universal religious sentiment. It could be found anywhere. It was an ingredient in natural religion. Conversely, by no longer privileging ancient Israel as the unique recipient of divine revelation, eighteenth-century theorists could argue that the original religion of the Jews was based on the worship of a national or tribal god. Like any tribal religion, they imagined, the religion of ancient Israel could be barbaric. As David Hume found, the religion of the ancient Israelites, as it was described in the Bible, was just as barbarous as the pagan religions of savages recounted in the reports of missionaries and travelers from all over the world. Therefore, in this eighteenth-century Christian reassessment of ancient Judaism, savages could be recognized as religious because the religion of ancient Israel appeared savage.[59]

On the Natal frontier, the religion of the "savages" was denied until, by the 1850s, the Zulu were recognized as living fossils of ancient Judaism. Certainly, other comparisons were drawn. Striking resemblances were noted between the Zulu and "the ancient Irish living under Behan Law and the Patriarchal System"; similarities were observed between their religion and modern European spiritualism.[60] But the most frequent and pervasive analogy was established between the Zulu and Jews. Although he did not originate this observation, since it had already become commonplace in the discourse of the frontier colonial administration by the time he arrived, Bishop Colenso was instrumental in working out the logical consequences of a comparison between the Zulu and Jews. The religion of the Zulu could be understood by reading the Bible. Accordingly, the Zulu had a God that was just like the God of the ancient Jews. uNkulunkulu was Jehovah; umVelinqangi was Elohim. Conversely, however, the character of the religion of ancient Israel, as reflected in the Bible, was revealed by comparison with living Zulu religion. With this comparative strategy, Colenso reinforced a certain kind of "universalism" with respect to the religions of the world. Following F. D. Maurice, Colenso was prepared to find "a light among the heathen." Significantly, John Kumalo remembered Bishopstowe as the "place of light," a place where the Zulu received enlightenment not only by learning reading, writing, and Christianity but also by recovering their forgotten history in the religious heritage of ancient Judaism.

While Maurice had promised the discovery of light among the heathens, he had also proposed that Europeans would find "the materials out of which the divine universe has been created." This primary religious material was precisely what W. H. I. Bleek thought he had discovered in southern Africa. Replacing ancient Jews with the Zulu in the reconstruction of human prehistory, Bleek interpreted Zulu ancestor worship as the primary matter out of which religion had evolved. In the 1850s Bleek developed a sophisticated philology of religion that located the origin of religion on the southern African frontier. In the beginning, Bleek suggested, all humanity had divided into Khoikhoi and Zulu, and their different grammatical structures had impelled human be-

ings to evolve religions based either on sidereal or ancestor worship. As the most primitive form of religion, which existed before
the sex-denoting languages, such as the Khoikhoi language, had
"filled the sky with gods," the Zulu stood at the origin of the
evolution of religion.

Henry Callaway resisted the strategies of comparative religion
advanced by both Colenso and Bleek. He refused to equate the
Zulu with Jews; he denied that the Zulu were an evolutionary
point of origin. Preferring the conventional frontier explanation,
Callaway argued that contemporary Zulu religion represented,
not the beginning of a process of human evolution, but the end
of a long history of degeneration. Nevertheless, especially after
his consecration as bishop of St. John's, Henry Callaway reflected
on the broader significance of comparative religion within the
colonial context. In a series of publications, he argued for the
universality of "religious sentiment" among all the people of
the world. Comparative religion, Callaway proposed, would enable Europeans to recognize the light of religious truth even in
the most remote and savage forms of religious life. In this context, Callaway did indulge in a pointed comparison with Judaism.
Rather than equating the Zulu with Jews, however, he recommended a broader, more inclusive approach to the study of religion because, he observed, the Jews were "wrong in being exclusive." By contrast, Callaway advocated a comparative religion
attuned to recognizing traces of divine truth that were already
present in "heathen" religions. "When we go among the heathen," Callaway entreated, "let us believe that God has gone before us. . . . Let us not for a moment adopt as a principle of action
the notion that . . . we are the first messengers of love and light,
and that all before was darkness and death." Even among "savages" such as the Zulu, Callaway concluded, comparative religion
should be able to discern fragments of universal religious truth.[61]

On New Year's Day 1901, conversing with James Stuart in room
12 of the Royal Hotel in Ladysmith, Lazarus Mxaba, John Kumalo, and Mabaso would have agreed with Henry Callaway
on that point. As they discussed Zulu history, Mabaso asked,
"Which of all the world's creeds, excepting those which have belief in God for their main doctrine, makes the nearest approach
to belief in God?" Elaborating his question, Mabaso observed that
while the Zulu believed in snakes, other people worshiped trees,
or stones, or the sun, or other things. Trying to be helpful, James
Stuart added that ancient Romans worshiped Jupiter, ancient

Egyptians worshiped cattle, and Buddhists believed in annihilation, while Socrates, Plato, and Muhammad came closest to the Christian belief in God.[62] However, Stuart admitted, "I found the question too difficult to reply to, simply because I did not know the various beliefs of the nations on earth." At this point, however, John Kumalo interrupted Stuart's inventory of religions to clarify the thrust of the question. What Mabaso meant, he explained, was, "Is there any nation that rises nearer to the idea of God than the Zulus?" To Stuart's surprise, Mabaso, Kumalo, and Mxaba all agreed that traditional Zulu religion, with its creator God, its national ancestors, its familial ancestors, and its snakes, came closest of all the religions of the world to a Christian belief in God. Even the ancestral snakes, as Mxaba explained, echoed the ancient Israelite serpent in the wilderness, which, analogically, prefigured the suffering of Jesus Christ on the cross. According to these comparative religionists, therefore, Zulu religion came closest of all the religions of the world to capturing the unknown God of Christianity. In this indigenous comparative religion on the frontier, the unknown God was relocated as central to Zulu history. Reclaimed by Zulu comparativists, the unknown God was not the sole property of the Christian mission and colonial administration. God also belonged to Africa.

5

SACRED ANIMALS

DURING 1894 the Boer forces of the South African Republic waged a military campaign against the Bagananoa people of Chief Malaboch, who had retreated into their mountain stronghold in the northern Transvaal. As only one of a series of military confrontations against African polities on the borders, this campaign against Malaboch reflected a concerted "native policy."[1] The two independent Boer republics, the Orange Free State, which was established in 1854, and the South African Republic in the Transvaal, established in 1868, conducted recurring and ongoing wars against neighboring Africans groups over land, cattle, and labor. During these struggles, most British commentators condemned the aggression of the Boer republics. They raised humanitarian, historical, and political arguments against Boer domination of the region. However, British reports also consistently mounted a particular kind of comparative religion against the Boers in which the British indicated that the Boers had walked straight out of the Old Testament. The Boers imagined that they were the "chosen people" of God. Not Africans, therefore, but these Boer ancestors of white Afrikaners were the ancient Jews on the northern frontier of southern Africa.

As previously indicated, earlier travel accounts had often depicted the religion of the Boers on the Cape frontier as "superstition." These frontier descendants of Dutch, French, and German immigrants might have been Christians, but they were nevertheless characterized as being as "superstitious" as Africans. One reason for leaving the Cape, according to Voortrekker leader Piet Retief, was "the unjustifiable odium which has been cast upon us by interested and dishonest persons, under the name of Religion." Following the Boer migrations into the interior of southern Africa of the 1830s and the formation of independent white states, British reports specified Boer religion as a kind of frontier Judaism. The missionary David Livingstone argued in 1857 that the Boers were like ancient Jews because they had assumed the mantle of divine election. "They, being the chosen people of God," as Livingstone represented their religion, thought that "the heathen are given to them for an inheritance, and that they are the rod of divine vengeance on the heathen, as were the Jews of old." Livingstone's negative depiction of the Boers influenced missionary opinion, and British attitudes generally, during the years leading up to the South African War. As British interests increasingly came into conflict with the Boer republics, this polemical construction of Boer religion was amplified in nearly all British reports about the northern frontier. Calling themselves Christians, Boers nevertheless preferred the Old to the New Testament, where they found that they were the "chosen people" of God called to exercise divine vengeance by destroying the African "Canaanites" of southern Africa.[2]

Sometimes this identification of Boers as Jews seemed as though it were intended to produce a comic effect. "It is a very curious thing," Thomas Baines observed in 1877, "what a Judaical or Old Testament tint all the ideas of these people have taken since their migration from the Colony, or, as they prefer to call it, their 'sojourn in the wilderness.'" For example, Baines reported, Transvaal Boers thought that the biblical land of Palestine was just beyond their northern border. Accordingly, when they found a tributary of the Limpopo, the Maghaliquain (Fierce Crocodile) River, that flowed north, they named it Nylstroom, mistaking it for the Nile River and thinking they could follow it up through Egypt to the ancient Promised Land. One group of Boers on the northern frontier in the 1860s were known as "Jerusalemgangers" because they thought they were approaching the sacred city.

When not designed to make them look ridiculous, however, the comparisons between Boers and Jews most often represented the Boer republics as extremely dangerous. Motivated by an archaic, irrational religious faith, the Boer republics were a threat to the modern political and economic order that was emerging under British control in southern Africa. In the decade before the South African War, British comparisons between Boers and Jews became increasingly strident. As H. Lincoln Tangye declared in 1896, their identification with ancient Jews was the key to understanding the Boers.

A strange faith is the keynote of their character, and one which has dominated their every act. Believing themselves to be a second edition of the Israelites, and drawing a parallel between their own circumstances and those of the chosen people, they take the Old Testament as their only guide, and openly assert that they are God's elect, and that the Hottentots, Bushmen, and Kaffirs are so many Canaanites, Amalekites, or Amorites, whom it is their right and duty to dispossess and subjugate or destroy; every bloody act committed and every tract of land wrested from the natives, has been said in devout language to be a duty directly imposed upon them and sanctioned by the Divine Being, and for every such deed and incident they will quote a dozen of the more sanguinary passages in the Old Testament.

Boers were not only ancient Jews, however. They were also savages. As white savages, Boers had reportedly embraced the African system of superstition and magic. They consulted African diviners for luck in hunting, to find lost cattle, or to counter the effects of witchcraft. Believing in the supernatural, they were enveloped in a world of dreams and delusions. As Tangye argued, the "Boers are the only example of a white race which has retrograded in the face of the savage." Echoing this assertion in London, H. H. Johnston reported in the *Fortnightly Review* that the Boers had relapsed into the condition of being "white savages." Isolated for so long from the improving effects of civilization, the Transvaal Boers in particular displayed a hatred of government, a harsh treatment of natives, and a lack of ambition for self-improvement that made them, in Tangye's terms, "almost purely animal."[3]

Boers had their defenders. The Portuguese hunter Major Serpa Pinto agreed that the Boers regulated their lives by the principles of the biblical patriarchs. However, he argued, their bad reputation had resulted from the polemic of British missionaries who had entered the Transvaal after the Boers had "succeeded in pacificating by force the warlike tribes which disputed their possession."[4] As an eyewitness to the Boer military campaign against the Bagananoa of Chief Malaboch, the Reverend Colin Rae argued that the militant native policy of the Transvaal Boers, in driving Africans from their strongholds and breaking the power of their chiefs, accomplished more for the cause of civilization than anything done by Christian missionaries. When they finally achieved victory over the Bagananoa in 1894, the Transvaal Boers imprisoned Chief Malaboch and apportioned the surviving women and children among the various districts of the Transvaal Republic to serve as forced labor for a period of five years. In that Boer victory, therefore, the independent polity of Malaboch, like so many other African chiefdoms, was finally broken.

By capturing the chief, however, the Boers also succeeded in capturing the most sacred symbol of his community. According to Rae, "A Kafir god, in the shape of a huge carved crocodile, was brought into camp to-day, amid much beating of drums and blowing of horns." Therefore, the Boers had defeated not only a chief but also a god, the sacred crocodile of the Bagananoa people of Chief Malaboch. Fashioned out of wood, this enormous crocodile, over six feet long, was a ritual object that had featured prominently in the rite of initiation marking a boy's passage into the status of a man and a warrior. Accordingly, its image also appeared on the captured weapons and war drums that the Boers paraded through the camp in celebration of their victory. Among the spoils of war, the sacred crocodile was eventually brought to Pretoria to be housed in the Transvaal museum. While Chief Malaboch was a political prisoner, the sacred crocodile was a religious prisoner in the confines of the public museum in Pretoria. Unable to recover from their political defeat, the Bagananoa nevertheless found a creative response to the desecration, confiscation, and capture of their sacred object. They carved another crocodile.[5]

In the earliest reports of Sotho-Tswana religion, sacred animals went unnoticed. From the 1840s, however, they formed a recurring feature in European accounts of the religious beliefs and practices of African people living on the northern frontier of the Cape Colony and along the new frontiers created by the migration of Dutch Boers into the interior of southern Africa. Apparently, sacred animals defined a system of allegiances, cutting across chiefdoms, that bound people together under the sign of a common object of communal reverence, honor, and praise. The term for praise, *seboko* (pl. *liboko*), was often used for the sacred animal. Or the animal was called *seano* (pl. *diano*) to indicate a sacred object of reverence. To have a sacred animal was to dance (*go bina*) that animal. At the same time, the object of reverence was also guarded by avoidances, particularly by the prohibitions of people under a particular *seboko* from killing or eating their sacred animal. European observers tried to document this system

Chief Malaboch imprisoned. (From Roberts, "The Bagananoa or Ma-Laboch")

The sacred crocodile "worshiped" by the Bagananoa of Chief Malaboch. (From Roberts, "The Bagananoa or Ma-Laboch")

of animal praise and avoidance. According to one account, the Bakuena had the crocodile (*kuena*); the Bataung, the lion (*taung*); the Batloung, the elephant (*tlou*); the Batsueneng, the baboon (*tsuene*); the Batlokoa, the wild cat (*quabi*); the Bapedi, the porcupine (*noka*); the Baphuti, the duiker, a small gazelle (*phuti*); and so on.[6] Comparative religionists tried to make sense out of this system of sacred animals as evidence of an African religion. Eventually, European theorists defined the nature of traditional Sotho-Tswana religious life on the basis of their regard for these animal emblems. By the beginning of the twentieth century, most accounts of Sotho-Tswana people found that they displayed a classic form of "savage" or "primitive" religion. They were totemists.

FURTHER DENIALS

As was the case on other frontiers, the earliest reports that emanated from the northern border of the Cape Colony denied the existence of any indigenous religion among the Sotho-Tswana people. During 1801 and 1802, the British traveler John Barrow entered the interior of southern Africa, further, he claimed, than any European had previously penetrated. There he discovered that the "Booshuana nation" did not appear to have any form of religious worship. Lacking any notion of a good Supreme Being, they could not have religion "in the strict sense of the term as applied by Europeans." Barrow noticed, however, that the "Booshuanas" observed certain customs, such as male circumcision and all-night dancing under the moon, which suggested that if they did not have religion, they did have superstition. Central to their superstition was the belief in the existence of an evil god. This discovery inspired Barrow to reflect upon the origin of religion. Most nations, he remarked, ascribed the powers of nature to good and evil spirits. The good spirit tended to be identified with the sun, moon, and fertilizing rain; the evil spirit with the frightening and destructive effects of thunder, lightning, and torrential storms. Barrow concluded by applying this natural dichotomy of good and evil spirits to the superstition of the "Booshuanas": "As fear is the parent of superstition, the evil spirit is usually found to be venerated in preference to the good one. This appears to be the case with the Booshuanas, and was in all probability the same in the early stage of all nations. The vices of Jupiter and his evil actions were most likely recorded before his virtues; just as his thunder terrified before his paternal protection inspired confidence."[7]

In this formulation, Barrow proposed a general theory of religion that was based on three propositions. First, he identified fear as the origin of superstition. Drawing upon an ancient theory of religion that can be traced back to Democritus, Barrow suggested that fear was the original motivation behind all the superstitious beliefs and practices of the world's religions. In this diagnosis, Barrow also followed David Hume, who had argued in 1755 in his *Natural History of Religion* that "the primary religion of mankind arises chiefly from an anxious fear of future events."[8] Second, Barrow suggested that superstitious hopes and fears were projected through the personification of natural forces. In all the superstitions of the world, good and evil spirits personified the beneficial and destructive forces of nature. Finally, since fear was primary, the veneration of evil spirits preceded any worship of a good God in the history of superstition. Fearing the destructive forces of nature, all nations had developed superstitious practices to appease the evil spirits that personified those forces. In Barrow's terms, these three principles outlined a theory of superstition. But they could just as easily provide the basis for a theory of the origin and development of religion. Finding these principles operating among the "Booshuanas," Barrow indicated that he was interested in more than merely denying, once again, that Africans had a religion. Like subsequent European observers on the northern frontier, Barrow used Sotho-Tswana beliefs and practices to illustrate or substantiate some more general theory of religion.

Travelers

As we recall, the traveler Henry Lichtenstein had found no religion among the Xhosa on the eastern Cape frontier. Instead, he found only a superstitious interest in a shipwrecked anchor. In 1807 Lichtenstein reported that the "Beetjuana" people of the north also lived in a world of magic and superstition. He observed the "superstitious faith which they have in the sacredly kept magic of their priests." Although uncertain whether they believed in a Supreme Being or in a life after death, Lichtenstein considered the possibility that they might have "a kind of religious conviction" that was evident in their ceremonies of initiation and cattle blessing. In particular, Lichtenstein was impressed by their practice of divination. This "sacred magic" of their priests was performed by casting and interpreting a set of bones. Their "divining dice" were probably sacred, Lichtenstein concluded, because the priests refused to sell them, but then he noted that the "Beetjuana" had absolutely no idea of how to conduct trade. If the set of divining dice was not sacred, therefore, it was only symptomatic of an ignorance of the value of trade goods in economic exchange. In either case, Lichtenstein cited the divining dice as another illustration, like the Xhosa anchor, of an African inability to value objects.[9]

During his travels into the interior of southern Africa, the naturalist William Burchell also found "no religion" among Sotho-Tswana people. Although his primary interests were zoology and botany, Burchell nevertheless made observations about African religion. Employing the distinction between religion and superstition, he discounted any genuine religious beliefs and practices among the "Bachapin" people on the northern frontier. In Burchell's terms: "The *superstition* of the Bachapins, for it cannot be called religion, is of the weakest and most absurd kind; and, as before remarked, betrays the low state of their intellect. These people have no outward worship, nor, if one may judge from their never alluding to them, any private devotions; neither could it be discovered that they possessed any very defined or exalted notion of a supreme and beneficent Deity, or of a great and first Creator (emphasis in original)." According to Burchell, this lack of religion resulted not merely from ignorance of revealed truth but from a basic mental incapacity in which they could exercise only the "weakest mind." The superstitious concepts and customs of the "Bachapins" revealed precisely "how low is the state of intellect and reason among these people." Out of that degraded mental condition, the "Bachapins" had produced the most absurd superstitions, especially the principal article of their "creed," witchcraft or sorcery. They did practice ritual circumcision, Burchell noted, but he insisted that the custom had no religious significance whatsoever because it was motivated by some "traditionary superstition" and therefore was performed for absolutely no reason. Since the "Bachapins" lacked religion, as well as reason, Burchell saw in their superstitious practice of circumcision no evidence of descent from "some more civilized Mahometan nation." Their beliefs and practices had not degenerated from previous contact with Islam. In any case, their close, woolly hair, the naturalist argued, provided stronger proof that the "Bachapins" were, and always had been, a "genuine African race." Therefore, William Burchell concluded, their superstitions could not be corruptions of some earlier or higher religion; they represented a genuine African absence of religion.[10]

However, Burchell observed that the "Bachapins" did seem to have some confused idea of a Supreme Power, which, although it had nothing to do with religion, nevertheless suggested some notion of a spiritual reality. He recorded the name of this being as "*Mulíimo (Mooleemo)*." This was not a good deity, Burchell advised, but an evil spirit that pervaded all their superstitions. In translating the "Bachapin" term for this spirit, Burchell's Khoikhoi interpreter used the Dutch word for "Devil." Accordingly, Burchell concluded that the "Bachapins" had no God, but they did hold a superstitious belief in the existence of a powerful demon, *Mulíimo*. Like Burchell, Protestant missionaries also discovered this term, appearing in various dialects also as *Morimo* or *Modimo*, among Sotho-Tswana people on the northern frontier. Certainly, they encountered considerable confusion when they tried to pinpoint its meaning. In the 1830s when Andrew Smith asked three "Baquana" men who attended his sermon, "they said they did not know the meaning of the word *moremo*." In Sotho-Tswana discourse, a rainmaker might be referred to as *morimo*. But even a European hunter, like Andrew Geddes Bain, could be hailed by that designation for his artistic ability. "The natives were always surprised at seeing me represent the different animals we shot, on paper," Bain recalled, "but with this they seemed particularly pleased and called me by no other name but *Moorimo* (god), for they said no mortal could make things live as I did on paper." When the word was used, therefore, it seemed to indicate some extraordinary power or effectiveness. Although Burchell's Khoikhoi interpreter translated *Mulíimo* as "Devil," the missionaries on the northern frontier, through a different act of translation and appropriation, consistently rendered the same term as "God."[11]

For the Supreme Being of the Christian mission, Protestant missionaries among Sotho-Tswana people consistently used variations of the same term, *Mulíimo*, that Burchell's interpreter had translated as "Devil." In reconstructing the history of these translations, the intervention of Khoikhoi and Sotho-Tswana interpreters is significant. Serving as multilingual mediators conversant both in Dutch and in Sotho-Tswana dialects, interpreters were obviously agents of cross-cultural translation. However, they were also used, in retrospect, to certify the authenticity of the missionary appropriation of an African term for God. As the missionary John Mackenzie explained fifty years later, the "invariable equivalent for *God* in Dutch, given by all interpreters, was *Morimo*. It was no suggestion of the missionaries: the Bechuana interpreters, after hearing concerning God in the Dutch language, said that their name for Him was Morimo." In this standard missionary account, *Morimo* was recognized, in the act of translation, as God. Although the interpreters, according to Mackenzie, knew nothing about *Morimo*, and Sotho-Tswana people, in general, had forgotten everything they might have once known about *Morimo*, the Christian mission could appropriate this name for their God because it "was found by the missionaries still floating in their language."[12] As a floating signifier in a frontier comparative religion, *Molimo*, *Morimo*, or *Modimo* eventually became the God of both the Christian mission and an African traditional religion.

Missionaries

In the 1820s, when the Wesleyan Methodist Missionary Society and the London Missionary Society sent their agents to the Orange River region, the missionaries also discovered an absence of religion. Arriving in 1821 to establish a mission among one Tswana polity, the Barolong, the Methodist missionaries Thomas Hodgson and Samuel Broadbent were convinced that they had entered a religious vacuum. According to Hodgson, the Barolong "appear to have no religious worship." Prior to the advent of the mission, Broadbent emphatically declared, the Barolong "*had no religion.*" In this respect, the Barolong were unlike most other "heathen" people. Having worked in Ceylon and Madagascar before coming to southern Africa, Broadbent was in a position to make this comparative observation on firsthand authority. Among the Barolong, Broadbent observed sorcerers and witchcraft, but he found no belief in God, no concept of immortality, no temples, and no outward forms of religious worship. Significantly, Broadbent reported that he had discovered another absence among the Barolong. In addition to lacking religion, "*they had no marriage,* nor any proper domestic order, nor acknowledged any moral obligation to the duties arising out of that relation." With-

out marriage and religion, the Barolong lacked the basic institutions that regulated human relations, as well as relations between
human beings and God, upon which the order of any society depended. As a result, Broadbent reported, the missionaries originally found the Barolong in a state of disorganization, anarchy,
and misery. His mission's response to this chaotic situation,
as Broadbent recalled, was to appropriate a local term, *Madeemo*,
which had come up in conversation when he asked, "Who was
the first?" Although he maintained that the Barolong had no
concept of a spiritual, invisible, or infinite Being, Broadbent determined, by a process of local comparison, that this term would
serve to represent the mission's "heavenly Father." Furthermore,
Broadbent, like other missionaries, took that term and put it in a
book, the Bible, which he declared was the "word of Modeemo."
Through such acts of comparison, translation, and symbolic
appropriation, therefore, Protestant missionaries on the northern
frontier created the lineaments of a religious system for people
who had previously had no religion, no marriage, and, as Broadbent emphasized, *"no book, no writing, nor any knowledge of
letters* (emphasis in original)."[13]

Like the Wesleyans, representatives of the London Missionary
Society also entered the region denying the existence of any indigenous religion among the Sotho-Tswana. Most prominent among
those early missionaries on the northern frontier, the LMS agent
Robert Moffat worked out the most detailed, elaborate, and
highly publicized missionary theory of comparative religion in
southern Africa. Son of a Scottish ploughman, Moffat was an apprentice hot-house gardener when he decided on a career as a missionary. After several years based in Cape Town, Moffat arrived
on the northern border in 1820, eventually establishing the LMS
mission to the Griqua and Sotho-Tswana based in Kuruman. In
Britain, Moffat was widely perceived as the archetypal missionary
hero, fighting back Satan's weeds to plant the seeds of the gospel in Africa. Moffat's dramatic account of his work, *Missionary Labours and Scenes in Southern Africa*, published in 1842,
greatly influenced British perceptions of the rationale and accomplishments of the Christian mission. At the same time, however,
Moffat articulated a theory of comparative religion. Not merely
denying the existence or validity of other religions, Moffat consistently argued that Satan had authored the world of religions.
Seeing himself on the front lines of the battle against Satan on
the southern African frontier, Moffat developed a theory that ac

counted for the origin, history, and structural relations of religions within a general, Satanic theory of comparative religion.[14]

SATANIC COMPARATIVE RELIGION

Like other missionaries on contested frontiers, Robert Moffat began with denial. Moffat's denial of any indigenous religion in southern Africa, however, was particularly thorough since he insisted in specific detail that no people, whether "Bushmen," "Hottentots," "Kafirs," "Zoolahs," or "Bechuanas," had any trace of religion. Based on his personal contacts with Bushmen on the Orange River and in Tswana territory, Moffat declared that they had no religion. As the lowest beings on the scale of humanity, they had no God, no shrines, and no hope of eternity. The Bushmen, according to Moffat, represented the image of an alternative world, a world that could only have been realized by people who had lived for the four thousand years since creation without the benefit of divine revelation. Concerning the Hottentots, Moffat repeated the denials that had been formulated in the 1780s by the Swedish naturalist Anders Sparrman. Although they might have come from China by way of Egypt, the Hottentots maintained no trace of religion. As for the Xhosa on the eastern Cape frontier, Moffat echoed the categorical denial that had been issued by his fellow LMS missionary, J. T. van der Kemp. Like the "Kafirs" on the eastern Cape frontier, the "Zoolahs" had no religion. Moffat regarded the "Zoolahs" as more savage than all the rest. They even competed "in fiercest barbarity," he asserted, with the barbarous inhabitants of the Pacific Islands. In their savagery, Zulus did perform ritual sacrifices that seemed similar to religion. However, Moffat insisted, those sacrifices, which honored the spirits or "manes of the dead," were nothing more than the glorification of ancient heroes.[15]

In his reconaissance of all the indigeneous people of southern Africa, Moffat found absolutely no religion. By explaining "Zoolah" sacrifies as celebrations of ancient heroes, however, Moffat did propose a theory of religion, the ancient theory of Euhemerus, which accounted for the origin of religion in the elevation of cultural heroes to divine status. According to Moffat, Euhemerism could explain any hint of worship that might be found among the indigeneous people of southern Africa. He held that the alleged

Robert Moffat. (Courtesy South African Library, Cape Town)

god of the Hottentots—*Tsui'kuap, Uti'kuap,* or *Uti'ko*—was only an "ancient hero." Among the frontier Xhosa, Moffat conjectured, the term *Uhlanga* referred either to the oldest of their kings or to "a deified chief or hero, like the Thor and Woden of our Teutonic ancestors."[16] In these terms, Robert Moffat advanced the strongest, most sustained explanation of African beliefs and practices as the result of the euhemeristic deification of ancient cultural heroes.

Against Natural Religion

Although this glorification of ancient heroes might sometimes look like religion, Moffat insisted that it was not in fact religion. Furthermore, even this semblance of religion, he argued, was absent from the Sotho-Tswana people among whom he worked on the northern frontier. The Bechuanas presented a unique and complete absence of religion. In this respect, Moffat held, they were "peculiar, differing, with slight exception, from any other among any nation on the face of the earth." While others had tried to deify their ancient heroes, the Bechuanas had done nothing that even slightly resembled religion. They were a religious wasteland. "Their religious system," Moffat observed, "like the streams in the wilderness which lose themselves in the sand, had entirely disappeared." They lacked any of the familiar, expected features of "pagan" or "heathen" religion. In dramatic, highly charged images, Moffat tried to evoke for his readers the unique situation of a Christian missionary who was faced with such a remarkable religious vacuum.

> [The missionary] has no idolatry to arrest his progress, and his mind is not overwhelmed with the horrors which are to be found in countries where idols and idol temples are resorted to by millions of devotees; his ears are never stunned by their orgies; his eyes are not offended by human and other sacrifices, nor is he the spectator of the unhappy widow on the funeral pile of her husband; the infant screams of Moloch's victims never reach his heart. He meets with no sacred streams, nor hears of voluntary victims to propitiate the anger of imaginary deities. He seeks in vain to find a temple, an altar, or a single emblem of heathen worship. No fragment remains of former days, as mementos to the present generation, that their ancestors ever loved, served, or reverenced a being greater than man. A profound silence reigns on this awful subject.

According to Moffat, therefore, the Bechuanas displayed not the slightest trace of religion. He envied missionaries in India, who could use local Hindu idols, altars, temples, or recollections of an "unknown God" as reference points in their work of Christian conversion. Among the Bechuanas, Moffat found none of these recognizable elements of religion. Even their few customs that might, at first glance, have seemed to be of "Mosaic or patriarchal origin," he explained, were only empty shells, containing no religious content. Therefore, Moffat concluded, while missionaries elsewhere might find traces of religion among "heathen" people, he had discovered among the Bechuanas that "nothing of this kind ever floated in their minds."[17]

Displaying broader theoretical concerns, however, Robert Moffat was interested in more than merely denying the religious character of Africans who were resisting colonial incursions on a contested frontier. Based on his southern African evidence, Moffat argued strenuously against any theory of natural religion. Reports from southern Africa, he argued, refuted any philosophical presumption about innate, intuitive, or natural religious ideas. From seventeenth-century Deists, many European theorists had absorbed the assumption that certain basic religious concepts and sentiments were inherent in human life around the world. Moffat was determined to lay that notion of natural religion to rest. Lending weight to his argument, Moffat revealed that he had embarked upon his mission firmly convinced of the existence of natural religious ideas among all people of the world. "Such were my own views when I left my native land," he claimed, "and entertaining such views, I persuaded myself, or rather tried to persuade myself, that I could discover rays of natural light, innate ideas of a Divine Being in the most untutored savage." However, his African experience dramatically altered his theoretical position on the universality of natural religion. In fact, in southern Africa Moffat was able to assemble the empirical proof that was necessary to refute it. The complete ignorance of religion among the Bushmen, for example, disproved any philosophical theory of "innate and intuitive ideas, and what some term natural light." If the Bushmen lacked religion, Moffat suggested, then any notion of universal natural religion or innate religious ideas was therefore invalidated.[18]

As if one instance could not disprove the rule, however, Moffat aggressively pursued his argument against natural religion by invoking the evidence that he had gathered from the Bechuanas. He had looked there, he confessed to fellow Christians, for "something analogous to our own faith." At first, Moffat recalled, he had thought that his failure to find any glimmer of religious concepts and practices among the Bechuanas was due to his unfamiliarity with their language or to the incompetence of his interpreters. However, after years of patient inquiry, he had been forced to conclude that the Bechuanas simply lacked any trace of religion. Therefore, like the Bushmen, the Bechuanas stood in evidence as a refutation of any claim to the universality of religious ideas or feelings in the world. Calling upon the evidence of the Bechuanas, in particular, Moffat dismissed the arguments of Samuel Clarke and his allies for the existence of innate religious ideas. Although Moffat claimed to have entertained such notions before arriving in southern Africa, he appears to have been more influenced by missionary theorists, such as William Roby, John Ellis, and Edward Edwards, who had argued that only revealed religion could count as religion. In his *Miscellaneous Observations,* for example, Edwards had used evidence from the reports of people all over the world to confute the philosophical assumptions of proponents of natural religion. By reason alone, Edwards had insisted, human beings could not naturally arrive at the truths of religion.

> What instance can be mentioned, from any history, of any one nation under the sun, that emerged from atheism or idolatry into the knowledge or adoration of the one true God, without the assistance of revelation? The Americans, the Africans, the Tartars, and the ingenious Chinese, have had time enough, one would think, to find out the right and true idea of God. . . . [but they persist in] the worship of stocks and stones and devils. How many thousand years must be allowed to these nations to reason themselves into the true religion?

Moffat thought that he had gathered evidence on the frontier that could be deployed against any theory of natural religion. Certainly, his argument was circular. If, by definition, the only genuine religion was revealed, then people who had never received that revelation could not possibly have religion. The circularity of Moffat's argument did not go unnoticed. The LMS administrator John Philip, for example, felt that Moffat had been prejudiced by the influence of the missionary theorist William Roby. In 1851 Philip noted that "Mr. Moffat honestly believed that he found them destitute of the idea of a God, of a future state, and the proper conception of sin; and he placed a veto on all future attempts at a reversal of his judgment." Without doubting Moffat's honesty, Philip nevertheless questioned the impartiality of his investigation. "*A priori* reasoning was exploded by Bacon," Philip remarked, but apparently, in Moffat's case, "not *a priori* observation." For his part, however, Moffat insisted that he was collecting data that disconfirmed the existence of natural religion. The only genuine religion was revealed religion, he argued, not merely by definition, but because the "multitude of ignorant savages to be found in the world corroborates this statement." Therefore, in Moffat's terms, the Bechuanas lacked religion not only because they lived without revelation but also because their "savage" ignorance disproved the existence of any natural religion.[19]

Satanic History, Satanic Structures

This denial of natural religion, however, did not necessarily entail a dismissal of all other religions. In his analysis, Robert Moffat was prepared to acknowledge the altars, temples, and "unknown God" of the Hindus as elements that constituted a religion. However, Moffat worked out an explicit theoretical account of the origin of religions that traced all religious diversity to the work of Satan. In effect, Satan was the author of other religions. Satan had proliferated deities all over the world. "Satan has been too successful," Moffat observed, "in leading captive to his will a majority of the human race, by an almost endless variety of deities." All these deities, the "horrid, the ludicrous, and the obscene," had been generated by Satan. At the same time, however, while Satan was authoring this multiplication of gods and goddesses, he was erasing any notion of a deity in the minds of the people of southern Africa. "While Satan is obviously the author of the polytheism of other nations," Moffat declared, "he has employed his agency, with fatal success, in erasing every vestige of religious impressions from the minds of the Bechuanas, Hottentots, and Bushmen." If Satan could be author, he could also be the eraser of religious ideas among the various people in the world. In fact, since Satan, according to Moffat, was the "god of this world," he could determine the entire course of the world's history of religions.[20]

Due to the influence of Satan, Robert Moffat held, a Christian missionary in southern Africa could make no appeal to local legends, or altars, or "an unknown God" that would establish any analogy between Sotho-Tswana religious concepts and Christian religious truth. However, a Christian missionary on the northern frontier of the Cape Colony could advance a general theory of the history of religions that was based upon an experience of the alleged absence of religion among the indigenous people in southern Africa. In formulating such a general theory of religion, Moffat proposed both a historical and a structural analysis of the diversity of religions in the world. In historical terms, Moffat outlined a scale of religious degradation from an original divine revelation. Instead of tracing the many religions of the world back to innate, intuitive, or natural religious ideas, Moffat derived religion from a primordial revelation. In the beginning, the revealed truth of religion was transmitted both in oral tradition and in writing. However, Satan intervened to distort revelation. As a result of Satanic influence, the original revealed religion degenerated by stages, on a continuum from the refined Greek paganism, through the proliferation of polytheisms and idol worship in India and China, to the barbaric religions of the most savage people around the world, the people of the Eastern Archipelago, the South Sea Islands, or the Americas who worshiped, not God, but "fetiches and charms." According to Moffat, therefore, "all knowledge of Divine things existing in every nation . . . is to be traced to Divine Revelation, whether written or traditional, and not to innate or intuitive ideas." However, Moffat claimed to have discovered people at the bottom of this great chain of degradation. At the lowest point on Moffat's scale of world religions, Satan had succeeded in entirely eliminating any trace of the original revelation among the indigenous people of southern Africa. Occupying a position on the bottom of the chain of being with the Bushmen, the Bechuanas had "lost all idea of the being of a God."[21]

Influenced by religious motives and colored by particular Christian assumptions about the efficacy of Satan, the missionary Robert Moffat nevertheless advanced a general theory of the history of religions. In the beginning, he proposed, there was one religion. Through a long, gradual process of historical diffusion, a process determined, in Moffat's reading, by Satanic influence, the one had become many; the religions of the world had proliferated. Repeatedly, Moffat asserted this theory of comparative religion, observing that "God originally imparted the knowledge of his own being to man, and that tradition has circulated the report through the nations of the earth, which has undergone, by satanic influence on the minds of fallen creatures, those modifications presented to us in the pantheon, or in the minds of savages."[22]

As a supplement to this theory of the history of religions, Robert Moffat also advanced a structural analysis of religious diversity. From his missionary perspective, relations between Christianity and other religions were defined as a kind of holy warfare. As he observed, "whoever goes to preach the unsearchable riches of Christ among the heathen, goes on a warfare . . . to wrestle and struggle, and toil, in pulling down the strongholds of Satan, whether in Africa, India, or the Islands of the Pacific." On those colonial frontiers, other religions necessarily appeared, in structural terms, as obstacles to the progress of the Christian mission. Accordingly, Moffat developed a structural theory of religions, a theory that depended heavily upon architectural metaphors to represent non-Christian religions as blocks, barriers, or obstacles to the advance of Christianity. On the northern frontier of the Cape Colony, Moffat observed that the "next barrier to be noticed," as he referred explicitly to the Bechuanas, was "the entire absence of theological ideas, or religion." Their lack of religion was a structural obstacle to the advance of Christian colonization. However, Moffat also developed a more subtle analysis of structural analogies between religions confronted on different European colonial frontiers. For example, Moffat highlighted the structural analogy between Bechuana customs, such as male and female initiation, and the Hindu caste system. Based on this structural analogy, he complained, "Of their customs they are as tenacious as the Hindoo could be of his caste, that dreadful barrier to evangelization in the East Indies." Although he envied Christian missionaries in India, Moffat could still find an analogy with their struggle against Hinduism. In Africa, as in India, he argued, such "ceremonies were prodigious barriers to the Gospel." In structural terms, therefore, Moffat found that African custom was exactly like the Hindu caste system because both blocked the Christian mission.[23]

Likewise, in structural terms, Robert Moffat insisted that the sacred specialist of the Bechuanas, the diviner, or *ngaka*, presented a serious obstacle to the Christian mission. Although he could easily dismiss them as witches, sorcerers, magicians, or fraudulent rainmakers, Moffat nevertheless had to come to terms with Sotho-Tswana *ngakas* within his general theory of religions.

Accordingly, Moffat determined that such indigenous sacred specialists, whether the *angekoks* of Greenland, or the *pawpaws* of North America, or the *greegrees* of West Africa, were the structural "pillars of Satan's kingdom." All over the world, indigenous sacred specialists had built the foundation of a global Satanic order. In his analysis of the sacred specialists of the Bechuanas, therefore, Moffat concluded that they were also implicated in upholding the evil structure of Satan's domain in the world. In a holy war against Satan, the missionary Robert Moffat had to counteract the kind of structural blocks, barriers, or obstacles presented by Sotho-Tswana sacred specialists.[24]

Although he confidently asserted this argument in Britain and vigorously pursued it on the frontier, Moffat was often frustrated by the conduct of the "pillars of Satan's kingdom" among the Sotho-Tswana people he was trying to convert. For example, a Barolong *ngaka*, described by Moffat as a "wily rainmaker," proposed a different comparative account of the history of religions. According to this rainmaker, the Supreme Being who created humans first produced the Bushmen, but did not like them because they were so ugly and their speech sounded like frogs. So, the Creator made the Hottentots but did not like them any better than Bushmen. Using all his knowledge and skill, he next made the Bechuanas, who he found to be a great improvement but still not the end of creation. Finally, the Supreme Being produced white people and sent them out into the world with ox-drawn wagons and plows. Moffat perceived this story as a countermyth, a direct challenge to his own account, because he expressed disgust that the "wily rainmaker's" story "received the applause of the people, while the poor missionary's arguments, drawn from the source of Divine truth, were thrown into the shade."[25] Like the "wily serpent" in the Garden of Eden, the Barolong rainmaker had transposed "Divine truth" to serve Satanic ends. In the northern Cape, however, such appropriations and transpositions of religious elements defined the local practice of a cross-cultural comparative religion on the frontier.

CONTESTED APPROPRIATIONS

The missionaries had determined that the term *Morimo* was analogous to the Christian term *God* by an exercise of comparison. At the same time, however, comparison had also been an act

No 39. Medicine man administering the Charm to Barolong warriors when going to battle 1834

No 40. Medicine man blowing counter charm towards the Enemy —

Barolong sacred specialists: (a) Ritual for strengthening warriors; (b) Ritual for weakening enemies. (Courtesy Museum Africa, Johannesburg)

of appropriation, as the missionaries captured the term from a Sotho-Tswana religious vocabulary and redeployed it for their own ends. Based on a questionable etymology, Moffat argued that the word *Morimo* was derived from combining the personal prefix *Mo* with *rimo*, from *gorimo*, meaning "above." Cognate with *legorimo* ("heaven"), *Morimo*, in Moffat's reading, therefore originally referred to a being who was above in the heavens. However, this interpretation contradicted, as Moffat recognized, what seemed to be the more general Sotho-Tswana understanding of *Morimo* as a mysterious being or force located underground. Nevertheless, he insisted, no one "disputed the propriety of our using the noun Morimo for the great Object of our worship, as some of them admitted that their forefathers might have known more about him than *they* did" (emphasis in original). In this formulation, Moffat assumed the role of their "forefathers." He insisted that the Christian missionaries knew more about the original meaning of traditional beliefs than Africans did. Accordingly, Robert Moffat saw no impropriety in turning their vocabulary into the property of the Christian mission.[26]

Actions and Counteractions

For their part, however, Africans developed countermeasures to contest the missionary appropriation of their religious vocabulary. Moffat found that his primary religious competitor, the wily rainmaker, contested the mission's appropriation of the term *Morimo*. The *ngakas*, Moffat complained, stole the term back from the Christian mission and used it for their own nefarious ends. According to Moffat, local rainmakers claimed access to the knowledge and power of Morimo, the governor of the heavens. If it rained, they took credit, attributing the rainfall to their ritual intervention with Morimo. However, if their rituals failed to produce rain, they blamed the Morimo of the mission. In this symbolic contest, Moffat observed, the rainmaker "showed his skill in the appropriation of our principles to serve his own purposes. He also exhibited considerable cunning in this transfer." Clearly, however, Moffat himself had displayed considerable cunning in appropriating and transposing the terms of a local African religious vocabulary. As he appropriated the word *Morimo* to signify the Christian God, Moffat simultaneously captured the Sotho-Tswana term for ancestors, *barimo*, and translated it as "demons." He recognized that *barimo* signified the *"liriti*, shades or manes of the dead," and, accordingly, played an important role in Sotho-Tswana ritual life. Nevertheless, in fashioning a Christian vocabulary out of local symbolic materials, Moffat elevated *Morimo* to the heavens and demoted *barimo* to the status of evil, demonic spirits.[27]

Sealing his capture of these local terms, Moffat locked them up in a book, giving his appropriation a kind of permanence through his translation of the Bible. Frequently, in response, Sotho-Tswana comparativists drew the analogy between the missionary's book and the *ngaka*'s instruments of divination. "My books puzzled them," Moffat reported; "they asked if they were my 'Bola,' prognosticating dice." John Mackenzie found a smiliar observation made by the Ndebele of Chief Mzilikazi. In an important sense, this comparison highlighted a useful analogy since both books and bones were "read" by specialists in their respective technologies of the sacred. Both required skilled interpretation, based on shared hermeneutical principles, before they could disclose their meaning and significance. However, Moffat resisted this analogy because he saw it as an instance of the extreme relativism underlying Sotho-Tswana comparisons between Christianity and their own tradition. As Moffat complained, they thought that Christian beliefs and practices were "very wonderful, but no more so than their own." Moffat cited this relativism as evidence of the "profoundest darkness" of African minds. However, Sotho-Tswana relativism reflected a more flexible, adaptive comparative religion that identified significant equivalences, such as the analogy between books and bones, in the symbolic elements of two religions.[28]

In other instances, however, Africans found no equivalence between the religion of the mission and local tradition. In some cases, their perception of incongruity was so great that it could only provoke laughter. As Moffat realized, African laughter was a challenge to the claims of the mission. On one occasion, a Tswana chief gathered together thirty men to tell them what the missionary had said about Morimo, the creation of the heavens and the earth, and the resurrection of the dead. "Did you ever hear *litlamane* (fables) like these?" the chief asked. "This was followed by a burst of deafening laughter," Moffat recalled, "and on its partially subsiding, the chief man begged me to say no more on such trifles, lest the people should think me mad!" From their perspective, therefore, many Sotho-Tswana people apparently

compared the missionary's curious appropriation of their religious vocabulary to a kind of madness. By manipulating their cultural symbols, he had produced a joke. Moffat's claims were often
met with laughter. When he related his "fables" to the chief of
the Ndebele, Moffat noticed that Mzilikazi thought he was jok-
ing. "He would stare at me," Moffat recalled, "to see if I maintained my gravity." When he told a group of women that they
should convince their husbands to do the agricultural work, thus
violating their gendered division of labor, Moffat found that his
suggestion "set them all into a roar of laughter." Although Moffat
interpreted this laughter as stubborn resistance to his gospel, it
might be better understood as the expression of a basic comparative observation. Their laughter suggested that they recognized
that the missionary's interventions involved crazy, illegitimate
transpositions of the fundamental symbolic categories of a local
African culture.[29]

Positions and Transpositions

Missionaries in Africa generally succeeded in imposing their
translations of indigenous terms. Backed up by colonial authority,
literacy, and guns, they enforced their translations upon an entire
field of discourse. As Rosalind Shaw has recently observed, "The
kind of cultural translation which characterized the Christian
missionary enterprise was very much a translation 'from above,'
a process of authorizing, selecting, editing, privileging and promoting certain African religious forms in favour of others." In
response to missionary translations "from above," Sotho-Tswana
people found new, creative ways to reappropriate crucial religious
terms. In the social relations of the northern frontier, however,
comparisons between religions were not only drawn by Europeans and Sotho-Tswana. Held in contempt by both, the Bushmen
proposed their own comparisons, developing a kind of comparative religion "from below." In their efforts to make sense out of
the new religion of the Christian mission, Bushmen translated
its strange practices into familiar terms. As the missionary John
Mackenzie reported, they compared Sunday worship to their own
rituals of purification and protection. In this Bushman comparative religion, therefore, the Christian ritual of prayers, sermons,
and songs was "the white man's way to make his encampment
pure and safe." In the battle over the term *Morimo*, the Bushmen

also advanced their own claim. According to Mackenzie, Bushmen also practiced divination by casting and interpreting a set of bones. When asked about their "divining dice," Bushmen explained them, in Setswana, as things of Morimo, or even by saying, "*Se se Morimo, se,*"—"This is God." Drawing their own comparison, therefore, the Bushmen proposed that their divining bones played the same role in their religious system as Morimo held in the Christian or Sotho-Tswana religions. Through this analogy, however, Bushmen also asserted their claim on the sacred power represented by the term Morimo within the contested religious vocabulary of the northern frontier.[30]

This Bushman comparative religion accounted for other symbolic elements that were floating in the religious life of the northern frontier. As Mackenzie observed, male Bushmen compared their own rite of passage into manhood, which was marked by piercing the cartilage of the nose, with the Sotho-Tswana ceremony of circumcision. They used the same Setswana term, *rupa,* for both rituals, indicating, as Mackenzie reported, that their ritual scarification was to them "what circumcision is to the Bechuanas." Apparently, Bushmen also drew a comparison between their own ritual regard for goats and the Sotho-Tswana system of sacred animals. Noting that the Bakuena, for example, said that they *bina* the crocodile, Bushmen seem to have observed that they *bina* the goat. In Mackenzie's account, at least, this comparison was obvious: "The Madenassana Bushmen 'bina' the common goat; that is to say, it is their sacred animal, as the 'kwena' or alligator is to the Bakwena. Now just as it would be hateful and unlucky to the Bakwena to meet or gaze upon the alligator, so the common goat is the object of 'religious' aversion to these Bushmen; and to look upon it would be to render the man for the time impure, as well as to cause him undefined uneasiness."[31]

As these multiplying analogies illustrate, comparative religion was by no means the sole preserve of the Christian mission. Practices of comparison proliferated all along the northern frontier. From different perspectives, Bushmen, Sotho-Tswana, and missionaries made claims and counterclaims about a common stock of religious symbols. As a result of these comparisons, a pattern of structural equivalences emerged. Comparison proceeded through the identification and transposition of analogous structural elements. The Sotho-Tswana *Morimo* was to the Bushmen divining bones, as the bones were to the Christian book, which in its turn was asserted by the missionaries as equivalent to the "word of *Morimo.*" As noted, Bushman comparative religionists interpreted the Sunday sermons and prayers of the mission as a rite of purification. Sotho-Tswana comparativists often interpreted mission services as rainmaking rituals. While Bushmen identified their ritual scarification with the Sotho-Tswana *rupa*, the missionaries maintained that circumcision was the structural equivalent of Christian baptism. In opposing circumcision, as Mackenzie recalled, the missionaries argued, "There are two ways and two rites: the way of God's Word and the way of heathenism; the rite of baptism and the rite of circumcision."[32]

Although the missionaries demanded that one rite had to be abandoned for the other, they nevertheless developed a comparative religion that recognized both as rites of passage. By adding their own rite of initiation to the mix, Bushman comparativists broadened the frame of reference of this northern frontier comparative religion. The structural relations in this intercultural comparative religion can thus be schematized:

Sotho-Tswana	*Bushmen*	*Mission*
Morimo	bones	book
rainmaking	purification	prayer
circumcision	scarification	baptism

However, in recognizing such structural similarities, the system of sacred animals posed a problem. Here was a system of differences, distinguishing people on the basis of animal emblems, that seemed to have no counterpart in the Christian mission. African comparativists must have asked: if the Bakuena *bina* the crocodile, and the Bushmen *bina* the goat, what do the European Christians *bina*? One solution to this problem in comparative religion on the northern frontier was posed by the Sotho-Tswana *ngaka*, the "wily rainmaker" recorded by Robert Moffat. In his creative improvisation on a traditional origin myth, Moffat's adversary suggested that the white people had emerged from the bed of reeds, like other human beings, with their particular sacred animal. In the beginning, they came out of the reeds with the ox-drawn wagon or the ox-drawn plow. According to the "wily rainmaker," therefore, the sacred animal of Europeans was the wagon or plow. Clearly, Moffat regarded the plow as a sacred emblem. He was fond of declaring that Africa would be regenerated by two sacred objects, the Bible and the plow. The ox-drawn wagon could also be regarded as a European sacred animal. As many Africans recalled, their first impression upon seeing an ox-drawn wagon was that it comprised a single, composite animal.[33] In the emergence myth told by the Sotho-Tswana *ngaka*, that animal was represented as the sacred emblem of Europeans. Therefore, in the comparative religion of the northern frontier a further set of structural resemblances could be established—crocodile : goat : wagon or plow. Significantly, therefore, the sacred animal of the European Christians on the northern frontier turned out to be a machine.

ANIMAL EMBLEMS

The French Protestants of the Paris Evangelical Mission Society, who in 1833 began their work in the mountain kingdom of Chief Moshoeshoe, also found no religion among Sotho-Tswana people. They had been preceded in the area by two Europeans, a "Rousseauite" in search of "noble savages" and an "Irvingite" who was looking for people speaking the "unknown tongue" of the Garden of Eden. The follower of Rousseau, a German naturalist by the name of Seidenstechter, stayed for a time with Moshoeshoe. Apparently, the chief's people had their own questions about nobility and savagery because when they saw Seidenstechter, they asked, "Is it a *man*, or a *god*, or a *beast*?" Martin, the English adherent of the millennial doctrines of Edward Irving, did not discover the "unknown tongue," but he did learn enough of the local language to go about exclaiming in Sesuto, "God—heaven—light—burning fire!" Unfortunately, the "Rousseauite" and the "Irvingite" never published the results of their investigations. Their "learned speculations" on African religion were lost because, according to the colonial official Joseph Millerd Orpen, they wandered north and were eaten by cannibals. However, the French Protestants did publish their own findings on the Basuto. For the most part, in their investigations of Basuto indigenous religion the French missionaries echoed the denials that had been issued by the British. They also found "no religion."[34]

According to Eugène Casalis, the "endemical atheism" of the Sotho-Tswana answered "one of the most interesting questions that ethnography can offer—Whether there really is a portion of humanity living in atheism, and among whom the religious instinct has been obliterated by absolute scepticism?" Like Moffat,

Casalis claimed to have found evidence among the Sotho-Tswana that refuted any notion of natural religion. As proof, Casalis pointed to the absence of any observable signs of religion. "The Hindu temples and the Marias [*marae*, or temples] of Polynesia," he noted, "had accustomed us to the idea that every pagan worship must necessarily show an altar and a visible god." Among the Sotho-Tswana, these visible signs were absent. At the same time, however, Casalis discounted any local beliefs and practices that could be discovered as lacking in genuine religious content. The "Basuto talk of God, and offer sacrifices," he argued, "without appearing to attach any religious idea thereto." Having learned these things from their forefathers, they could give no reason to explain why they talked about God or offered sacrifices. Without reasons, Casalis concluded, these beliefs and practices could have nothing to do with religion. In these terms, Eugène Casalis reported his discovery of "no religion," a discovery that was based not only on the lack of observable signs of religion but also on the inability of Africans to provide acceptable reasons for any signs of religion that did appear.[35]

Animal Gods

Although they found no religion, the French missionaries did discover a remarkable system of animal symbolism, myth, and ritual among the Sotho-Tswana. During the 1840s, their reports provided details of local regard for animal emblems. Samuel Rolland recorded the myth that traced the sacred animals back to the original emergence of humanity. When human beings emerged from Molimo through a marsh covered with reeds, Rolland related, "each tribe received a different animal as an emblem which would be for it a god-protector. These animals are held sacred by the Basuto up to this day." Sacred animal emblems were used to mark cattle, weapons, shields, skin cloaks, and household implements. Members of a tribe swore oaths by their designated animal. In relation to their sacred animal, each group observed special ritual prohibitions that prevented them from killing or eating it. "If any one ate such an animal during famine," Rolland observed, "he was looked upon as sacrilegious and worthy of punishment by the gods." If anyone should come upon a sacred animal dead in the field, he was bound by ritual propriety to approach it backwards, open its cranium, take out its brain, and rub it on his eyes. Otherwise, people feared going blind if they neglected this duty. Thomas Arbousset and François Daumas reported that the Bataung would never kill or eat their sacred animal, the lion. "They would not eat the flesh, though other tribes did so with relish," he reported, "for fear of eating an ancestor." If they found a dead lion, or killed one by accident, they rubbed their eyes with its fur to avoid being struck blind. Likewise, Arbousset and Daumas reported that a Pedi group, known as Banoku, the people of the porcupine, "feast, worship, or revere that animal." If they found a dead porcupine, they rubbed their eyes with its quills. Worshiping the porcupine, the Banoku lived with "the fear that they will die if they eat the flesh of one." Others worshiped the monkey or baboon through similar acts. Prosper Lemue recounted the same sacred regard for the crocodile by the Bakuena. Noting that they danced to its honor, Lemue speculated that "it is, no doubt, in order to appease the fury of this redoubtable amphibious animal, that these people praise its strength and ferocity in their songs." Not only honoring it in dance and song, the Bakuena avoided killing the crocodile because they feared that destroying their sacred animal would prevent rain.[36]

In these accounts, Sotho-Tswana sacred animals appeared not only as ancestral emblems but as gods or god-protectors. People who were supposedly without a God suddenly turned out to have many gods. They were polytheists. Their animal gods enforced a system of divine sanction. If the god's sacred obligations and prohibitions were observed, it granted protection. If not, it brought punishment, especially blindness, upon those who failed to show the proper respect to their animal god. According to the French missionaries, therefore, the system of sacred animals was based essentially upon fear. Invoking this familiar theory of religion, which had been proposed by David Hume in London as well as by John Barrow on the northern frontier, they accounted for the observance of animal emblems as a way of avoiding the anger of the gods. Ritual practices relating to the animal emblems were allegedly designed to deflect the fury of the gods and thereby avoid divine punishments. Therefore, the entire system of animal symbolism was motivated by emotions of sacred dread or holy terror. In this explanation, the French missionaries found evidence for a theory of religion that held that the basic human emotion of fear had been projected in the formation of Sotho-Tswana beliefs and practices.

At the same time, however, European commentators were intrigued by the apparent similarity between these sacred animals and animal gods in the religion of ancient Egypt. As Prosper Lemue observed, the Bakuena, by having the crocodile as their sacred animal, "resemble the ancient Egyptians, who rendered it divine honours." With respect to the importance of sacred animals among Sotho-Tswana people more generally, Henry Methuen suggested that an investigation of similarities or connections with ancient Egypt was an avenue for fruitful research. As he observed, "How far this custom indicates an Egyptian source, or what resemblance it may have to any practice in North Africa, is an interesting matter of research. . . . The sacred animals and birds of the East are familiar to all who have read accounts of that quarter." Napoleon's Egyptian expedition, the discovery of the Rosetta Stone, and the subsequent publication of the twenty-volume *Description de l'Egypte* (1809–22) had stimulated interest in the religion of ancient Egypt. Methuen was inspired by the possibility of an Egyptian connection to reflect on the importance of animals in African myths and rituals. Throughout southern Africa, he observed, indigenous people related a myth about the origin of death that featured two animal messengers, the chameleon and the lizard. The Hottentots reportedly worshiped an insect; the Zulu worshiped snakes. In developing their system of sacred animals, therefore, the Sotho-Tswana were demonstrating a more general tendency to deify animals that could be found all over southern Africa. Did this practice originate in ancient Egypt? If it did, Methuen suggested, then the ancient Egyptian animal worship had degenerated in the course of its migration into southern Africa. The sacred animals were no longer worshiped. As proof, Methuen revealed, "I have shot the crocodile in presence of Baquaines without their uttering a syllable, and have known the baboon shot in the same way at Mabotsa." Through such an empirical test, therefore, Henry Methuen could conclude that the Sotho-Tswana sacred animals were no longer worshiped as they might once have been in ancient Egypt.[37]

The assumption that the Sotho-Tswana could be traced back to ancient Egypt became common in frontier comparative religion. Citing the authority of the Berlin Missionary Society agent Alexander Merensky, who worked among the Pedi on the northern frontier, J. E. Carlyle observed that all "the traditions point to the North-east—Egypt or the source of the Nile—as the cradle of their race." Not only their veneration of sacred animals but also their practice of burying their dead with their faces turned toward the northeast indicated the Egyptian origin of the Bechuanas. While the worship of animals could be connected to ancient Egypt, however, the worship of sacred plants, trees, and fires recalled pagan Europe. In one Sotho-Tswana community, which worshiped the rietbok, a type of antelope, Arbousset and Daumas also found the veneration of a wild vine. Holding it sacred, the people never used the wood from that vine. If it should burn, they would never take a light from its fire but would gather the ashes and anoint their foreheads and temples "in token of grief." In these practices, Arbousset and Daumas supposed, Sotho-Tswana veneration of a sacred vine "resembles in some respects the worship rendered by the Druids to the mistletoe." Some years later, John Mackenzie found Sotho-Tswana who periodically entered the densest part of a forest, found the largest tree, and prostrated in prayer before it. This practice reminded him of the "grove worship" of pagan Europe. Mackenzie also observed a sacred fire ceremony that seemed "to be the African version of the fire which was represented to come down annually from Jupiter in Southern Europe, and almost the same as the sacred fire which was dealt out to our own forefathers in ancient Britain by their priests." Like pagan Romans, or ancient Druids, African priests lit the hearths of every household from a single sacred fire. Reminiscing about his Scottish childhood, Mackenzie recalled that such a ceremony had persisted in the Highlands as Beltaneday, the day of Baal's fire. "We did not know, as children," he noted, "that we were taking part in the lingering Pagan worship of our rude forefathers." Significantly, however, no European commentator deduced from these comparisons that the Sotho-Tswana shared the same "rude forefathers" as the Europeans. No theory of historical diffusion was proposed that derived African religious practices from pagan Romans, Gauls, or Druids. Although many imagined that their worship of animals might have come from ancient Egypt, no observer proposed that the African worship of sacred plants, trees, or fires had originated in ancient Europe.[38]

The Closing Frontier

Sacred animals and objects appeared in these accounts as religious fragments, perhaps, but not as elements that comprised a coherent religious system. European observers on the northern frontiers persisted in denial. For example, the German Dr. Emil

Holub, who spent seven years in southern Africa during the 1870s, continued to find no religion among the Sotho-Tswana. "In the strict sense of the word," Holub insisted, "the Bechuanas . . . cannot be said to have any religion at all." He found that they did exhibit certain beliefs and practices, such as their beliefs in Morimo, barimo, and sacred animals, or the practices of their priests and ceremonies, "which amongst other people professing polytheism would be regarded as religious rites." However, even this evidence was insufficient for European comparativists to attribute a religious system to the Sotho-Tswana because, as Holub dogmatically concluded, "they cannot be said to have any actual religion."[39] In this categorical denial, a denial so absolute that it could even disregard evidence that would be acknowledged as proof of the existence of religion elsewhere, European comparativists persisted in finding an absence of indigeneous religion among Africans on the northern frontier.

Since the northern region remained a contested frontier into the 1890s, acknowledgment of the existence of a Sotho-Tswana religion was postponed longer than on any other frontier in southern Africa. As relatively independent African polities held out on the northern frontier, European observers tended to perpetuate the denial of any indigenous Sotho-Tswana religion. In the end, however, the colonial containment of African populations was accomplished through the native "reserve system." Combining the functions of containment and surveillance, native reserves also provided farming and industry with a reservoir for cheap, exploitable labor. Although a native reserve system for the northern frontier was designed in the 1890s, it was not fully implemented until the reconstruction that followed the South African War in the early 1900s.[40] As on other frontiers, once the boundaries of a native reserve system were drawn around the Sotho-Tswana, and they were effectively brought under a system of colonial containment, they were found to have a religious system.

The historical process that led to the "discovery" of a Sotho-Tswana religion can be suggested by the work of the LMS missionary John Mackenzie. From the 1870s, Mackenzie was engaged in a concerted propaganda effort for the creation of an imperial "Territory" or "Protectorate" that would establish direct British control over the Bechuanas. In his extensive reports from southern Africa, Mackenzie provided detailed accounts of "native worship and superstition." But he did not call it religion. In his voluminous writings, Mackenzie avoided using the term *religion* for

African beliefs and practices until after the establishment of the protectorate of British Bechuanaland in 1884. In fact, Mackenzie did not identify those beliefs and practices as religion until the last Sotho-Tswana resistance, the Langeberg Rebellion, had been suppressed in 1897. Only then was Mackenzie prepared not only to recognize but even to insist that the Bechuanas had indigeneous beliefs and practices that counted as religion.[41]

In a lecture that was published the year of his death in 1899, John Mackenzie noted, as he had often observed before, that "the Bechuanas were ancestor-worshippers, and believers in fetiches, charms, and spells." However, for the first time, Mackenzie asserted that this "native worship and superstition" had to be regarded as a religion. Like Joseph Cox Warner on a different frontier in the 1850s, Mackenzie was aware that he was departing from the customary European practice of designating African beliefs and practices on the northern frontier as superstition rather than religion. Mackenzie recommended that the long denial of Sotho-Tswana religion should come to an end. Their "hoary superstition or religion," he announced, "merits the latter name." In arguing that the Bechuanas had a religious system, Mackenzie explained their ethical and ritual regard for ancestors as a moral force that often restrained them from evil conduct. Their religious veneration of ancestors, he suggested, also maintained social stability. In highlighting these religious functions of moral restraint and social order, functions that were performed by any religious system, Mackenzie also followed Warner in advancing a functionalist definition of religion. On the grounds that they operated to reinforce personal morality and social order, therefore, Mackenzie finally concluded that the beliefs and practices of the Bechuanas actually constituted a religious system.[42]

Significantly, Mackenzie's recognition of the religion of the Bechuanas had been delayed until the political independence of all African chiefdoms on the northern frontier had finally been destroyed. In 1898 a contingent of four thousand Boers, with African allies, conquered the Venda chiefdom, thus shattering the only remaining independent African polity in southern Africa. Apparently, the final frontier was closed. A year later, however, the closed frontier reopened with the outbreak of the South African War. Not only pitting Boer against Briton, the war involved and affected everyone in southern Africa. In reconstructing a single political order after the war, High Commissioner Alfred Milner appointed the South African Native Affairs Commission in 1903 to work out a common "native policy" for all the regions of the country. Published in 1905, the commission's reports advocated urban racial segregation and separate rural territories for Africans. While denying African political rights, British government reports found that African religion might provide building blocks for reconstructing a racially segregated and separated South Africa. Ironically, after a century of denial, the government found not only that Africans had a religion but that they had a useful religion to the extent that religious beliefs and practices kept the tribal system intact.

A report submitted in 1905 by the general staff of the War Office observed that the system of separate African tribes might very well disintegrate under the impact of civilization. "Such a consummation does not, however, seem altogether desirable," the report warned, "for a general fusion of hitherto antagonistic tribes would then be possible, and this would constitute a far greater danger to the white community than is to be apprehended from any of the present tribes." In order to discourage separate tribes from forming a common front, religious differences had to be preserved. According to the War Office, certain features, such as beliefs in spirits, veneration of chiefs and ancestors, and ritual sacrifices, appeared all over southern Africa and constituted a generic "Bantu religion." However, a religious basis for specifying and reinforcing tribal differences could be found in the system of sacred animals. The report explained that in the most ancient "Bantu religion," Africans believed that deceased friends and relatives regularly visited them in the form of animals. Each tribe, however, regarded a different animal as the one selected by its ancestral ghosts. For Zulu, Xhosa, and other coastal tribes, that sacred animal was a certain species of snake. For the Sotho-Tswana, each tribal subdivision had its own specific animal, whether the crocodile, the lion, the hyena, or some other creature, through which the spirits of its ancestors appeared. As the report of the War Office noted, sharing a sacred animal linked people of the same tribe, even if they lived far apart. However, by implication, this system of sacred animals also separated Africans, even when living close together, along distinct tribal lines. Therefore, the report of the War Office suggested that the system of sacred animals could play a significant religious role in the political separation of African "tribal" groups in southern Africa.[43]

The general staff of the War Office had a new term at its disposal for the sacred animals. They were *totems*. In using this term, the War Office was incorporating a line of analysis that had become firmly fixed in the European study of religion by the turn of the century. Although the word was introduced into European vocabularies a century earlier from reports about North American Indians, totemism eventually came to be regarded as a general feature of "savage" or "primitive" religion. In his influential essay on "The Worship of Animals and Plants," which appeared in the *Fortnightly Review* (1869–70), the lawyer and legal scholar John Ferguson M'Lennan had placed totems in an evolutionary framework by identifying a primitive "totem stage of development" through which all nations passed. Major European scholars of religion, such as W. Robertson Smith, James Frazer, and Émile Durkheim, pursued the analysis of totemism as an early stage in human evolution. On the southern African periphery, however, the doctrine of evolution had not yet taken hold in the study of religion. The War Office, for example, was interested in totemism, not as a stage of evolution, but as a system of tribal separation. Although evolutionary theory held that totemism was destined to be replaced, the War Office found that totemism, as a "tribal" system, needed to be restored for effective "native" administration.

At the beginning of the twentieth century, two missionary theorists of comparative religion, the London Missionary Society agent William Charles Willoughby and the Paris Evangelical Mission Society agent David Frederic Ellenberger, took up the study of Sotho-Tswana totemism. Both tried to uncover an ancient, original religion underlying the traditional symbolism of sacred animals. Their inquiries, however, produced strikingly different results. While Willoughby found an ancient system of ox worship, Ellenberger discovered the "unknown God" at the basis of Sotho-Tswana totemism. Nevertheless, these comparative religionists agreed on one point: Sotho-Tswana people did in fact have a traditional religious system.

Totemism

Born in Cornwall in 1857, William Charles Willoughby arrived in Bechuanaland in 1893, where he was stationed as the agent of the London Missionary Society at the capital of the Christian chief, Khama III. Willoughby served not only as missionary but also as political adviser to Chief Khama in successfully resisting the at-

W. C. Willoughby. (Courtesy South African Library, Cape Town)

tempt by Cecil Rhodes to incorporate the chief's territory into the British South African Company. In 1904 Willoughby assumed the position as principal of a new educational institution, Tiger Kloof, which was established just below the border of the Bechuanaland Protectorate in the northern Cape. Combining scholastic and practical education, Tiger Kloof provided training, in particular, for "native" teachers and ministers, but also industrial education for "native" craftsmen and women.[44]

The curriculum emphasized religious education. In addition to biblical studies, Old and New Testament history, Christian doctrine, church history, church polity, ethics, and hygiene, the curriculum also included the subject of comparative religion. At Tiger Kloof, comparative religion took two forms: the investigation of world religions and the study of "the relation of Bantu religion and customs to Christian thought." Emphasizing comparative religion, Willoughby noted that "non-Christian religions were, of course, our main work." In a 1911 report on Tiger Kloof he observed that his class of fourteen Bechuana Christian students "devoted the time to sermons, public reading, and the study of non-Christian religions." At one point, Willoughby wanted to "confine the work of this class to the study of Buddhism." However, his students encouraged him to treat non-Christian religions in such a way as to show how they "led either to old Bantu religious beliefs and practices or else to Christianity." Therefore, Willoughby and his students found ways at Tiger Kloof to integrate Buddhism and other religions into comparisons between African and Christian religious ways of life.[45]

After leaving South Africa in 1919, Willoughby pursued his interest in comparative religion as professor of African missions at the Kennedy School of Missions at Hartford Theological Seminary in Connecticut. During his tenure there, he published three books—*Race Problems in the New Africa* (1923), *The Soul of the Bantu* (1928), and *Nature Worship and Taboo* (1932)—that tried to place "Bantu religion" in the broader context of a global comparative religion. While still at Tiger Kloof, however, Willoughby identified totemism as the interpretive key for understanding "Bantu religion." In 1905 Willoughby summarized his findings in a paper, "Notes on the Totemism of the Becwana," which he presented to the joint meeting of the British and South African Association for the Advancement of Science. In analyzing the vocabulary of "Becwana" totemism, Willoughby identified *sereto*, signifying "friendship," and *seano*, meaning "the sacred thing," as synonyms for "the tribal totem." The expression go bina signified allegiance to a tribal totem, as "go bina phuti (to dance to the duyker) is the ordinary phrase for having the duyker [a small gazelle] as a tribal totem." Although each "tribe" had its totem, two sacred animals deserved special mention: the crocodile, because it was held in respect by all tribes, even when it was not a tribal totem, and the hare, because that clever animal of "Becwana" folktales was thought to bring good luck. Like earlier commentators, Willoughby noted the ritual observances and avoidances that were required by allegiance to a sacred animal. Although the whole system seemed to be in decay, as tribes had been reorganized or relocated, Willoughby found that all the "Becwanas" still knew and respected their particular tribal totem.

However, Willoughby's most remarkable discovery was that the current system of sacred animals was a relatively recent form of totemism. He observed that the sacred animals were not integrated into the major "Becwana" rituals and customs. They played no role in rites of passage at birth, initiation, or death, nor did they feature in rites of crisis during warfare, drought, or famine. The sacred animals did not appear in the sacrifices and sacrificial meals that were so prominent in "Becwana" ritual. From this evidence, Willoughby argued that "the present totems are of comparatively recent date; that when they were adopted by the Becwana an older ritual was in secure possession of the field; and that the new totems have failed to modify this older ritual even in the slightest degree." The more recent system of sacred animals identified tribal totems with wild animals. According to Willoughby, however, a more ancient totemism appeared in rituals involving domesticated animals. Cattle were at the center of "Becwana" ritual. The ox was the supreme ritual animal that was killed in sacrifices and eaten in sacrificial meals. As Willoughby argued, "this older ritual is totemistic," a totemism more authentic than the system of tribal totems that featured the sacred animals. Their original totem, therefore, must have been the ox.

Willoughby observed that all "Becwana" tribes, regardless of their sacred animal, participated in "the totemistic ritual of the ancient ox-totem." At some length, he supplemented his discovery of this domesticated animal totem with an analysis of domesticated plant and cereal totems in the women's initiation ritual. Willoughby argued that "just as we find survivals of the ox-totem in the ritual that is peculiar to the men, so we find survivals of the gourd and the Kaffir-corn totems in the ritual that is peculiar

to the women." This duality of totems seemed to correspond to
the gendered division of labor in traditional "Becwana" society.
However, Willoughby was not interested in analyzing relations
between ritual and society. Rather, he was concerned with tracing
the ancient history of a primordial totemism underlying all "Becwana" ritual. If cattle, rather than the sacred totemic animals,
played the central role in the ritual practice of all major "Becwana" ceremonies, Willoughby submitted that "this can only be
explained by assuming that the ritual came from a far-distant past
when the ox was the totem of the people, and that all the present
totems are mere modern accretions."[46]

Willoughby conducted his analysis of totemism like an archae-
ological investigation. He treated current ritual practices as fossilized remnants of a prehistoric "Becwana" religion, arguing that
"the fossil is a stone with a tale to tell for those who have ears
to listen—the fossil ritual as well as the fossil shell." Beneath the
more recent strata of sacred animals that divided "Becwanas"
into different tribal totems, Willoughby thought he had uncov-
ered a primordial totemism of the ox that unified all "Becwanas,"
and perhaps all Bantus, in southern Africa. The notion of a generic Bantu religion arose in the context of the changing social
conditions at the beginning of the twentieth century that appeared to be rapidly eroding the traditional tribal system. Under
new conditions of urban life, rural poverty, and migrant labor,
even the ritual fossils of African tribal religion seemed to be vanishing. As Willoughby warned, "The ceremonies of an animistic
faith used to hold the African in awe of unseen powers, and cast
their halo around the sanctity of tribal morality; but tribal morality can hardly exist without the tribe, and animistic religion
is shifted in the atmosphere of materialistic civilization." In response to the challenge posed by the breakdown of tribal religion
and morality under modernization, Willoughby advocated salvage
research. "In the interest of anthropology," he urged, "it would be
well if these people were studied before it is too late." Certainly,
Willoughby displayed a nostalgia for what he imagined as traditional African tribal life. However, he did not call for its reconstruction. At a level more basic than the relatively "modern accretions" of tribal totems, Willoughby thought he had found the
primordial foundation of a unifying religion. Adapting terms current in European scholarship, he identified that unifying foundation as animism or totemism. In either case, however, the result
was the invention of a generic Bantu religion.[47]

Iconology

As a missionary for the Paris Evangelical Mission Society, David Frederic Ellenberger worked for over forty-five years in Basutoland. After his retirement, Ellenberger published some of his observations on Basuto traditions and customs in *History of the Basuto: Ancient and Modern* (1912). Translated from French into English by James Comyn Macgregor, who was assistant commissioner of the Leribe district of Basutoland, as well as an authority on Basuto traditions in his own right, Ellenberger's book claimed to provide a record of a disappearing way of life. As the resident commissioner of Basutoland Sir Herbert Cecil Sloley observed, traditional life was vanishing so rapidly under modern conditions that the salvage of Basuto history and customs was "clearly a case of now or never." In that rescue operation, Ellenberger devoted a long appendix to the recovery of the "religion of the early Basuto." While his French evangelical predecessors had refused to designate Sotho-Tswana beliefs and customs as religion, Ellenberger identified them as a coherent religious system. In outlining that system, he devoted considerable space to an analysis of the animal emblems or totems in Basuto religion. His aim, however, was not merely to record the traditional system of sacred animal totems. Ellenberger proposed a new and surprising theological interpretation of that system. Like his predecessors, he considered the possibility that the animal emblems were projections of fear or derived from ancient Egypt. However, Ellenberger revealed that the emblems actually had a specific religious content. Ironically, according to Ellenberger, the sacred animals of people who supposedly had no God turned out to be icons of the one supreme God.

Ellenberger noted that the "cult of the totems" played an important role in traditional Basuto life. Although they never performed sacrifices for their totemic animals, the Basuto swore by them, praised them, and venerated them in song and dance. Each group had derived its sacred animal from the fact that it originally lived in a district abounding with that particular wild animal. Accordingly, both the district and its inhabitants came to be known by the name of the specific "animal of their worship." Contrary to previous reports, Ellenberger argued that the "cult of the totems" was not motivated by fear of wild animals or whatever supernatural force they might represent. Nor did Ellenberger find their significance in any link with ancient Egypt, although he did notice a resemblance with the *nomes*, or administrative districts, and the animal gods that had symbolized "the great divinities of Mitsraim [Egypt]." Furthermore, Ellenberger emphatically denied the charge that the animal totems constituted a Basuto polytheism. By analogy, he noted that in ancient Israel King Jeroboam had set up a golden calf, which, although an act of idolatry, was not polytheism because that sacred animal had been dedicated to the one true God. "In the same way the Basuto, with their numerous symbols of the same Invisible Being, which they worshipped with noisy and coarse ceremonies, were indeed idolaters," Ellenberger argued, "but by no means polytheists." Remarkably, therefore, Ellenberger found that people who had been described in all previous reports as having no idols were idolaters. Even more astounding, he discovered that people who supposedly had no concept of God were actually monotheists.[48]

In Ellenberger's theological reading, the sacred animals were icons that symbolized *Molimo oa khale*, the "God of old." Each animal, whether crocodile, lion, or duiker, represented the same God. As symbols for the supreme God, the animal totems were interchangeable. People could change their totems with little consequence because "one animal was as good as another for the purpose of symbolising Him who created them all." Although their original meaning had been largely forgotten, the sacred animals stood as evidence, according to Ellenberger, of a primordial monotheism. In this respect, the animal totems had been motivated, not by any fear of the forces of nature, but by the fear of God. Ellenberger proposed that the "cult of the totems" was the "remnant of an ancient and forgotten fear of God which caused each tribe to dread to offend the sacred animal by which, without knowing it, they symbolised Him—'*The Unknown God*'" (emphasis in original). Once again, therefore, the unknown God surfaced in a missionary theory of comparative religion as Ellenberger insisted that the sacred animal totems were actually symbols of an original monotheism.

Ellenberger extended the significance of his findings about "the cult of the totems" among the Basuto by suggesting that his discovery of their original monotheism also applied to a generic Bantu religion. Furthermore, he argued that the same original monotheism could also be discerned in the totems of other "savage" religions. Ellenberger insisted that no "savage tribe" existed without some sacred totem, whether an animal, a plant, a metal, or a star, to which it traced its origin. Therefore, "the cult of *liboko,* or totems, was not peculiar to the Basuto, or even to the Bantu," he concluded. "In some form or other it is common to most savage peoples, even to the aborigines of America." If the sacred animals of the Basuto pointed to the "unknown God," then the totems of all "savage" religions could be understood as icons of the one God. In support of this argument, Ellenberger cited the French philosopher Frederic de Rougement. "If the ancient symbols are essentially religious," De Rougemont had proposed, "it is because antiquity brought everything back to God." According to Ellenberger, therefore, the sacred animals of Bantu religion, like the sacred totems of all "primitive" religions, ultimately referred back to the same original God.[49]

SACRED ANIMALS

Prior to his defeat and capture in 1894, Chief Malaboch of the Bagananoa had received regular visits from the missionary Christopher Sonntag, who observed on his first visit that people addressed their chief with ceremonial praise names, such as Great Lion, Awesome Monster, Fiery Dragon, or Mighty Ox. In these animal titles, people expressed their respect for the political authority of their chief. As they grew accustomed to Sonntag's presence, the Bagananoa also bestowed a special praise name upon the missionary. They gave him "the most impressive of all," Sonntag reported, "Ape." Under normal circumstances, he noted, he would have been offended by receiving such a title. Back in Europe, he certainly would have been dismayed if anyone had called him an ape. In southern Africa, however, animals were not the same as they were in Europe. They could be sacred. At the royal kraal of Malaboch, the ape was the chief's sacred "coat-of-arms." By being addressed as Ape, Sonntag felt he was being accepted into the chief's household. "For this reason," he explained, "the title 'Ape' sounded like heavenly music in my ears."[50]

Throughout southern Africa, animal symbols permeated the discourse of politics as well as religion. In praise names, animal symbols configured power relations of alliance and hierarchy. If animal titles could elevate, however, they could also subordinate. The epithet *dog,* for example, often operated as a sign of incorporation and subordination when applied to a chief's subjects. But it also served as a sign of exclusion and denigration when referring to enemies or, as it was systematically applied on the northern frontier, to designate Bushmen as "a mongrel race." Animal praises, animal insults, and the system of Sotho-Tswana sacred animals were all affected by the closing of the northern frontier. In 1914 the missionary Johannes August Winter, who had worked on behalf of the Berlin Missionary Society in the northeastern Transvaal for nearly fifty years, recorded the conclusions he had drawn on the mental and moral capacity of "the natives" in the Union of South Africa. "Capabilities our natives have, undoubtedly," Winter observed. "So, too, have even our baboons." By the second decade of the twentieth century, therefore, a former name of praise had become an insult. No longer the "heavenly music" of high honor, the title *ape*, in Winter's usage, signified the incorporation and subjugation of Africans in a new political economy.[51]

During the nineteenth century, European analysis of Sotho-Tswana sacred animals reproduced a range of disparate theories of religion. As noted, the system of sacred animals could be explained as a product of fear. Drawing upon what has been called "the most ancient theory of religion," European comparativists could identify a motive in the human emotions of awe and terror before the wild, uncontrollable forces of nature. At the same time, many European observers speculated that the system of sacred animals migrated from ancient Egypt. In their efforts to trace the historical origin of Sotho-Tswana beliefs and practices, no European theorist on the northern frontier suggested that they had originally come from ancient Jews, Muslims, or Arabs. A few reports made passing mention of apparent similarities between certain Sotho-Tswana customs and "Mosaic" or "Levitical" laws of the Old Testament. But they argued for no direct historical link. The traveler and hunter Henry Anderson Bryden considered the possibility of a Semitic origin but concluded that "still more probably they were very anciently allied to the Egyptians and Abyssinians."[52]

Instead, British reports found that Boers, not the Sotho-Tswana, were the ancient Jews on the northern frontier. In one exceptional case, the Lemba of the northern Transvaal were often traced back to an Islamic origin. As early as 1850, Boers in the frontier town of Potchefstroom described the Lemba as "the Slaamzyn (Islaams or Mahomedans) Kafirs" beyond the Soutpansberg. Scholars continued to find Muslim influences, and Arabic traces, in Lemba religious practices in the twentieth century. In any event, theories of historical diffusion seem to have had their greatest impact as instruments for distinguishing among the indigenous people on different southern African frontiers. As noted, the most popular nineteenth-century theories in the eastern Cape and Natal found that the Xhosa were Arabs and the Zulu were Jews. On the northern frontier, Sotho-Tswana people turned out to be ancient Egyptians, at least to the extent that their system of sacred animals could be compared with or traced back to an ancient Egyptian religion of animal worship. Remarkably, therefore, the comparative history of religions provided a symbolic vocabulary, like the animal emblems, that marked differences among African people on all the frontiers of southern Africa.[53]

After the closure of the northern frontier, European theorists tended to explain the Sotho-Tswana system of sacred animals as totemism. As we have seen, however, totemism could mean different things. In Europe, following John M'Lennan's formula, totemism might signify a symbolic system that merged fetishism with exogamy, thereby combining the worship of plants and animals with the obligation to marry outside of a totemic group that worshiped the same object. In southern Africa, however, totemism was given much more fluid renderings. It could signify a stable, organic "tribal" system, or a fossilized remnant of ancient animal worship, or even the symbolic expression through animal icons of reverence for the supreme "unknown God."

The Reverend Noel Roberts submitted a report in 1915 on the Bagananoa of Chief Malaboch, who had been conquered by Boer forces in 1894, and their system of sacred animals. Although their original sacred crocodile remained imprisoned in the Transvaal Museum in Pretoria, Roberts observed that the Bagananoa had made another for use in their male initiation ritual. Echoing earlier speculations about an Egyptian connection, Roberts highlighted what he thought was a striking resemblance between Bagananoa and ancient Egyptian ritual. "The most interesting point to be observed in these customs," Roberts proposed, "is to be found in the apparent resemblance to some ancient rites which became crystallized in the Egyptian Ritual, and which are recorded in 'The Book of the Dead.'" In the Egyptian myth of Seth and Horus, Seth turned into a snake, disappeared into a hole in the ground, and was imprisoned there by Horus, the god of light. Certain elements in this story—a snake, a hole in the ground, and the victory of light over darkness—also appeared, with some modification Roberts found, in the Bagananoa initiation ritual. The snake had been replaced by the crocodile, who was known

The sacred crocodile upside down. (From Roberts, "The Bagananoa or Ma-Laboch")

among the Bagananoa as "the father (or grandmother) of the Snake." During the ritual, the crocodile was taken out of a hole in the ground to be worshiped, but it was then turned upon its back and kept in a special place that was associated with the source of all knowledge and light. In conclusion, Roberts demanded, "Is not this symbolic imagery of the victory of Horus?"

Noel Roberts hoped that the possibility of some historical connection with the esoteric mysteries of ancient Egypt would inspire further studies of African religion in southern Africa. Whether on the Nile or the Nylstroom, the crocodile was a sacred animal. In addition to the crocodile, however, the Bagananoa also revered the baboon and the duiker. From this animal evidence, Roberts proposed that the history of the Bagananoa "tribe" could be reconstructed. Since the baboon was the sacred animal of the Bahurutsi, at some point the Bagananoa must have broken off from the Bahurutsi. Retaining the Bahurutsi baboon as a sacred emblem, the Bagananoa subsequently added the duiker to distinguish themselves from their original tribe. In this manner, the history of any tribe could be discovered by referring to its sacred animal emblems. Sacred animals, therefore, provided evidence for reconstructing the organic unity of African tribes in southern Africa. As Roberts suggested, each sacred animal represented a particular tribal specification of the generic Bantu religion. "The Bagananoa, like other Bantu tribes," he reported, "regard themselves as a distinct species of the genus *Bantu*, and the conception of a Specific or Tribal Spirit or Soul, uniting all members of the tribe is strongly developed."[54] On the closed frontier of the early twentieth century, therefore, as Roberts's work indicated, comparative religion in southern Africa assumed a dual mandate: it could reconstruct "tribal" religions on the premise that each had its own "Specific or Tribal Spirit or Soul," but it could also abstract the outlines of a generic Bantu religion that supposedly encompassed all Africans living in southern Africa.

6

BEYOND THE FRONTIER

IN SOUTHERN AFRICA, comparative religion was conducted on frontier battlefields. Comparisons were not merely intellectual exercises. They were entangled in the European conquest and subjugation of Africans. Initially, European observers denied the existence of any indigenous African religion. The enemy had no religion. Under colonial control, however, Africans were recognized as having a religion that could be inventoried and analyzed. In the Cape, the Hottentots gained, lost, and regained that recognition with the fluctuations of an advancing colonial border. On other frontiers, European recognition of an indigenous African religion likewise depended upon colonial domination. The annexation of Zulus in Natal in 1843, the destruction of Xhosa independence following the Cattle-Killing in 1857, and the conquest of the last independent polities on the northern frontier in the 1890s all produced new discoveries of religion. Since the advance of colonial control was uneven, so was European acknowledgment of the existence of indigenous African religions. By the turn of the century, however, all Africans were credited not only with having indigenous religious systems but with sharing a generic Bantu religion that supposedly defined the beliefs and practices of all Africans in southern Africa. Having lost their political independence, Africans acquired this small compensation: they had a religion.

On the closed frontier of the twentieth century, European comparativists were able to fix Africans in place, and to freeze them in time, by reconstructing the contours of their traditional religious life. In providing an inventory of "Uncivilised Man" in southern Africa for a scientific handbook published in 1905, W. Hammond Tooke, who was serving as assistant under secretary for the Department of Agriculture of the Cape Colony, fixed and froze the Bantu in a timeless past. Tooke explained that he intended to describe Africans only "as they were before they were influenced in their character and habits by intercourse with the white man." Religion played an important role in that redescription. Hottentots and Bushmen worshiped nature, whether astral or animal, while the Bantu worshiped their ancestors. Terms for a god, a chief spirit, or an ancestral progenitor appeared in Bantu vocabularies, but their meanings were uncertain. In a systematic, purely factual manner, Tooke described the traditional beliefs, dispositions, and customs of the "uncivilised" as they supposedly had lived in a distant, precolonial past. As Tooke advised, "To describe them as they now are—in Reserves, Locations, or Compounds—is foreign to the writer's present purpose." Nevertheless, in all his descriptions of the Bantu, Tooke employed the present tense. "Thieving is with them a laudable achievement," he stated, for example, "and lying an elegant accomplishment." As Johannes Fabian has argued, the rhetoric of the ethnographic present has generally operated in anthropological discourse as an implicit strategy for denying the coeval temporality of the Other. On the closed frontier in southern Africa, however, the ethnographic present was a discursive strategy that also duplicated the reserves, locations, and compounds in the systematic containment of Africans. Confined in space, frozen in time, Africans were enclosed in the present tense of a new kind of comparative religion.[1]

South Africa's preeminent historian of the closed frontier was the Canadian emigrant, George McCall Theal. Avoiding the ministerial career that his father had intended for him, Theal came to the Cape and established himself as a diligent archivist. His publications were prodigious. Often characterized as a "settler historian" because he adopted a colonial perspective on every historical conflict in the region, Theal also tried to produce an authoritative historical ethnography of precolonial southern Africa. In his *Ethnography and Condition of South Africa before* A.D. *1505,* Theal inventoried the "native races" of the region, with special attention to religious beliefs and practices, as they supposedly had existed before European contact. Theal's work embodied both the containments and the contradictions of comparative religion on the closed frontier. On the one hand, all the indigenous people of the region—the Bushmen, the Hottentots, and the Bantu—could be contained within the ethnographic terms of their religious systems. In other words, their human characteristics could be defined and delimited by their religions. On the other hand, however, Theal affirmed the existence of African religions by using the same evidence with which they had previously been denied. For most of the nineteenth century, European findings about African fear or ignorance, childishness or degeneration, had constituted proof of an absence of religion. In Theal's treatment, these were the basic ingredients of African religious systems.

According to Theal, the Bushmen had a religion. They believed in a powerful being, known as 'Kaang or 'Cagn, and had some expectation of immortality that was demonstrated by their burial practices. They performed ritual dances and offered prayers to the moon and stars. However, Theal observed, "everything connected with their religion—that is, their dread of something outside of and more powerful than themselves—was vague and uncertain." This unclarity in Bushman religion, Theal explained, resulted from their endemic ignorance. The Bushmen were "as credulous in such matters as infants could be." Comparing Bushmen to European children, Theal observed that their "power of thought on subjects of any nature outside their ordinary occupations is not greater than that of a European child of six or seven years of age, and they have all the credulity of such a child." Their religion, therefore, was a product of childish credulity and ignorance. In this conclusion, Theal proposed not only a description of their mentality but also a historical genealogy of the Bushmen. They had much in common, he noted, with the Philippine, Andamanese, and Semang people of the Malay Peninsula. They shared common physical and linguistic traits. "Mentally especially this is the case," Theal concluded, that the Bushmen could be shown to be of the "same stock" as the indigenous people of Malaysia. On the basis of their shared religious mentality, therefore, Theal could conceptually relocate the Bushmen with the "pagan races of the Malay Peninsula" in their "common primeval home."[2]

Significantly, this conceptual removal of the Bushmen from the distant past of southern Africa resonated with Theal's settler interpretation of their historical destiny. According to Theal, the Bushmen were destined to be removed from southern Africa in the present in order "to satisfy God's law of progress." Under God's law, entitlement to the land depended upon a higher intelligence and greater strength than was evident in the religion of the Bushmen. As Theal declared the demands of God's law: "A struggle for the possession of the fairest tracts of country took place, and the more intelligent and consequently the stronger races were the victors. It was for the good of all the world that it should be so. It seems to be God's law that man must raise himself constantly higher, and he who cannot as well as he who will not conform to that law must pass out of existence." Like the ancient paleolithic cave dwellers of Europe, the Bushmen of southern Africa were destined to disappear. As Theal insisted, their removal from the land in southern Africa was according to divine law and for the greater good of the entire world. In his comparative religion, however, Theal had already conceptually removed the Bushmen from southern Africa not only by tracing them back to Malaysia but also by diminishing them as people with a religion based on a childish mentality.[3]

Similarly, Theal described the religion of the Hottentots as a system of childish morphology and foreign genealogical origin. As Theal recounted, the Hottentots venerated the mantis, worshiped the moon with singing and dancing, and revered the "mythical hero" Heitsi-eibib by building stone cairns around the Cape. They told a myth about a Supreme Being, Tsui-\\Goab, who had engaged in battle with an evil being, \\Gaunab. Theal was aware that the missionary ethnographer Theophilus Hahn had interpreted this story, under the influence of F. Max Müller, as a solar myth about the conflict between light and darkness at dawn. If that interpretation was correct, Theal remarked, then the Hottentot myth would have "had an origin as lofty in ideal as that of many of the Aryans." However, Theal found that such an exalted origin was impossible because "the credulity of the Hottentots was that of children." With their "childlike simplicity," the Hottentots displayed an inveterate ignorance in their religion, an ignorance so pervasive that "the system of religion of the Hottentots could not be explained by themselves."[4]

If the Hottentots could not understand their own religious system, how could European comparativists explain it? As Theal proposed, the ancient origin of Hottentot myth and religion could be found, not by comparison with Aryan solar mythology, but through the analysis of language. In 1851, Theal recalled, the Reverend Dr. James R. Adamson, the first minister of the Presbyterian Church in Cape Town and professor of mathematics at the South African College, had reported to the Syro-Egyptian Society that a close affinity could be established between the Hottentot language and "Old Egyptian." Perhaps influenced by the researches of W. H. I. Bleek, who made a similar finding in his doctoral dissertation, Adamson identified the Hottentots on linguistic grounds with ancient Egypt. Following this lead, Theal concluded that the Hottentots had "descended from men who once resided on or near the other extremity of the continent." In Theal's comparative account of language and religion, therefore, the Hottentots could also be conceptually displaced to a remote region of the world.[5]

Turning to the Bantu, Theal assumed, along with other European comparativists on the closed frontier, that Africans had a generic indigenous religion. "The religion of the Bantu," Theal observed, "was based upon the supposition of the existence of spirits that could interfere with the affairs of the world." In other words, Bantu religion was based on ancestor worship. Theal provided a thorough, detailed inventory of Bantu religion, along with an account of the "Superstitions and Customs of the Bantu" and "Specimens of Bantu Folklore." Although he placed less stress on the childishness of Bantu mentality, Theal framed his entire discussion of this religious system in terms of a historical reconstruction of African migrations from an ancient cultural center. As noted, frontier comparativists had also traced genealogies that placed indigenous southern Africans in ancient Arabia, Israel, or Egypt. Likewise, Theal supposed that the Bantu were recent arrivals in southern Africa. "At some time not exceedingly remote," he observed, "a band of people speaking the parent language of the various dialects now in use, and having ancestor worship as their religion, must have entered North-Eastern Africa." Surprisingly, however, Theal opted for none of the points of origin in the ancient Near East that had been so popular in the theories of frontier comparative religion. Instead, based on his analysis of their religion, Theal located the primordial home of the southern African Bantu not in the Near but in the Far East. As Theal explained:

In addition to language, religion must be taken into consideration when dealing with the past history of these people. It consists of a mixture of ancestor spirit worship and fetishism, in different proportions in different tribes. The first of these elements must have been brought from Asia, for it is widely prevalent there, and it is inconceivable that it could have had its origin in Central Africa. Fetishism was developed after their arrival in this continent, particularly by the tribes that mixed their blood with that of the more degraded negroes who were here before them.

As this formulation suggests, the key term in Theal's reconstruction of Bantu religion was *mixture*. According to Theal, Bantu religion had been constituted by the racial mixture of blood, the geographical mixture of separate peoples, and the illicit mixture of the two distinct forms of religion identified as ancestor worship and fetish worship. Lacking any inherent integrity or authenticity, Bantu religion was an aberration that had been produced by mixing race, region, and religion. As a result, its historical formation, according to Theal, had been a process of degeneration, as the ancestor worship of Asia became mixed with the degraded fetishism of Africa.[6]

Theal was well aware that European Christians in southern Africa at the beginning of the twentieth century were alarmed by recent African initiatives in forming independent Christian churches. The Ethiopian movement, which had started in the 1890s in Johannesburg and Pretoria, represented an innovation in African Christian leadership and theology that was outside the control of the European mission churches or colonial administration. In response, white church leaders accused this movement of engaging in an illicit mixture of Christian and African religion. Eventually, scholars applied the term *syncretism* to this phenomenon, ostensibly in explanation but also as a modulation of the same accusation. Addressing this issue directly, Theal proposed that syncretism, the illicit mixture of African and Christian forms of religion, appeared not only in the Ethiopian movement but also among the African converts of Christian missions because, he argued, their minds were "shackled by hereditary superstition."[7] In the context of this controversy about illicit religious mixtures, however, Theal had already established that African religion was itself a mixture, an inauthentic, degraded by-product of Bantu historical migrations.

Like the missionary and settler comparativists of the first half of the nineteenth century, Theal adopted a theory of degeneration to account for African religion in southern Africa. Likewise, he conjectured that Africans could be traced back to some distant geographical point of origin, thereby conceptually displacing them from southern Africa. Under the terms of the new Union government's Land Act of 1913, the displacement of Africans from most of the territory of the region carried the force of law. Although government land policy did not depend upon his legitimation, Theal nevertheless practiced a comparative religion that justified this dispossession. Bantu religion, as reconstructed by Theal, defined Africans as people with no historical entitlement to land in southern Africa since the syncretistic character of Bantu religion revealed that their original homeland was in Asia and that they had degenerated during the course of their racial mixtures and recent migrations into Africa. As both distant and degraded, Africans in southern Africa were represented in Theal's comparative religion as barbarians with no legal or political rights. He made this conclusion explicit. Invoking the law of God and history, Theal asserted the "right of civilised men to take possession of land occupied by such a race." Unfortunately, he added, "to the present no-one has devised a plan by which this can be done without violence."[8] As a strategic exercise of covert violence, however, the comparative religion advanced by George McCall Theal on the closed frontier of a new South Africa was already a violation of Africans. Without legal rights or political representation, Africans had to suffer Theal's historical representation of them and the effects of that representation. Clearly, if Theal set the standard for the practice of comparative religion on the closed frontier, no one had yet devised a plan by which comparative religion could be done without violence.

LAUGHTER AND PAIN

Although they were subjected to this process of colonial conquest, classification, and representation, Africans were certainly not passive victims. As noted, independent African initiatives also shaped the contours of frontier comparative religion. In resistance, accommodation, and creative improvisation, Africans conducted countermaneuvers on the battlefield of comparative religion in southern Africa. As Jean and John Comaroff have proposed, the nineteenth-century colonization of southern Africa can be seen as an intercultural exchange, a "long conversation," in which both African and European subjectivities were renegotiated in relation. In this regard, comparative religion was also negotiated and renegotiated in dialogical exchanges. Partners in conversation have been preserved in the historical record. We have heard the voice of the Hottentot traveler Coree in conversation with the British traveler Thomas Herbert. We have listened to interchanges between Ngqika and Van der Kemp, Ngidi and Colenso, Mbande and Callaway, Mxaba and Stuart, the "wily rainmaker" and Moffat, among many others, all struggling to work out religious comparisons in dialogue. As the work of Mpengula Mbande suggests, the most vital, crucial conversations were con-

ducted among Africans, as people debated, argued, and reconfigured their identities in new religious idioms. Although most of
these conversations have been lost or submerged in the historical
record, they must have engaged comparisons that profoundly affected African self-understanding. As elsewhere in the nineteenth
century, African religious understanding increasingly depended
upon a comparative religion, and the character of comparative
religion depended upon ongoing cross-cultural conversations.

A comparative religion, therefore, was forged in those conversations. They were serious conversations. Lives and life-ways depended upon their outcome. Why, then, was laughter a recurring
feature? Frequently, the historical record captures the sudden
smile, the loud laugh, the peal of mirth, the general merriment,
and even the ludicrous mimicry through which Africans compared the religion of the Christian mission with their own religious way of life. Robert Moffat was by no means the first European comparative religionist to inspire laughter by confusing the
categories of local culture. As mentioned previously, François Le
Vaillant testified that when he read Peter Kolb's account of Hottentot customs to Khoikhoi people, "They laughed in my face."
In turn, however, Le Vaillant himself was a target for Xhosa jokes.
According to Van der Kemp, "It was only to deceive Mr. Vaillant
and to amuse themselves at his expense, if the Caffrees whom he
met with, offered him milk in a basket, washed out with their
urine, to make him believe that this was customary among
them." In the context of intercultural contact, laughter echoed.
What did laughter signify in the frontier comparative religion of
southern Africa?[9]

Laughter

On some occasions, laughter certainly signified a rejection of the
religious claims of the Christian mission. On his journey through
Natal and Zululand in the 1830s, Allen Gardiner recalled that
Mfengu refugees patiently listened to his lecture on the Christian
doctrines of God, immortality, the resurrection, and the last judgment, "but an audible laugh instantly proceeded from all who
were present, on my telling them that God had declared in his
Word that man's heart was full of sin." In this case, laughter
served a critical function in rejecting a theological assertion that
the Mfengu perceived as absurd. Sometimes, this rejection of

Christian claims was amplified and modulated by satirizing the religious notions or practices of the Christian mission. For example, Archdeacon Nathaniel J. Merriman, on a tour of the eastern Cape in 1849, recorded a conversation with a Xhosa chief, Umhala. When Merriman refused the chief's request for a blanket, Umhala launched into a theological satire that mocked the religious assumptions of the Christian mission. As Umhala proclaimed, "he knew God was good; He gave them water; He gave them grass, He gave them gum; and would I give him a blanket?" As Merriman still refused to give him a blanket, Chief Umhala laughed and changed the subject. Merriman was left at a loss to make sense out of Umhala's sense of humor in this exchange. For another example, African imitations of the practices of the mission on the northern frontier frequently produced laughter. As James Chapman observed, people in one Bechuana town "laugh at Livingstone telling them about God, mimic him preaching and singing, and the chief and his councillors fill the air with shouts and yells." During his mission to the Ndebele of Chief Mzilikazi, John Mackenzie learned "that the chief, after we left his presence, proceeded, amid the merriment of his attendants, to draw a ludicrous picture of the state of Matabele [Ndebele] society were the Christian views adopted."[10]

At the very least, such jokes and mimes revealed the possibility that frontier comparative religion could actually be funny. In the play of difference, people smiled. In the recognition of incongruity, they laughed and shouted at the absurdity. Since comparative religion required people to reflect upon alternative realities, some of the alternatives provoked laughter. Humor played a critical, reflective role in intercultural contact. From the sudden peal of mirth to the satirical mimicry, African comparativists advanced critical responses to the intercultural encounter of different religions. Amidst the widespread confusion of cultural categories, laughter attended the comparison of different religious beliefs, practices, and forms of social organization on southern African frontiers.

However, in their frequent complaints about this practice, as in the case of Robert Moffat, nineteenth-century missionaries interpreted African laughter only as an ignorant, stubborn resistance to their gospel. While maintaining their gravity, the missionaries were often met with humorous responses that they interpreted as ridicule. Not only worrying about African laughter, Moffat also looked back over his shoulder to those scoffers in Europe who have "laughed to scorn every article of our creed, and have died martyrs to atheism!" Clearly, the missionaries displayed a strong apprehension about being mocked by laughter. As a result, they could only experience laughter as mockery. Moffat seemed particularly sensitive about Africans laughing at his religious concepts, his proposals for rearranging gender roles, and even his foreign notions about hygiene. Moffat's insistence that people should wash their bodies with soap and water, instead of lubricating them with animal fat and red ocher, "contributed to their amusement in no small degree." On one occasion, Moffat told his Tswana cook to turn the meat on the fire with a stick or fork instead of his greasy hands. "This suggestions made him and his companions laugh extravagantly," Moffat recalled, "and they were wont to repeat it as an interesting joke wherever they came."[11]

Although Moffat also repeated this joke by publishing it, he took no delight in the interplay of its humor. He followed a much more serious agenda. In the face of African laughter, the missionaries could draw some consolation from contemplating the ultimate revenge that would be exacted on anyone who laughed at their religion and culture. When the missionary Thomas Hodgson warned the Tswana chief Sefunelo that God would punish people who presumed that they could affect the rains through ritual acts, Sefunelo responded with laughter. "He laughed," Hodgson reported, "at the idea of the Almighty being angry with him for attempting such a presumptuous act." The African chief might respond with laughter, but the missionary anticipated that in the end he would have the last laugh, as Hodgson informed Chief Sefunelo "that he would see things in a different light when he died."[12] Obviously, therefore, from the Christian missionary perspective, comparative religion was no laughing matter.

Only rarely did a European observer suspect that laughter was evidence of comparative religion. At the beginning of the nineteenth century, the traveler Henry Lichtenstein observed that the "Beetjuana" people were always in a good mood, laughing easily and loudly at anything that surprised them, especially if they wanted to show their appreciation. As Lichtenstein observed, the missionaries were distressed by African laughter. He noted that the missionaries "maintained that they could achieve nothing because the Beetjuanas ridiculed divine service and laughed about the teachings of Christianity." However, instead of interpreting this laughter as a symptom of stubborn resistance or inveterate ignorance, Lichtenstein proposed that people laughed because they were comparing Christianity to their own beliefs. If that was the case, their laughter indicated that Africans might after all hold "a kind of religious conviction."[13] In raising this possibility, therefore, Lichtenstein suggested that laughter might be understood as evidence of an African practice of comparison. In the juxtaposition of different beliefs and practices on the frontier, laughter might be a reflex that registered the existence of a kind of comparative religion. This interpretation of laughter as an index of comparison was one of the lost opportunities of frontier comparative religion in southern Africa.

Why do people laugh? In his book-length analysis of laughter, the French philosopher Henri Bergson proposed that people laugh when they observe human beings behaving like machines. The fundamental basis of laughter, Bergson argued, is the sudden, surprising perception of incongruity that occurs whenever human beings are observed acting with the inflexibility or absent-mindedness of a mechanical object. In this analysis, Bergson located the source of humor in the contradiction that arises whenever humans behave in unconscious, automatic, or inflexible ways like machines. When a human acts like an automaton, people laugh. We can find evidence of this phenomenon on southern African frontiers. For example, the LMS missionary John Campbell complained in 1815 that Bechuana boys and girls followed him, asked him questions, and laughed at him as he continued walking without answering. "I was grieved I could not understand a single word," Campbell recalled, "but this very circumstance afforded them much entertainment." Inflexibly, absent-mindedly, the missionary produced laugher by acting like a machine.[14]

As already noted, however, this identification of the European Christian missionaries with machines was an important feature of African comparative religion in southern Africa. Robert Moffat's adversary, the "wily rainmaker," delighted the crowd by asserting that the sacred emblem of the Europeans was a machine. In the beginning, Europeans had emerged from the bed of reeds under the sacred sign of a mechanical device, the wagon or the plow. They were, accordingly, the people of the machine. In the interplay of intercultural relations, therefore, Europeans provoked laughter because they behaved in ways that were as inflexible and automatic as any machine. Although they might be powerful and dangerous, Europeans were also funny because they did not act like human beings. Africans noticed and responded by laughing.

In the sound of their laughter, significant questions about what it might mean to be a human being were put into play in the practice of frontier comparative religion.

Pain

While Henri Bergson's philosophical analysis of laughter was being serialized in the *Revue de Paris*, his compatriot, the anthropologist and philosopher Lucien Lévy-Bruhl, was pursuing research that culminated in 1910 in the publication of his first book on "primitive mentality," *Les Fonctions mentales dans les sociétés inférieures*. Analyzing "how natives think," Lévy-Bruhl proposed that "primitive" people "do not seem to us to rise to the level of what we properly term 'thought.'" Instead, they display a "prelogical" or "mystical" mentality. Lacking any trace of scientific rationality, that primitive mentality, according to Lévy-Bruhl, followed its own "law of participation," which assumed that the world was permeated with unseen forces. Basically, primitive mentality confused thoughts and things, so "primitives," as a result, were unable to make rational distinctions. Although he collected evidence from all over the world, Lévy-Bruhl made considerable use of southern African data in building his model of "primitive mentality." As a result, he reinscribed the reports of nineteenth-century travelers, missionaries, and colonial agents into his scientific theory of primitive religion and thought. For example, as proof of the existence of a prelogical mentality in Africa, Lévy-Bruhl repeated the assertion by LMS official John Philip that southern Africans lived in a complete "state of ignorance."[15]

According to Lévy-Bruhl, African ignorance was demonstrated by their propensity for laughter. In arguing that Africans, like other "primitives," were incapable of abstract thought, Lévy-Bruhl invoked the testimony of the missionary Thomas Arbousset. "In the midst of the laughter and applause of the populace," Arbousset had reported, "the heathen inquirer is heard saying: 'Can the God of the white men be seen by our eyes? . . . and if *Morimo* (God) is absolutely invisible, how can a reasonable being worship a hidden thing?'" Certainly, the laughter in this case could be subjected to various interpretations. Was it inspired by a shared perception of incongruity in the context of an interreligious argument? Was it a reasonable response to the perceived irrationality of the mission? Was it a psychological defense against the encroachments of a Christian mission that was confusing and disrupting indigenous cultural categories? Or was it simply a popular response to a playful joke at the expense of the missionary? Taking sides with the missionary, however, Lévy-Bruhl froze African laughter by concluding that it was only evidence of a "lack of serious thought and an absence of reflection." Instead of recognizing laughter as a significant comparative impulse, and therefore as an act of rational reflection on cultural and religious difference, Lévy-Bruhl perpetuated the seriousness of the missionaries. Like Robert Moffat, Lévy-Bruhl maintained his intellectual gravity by refusing to hear any rationality in the sound of African laughter. Ironically, therefore, while Bergson was arguing that people laugh at human beings who act like absent-minded machines, Lévy-Bruhl insisted that primitives only laugh because they are themselves essentially absent-minded.[16]

However, Africans did not only laugh; they also experienced pain in their encounters with Europeans. The naturalist William J. Burchell reported about his African companion that "abstract questions of the plainest kind soon exhausted all mental strength and reduced him to the state of a child whose reason was yet dormant. He would then complain that his head began to ache." Similarly, the missionary and ethnographer H. A. Junod recounted that abstract thought caused pain among Africans. "When requiring reasoning," Junod observed, "it is a painful occupation." In citing and repeating these claims by travelers and missionaries, Lévy-Bruhl concluded that primitives avoided thinking and reasoning because it was painful. Although encounters with Europeans actually caused real pain and suffering for Africans, he used their pain as evidence of an absence of rational thought. Pain provided further proof that Africans did not rise to the level of rationality.[17]

African laughter and pain, therefore, were taken by Lucien Lévy-Bruhl as proof of a primitive mentality. Like laughter and pain, African bafflement before new European technology, especially the technologies of literacy and warfare, also demonstrated, according to Lévy-Bruhl, an absence of rational thought. "Printed books and writing," he observed, "are no less astonishing to primitives than are firearms." In southern Africa, he noted, literacy was confusing. "My books puzzled them," the missionary Robert Moffat had reported. However, Lévy-Bruhl was aware that Africans consistently explained books, particularly the Bible, in local idiom, as "instruments of divination." By comparing books to divining bones, which was a perceptive analogy, Africans certainly evidenced skills in analogical reasoning. According to Lévy-Bruhl, however, following the interpretation of the missionaries once again, this analogy was evidence of an African inability to understand literacy or any other form of European technology. "The primitive no more tries to explain it," he concluded, "than he does to find out why the rifle and cannon carry death to so great a distance." As a subtext in his analysis of primitive mentality, therefore, Lévy-Bruhl dismissed the useful analogy between books and divining bones by drawing his own analogy between books and guns, two technologies that signified and demonstrated European power in Africa.[18]

Finally, he concluded that Africans had no appreciation for detached or disinterested scientific rationality. Missionaries complained that Africans were suspicious about modern science and, in particular, about scientific medical practice. In 1908, as Lévy-Bruhl recalled, the missionary Henri Dieterlen reported that "the blacks think the whites wish to injure them, or wish them no good. They do not believe in their disinterestedness. They are distrustful, for fear of being deceived, despoiled, injured, and led into misfortune. These feelings are innate and quite natural to them; they are irresistible and ineradicable." African mistrust of European medical practice was abstracted by the missionary from its historical context. It was characterized as an "innate" feeling, as "natural," and, in terms that Lévy-Bruhl repeated, as an "ineradicable" feature of a primitive mentality. However, in historical context, African disbelief in European "disinterestedness" was understandable because people had in fact been "deceived, despoiled, injured, and led into misfortune." Nevertheless, Lévy-Bruhl persisted in reading justifiable suspicion as primitive superstition. It was an "innate" primitive mentality that was "natural" among the indigenous people of southern Africa and elsewhere in the colonized world.[19]

For whatever reasons this caricature of "primitive mentality" might have been attractive in Europe, it was produced and reproduced on the southern African periphery in stereotypes of the "Essential Kaffir" or the "Bantu mind."[20] These stereotypes gave the model of primitive mentality its local significance as a symbolic instrument of social segregation, economic exploitation, and political control that could easily be transposed from justifications of nineteenth-century colonial domination to the implementation of twentieth-century apartheid. The roots of these notions, however, run deep in the frontier comparative religion of nineteenth-century southern Africa. In many respects, the idea of a primitive mentality was built on the foundations laid by travelers, missionaries, and colonial agents. It might be useful, therefore, to review the comparative strategies that they developed in pursuing a comparative religion on the frontier battlefields of southern Africa.

COMPARATIVE STRATEGIES

European comparative religion developed a repertoire of comparative procedures to account for religious resemblance and diversity.[21] On southern African frontiers, however, these procedures were exercised in specific social, economic, and political contexts. As previously noted, the earliest comparative strategy was denial. From 1610 to 1654, from 1685 to 1700, and from 1770 to 1800, European comparativists denied that Hottentots had any religion. Often the lack of religion was identified as only one aspect of a more general absence of basic human features such as language, law, or marriage. Increasingly, however, European observers pointed to the absence of specific religious doctrines or practices. As the traveler Thomas Herbert insisted, the Hottentots had no God, heaven, hell, temples, worship, ceremonies, sabbath, shame, or truth. Such denials were repeated on every frontier. Van der Kemp, Lichtenstein, and Alberti reported that the Xhosa had no religion. Isaacs claimed that the Shaka's Zulu lacked religion. Casalis and Moffat insisted that the Sotho-Tswana were "endemical atheists" from whom every trace of religion had been erased. Sometimes these denials were framed as an argument against the notion of natural religion. Missionary comparativists, in particular, used southern African data to refute the hypothesis that innate religious ideas or sentiments could be found among all human beings. In southern Africa, they had made the remarkable discovery of people with no religion.

What did these denials signify in the frontier context? Certainly, they indicated that European comparativists were operating with a single set of criteria for what counted as religion, criteria that in most cases were defined by Protestant doctrine and worship. In performative terms, denial reinforced the power and scope of that single construction of religion. However, denials of African religion also implied that Africans were not fully human since they allegedly lacked such a crucial defining feature of humanity. In the 1870s Henry Callaway came to recognize that these earliest denials had in fact suggested that Africans were "not human beings, but a lower class of animal with the form, but without the mental characteristics of man." Through the denial of religion, European observers represented Africans as an empty space. "What a blank is the life of man," Allen Gardiner had exclaimed, "without a knowledge of God!"[22]

Lacking a knowledge of God, or any other feature of religion, Africans appeared as precisely such a blank, empty space. But then so did their land. The European "myth of the vacant land" depicted the frontier as an empty territory waiting for colonial settlement. As that "vacant" space was filled with European settlers and controlled by colonial administrations, it was also filled and controlled conceptually by European comparative religionists. As Henry Methuen declared in 1846, "There is a blank on the maps to be filled up: there are numerous tribes whose names, probably, have never been heard, and whose customs can only be imperfectly imagined by the analogy of kindred races: there is fallow ground for the naturalist and the philosopher."[23] That blank space was eventually filled with religions not merely by exploring, collecting data, and gaining familiarity but through procedures of comparison and generalization. As noted, however, the "discovery" of religions depended upon the closing of frontiers. As European hegemony was established, denial lost its strategic value and was replaced by the production of knowledge about religion and religions that was suited to the interests of colonial management and control. Although missionaries, philosophers, and naturalists contributed to the production of useful knowledge about African religion, the supreme authorities on comparative religion were colonial agents and agencies, from Joseph Cox Warner to the British War Office, who could put that knowledge to use in "native" administration.

As a comparative strategy, the distinction between religion and superstition also served the interests of denial. In ancient Roman usage, as Emile Benveniste noted, the piety of *religio* was defined as the contrary of the fear and ignorance of *superstitio*. The "notion of 'religion' requires, so to speak, by opposition, that of 'superstition.'" Only rarely did Europeans notice the inherently oppositional character of their notions of religion and superstition.

As Thomas Hobbes observed, the "fear of things invisible is the natural seed of that, which everyone in himself calleth religion; and in them that worship or fear that power otherwise than they do, superstition." Having a long history in European comparative religion, this opposition between religion and superstition was consistently deployed on contested southern African frontiers. François Le Vaillant was alone in suggesting that superstition was an inevitable by-product of religion. Every other observer insisted on the categorical opposition between genuine religion and spurious superstition. Identifying superstition, therefore, was the equivalent of denying the existence of religion. Not merely an act of denial, however, the designation of beliefs and practices as "superstition" resonated with key terms in Protestant anti-Catholic polemic. From the perspective of the London Missionary Society, superstition reigned in Catholic France as it did in heathen Africa. Like pagano-papism, African superstition was characterized as an ignorant, fearful, and magical regard for objects and the dead. Eventually, during the nineteenth century, these same categories came to constitute the basic ingredients for scholarly representations of African religion.[24]

Representations of African Religion

Drawing on a long heritage of European theory, comparativists in southern Africa could explain African religion as ignorance, fear, imposture, the elevation of the dead to divine status, or the deification of natural objects. All these explanations, at one time or another, were deployed on southern African frontiers. Ignorance and fear, for example, were commonly invoked as explanations for the origin of African superstition. As John Philip proposed, all superstitions had originated in ignorance, in "confused ideas of an invisible agency." John Barrow held that "fear is the parent of superstition." Having venerable ancient Greek antecedents, these explanations for the origin of religion had been revived and popularized during the eighteenth-century Enlightenment. On southern African frontiers, however, they had a more specific, localized import. Explanations of superstition reinforced the frontier stereotype of Africans as permanent children. Because they were supposedly as stupid and frightened as children, Africans had developed superstitions that were based on ignorance and fear. As long as Africans persisted in such childish beliefs and practices, they had no adult rights to land, livestock, or political autonomy that had to be respected by Europeans. In this regard, comparative religion was complicit in the Africans' displacement and dispossession.[25]

In addition, these explanations supported the impression that the heart of African religion was "savage" terror. As William Holden described an African ritual conducted by a Zulu sacred specialist, "The spectacle is one of terror and dismay, differing from those of Greece and Rome, where the priests or vestals performed their sacred rites amidst the most profound awe, and the mysterious solemnities of their hallowed temples; whilst the vulgar, common horde were not permitted to enter the god-honoured enclosures, only the privileged few being admitted there." Unlike the solemn dignity of ancient Greek ritual, a dignity ensured by rigid class distinctions, African ritual evoked only mass hysteria and wild fear, with "the multitude looking on with astonishment and terror, whilst the frenzied being professes to hold audience with the spirits of the departed." If African religion was based on mass terror, some comparativists concluded that it had to be combated by a greater terror in the frontier campaign to establish "Christian civilization." As the British settler John Mitford Bowker put it, the colonial government had to use military force to cause the "savages" to "fear and respect, to *stand in awe* of a nation whose manners and customs, whose religion, it is beneficial and desirable for them to adopt" (emphasis in original). In this frontier calculus of terror, the "fear theory" of the origin and persistence of religion assumed a specific local significance. Since African superstition was supposedly based on terror, the military exercise of terror against them by a Christian government could be justified as an appropriate means for replacing superstition with religion.[26]

If ignorance and fear were the roots of African superstition, its branches were found in the deification of the dead and of natural objects. The identification of these two aspects of superstition also could rely upon ancient Greek theories. Around 300 B.C.E., Euhemerus lent his name to a theory of the origin of religion by proposing that the Greek gods and goddesses had once been men and women. As benevolent rulers, they had been held in such high esteem that they continued to be worshiped as divine beings after their deaths.[27] This euhemerist explanation was adopted by such frontier comparativists as Stephen Kay, Thomas Pringle, and Robert Moffat to explain African divine beings as deified ancient heroes. While pursuing this demythification of African divine beings, however, frontier comparativists often referred to the ancestors who were venerated in ritual as African gods. Ironically, therefore, African divine beings were interpreted as ancient heroes, while their ancient heroes were identified as gods who were propitiated by gifts and sacrifices. In either case, however, African superstition was reduced to the deification of the dead.

Concerning the deification of natural objects, most European comparativists entered the frontier with the assumption, as the magistrate Ludwig Alberti put it, that there were people in the world who worshiped the sun or other natural objects. Here as well an ancient Greek theory could be invoked. The sophist Prodicus of Ceos found the origin of religion in the linguistic process that turned words for objects into proper names, personified those proper names, and then transformed those personifications into gods. As the Greeks had substituted the proper name *Haphaestos* for *fire* and then worshiped that personification of fire under that proper name, so had all the gods and goddesses been created by the deification of objects. A version of this theory was revived in Europe during the nineteenth century by F. Max Müller, and it also appeared in southern Africa in the comparative philology pursued by W. H. I. Bleek. However, most frontier comparativists did not require the linguistic sophistication of this theory to find the deification of objects in African superstition. In report after report, European observers claimed to have discovered that Africans worshiped the moon, insects, birds, animals, trees, bones, piles of stones, and even an anchor that had been washed ashore on the eastern Cape coast. Along with the worship of the dead, therefore, this propensity to deify natural objects became the other major defining feature of African superstition or religion.[28]

Global Comparison

Frontier comparative religion, however, was not only engaged in defining African religion. It also produced and reproduced knowledge about all the religions of the world. In order to discover one new religion, frontier theorists had to establish comparisons between the one and the many, the new and the old, the strange and the familiar. In the process, they effectively reinvented all the world's religions. At the end of the eighteenth century, knowledge about Judaism, Islam, Roman Catholicism, and the religions of ancient Israel, Greece, and Rome all had to be reproduced in the Cape in order to make sense out of the invented religion of the forger Stephanos the Pole. A similar body of knowledge had to be reproduced in order to discover the religion of the Hottentots. Although they might not have been idolaters like the Hindus and Buddhists of Asia, Africans did have beliefs and practices that seemed to resemble those of other religions, especially if the Xhosa could be identified as "Ishmaelitish sons of Abraham," the Zulu as lost tribes of Israel, or the Sotho-Tswana as ancient Egyptians. In these "learned speculations," with their play of similarity and difference, a frontier comparative religion in southern Africa developed global strategies for the comparison of religions. Three basic kinds of global comparison—taxonomy, genealogy, and morphology—can be isolated for review.

In natural history, the Swedish scientist Linnaeus established taxonomy as the basic comparative principle for the organization of plants, animals, and humans into *genus* and *species differentia*. As noted, his students Anders Sparrmann and C. P. Thunberg visited the Cape to collect data that could be fitted into the Linnaean taxonomy. Although the *differentia* of the *species Homo Africanus* had prepared them to find people who were phlegmatic, relaxed, and governed by irrational caprice, the natural scientists reproduced frontier prejudices against Hottentots who were regarded as lazy because they resisted working for the colonists and stupid because they did not appreciate the trade value of cattle. In the global taxonomy of natural history, however, these local realities were erased as Africans were abstracted and incorporated as a distinctive species of human being.

Similarly, during the eighteenth century, European comparativists regarded religion as a *genus* divisible by *species differentia*, particularly into the *species* of Christianity, Judaism, Islam, and Paganism. On southern African frontiers, however, a different taxonomy began to emerge by the middle of the nineteenth century. The incorporation of an African religious system required the reconfiguration of the global taxonomy of the religions of the world. Using "worship" as the *genus*, frontier theorists identified three basic types of religion in the world: God, idol, and ancestor worship. As a result, Christianity, Judaism, and Islam were collapsed into one species of religion, God worship. While searching for the "unknown God" in Africa, frontier comparativists discovered that three different religions actually belonged to the same monotheistic species of religion. The category of Paganism, however, was divided into Asian and African religions. In many cases, African religion was further divided into the fetish worship of West Africa, the sidereal worship of the Hottentots, and the ancestor worship of the southern African Bantu. We have seen how the distinction between sidereal and ancestor worship was crucial to Bleek's linguistic theory of the origin of religion. Frequently, however, missionaries and magistrates used this taxonomy to locate the Africans under their jurisdiction between two evil extremes, the fetish worship of West Africa and the idol worship of Asia. Southern African ancestor worshipers might be pagans, they suggested, but they were not as degraded, nor as resistant to colonial management and control, as were fetish and idol worshipers. With some variation, this taxonomy remained implicit in the discourse of comparative religion in southern Africa throughout the second half of the nineteenth century and well into the twentieth century.

Frontier comparativists were also interested in tracing the religious genealogy of the indigenous people of southern Africa. Many favored a theory of historical degeneration from some ancient, original religion. Missionary theorists, including the prominent comparative religionist Henry Callaway, were especially fond of a three-stage theory of the history of African religion. This missionary explanation posited an original revelation, which was forgotten during a long historical process of degeneration, but which was gradually being recalled under the recent influence of the Christian mission. On the contested frontier, however, the degenerate was also a synonym for the dangerous. Settlers such as Robert Godlonton and John Bowker repeated the historical argument about African religious degeneration in their appeals for British military intervention in the eastern Cape. Accusing the mission of failure, they insisted that the degraded and dangerous Africans had to be civilized, by destroying their political independence, before they could be Christianized. This argument was repeated on other frontiers as settlers and missionaries often drew different practical implications from the same historical theory. As a genealogical hypothesis, therefore, the theory of African degeneration from an original revealed religion was entangled in strategic debates about the most effective means of advancing Christian civilization in southern Africa.

As previously described, however, Africans on different frontiers were often thought to have degenerated from specific ancient religions. Although undisciplined or idiosyncratic, the intensive study of languages, customs, and religions supported historical reconstructions that traced Africans back to some original home. Peter Kolb self-consciously employed comparative religion to establish that the Hottentots had originated in ancient Israel, by way of the Troglodytes, as children of Abraham. Mentzel speculated that their original home must have been in Carthage, Phoenicia, Tyre, Sidon, or, perhaps, ancient Israel. Years later, Moffat, Colenso, and Bleek, also employing comparative methods, argued that Egypt was the ancient home of the Hottentots. Likewise, frontier theorists retraced the genealogy of the Xhosa to ancient Arabia, the Zulu to ancient Israel, and the Sotho-Tswana to ancient Egypt. In the comparative religion of colonial frontiers, what was the significance of such genealogies? If Africans could be traced back to some original homeland, then southern Africa was not their real home. The indigenous people were not indigenous. Africans, like the colonizers, could be understood as relatively recent intruders in the region, with no ancient genealogical claim to the land. The frontier genealogy of religions, therefore, contributed to the production, as Sir Bartle Frere observed at the first meeting of the South African Philosophical Society, of "the well-ascertained fact that the Kafir races are recent comers into this part of South Africa."[29]

A very different kind of genealogy emerged in the work of W. H. I. Bleek. Against the general trend of finding African evidence for religious degeneration or historical diffusion, Bleek argued that Africans represented a preservation of the origin of religion. In southern Africa, the Bantu and Khoisan had preserved religion's dual origin. By analyzing the different grammatical structures of their languages, Bleek was able to propose that they exemplified the original ancestor worship and sidereal worship of humanity. Bleek introduced an evolutionary scheme that traced the genealogy of all religion back to a primordial ancestor worship. From that origin, religion had evolved through the worship of heavenly bodies, the proliferation of sky gods, and the gradual emergence of monotheism. In southern Africa, therefore, Bleek found the raw materials for reconstructing the evolution of religion. Bleek's work on evolution was intended to reconstruct the religious genealogy, not of Africans, but of humanity in general and, more specifically, of "civilized" Europe. He tried to demonstrate "how essential is a comparison of the branches of humankind spread over Africa, to an investigation of the earlier developments of our race." Therefore, Bleek's comparative philology and comparative religion were techniques that ultimately revealed a European genealogy.[30]

In conversation with international scholarship, Bleek was aware of the general shift from taxonomy to genealogy in European comparative religion. The earlier inventory of four world religions had been replaced by the Comtean developmental sequence of fetishism, polytheism, and monotheism. However, Bleek's evolutionism was extremely rare in southern African comparative religion until the beginning of the twentieth century. In southern Africa, evolution was a theory of comparative religion best suited to the conditions of the closed frontier. Displaced and dispossessed under colonial control, Africans suddenly appeared as living fossils for an evolutionary theory of religion. However, from the perspective of evolutionists, Africans also seemed to be disappearing. By the turn of the century, salvage ethnography undertook the task of recording traditional beliefs and customs that appeared to be rapidly vanishing under the impact of modern social transformations. Accordingly, at the beginning of the twentieth century, an evolutionary comparative religion tried to provide a new religious genealogy for Africans. In its dual mandate, evolutionary comparative religion reified tribal religious differences and abstracted a "primitive mentality" that defined a generic Bantu religion. However, this evolutionary comparative religion also reinforced the displacement of Africans in southern Africa. Put bluntly: if the earlier frontier genealogies, which traced Africans back to the ancient Near East, implied that Africans did not belong *here*, this new evolutionary genealogy suggested that Africans, as fossils of the tribal and the primitive, did not belong *now*. Once again, therefore, comparative religion was entangled in local conflicts over land in southern Africa.

Finally, frontier theorists developed morphological comparisons in southern Africa that identified the basic forms, structures, or functions of religion. Like genealogy, morphology was also a global comparison. In principle, it allowed comparisons to be drawn between religious forms from all over the world that were otherwise unconnected by geographical proximity or historical process. Through morphology, comparativists could establish formal, structural, or functional resemblances. As we have seen, the primary archetype in frontier comparative religion was the "unknown God." One biblical text from the Book of Acts (17:23–24) was sufficient to provide a charter for missionary comparative religion in nineteenth-century southern Africa. Although Robert

Moffat bemoaned the absence of any unknown God among indigenous people, Colenso found it among the Zulu, Callaway among the Xhosa, and Ellenberger among the Sotho-Tswana. However, even when they found the unknown God, comparativists decided that the pure archetype had been so mixed with other religious forms, especially with ancestor worship, that African religion could not be identified as a monotheism.

If the unknown God was the primary archetype, then Satan was the secondary form of religion identified in the morphological analysis of frontier comparative religion. In the Satanic structuralism of Robert Moffat, the basic forms of the religions of the world had been authored by Satan as obstacles to the Christian mission. The explanation of religions as products of evil forces was popular with early Church Fathers, who often identified pagan gods as demons. Moffat entrenched a similar comparative strategy in southern Africa not only by insisting on Satan's evil agency in the production of religions but also by translating the Sotho-Tswana term *barimo* as "demons." But Moffat's morphological comparison also identified the crucial structural position of local African sacred specialists, who, like the *angekoks, pawpaws,* or *greegrees* that missionaries had encountered elsewhere, were the formal "pillars of Satan's kingdom" of religions. In architectural terms, Moffat compared basic forms of religion as structural barriers. Religious forms were comparable to the extent that they assumed similar roles in blocking the advance of the mission. On this basis, for example, missionary comparativists could equate African custom with Hindu caste. They were equivalent, in structural terms, as religious obstacles to the gospel.[31]

As a supplement to this Satanic structuralism, a Satanic functionalism appeared on the eastern Cape frontier during the 1850s in the work of Joseph Cox Warner. Although he was the first to designate Xhosa superstition as a "religious system," Warner nevertheless assumed that it was a false religion "under Satanic influence." Even a false religion, however, met basic human needs. In satisfying the needs for psychological comfort and social stability, Xhosa religion operated as a functional system. In functional terms, Warner could also draw a morphological comparison between African custom and Hindu caste. They were not equivalent structures, however, but institutions that performed the same psychological and social functions. Like Moffat, Warner also concluded that African religious systems represented structural obstacles to the advance of "Christian civilization." He proposed that only military force would eventually succeed in breaking them up. In the meantime, however, it was essential that the magistrate should know how African religious systems worked. To enforce more efficient management and control, colonial agents had to understand African religions as functional systems.

At the highest degree of formal abstraction, theorists eventually invented a generic Bantu religion that was suited to the conditions of the closed frontier at the end of the nineteenth century. Once all independent African polities had been broken, comparative religion provided the resources for defining the religion that was common to all Africans under colonial control. Ironically, therefore, indigenous religion, which was allegedly absent at the beginning of the century, was declared universal among Africans by the end of the century. In many respects, this generic religion was similar to earlier constructions of African superstition. The Bantu religion was supposedly based on ignorance, fear, magic, the worship of the dead, and the deification of objects. In abstracting that generic religion, however, theorists could draw inspiration from the new procedures that had been developed in European comparative religion. In that comparative method, the notion of superstition had been redefined. Not merely ignorance or fear, superstition was a survival, literally a "standing over," from the prehistoric origin and early development of humanity.[32] Comparativists could identify the superstitious beliefs of modern children, women, peasants, the urban underclass, and colonized subjects as "survivals" from the prehistoric past of humanity. But what had survived? What original trace lingered in the superstitious beliefs and practices of colonized people that had been recorded by travelers, missionaries, and colonial agents from all over the world? It was neither the presence of the unknown God nor the authorship of Satan. It was not evidence of a process of historical diffusion through which religions had migrated from ancient cultural centers. It was not even the basic forms, structures, or functions of religion. What survived in primitive religion was a mentality.

THE UNANCHORED MENTALITY

If we return for a moment to the eastern Cape at the beginning of the nineteenth century, we recall the fascination with which a shipwrecked anchor was discovered by the missionary Van der Kemp, the traveler Lichtenstein, and the colonial magistrate Alberti. They reported that the anchor stood at the mouth of a river that had been named Keissi, or Keiskamma, by the Hottentots. When the Xhosa chief Rharhabe, the grandfather of the contemporary chief Ngqika, had a piece of the anchor broken off, the person who removed it died shortly afterwards. Perceiving the anchor as an enchanter, who had power or dominion over the sea, the Xhosa apparently concluded that the anchor was angry at the offense. Conferring a special name upon the anchor, they saluted it whenever they passed. As we recall, the missionary, traveler, and magistrate used this anchor as evidence for the absence of religion among Xhosa-speaking people in the eastern Cape. They used the anchor to punctuate the theoretical opposition between religion and superstition. If the Xhosa displayed such superstitious behavior as they seemed to do before the anchor, European observers insisted that they could not possibly have any religion. Whatever the anchor might have meant to the people of Ngqika, European comparative religionists in the eastern Cape concluded that it stood as a monument to their lack of religion.[33]

The Anchor's Return

Remarkably, however, the anchor resurfaced many years later in Europe as a classic piece of evidence for the origin of religion. In the 1870s the anchor reappeared far away in London in one of the most popular accounts of the evolutionary rise of humanity, John Lubbock's *Origin of Civilization and the Primitive Condition of Man.* Drawing on Auguste Comte for inspiration, Charles Darwin for conversation, and Edward B. Tylor for corroboration, Lubbock outlined successive stages in the evolution of religion, beginning with Atheism, "the absence of any definite ideas on the subject," moving to Fetishism, the deification of objects "in which man supposes he can force the deities to comply with his desires," and proceeding through Nature Worship (or Totemism), Shamanism, Idolatry (or Anthropomorphism), until culminating in "the gradual evolution of more correct ideas and of nobler creeds." Relying on Lichtenstein's report, Lubbock invoked Xhosa-speaking people of the eastern Cape to exemplify the first two stages of this evolutionary scheme. Ironically, they served to illustrate both an original absence of religion and the origin of religion in the emergence of fetishism.

"Among the Koossa Kaffirs," Lubbock noted, "Lichtenstein af-

firms that 'there is no appearance of any religious worship whatever.'" Although repeating Lichtenstein's denial, Lubbock obviously drew a different conclusion in holding that Xhosa-speakers
in the eastern Cape represented a survival of the original stage of
Atheism in the evolution of human civilization. Where Lichtenstein, like Van der Kemp and Alberti, had found merely an
absence, Lubbock found an origin, the primordial point of departure for the process of human evolution. The anchor at the mouth
of the Keiskamma River marked the next stage, signifying not
merely superstition but the crucial transition, according to Lubbock's evolutionary scheme, from Atheism to Fetishism. While
the absence of religion represented the primitive origin of humanity, the anchor marked the origin of religion. In Lubbock's analysis, the anchor illustrated the origin of "the savage notion of a
deity," which he insisted was "different from that entertained by
higher races" because, rather than being supernatural, this deity
"is merely a part of nature." Again, citing Lichtenstein, Lubbock
pointed to the anchor as an example of the primordial and primitive tendency to deify natural objects. "A good illustration," Lubbock reported, "and one which shows how easily deities are created by men in this frame of mind, is mentioned by Lichtenstein.
The king of the Koussa Kaffirs having broken off a piece of a
stranded anchor, died soon afterwards, upon which all the Kaffirs
looked upon the anchor as alive, and saluted it respectfully whenever they passed near it."[34]

Whether consciously or not, Lubbock clearly engaged in some
substantial subtractions and modifications in transmitting Lichtenstein's account of the anchor. His rewriting reveals something
about his interest in the story. Some of the changes in his ren-
dition are curious, but perhaps accidental. Lubbock replaced
enchantment with *alive*, omitted any reference to *anger*, and
completely removed the naming of the anchor or the practice of
saluting it by its name. More dramatically, Lubbock inexplicably
killed the king, recounting that the king, rather than the person
commanded by the king, died as a result of breaking off a piece
of the anchor. Perhaps an unintentional mistake, the removal of
the king nevertheless worked in Lubbock's retelling of the story
to divorce the anchor from its role as a symbol of political authority. Most of Lubbock's alterations had this effect. They separated
the anchor from its political ground.

Accordingly, other changes in the story more directly decontextualized the anchor. Lubbock's subtractions enabled him to clear

the geographical, historical, and social space around the anchor so that he could use it as evidence for his theory of religious evolution. First, Lubbock removed the precise location of the anchor, divorcing it from its specific, geographical habitat by the mouth of the Keiskamma River. Second, by erasing the name of King Chachábe (Rharhabe), as well as that king's relation to his grandson, Ngqika, reigning at the time of Lichtenstein's report, Lubbock divorced the anchor from its temporal, historical location in the period from the 1780s to the early 1800s. Third, Lubbock elided the Khoikhoi, along with their naming of the river, thus obscuring the plural, diverse social field in which the anchor stood. Finally, Lubbock subtracted what must have been the anchor's primary symbolic significance for the local Xhosa-speaking people, or at least for Ngqika, who claimed ownership of the anchor, by removing any reference to the anchor's "power over the sea." Like killing the king, this modification in Lubbock's account eliminated the political context in which the anchor operated as a ritual object. By these textual omissions, therefore, any hint of a contextual, relational, or political significance for the anchor was entirely erased. Torn from its context, the anchor could be employed as a free-floating emblem of the origin of religion.

After all these subtractions and modifications, what remained? According to Lubbock, the anchor remained as evidence of a "frame of mind" and a "tendency to deification" that represented the primordial origin of religion. Divorced from any geographical, historical, or political context, this "frame of mind" could be imagined as an explanatory constant. In this respect, according to Lubbock, the anchor was evidence of a mentality that attributed life to inanimate objects. Primitives, savages, and, not incidentally, animals shared this mental framework since, as Lubbock observed in a footnote, "Dogs appear to do the same."[35] According to Lubbock, not only did Xhosa-speaking people in the eastern Cape have this "frame of mind" that attributed life to inanimate objects, but they also demonstrated the evolutionary leap, from regarding objects as alive to deifying them, that was necessary for the origin of religion. Having perceived the anchor as alive, they began saluting it with the kind of respect due to a deity. Thus, according to Lubbock, religion was born.

The Floating Anchor

Following Lubbock, subsequent commentators on the anchor persisted in divorcing it from its geographical, historical, or political context. In European reflections on the origin of religion at the turn of the century, the anchor continued to stand, or, more accurately, to float, as a symbol of a mentality. That mentality could be found at the origin of religion, but it also persisted in the "child-like" thought processes attributed to colonized people all over the world. The primitive mentality could be found in colonized people abroad but also among children, women, rural peasants, the working class, criminals, the insane, and, following Lubbock, even animals in Europe.

In his 1885 book, *Myths and Dreams*, Edward Clodd used the anchor as evidence of "the confusion inherent in the savage mind between things living and not living, arising from superficial analogies and its attribution of life and power to lifeless things." Like Lubbock, Clodd killed the king, while adding the notion that the Xhosa regarded the anchor as "a vindictive being." Nevertheless, Clodd cited the anchor to illustrate a confused primitive mentality that was incapable of distinguishing between animate and inanimate objects. More significantly for the study of religion, the anchor reappeared in the 1896 Gifford lectures delivered by the Dutch historian of religions, C. P. Tiele. Along with F. Max Müller, Tiele has often been identified as a founder of the European science of comparative religion. Although he specialized as an Egyptologist, Tiele provided a more general overview of the field in his lecture series, "Elements of the Science of Religion." In outlining the elements of the "lowest Nature-Religions," Tiele reinforced the frontier stereotype of "savages" as permanent children. Their religion corresponded to the basic needs of "the childhood of humanity." Their animistic worship of natural objects was a "childish philosophy" motivated by childish self-interest. Under what conditions, Tiele asked, would "primitives" or "savages" worship an object?

Only—for primitive man is as selfish as an untrained child—only when he has an interest in doing so, only when he is satisfied that the object in question is more powerful than he, and that he has something to hope or to fear from it. An anchor is washed up on the African coast. Such an object has never been seen there before. The natives approach it cautiously; but when it lies quiet and hurts nobody, they suspend their judgment and go away. But some free-thinker in the kraal has observed that it is made of iron, and as he is just in want of a bit of iron, he ventures to break off a fluke of the anchor. Just as he is busy forging it, an accident happens to him and he dies. And now the matter is clear. In the unknown object dwells a spirit, which has thus avenged the insult offered to it, and henceforth the spirit is propitiated with gifts and sacrifices.

In this fanciful retelling of the tale of the anchor, Tiele replaced the king with a childish freethinker of the kraal who desired a bit of iron. He also invented the ritual propitiation of the anchor with gifts and sacrifices. In Tiele's account, the anchor demonstrated the childish hopes and fears that caused primitives to perform ritual acts of worship before unknown and mysterious objects. However, although he also divorced the anchor from its historical context, Tiele was more sensitive than most theorists to the polit-ical significance of the primitive worship of natural objects that was exemplified by the anchor on the African coast. Addressing the imperial patriotism of his British audience, the Dutch com-parative religionist observed that "Your Union-Jack and our Tri-colour are looked upon by the Negroes as sacred fetishes." Like the anchor, these flags were sacred objects, but, Tiele insisted, they were fetishes "in the noblest sense." They were emblems of European national identity and power. It was only natural, he con-cluded, that the adherents of African "Nature-Religions" should worship such powerful imperial objects.[36]

In a general introduction to the history of religion that first appeared the same year as Tiele's Gifford lectures of 1896 and that had gone through eight editions by 1921, comparative religionist Frank Byron Jevons also invoked the anchor as a crucial piece of evidence. He referred to the anchor in the context of a theoretical discussion of the difference between primitive magic and scien-tific explanations of the relation between cause and effect. Like Lubbock and Tiele, Jevons invoked the anchor to illustrate a men-tality; in this case, a kind of magical thinking in which a single instance, rather than a body of evidence, was sufficient to impute causal powers to an object. "Thus," Jevons observed, quoting, in this case, not Lichtenstein but Lubbock, "'the king of the Koussa Kaffirs having broken off a piece of a stranded anchor died soon afterwards, upon which all the Kaffirs looked upon the anchor as alive, and saluted it respectfully whenever they passed it.'" Ironically, in an introduction to religion, Jevons concluded that the anchor had nothing to do with religion as such. It was evidence of neither the absence of religion nor the origin of religion. Rather, the anchor was evidence of the kind of logical error that Jevons attributed to the practice of sympathetic magic, which, in his scheme, was a prereligious, nonreligious, or anti-religious way of thinking and acting. Therefore, the anchor was evidence of nothing more than mistaken reasoning. "Here the Kaffirs' error," Jevons argued, "consisted in jumping to the conclusion that the molestation of the anchor was the cause of the king's death." According to Jevons, that error—the magical mentality that misunderstood empirical, scientific relations between cause and effect—could only be corrected by proper logical induction. In the hands of Frank Byron Jevons, therefore, the anchor assumed a new significance. For Van der Kemp, Lichtenstein, and Alberti it had represented the absence of religion. Now it represented the absence of science.[37]

In 1906 anthropologist Alfred C. Haddon published a brief analysis of the origin of religion, *Magic and Fetishism*. Arguing against the theory of "animism" associated with Edward B. Tylor, Haddon relied on a more recent German theory of primitive psychology to build an account of the evolution of fetishism, the supposed origin of religion. Following the psychology that Fritz Schultze had elaborated in his *Psychologie der Naturvölker*, Haddon outlined what he regarded as the basic developmental pattern of primitive psychology. First, "uncultured man" attributed exaggerated value to objects, especially when they were "conspicuous, unusual, or mysterious." Second, "primitives" attributed human characteristics to natural objects. Third, they associated objects with auspicious or inauspicious events, thereby attributing a causal influence over those events to objects. Fourth, and finally, a belief in the causal, influencing power of objects led "uncultured man" to revere specific objects and to attempt to engage the power attributed to those objects through acts of worship.

Adopting this four-stage outline of primitive psychology, Haddon matched a German psychology of "Naturvölker" with evidence from Xhosa-speaking people in the eastern Cape of southern Africa. "As an example," Haddon observed, "the anchor cast up on the beach of the river Keissi may be cited." Although Haddon bypassed Lubbock to rely more directly on Lichtenstein's account, his analysis also cast the anchor adrift from its geographical, historical, or political moorings. Once again, the anchor became shipwrecked evidence of a free-floating, primitive mentality. Mechanically, Haddon drew upon the anchor to illustrate Schultze's four psychological stages of a primitive "frame of mind."

1. The anchor was an unusual object, and was therefore credited with an exaggerated value and regarded with great interest.

2. It was believed to possess a life of its own, a soul or spirit, somewhat analogous to man's.

3. A Kaffir broke off a piece of the anchor, and he soon afterwards died. The two events were associated with one another, and the breaking of the anchor was believed to have caused the death.

4. The power of the anchor-spirit was thus established, and the natives worshipped it in fear and hope.

"Thus," Haddon declared decisively and triumphantly, "the fetish was evolved." In Haddon's analysis, therefore, Xhosa regard for the anchor represented evidence of the origin of religion. Like Lubbock, he placed the anchor at the beginning of an evolutionary sequence beginning with fetishism. More emphatically, however, Haddon made this fetishism the basis of a "primitive psychology," a mentality characterized not merely by beliefs in spirits but, most decisively, by the "low grade of consciousness" demonstrated in the inability to value or evaluate objects. Therefore, like Jevons, Haddon used the anchor to mark a line that distinguished primitive magic from modern science. The anchor stood as a sign of a disembodied mentality, a primitive psychology incapable of logical induction and, accordingly, not anchored in the real world.[38]

Imperial and Apartheid Comparative Religion

Obviously, comparative religionists in European centers of theory production found their raw materials in the reports of travelers, missionaries, and government agents from colonized peripheries all over the world. As a result, people on the southern African periphery became incorporated into their theories of religion. The Xhosa, who supposedly worshiped an anchor, became a classic illustration of fetishists in European comparative religion. Zulus featured even more prominently in nineteenth-century comparative religion, as Henry Callaway's collection in particular carried authority because it seemed to present authentic Zulu "natives" speaking in their own voices. Zulus, however, were animists. As the prominent folklorist, anthropologist, and comparative religionist Andrew Lang observed, "The Zulus are the great standing type of an animistic or ghost-worshipping race without a God." And, as we might expect, the Sotho-Tswana were distinguished from Xhosas and Zulus by being designated as a classic example of totemists. In his 1905 presidential address before the Anthropology section of the British Association, which was meeting that year in Cape Town, Alfred C. Haddon observed that "the Be-Chuana must have crossed the Zambesi from the north at a very early date, because of all the south Bantu groups they alone have preserved the totemic system." In the frontier comparative religion of southern Africa, these same people had supposedly degenerated, respectively, from ancient Arabia, ancient Israel, and ancient Egypt. Now, however, they were incorporated into what might be called an imperial comparative religion, which found that they had preserved the original religious mentality, whether that primitive mentality was identified as Xhosa fetishism, Zulu animism, or Sotho-Tswana totemism.[39]

More research and reflection needs to be done on the complex relations between European centers of theory production and colonized peripheries in the history of comparative religion. The fate of the shipwrecked anchor recalls one trajectory in those relations between center and periphery. Cited as evidence for the absence of religion on the frontier periphery, the anchor became evidence for the origin of religion at the European center. At every stage in its history, however, the anchor marked significant theoretical oppositions in comparative religion. Perhaps originally used to signal an indigenous African distinction between sea and land, the anchor was subsequently employed by European comparativists to mark oppositions between religion and superstition, between the civilized and the primitive, and, ultimately, between a scientific rationality and an abstracted, disembodied, and decontextualized primitive mentality that was out of touch with the real world.

Whatever impact they might have had in Europe, these theoretical oppositions returned to southern Africa with a vengeance under the reign of oppression known as apartheid. In apartheid comparative religion, the land remained the primary battlefield for the study of religion. Although a more detailed development of this argument will have to await another occasion, its basic contours can be suggested by a brief look at the work of W. M. Eiselen, Afrikaner anthropologist, apartheid theorist, and, eventually, administrator with the Bantu Affairs Department in the 1950s during the implementation of "Grand Apartheid." In the 1920s Eiselen established a reputation as the leading academic expert on the indigenous religion of South Africa. In 1932 social anthropologist Isaac Schapera noted that "Eiselen is now engaged in writing a book on the religious life of the Southern Bantu which, if it includes an equally authoritative analysis of magic and witchcraft, should make this aspect of Bantu life one of the best known." Although that book was never written, Eiselen's work exerted considerable influence on the development of an apartheid comparative religion, which, in its analytical strategies, recapitulated the history of interpretations that we have reviewed by focusing on the anchor. Recalling the treatment of the anchor in frontier comparative religion, apartheid comparative religion denied the authenticity of African religion, even occasionally refusing to designate African beliefs and practices as religion. However, like the analysis of the anchor in imperial comparative religion, it presumed that Africans were evidence for the origin and evolution of religion. Likewise, it attributed to Africans a disembodied primitive mentality that had supposedly survived from human prehistory. These three themes—denial, evolution, and primitive mentality—were basic ingredients in apartheid comparative religion.[40]

Following the lead of the missionary Van der Kemp, the traveler Lichtenstein, and the magistrate Alberti, apartheid ideologues often denied indigenous African beliefs and practices the designation *religion*. For example, Eiselen argued that Africans throughout the continent did not have religion. In the 1920s he insisted that the term *religion* should be reserved only for the beliefs of an "elevated culture." Accordingly, since Africans supposedly lacked such an "elevated culture," Eiselen insisted that they had "forms of belief" (*geloofsvorme*) but no religion (*godsdiens*). This leading expert on Bantu religious life, therefore, recast the early-nineteenth-century gesture of dismissal as a sweeping denial of African religion and culture.

Like Lubbock, however, Eiselen found among the Bantu not merely an absence but also a point of origin for an evolutionary development. "The Bantu is no longer a primitive in the true meaning of the word," Eiselen observed. "The level of development that he has reached we usually call the Totem-culture." Presuming an evolutionary scheme similar to Lubbock's, therefore, Eiselen placed Africans on a stage of development just above fetishism. To evolve to the next level, the Bantu required, according to Eiselen, Christian civilization. "Christian education," Eiselen proposed, "is the only way to make the Kaffer a useful inhabitant of our Union." Clearly, evolution and exploitation, turning people into "useful" subjects, went together in Eiselen's comparative religion.

Finally, Eiselen abstracted a primitive mentality that was suffused with magic and superstition and attributed it to Africans in southern Africa. The Bantu, according to Eiselen, was not "rational." For evidence of this supposed lack of rationality, Eiselen compared European and African agricultural methods. White Afrikaans-speaking farmers, he held, made use of rational techniques, such as irrigation or storage, in addition to prayer. However, according to Eiselen, African farmers, not being rational, used only prayer or its equivalent, rainmaking ritual. From such suspect, anecdotal evidence, Eiselen concluded that the "Bantu mind" lacked "causal reasoning." By reifying this unanchored mentality, Eiselen and other apartheid ideologues inscribed the opposition between scientific rationality and primitive mentality into the design of apartheid. Dispossession and exploitation of Africans could be justified by referring to this primitive mentality. As the government's Tomlinson Commission found in 1955, "inadequate use of land and employment opportunities are due to the limited world-view of the Bantu." Therefore, the relegation of 80 percent of the population to 13 percent of the land could be justified in terms of the comparative findings of the modern study of religion. Once again, comparative religion was entangled in a battle over land.[41]

NEW FRONTIERS

As a strategic act, the denial of religion has certainly operated on other frontiers, even on frontiers that have been closed under an established hegemony. Modified and modulated under local circumstances, this denial has registered performative effects. In modern North America, as in nineteenth-century southern Africa, the very term *religion* has been entangled in the interplay of strategic maneuvers on battlefields of religious conflict. The history of the U.S. government's suppression of American Indian beliefs and practices recalls one battlefield on which the recognition of an indigenous religion has been denied. Even after the passage of the American Indian Religious Freedom Act of 1978, legal conflicts over the ceremonial use of peyote, access to sacred sites, protection of burial grounds, and Indian land claims have continued to call into question government recognition of American Indian religions. In response to the emergence of new religious movements in the 1960s and 1970s, anti-cult propaganda denied their religious status by labeling them as entrepreneurial businesses, as subversive political organizations, or as brainwashing "cults." Anti-cult polemic along these lines even seemed to influence the academic analysis of new religions. During the 1980s, the religious character of fundamentalism, especially in its Muslim variety, was also dismissed, even in academic discourse, by strategic reductions that explained it as a social reaction to modernization or a psychological aberration of fanaticism and mass hysteria. In public and potent ways, therefore, the definition of religion has been as intensely contested in modern American culture as it has been as elsewhere in the world.[42]

If *religion* has been a contested category, a term that has been historically produced and situationally deployed, then a single, incontestable definition of religion cannot simply be established by academic fiat. In the study of religion, a minimalist definition, such as the definition of religion as relations with supernatural agents, which was recently defended by E. Thomas Lawson and Robert N. McCauley, might deny the religious status of Buddhism. A maximal definition, like the useful dimensional map developed by Ninian Smart, might include not only Buddhism but also secular worldviews such as nationalism, humanism, and Marxism within the orbit of what counts as religion. In either case, however, academic debates about the definition of religion have usually ignored the real issues of denial and recognition that are inevitably at stake in situations of intercultural contact and conflict. As we have seen, the frontier has been an arena in which definitions of religion have been produced and deployed, tested and contested, in local struggles over power and position in the world. In such power struggles, the term *religion* has been defined and redefined as a strategic instrument. We can only expect those struggles to continue.[43]

In tracing the trajectory from the denial to the discovery of indigenous religions on southern African frontiers, we have been able to correlate the crucial historical moment of recognition with the establishment of a local system of colonial control. Under the magisterial system, the location system, or the reserve system, Africans were suddenly discovered to have an indigenous religious system. This linkage between the discovery of a local religion and the establishment of local control suggests that knowledge about religion and religions has depended upon the power relations reinforced by colonial enclosures. Well into the twentieth century, the struggles we have observed in southern Africa over denial and discovery, over inventory and intervention, over closure and conversion, have continued to be replayed in other colonial contexts. Here in conclusion I recall only two further illustrations of this process from recent colonial history.

Mau Mau and Cargo

In the early 1950s the breakdown of colonial order in Kenya was identified with the emergence of the "Mau Mau secret society." As violent acts of resistance increased, the colonial governor of Kenya declared a state of emergency in October 1952. Addressing this disturbance of colonial rule, the anthropologist and archaeologist Louis Leakey published a book in December of that year, *Mau Mau and the Kikuyu*, that attempted to allay white fears of a Kikuyu uprising. In that volume Leakey explained the Mau Mau as a political movement—an African nationalist organization aligned with the underground Kikuyu Central Association, which had been banned in 1940, and the Kenya African Union, which had been formed after World War II. As a nationalist political movement, Leakey argued, the Mau Mau movement was inconsistent with both the traditional religion and the Christian religious values that many Kikuyu had adopted. In other words, the Mau Mau movement was not a religion but the antithesis of local religion. Therefore, since it could not be expected to draw support from either traditionalist or Christian Kikuyu, the Mau Mau movement was bound to fail.[44]

Two years later, however, Leakey published a second account of the movement, *Defeating Mau Mau*, that registered the remarkable discovery that it was actually a religious movement in its own right. Although he regarded it as a perverse religion, Leakey nevertheless insisted that the Mau Mau movement had to be regarded as a religion. Looking back to his earlier work, Leakey reflected upon this change of perspective. "What I did not realize then, and in fact have only come to appreciate fully in the past few months," he revealed, "*was that Mau Mau was in fact a religion and that it owed its successes to this fact more than anything else at all*" (emphasis in original). As a religion, the Mau Mau movement was a syncretism, "a very strange blend of pseudo-Christianity and utter paganism." As we have seen in southern Africa, this depiction of a local religion as a syncretism, as an illicit mixture, was a strategy for denying the authenticity of a religion even in the act of discovering that it existed. Not only deviant, this religion was also dangerous. It was the "force that turned thousands of peace-loving Kikuyu into murderous fanatics"; it was the religious impetus that transformed Africans "into fanatical murdering maniacs."[45]

In the midst of a war zone, therefore, Louis Leakey tried to reinforce a colonial conceptual closure around the Mau Mau movement by designating it as a religion. This conceptual containment coincided with the literal containment of tens of thousands of Kikuyu in prisons and "rehabilitation" camps. As in southern Africa, a theory that explained a religion as based on fear could easily become part of a colonial calculus of terror. According to one commandant, since "Mau Mau was built on fear we had to create a greater fear of our camp." Defined as a mixture of pagan and Christian elements, the Mau Mau movement could appear as an illegitimate but understandable religious movement. Although he represented it as an irrational aberration within the modern, progressive, and normalized domain of colonial control, Louis Leakey nevertheless tried to explain and contain the Mau Mau movement as a religious system. However, Kenya in the 1950s, unlike the eastern Cape of southern African a century earlier, could not be so easily managed by imposing a colonial system, whether by enforcing an administrative system or by conceptually inventing a religious system. Nevertheless, although its adherents escaped the immediate effects of colonial enclosure when Kenya achieved independence in 1963, the Mau Mau movement, following the polemic of Louis Leakey, has continued to be defined as a religious movement in the literature of the study of religion.[46]

For a second recent example of the discovery of religion in a frontier zone, we might reflect briefly on the twentieth-century emergence of "cargo" movements in the Pacific. Under conditions of intercultural contact, Melanesian islanders developed complex beliefs and practices in relation to the material goods brought by white merchants, missionaries, and colonizers. Refusing to accept the "rationality" of the economic relations and political administration imposed upon them, adherents of the cargo movements anticipated a dramatic change in the immediate future that would bring material prosperity and political autonomy. Expecting the imminent return of ancestors bearing the "cargo," these moments promised redemption from colonial domination.

In his classic analysis *Road Belong Cargo*, Peter Lawrence, like Joseph Cox Warner on the eastern Cape frontier, insisted that the cargo movement should be understood not as superstition but as a religious system. According to Lawrence, "we are dealing not with a farrago of superstition but with a coherent system." Under colonial enclosure, that system could be analyzed and inventoried; its psychological and social functions could be explained. The discovery that it was a religious system, rather than superstition, meant that the cargo movement could be conceptually contained. Furthermore, again like Warner, Lawrence proposed that the recognition of this local religious system was essential for effective intervention and conversion. Warner had argued that colonial administration and Christian conversion had been frustrated by a failure to recognize that the Xhosa had a religious system. Once that system was acknowledged, however, magistrates and missionaries could gain enough knowledge about Xhosa religion to destroy it. Likewise, Lawrence asserted, once the cargo movement was recognized as a coherent religious system, "we should seek out carefully its weakest point for the spearhead of our attack." Not content with its colonial containment, Lawrence also advocated the destruction of the coherent religious system he had discovered.

Remarkably, therefore, a century after the work of Joseph Cox Warner, comparative religion, moving from denial to discovery, was pursued on the battlefield of another frontier zone. On the beaches of Melanesia, this frontier comparative religion was also entangled in local conflicts over the ownership of land, access to wealth, freedom of labor, and political autonomy. As noted, Warner had entered the battlefield of the eastern Cape frontier under the banner of "Christian civilization." In dealing with the Xhosa, he insisted, colonial power had to "break them up as tribes, and destroy their political existence; after which, when thus set free from the shackles by which they are bound, civilization and Christianity will no doubt make rapid progress among them."

While Warner proclaimed the advent of Christian civilization, Peter Lawrence advanced his attack on the cargo movement in the name of a new global mission, economic development. "We must so co-ordinate and introduce our programmes of development," he advised, "that the mass of the people have no alternative but to accept them as the only logical solution to the problems of modern living." Although he did not advocate military force, which Warner had invoked as God's "sword" in the work of conversion, Lawrence did imply an element of coercion by asserting that policies of economic development should permit no alternative. However, even if this implication was unintended, Lawrence seemed to share Warner's assumption that people with a recognized religious system could be more effectively contained, controlled, and converted. Whether the mass of people was coerced into Christian civilization or economic development, conversion had to be guided by the knowledge gained through discovering their local religious system.[47]

As these two illustrations drawn from research on the Mau Mau and cargo movements should suggest, frontier comparative religion continued into the twentieth century to be advanced in contested zones of intercultural conflict. Providing a measure of local control, even if only conceptually, the study of religion in frontier situations has repeated and reinforced strategies of colonial enclosure. As bounded and contained systems, local religions have been discovered; their contours have been outlined and their contents enumerated. Once delimited and defined, however, local religious systems have been marked for colonizing intervention. In South Africa they continued to be targeted for destruction. In the 1980s, for example, experts on African religion could identify three coherent worldviews, or "cognitive systems," in South Africa: the traditional African, the Christian, and the worldview of international business. In the interest of economic development, the traditional African worldview, which could still be inventoried in the terms—superstition, magic, failure to evaluate objects, and worship of the dead—that had been used to invent it in the nineteenth century, had to give way to Christian conversion in order to prepare Africans to enter the modern world of "international business culture."[48] In this formula, with its colonial conceptual containment and missionary program for conversion, the basic terms and conditions of a frontier comparative religion continued at the end of the twentieth century to be reinstated and reinforced in southern Africa.

New Horizons

What does the future hold? Is there a postcolonial, postapartheid, or postmodern comparative religion on our horizon? Or are we condemned to repeat the colonial encounters and reinforce the colonial enclosures that have been established on the frontiers of our history? If we are to reopen what colonialism has closed, then the study of religion itself must be open to new possibilities. After reviewing the history of their colonial production and reproduction on contested frontiers, we might happily abandon *religion* and *religions* as terms of analysis if we were not, as a result of that very history, stuck with them. They adhere to our attempts to think about identity and difference in the world. Although scholars in the human sciences might try to fix their reference, the terms *religion* and *religions* do not belong solely to the academy. They also belong to a history of encounter and contact. Outside of the academic arena, these terms have been taken up and mobilized in conflicts over legal recognition and political empowerment. They have been entangled in the kinds of historical struggles of possession and dispossession, inclusion and exclusion, domination and resistance, that we have tracked on southern African frontiers.

Obviously, we would like to avoid the mistakes of the past, to diminish the violence that has been committed under the aegis of these categories, especially when they have been deployed to reify, separate, dispossess, and exclude. Toward that end, two recent conceptual innovations seem promising. First, a redefinition of definition itself has led to proposals for an open, multiple, or polythetic definition of religion. Instead of trying to establish a single, monothetic essence of religion, whether that essence is stipulated as beliefs in supernatural beings or relations with the sacred, as ultimate concern, symbolic orientation, or the depth dimension of human existence, a polythetic definition supports ongoing inquiry into the "family resemblances" through which identifiable aspects of religion might constellate. As a cluster concept, religion signifies an open set of discursive, practical, and social strategies of symbolic and material negotiation. In this respect, religion is not the object of analysis; it is an occasion for analysis, an opening in a field of possible relations. However fuzzy and blurred the term might be, however multivalent or subject to contestation, *religion* nevertheless provides a significant focusing lens for reflecting on human identity and difference.

Since, for better or worse, we are in fact stuck with the term *religion*, we should work to minimize the structural violence that has inhered in the category of religion by being open to its open redefinition.[49]

Second, with respect to the notion of *religions*, open redefinitions of religious traditions have also recently been proposed. Religions have been reopened as invented traditions or as imagined communities. In recent cultural analysis, the previously comfortable assumptions about pure cultures, languages, peoples, or religions have receded before the recognition that there are no purities in the world. There are no pure, homogeneous cultural systems. It is not only in a postmodern world that "pure products go crazy." Bricolage and creole, mixture and exchange, have always been the norms of cultural production. Not merely a postmodern fashion, therefore, this rejection of the notion of the organically coherent or mechanically integrated cultural system, which was in any case a product of colonial containment, presents new opportunities for recovering the dynamics of cultural relations. Rather than bounded cultural systems, religions are intrareligious and interreligious networks of cultural relations. Recent advances in the study of culture, as Renato Rosaldo has observed, have encouraged analysts to "look less for homogeneous communities than for the border zones within and between them. Such cultural border zones are always in motion, not frozen for inspection." Back on the open frontier, in multiple and contested border zones, the study of religion will have to resituate itself as a human science of contact. Whether cooperative or conflictive, contacts on an open frontier, as Rosaldo has noted and as we have seen repeatedly in southern Africa, are inevitably "saturated with inequality, power, and domination." In any frontier zone, conflicts of interpretation intersect with contests over domination and resistance. Discourse and force inevitably overlap. Nevertheless, beyond colonial enclosures, intrareligious and interreligious relations become occasions for analyzing the fluid, mobile dynamics of the production of meaning and the contestation of power in situations of cultural contact.[50]

How can an academic study of religion reconstitute itself in these new frontiers? If, as I have suggested, the categories of *religion* and *religions* are not objects but occasions for analysis, then the focus of inquiry shifts to their aspects, such as symbol, myth, ritual, and tradition. Here, as well, open definitions are possible, redefinitions that might best be formulated in negative terms.

First, a symbol is not a sign with a fixed referent. What did the Xhosa anchor signify? What did the Zulu uNkulunkulu signify? What did Sotho-Tswana animal emblems signify? Like any symbol, they signified both an argument over definition and a contest over appropriation. Although frontier comparativists tried to fix their referents, symbols resisted their fixation and remained available for reinterpretation. Not only made meaningful through acts of interpretation, however, symbols are also invested with power through competing claims on their ownership. The symbolic dynamics of religion appear in the cultural process of stealing back and forth sacred symbols, symbols that are made sacred by the highly charged activity of appropriating and reappropriating them. Therefore, if we are attentive to both meaning and power on new frontiers, our definition of symbolic practices and processes must be reopened by recognizing that no religious symbol has a fixed or stable referent. Defying all claims to privileged, exclusive ownership, symbols are always available for new appropriations and new interpretations.[51]

Second, a myth is not a story with canonical closure. Rather than being subject to timeless repetition, a myth is opened and reopened by interpretation. As a result, myth is a type of ongoing cultural work. In recalling the myths told on southern African frontiers, we have observed how a Zulu creation myth or a Sotho-Tswana emergence myth could provide symbolic terms and narrative structures for making sense out of the nineteenth-century colonial situation. In this respect, myth was not a closed canon for repetition but an open repertoire of cultural resources. Not only open, however, these stories were also relational. They evoked intrareligious arguments over their significance and also embodied interreligious and intercultural relations. Recognizing this relational character of myth, the Zulu comparativist Mpengula Mbande even prefaced his version of a Zulu creation narrative by noting that it was the "account which black men give white men of their origin."[52] Open to reinterpretation, myth is also open to redeployment in frontier zones of intercultural and conflictual human encounter. This open and situational work of myth, however, has certainly not been confined to the stories told on southern African frontiers. It has defined the cultural enterprise of myth in the history of religions. A myth, therefore, is never a closed story. It is always open to retelling, reinterpretation, and redeployment in the context of intercultural relations.

Third, a ritual is not the reenactment of an authenticating original. Rather, as a dynamic, embodied practice, every ritual act is a new performance. Since ritual might invoke superhuman powers, signal a transition, reinforce political authority, or express emotion, its significance cannot be captured by regarding it only as a mechanical repetition of some original meaning. Frontier comparative religion tried to contain ritual in terms of both origin and meaning, especially if its original meaning, as in the case of circumcision, could be traced back to the ancient Near East. However, European comparativists were particularly frustrated by trying to elicit the originating meaning of the widespread African practice of placing stones or sticks on cairns. This ritual practice defied interpretation because no one knew what it meant; it defied explanation because no one could give reasons for doing it. People performed this ritual act for absolutely no reason. Beyond interpretation or explanation, the analysis of ritual must begin precisely at this point, at the juncture of thought, feeling, and action that coalesces in embodied practices that mark out the world. In each act of placing a stone on a cairn, people did not reenact some original meaning. Rather, they marked a new crossing, a new transition, a new journey. Through embodied practice, they redrew the map of their world. If the reality of southern African cairns, instead of theological assumptions about ancient Near Eastern circumcision, can serve as our model, we can recognize that in ritual human beings do not repeat old patterns; they move through the reorganized space of new worlds. Not a repetition of an original, every ritual act is a new act.[53]

Finally, a religious tradition is neither uniform in the present nor continuous with the past. Comparativists on open frontiers occasionally expressed frustration that not everyone within a particular African community shared the same religious beliefs and practices. As Peter Kolb observed, "with the Africans, as with ourselves, religious knowledge is not universal."[54] Nevertheless, as frontiers closed, comparative religionists invented religions, even a generic Bantu religion, based on the presumption that their beliefs and practices were in fact universally shared by every African man, woman, and child. In the invention of African religions, from Hottentot to Bantu religion, European comparativists presumed that Africans manifested a uniformity that was not "as with ourselves." Not only uniform in the present, African religion was assumed to be continuous with a timeless past. Whether degenerated from ancient origins or perpetuated from time immemorial, African religion was defined as a continuity with the past.

Obviously, these assumptions of both uniformity and continuity obscured the historical reality of African religious traditions. Not handed down unchanged from the past but always taken up and mobilized in the present, a religious tradition, comprised of open symbols, myths, and rituals, is necessarily a shifting, fluid ensemble of cultural resources. If nothing else, a study of religion must come to terms with this reality of tradition.

Frontier comparative religion, however, tried to identify uniformity and continuity through the comparative procedures of morphology and genealogy. It assumed uniformity by tracking analogies, continuity by tracing descent. Through these comparative procedures, it tried to fix religions in space and time as enclosed, yet comparable, systems. "When records are wanting, and tradition is grown a blind matter," Peter Kolb observed, "all that can be done is to compare that tradition, together with the histories, institutions, and customs of other nations, and fix it, if nothing shall hinder, where the parity most appears." To make the most of his silent, sightless evidence, Kolb proposed a comparative method. However, even in relation to written records or oral traditions, comparison is unavoidable. Since the very categories of analysis—religion and religions; symbol, myth, ritual, and tradition—have emerged from comparison, all that can be done, as Kolb insisted, is to compare. As David Hume proposed, "All kinds of reasoning consist in nothing but a *comparison*" (emphasis in original); and with respect to religion, as F. Max Müller specified, "All higher knowledge is acquired by comparison, and rests on comparison." If we are to reason at all or know anything about religion, therefore, we must somehow engage the problem of comparison. Otherwise, forsaking reason, we will know absolutely nothing about either religion or religions.[55]

But must the goal of comparison be "to fix" religions on the basis of similarity? Is comparative religion necessarily devoted to demonstrating parity among religions? In Peter Kolb's case, the establishment of parity between Jews and Hottentots was not an end in itself. The logic of comparison, as Jonathan Z. Smith has noted, requires that the comparison of two things must always be made in respect to some third. "In the case of an academic comparison," according to Smith, "the 'with respect to' is most frequently the scholar's interest, be this expressed in a question, a theory, or a model."[56] Certainly, Kolb had theoretical questions that anchored his methodological procedures of observation, conversation, and exchange. However, Kolb's comparative religion

was also a strategic and polemical imputation to Jews and Hottentots not merely of parity but of a shared difference in relation to
the Protestant Christians who had secured their early-eighteenth-
century colonial settlement in the Cape. The colonists represented the implicit third term in Kolb's comparison between Hottentots and Jews. During the nineteenth century, Protestant colonists continued to represent the silent third term in comparisons
between Africans and Roman Catholics, Xhosa and Arabs, Zulu
and Jews, Sotho-Tswana and ancient Egyptians. In all these cases,
parity was asserted on the basis that any two of these religions
were like each other because they differed in some respect from
Protestant Christianity. Therefore, Kolb and other frontier comparativists advanced a comparative religion not only in the service of a "theoretical" project but also in support of the practical
interests of Protestant colonists in southern Africa.

Kolb's formula for comparative religion had a long afterlife. In
the 1870s it was quoted in the preface of the first British publication devoted to providing an overview of African religion,
Henry Rowley's *The Religion of the Africans*. Surprisingly, Rowley
used this comparative method to discover that Africans all over
the continent held indigenous beliefs in God. "'I believe in God,'
—an uncreated Supreme Spiritual Being," Rowley declared, "is
the creed which underlies all else that the Africans believe." In
this respect, therefore, Africans were like Protestant Christians.
Where parity broke down, however, was on the basis, not of religion, but of race. Reciting Mbande's story about the origin of
black and white people, Rowley concluded that this creation
myth "is valuable only as showing the workings of the native
mind when brought into contact with the superiority of Europeans."[57] In this imperial comparative religion, therefore, the principle of parity only served to reinforce a fundamental disparity
between "primitives" and civilized Europeans. Africans might
have a religion, like Protestants, but they were nevertheless differentiated in this imperial comparative religion by virtue of their
supposedly inferior mentality.

Back in South Africa, Peter Kolb's formula for comparison was
quoted again in 1914 by the mining magnate Sidney Mendelssohn
in a two-part essay titled "Judaic or Semitic Legends and Customs
Amongst South African Natives" that was published in the *Journal of the African Society*. Two centuries after Kolb had advanced
his polemical comparison between Hottentots and Jews, Mendelssohn cited his authority to argue in considerable detail for both
formal analogies and common descent between Jews and all the

indigenous people of southern Africa. Ultimately, however, Mendelssohn suggested that Africans were like Jews, not because they presented a similar obstacle to the advance of Protestant Christianity, but because they had both been overwhelmed by its global expansion. Like Kolb, Mendelssohn found that indigenous evidence for comparative religion in southern Africa was silent. "When I first went to South Africa, over a third of a century ago," he recalled, "it was already late in the day to make inquiries of the natives, even if I could have spoken their language, of which I have no knowledge." On the closed frontier of the 1890s, Mendelssohn discovered that Africans, who had only recently been credited with having a Bantu religion, were already losing it under the impact of modernization, industrial capitalism, and Christian conversion. Although he could not hear their traditions, Mendelssohn recalled that he could nevertheless see African faces. While watching the laborers in the gold mines or in the diamond fields, he reported, "in the great sea of black faces I have seen men of such an unmistakably Jewish cast of features that I have almost felt inclined to greet them as strangers in a strange land." Having documented the Jewish forms and roots of African religion, Mendelssohn ended his treatise on comparative religion on a note of loss. Of the traditions once practiced by these "strangers in a strange land," he concluded, "practically little is left today, and that little will disappear with the probably gradual conversion to Christianity of the whole of the South African races." In Mendelssohn's comparative religion, the third term in the comparison of Jews and Africans remained Protestant Christianity. Parity between Jews and Africans could be established, however, not because they were obstacles, but on the basis that both were alien and alienated with respect to the expanding Christian society in South Africa.[58]

Using the same formula, therefore, the comparativists Kolb, Rowley, and Mendelssohn arrived at very different results. Nevertheless, a common pattern emerged. Each began with a formula for establishing similarity but ended by asserting that Africans represented an unassimilable difference—an obstacle, an inferiority, an estrangement—in relation to the implicit third term in their comparisons, Christian civilization. Arguably, each discovery of difference, in different ways, served the colonial project. If the practice of comparative religion is to enter a postcolonial era, it must certainly abandon this third term as the basis for making meaningful comparisons between religions.

However, as I have tried to suggest throughout this book, comparative religion does not necessarily compare religions. Beyond colonial containments, it can compare the situational, relational, and strategic practices of comparison that have produced *religion* and *religions* as objects of knowledge and instruments of power. In this work of comparing comparisons, comparative religion confronts the play of similarity and difference as a historical problem that can be situated within specific intercultural relations. Neither similarities nor differences are simply given in the world. They are produced through the practices of comparison and generalization that we have surveyed in this history of comparative religion in southern Africa.

Although this book has located a history of comparison within the colonial conditions of southern Africa, I believe that its findings have wider significance for the study of religion. As noted, similar discourses of denial and discovery, similar gestures of dismissal, policies of containment, and assertions of difference, can be observed all over the world. These practices of comparison carry colonial histories that need to be confronted. However, the relevance of that historical confrontation will register only if it enables us to move forward into a postcolonial comparative religion. The way forward, I would suggest, might be found by going backwards. We can journey back through the historically situated discourses and practices of comparison that have constituted frontier, imperial, and apartheid comparative religion and find ourselves once again on the frontier. As we have seen, a frontier is a zone of conflict; but it can also be a zone of reciprocal exchanges, creative interchanges, and unexpected possibilities. We might very well be faced with a frontier future. By going back through the history of situated comparisons to the frontier, it is possible that we might clear a space—perhaps even a postcolonial, postimperial, or postapartheid space—where something new in the study of religion can happen.

NOTES

Preface

1. Hume, *Treatise of Human Nature*, 1:375; Preus, *Explaining Religion.*
2. Müller, *Introduction to the Science of Religion*, 9; Sharpe, *Comparative Religion*, 35.
3. Capps, "Evaluation of Previous Methods," 180.
4. Long, *Significations*, 3–4.
5. Jonathan Z. Smith, *Drudgery Divine*, 34.
6. Bhabha, *Location of Culture*, 38–39.
7. Ackerman, *J. G. Frazer*, 192.

1. Frontiers of Comparison

1. Wallerstein, *Modern World System*, 66–129.
2. Foucault, *Order of Things*; Said, *Orientalism.*
3. Rosaldo, "Rhetoric of Control," 240–57.
4. Leopold, *Culture in Comparative and Evolutionary Perspective*, 66; Hind, "'We Have No Colonies,'" 3–35.
5. Jordan, *Comparative Religion*, 377–84, 580–604; Sharpe, *Comparative Religion*, 35; John Henry Barrow, *World's Parliament of Religions*, 1:583.
6. Leach, "Anthropology and Religion," 218–19. See, for example, Knight, *Inquiry into the Symbolical Language*, 78; Dupuis, *Origine de tous les cultes*; Manuel, *Eighteenth Century Confronts the Gods*, 259–70; and Lubbock, *Origin of Civilization*, 217.
7. On travel literature and ethnography, see Mary Campbell, *Witness and the Other World*; Daston, "Marvelous Facts"; Defert, "Collection of the World"; Frantz, *English Traveller*; Greenblatt, *Marvelous Possessions*; Harbsmeier, "Elementary Structures of Otherness"; Ryan, "Assimilating New Worlds"; and Glyndwr Williams and P. J. Marshall, *Great Map of Mankind.* On monsters, see Friedman, *Monstrous Races*; Mason, *Deconstructing America*; Park and Daston, "Unnatural Conceptions"; and Wittkower, "Marvels of the East." On wild men, see Dudley and Novak, *Wild Man Within.* On noble savages, see Fairchild, *Noble Savage.* On earthly paradises, see Baudet, *Paradise on Earth.* For discussions of conquest and representation, see Hanke, *Spanish Struggle*; Jennings, *Invasion of America*; O'Gorman, *Invention of America*; Pagden, *Fall of Natural Man*; and Pag-

den, *European Encounters*. On the centering of Europe, see Baritz, "Idea of the West"; Hay, *Europe*; and Trouillot, "Anthropology and the Savage Slot."

8. Pratt, "Scratches on the Face of the Country," 139. See Pratt, *Imperial Eyes*; and Fabian, *Time and the Other*.

9. Galton, *Narrative of an Explorer*, 53; see Fabian, "Hindsight." Galton, *Art of Travel*, 60–64; Stocking, *Victorian Anthropology*, 93.

10. Fardon, *Localizing Strategies*. See Bonsen, Marks, and Miedema, *Ambiguity of Rapprochement*; Brian Du Toit, "Missionaries, Anthropologists, and the Policies"; Fabian, "Religious and Secular Colonization"; and Van der Geest, "Anthropologists and Missionaries."

11. John W. D. Moodie, *Ten Years in South Africa*, 1:238–39; Lovett, *History of the London Missionary Society*, 1:120–21.

12. Christopher Herbert, *Culture and Anomie*, 150–203.

13. Henry, *Intoxication of Power*, 25; Du Plessis, *History of Christian Missions*, 21.

14. George Grey, *Journal of Two Expeditions*, 2:201; Grey, *Vocabulary*; Grey, *Journal of an Expedition*; Grey, *Ko Nga Mahinga*; Bleek, *Library of His Excellency Sir George Grey*; Rutherford, *Sir George Grey*.

15. Asad, *Anthropology and the Colonial Encounter*, 17. See Berreman, *Politics of Truth*; Gough, "Anthropology and Imperialism"; Hymes, "Use of Anthropology"; Scholte, "Discontents in Anthropology"; and Stocking, *Colonial Situations*.

16. Lubbock, *Prehistoric Times*, 589–93; Lubbock, *Origin of Civilization*, 212–17.

17. Jane, *Journal of Christopher Columbus*, 194–200; Vespucci, *Mundus Novus*; Berkhofer, *White Man's Indian*, 6–8.

18. Chidester, *Patterns of Power*, 113; Léry, *History of a Voyage*, xlix; Rau, *Articles on Anthropological Subjects*, 32; Wroth, *Voyages of Giovanni da Verrazzano*, 141; Thwaites, *Jesuit Relations*, 8:121; Force, *Tracts and Other Papers* 2 (5) : 21; Keen, *Aztec Image*, 113–16; MacCormack, *Religion in the Andes*, 55–63.

19. Callender, *Terra Australis Cognita*, 2:308; Hezel, *First Taint of Civilization*, 54; Bernard Smith, *European Vision and the South Pacific*, 147; J. D. Lang, *Queensland*, 374; Collins, *Account of the English Colony*, 354.

20. Diodorus, *Diodorus of Sicily*, 2:109; Snowden, *Blacks in Antiquity*, 146; Roussier, *L'Establissement d'Issiny*, 213; William Smith, *New Voyage to Guinea*, 26; Burton, *Lake Regions of Central Africa*, 2:341–57; Grant, *Walk across Africa*, 145; R. Caillié, *Travels through Central Africa*, 1:303; Richard Cope, "Christian Missions," 7; Donovan Williams, "Missionaries on the Eastern Frontiers," 294.

21. Andrewes, *Pattern of Catechistical Doctrine*, cited in Thomas, *Man and the Natural World*, 21; Hobbes, *English Works*, 3:125; Gray, *Good Speed to Virginia*, cited in Vaughan, "'Expulsion of the Salvages,'" 61.

22. See Pietz, "The Problem of the Fetish," parts 1, 2, and 3a.

23. Miller, *Blank Darkness*, 47. See Thornton, "Narrative Ethnography in Africa"; and Clifford and Marcus, *Writing Culture*.

24. Brerewood, *Enquiries Tracing the Diversity*; Harrison, "Religion" and the Religions, 39–45.

25. Huddleston, *Origins of the American Indians*, 70–71; Eilberg-Schwartz, *Savage in Judaism*, 32–37; Forster, *Observations Made during a Voyage*, 295, 300–301.

26. Lafitau, *Customs of the American Indians*, 1:27. See Hodgen, *Early Anthropology*, 348.

27. Diderot, *Supplément à L'Encyclopédie*, 1:194; Lubbock, *Origin of Civilization*, 215; Henson, *British Social Anthropologists*, 30.

28. Stoler, "Rethinking Colonial Categories," 134.

29. Lamar and Thompson, *Frontier in History*, 7.
30. MacCrone, *Race Attitudes in South Africa*.
31. Legassick, "Frontier Tradition," 65; Fawcett, *Account of Eighteen Months' Residence*, 87.
32. Wolf, *Europe and the People without History*, 6.
33. Braudel, *Mediterranean*, 1:18.

2. Inventing Religion

1. John Barrow, "Account of a Journey," 426; Borcherds, *Autobiographical Memoir*, 121–22; Burchell, *Travels into the Interior*, 1:252.
2. John Barrow, "Account of a Journey," 426; Kicherer, *Narrative of His Mission*, 22–23, 30–32.
3. Sparrman, *Voyage to the Cape of Good Hope*, 1:213–24; Du Plessis, *History of Christian Missions*, 50–60.
4. Needham, *Exemplars*, 75–116; Somerville, *Narrative of His Journeys*, 98; Kicherer, *Narrative of His Mission*, 30.
5. John Barrow, "Account of a Journey," 426; Borcherds, *Autobiographical Memoir*, 122; Krüger, *Pear Tree Blossoms*, 19.
6. Elphick, *Kraal and Castle*, 217; Guelke, "Freehold Farmers and Frontier Settlers," 73.
7. Raven-Hart, *Before Van Riebeeck*, 47, 57, 60, 70, 77, 101, 128, 140, 156.
8. Terry, *Voyage to East India*, 22. See John Cope, *King of the Hottentots*; and Varley, "Note on Coree."
9. Purchas, *Purchas His Pilgrimage*, 4:208; Terry, *Voyage to East India*, 16; Thomas Herbert, *Relation of Some Yeares Travaile*, 18; Tavernier, *Six Voyages*, 2:206.
10. Mandelslo, *Gedenkwaardige see en Landt Reyse*; Thomas Herbert, *Relation of Some Yeares Travaile*, 14; Thomas Herbert, *Some Yeares Travels*, 19.
11. Thomas Herbert, *Relation of Some Yeares Travaile*, 14; Purchas, *Purchas His Pilgrimage*, 4:148.
12. Raven-Hart, *Before Van Riebeeck*, 58; Heylen, *Cosmography*, 64.
13. Edward Herbert, *De veritate*, 121; Nieuhof, *Gedenkweerdige Brasiliaense*, 14.
14. Heeck, *Uit die "Journale*," 171; Herport, *Riese Nach Java*, 21; Meister, *Der orientalisch-indianische Kunst- und Lust-Gärtner*, 34; Vogel, *Oost-Indianische Reise-Beschreibung*, 75; Hoffmann, *Reise Nach dem Kaaplande*, 20; Schweitzer and Fryke, *Relation of Two Several Voyages*, 239.
15. Cowley, *Voyage*, 93; Schapera, *Early Cape Hottentots*, 75, 146; Dapper, *Naukeurige Beschryvinge*, 653; Dapper, *Description de l'Afrique*, 389–90; Schreyer, *Neue Ost-Indianische Reisz-Beschreibung*, 58.
16. Nieuhof, *Gedenkweerdige Brasiliaense*, 14; Bolling, *Frederici Bollingii*, 315–16; Loubère, *New Relation*, 2:184; Schreyer, *Neue Ost-Indianische Reisz-Beschreibung*, 58.
17. Tachard, *Voyage de Siam*, 1:96; Tachard, *Relation of the Voyage to Siam*, 71; Raven-Hart, *Cape of Good Hope*, 2:269, 264, 297. See Strangman, *French Callers*.
18. Elphick, *Kraal and Castle*, 112–14; Elphick and Malherbe, "Khoisan to 1828," 13. See Marks, "Khoisan Resistance"; and A. B. Smith, "Disruption of Khoi Society."
19. Raven-Hart, *Cape of Good Hope*, 1:192.
20. Dampier, *New Voyage*, 541; Raven-Hart, *Cape of Good Hope*, 2:388; Oving-

ton, *Voyage to Suratt*, 489; Langhansz, *Neue Oost-Indische Reise*, 634–38; Schapera, *Early Cape Hottentots*, 207; Leguat, *New Voyage*, 230.
21. Dampier, *New Voyage*, 541; Ovington, *Voyage to Suratt*, 489.
22. Meister, *Der orientalisch-indianische Kunst- und Lust-Gärtner*, 30; Langhansz, *Neue Oost-Indische Reise*, 634–38. See Coetzee, "Idleness in South Africa"; Coetzee, *White Writing*, 12–35; and Alatas, *Myth of the Lazy Native*.
23. Ovington, *Voyage to Suratt*, 489; Raven-Hart, *Cape of Good Hope*, 2:423.
24. Elphick and Malherbe, "Khoisan to 1828," 18; Luillier, *Voyage*, 16; Bogaert, *Historische Reizen*, 113; Wintergerst, *Reisen*, 2:21–22.
25. Elphick and Malherbe, "Khoisan to 1828," 21–22; Hoge, "Personalia of the Germans," 212; Schapera, "Present State," 233.
26. Kolb, *Present State of the Cape*, 56, 37, 91, 102–3, 109.
27. Kolb, *Present State of the Cape*, 29.
28. Diodorus, *Diodorus of Sicily*, 2:171–75. See Allen, *The Legend of Noah*.
29. Kolb, *Present State of the Cape*, 97–98.
30. Kolb, *Present State of the Cape*, 99, 102.
31. Kolb, *Present State of the Cape*, 105–7.
32. Kolb, *Present State of the Cape*, 316; Greenblatt, "Filthy Rites."
33. Kolb, *Present State of the Cape*, 135, 38.
34. Penn, "Land, Labour, and Livestock," 14; Newton-King, "Enemy Within," 382–94.
35. John Barrow, *Account of Travels*, 1:93; Macmillan, *Cape Colour Question*, 154, n. 1; Sales, *Mission Stations*, 79–100; Philip, *Researches in South Africa*, 1:204–6, 216–17; Elbourne, "Early Khoisan Uses of Mission Christianity."
36. Broberg, *Linnaeus*; Frangsmyr, *Linnaeus*; Goerke, *Linnaeus*.
37. Boorstin, *Discoverers*, 16; the term *Chinese* appears in Sparrman, *Voyage to the Cape*, 2:113; Robert Jacob Gordon, *Cape Travels*, 1:71, 79. On distinguishing between Khoi and San, see M. L. Wilson, "Khoisanosis"; A. B. Smith, "On Becoming Herders"; and Barnard, *Hunters and Herders*, 3–11.
38. Sparrman, *Voyage to the Cape*, 1:207–8, 211–12.
39. Thunberg, *Travels in Europe, Africa, and Asia*, 1:317, 316.
40. Le Vaillant, *Travels into the Interior Parts of Africa*, 1:82, 2:30, 2:29–30, 2:48. See Meiring, *Truth in Masquerade*.
41. Hoge, "Personalia of the Germans," 267–68; Nicholas Caillé, *Journal historique du Voyage*, 156–57; Schapera, *Early Cape Hottentots*, 162–67; Mentzel, *Geographical and Topographical Description*, 4:19, 3:266.
42. Mentzel, *Geographical and Topographical Description*, 3:301–5, 281, 299.
43. Mentzel, *Geographical and Topographical Description*, 3:281, 304–5, 264–65.
44. Mentzel, *Geographical and Topographical Description*, 3:283, 267–70.
45. Mentzel, *Geographical and Topographical Description*, 3:270, 272, 275.
46. Hahn, *Tsuni-//Goam*, 36; Bleek, *Brief Account of Bushman Folklore*; see Thornton, "'This Dying Out Race.'" Hoernlé, "Certain Rites of Transition," Hoernlé, "Hottentot Rain Ceremony"; Hoernlé, "Expression of the Social Value of Water"; Schapera, *Khoisan Peoples*, 374, see also 160–201, 357–99.
47. Appadurai, "Theory in Anthropology," 360.
48. John Barrow, *Account of Travels*, 2:427; Mentzel, *Geographical and Topographical Description*, 1:128–32.
49. Tooke, "Notes on Some of the Earlier Contributors," 351; John Barrow, *Account of Travels*, 1:238–39; McKay, *Origin of the Xosas*, 41–42, 53. On Buddhist cave art, see Abe, "Art and Practice"; on Bushman rock art, see Dowson and Lewis-Williams, *Contested Images*.
50. Jonathan Z. Smith, *Imagining Religion*, xi.

3. The Religion of Unbelievers

1. Saunders, "Hundred Years' War"; Mentzel, *Geographical and Topographical Description*, 3:266–67; Pinkerton, *General Collection*, 16:682–87.
2. Hondius, *Klare Besgryving van Cabo de Bonna Esperança*, 9; Burchell, *Travels into the Interior*, 1:530; Mentzel, *Geographical and Topographical Description*, 3:260.
3. John Barrow, *Account of Travels*, 1:214–15.
4. Van der Kemp, "Account of the Religion," 432–33. On Van der Kemp, see Cuthbertson, "Van der Kemp and Philip"; Elbourne, "Concerning Missionaries"; Enklaar, *Life and Work*; and Freund, "Career of Johannes Theodorus van der Kemp."
5. Lichtenstein, *Travels in Southern Africa*, 1:298, 311, 301, 313, 312.
6. De Mist, *Diary of a Journey*, 48–49; Alberti, *Tribal Life*, 47–48.
7. *Morning Chronicle and London Advertiser* (25 April 1783); Kirby, *Source Book on the Wreck of the Grosvenor*, 10. See Botha, *Wreck of the Grosvenor*; and Kirby, *True Story of the Grosvenor*.
8. Crais, *Making of the Colonial Order*, 28–29; Giliomee, "Eastern Frontier," 441; Peires, *House of Phalo*.
9. Philip, *Researches in South Africa*, 1:118; Hopper, "Xhosa-Colonial Relations," 131; Chidester, *Religions of South Africa*, 13–17.
10. John Campbell, *Travels in South Africa*, 513, 518, 526.
11. Bleek, *Zulu Legends*, 3–4.
12. Jonathan Z. Smith, *Imagining Religion*, 66–101; Van der Kemp, "Transactions," 426–28; see Reyburn, "Missionary as Rainmaker". Donovan Williams, "Missionaries on the Eastern Frontiers," 71; Peires, *House of Phalo*, 67.
13. Peires, "Nxele, Ntsikana, and the Origins"; Hodgson, "Study of the Xhosa Prophet Nxele," parts 1 and 2.
14. Chapman, *Travels in the Interior*, 1:18; Percival, *Account of the Cape of Good Hope*, 185; see Streak, *Afrikaner as Viewed by the English*. Gardner, *Faiths of the World*, 260.
15. Harrison, *"Religion" and the Religions*, 39; Jonathan Z. Smith, *Drudgery Divine*, 20–25; London Missionary Society, "Report concerning the State of Religion," 510, 513.
16. Brain, *Cape Diary*, 130. See Ricards, *Catholic Church*.
17. Van der Kemp, "Transactions," 419; Van der Kemp, "Account of the Religion," 432; Alberti, *Tribal Life*, 52. See Harinck, "Interaction between Xhosa and Khoi."
18. Warner, "Mr. Warner's Notes," 76. See Crais, "Vacant Land."
19. Donovan Williams, *When Races Meet*, 88; Steedman, *Wanderings and Adventures*, 1:36–37.
20. Philip, *Researches in South Africa*, 1:ix–x, ix. See Ross, *John Philip*; and Cuthbertson, "Van der Kemp and Philip."
21. Philip, *Researches in South Africa*, 1:8; 2:116. On *Uhlanga*, see George Thompson, *Travels and Adventures*, 448.
22. Philip, *Researches in South Africa*, 2:116, 364.
23. Rose, *Four Years in Southern Africa*, 77–78.
24. Crais, *Making of the Colonial Order*, 101; William Shaw, *Story of My Mission*, 188, 189.
25. John Barrow, *Account of Travels*, 1:212; Kay, *Travels and Researches*, 107; Appleyard cited in Fleming, *Southern Africa*, 158; Ward, *Five Years in Kaffirland*, 137–39; Fleming, *Kaffraria*, 117; Fleming, *Southern Africa*, 197. See also Martin, *History of Southern Africa*, 187; and Pringle, *Narrative of a Residence in South Africa*, 413.

26. Van der Kemp, "Transactions," 412; Napier, *Excursions in Southern Africa*, 2:301–3; Ward, *Five Years in Kaffirland*, 57–58; Sutherland, *Original Matter*, 159; Cole, *Cape and the Kafir*, 42. For nineteenth-century accounts of Muslims in South Africa, see Aspling, *Malays of Cape Town*; Davids, "Muslim-Christian Relations"; and Mayson, *Malays of Cape Town*. Van der Kemp's term—"Mahometan Hindoo"—was commonly used to designate a Muslim from India; see Frykenberg, "Constructions of Hinduism," 525.

27. Barnabas Shaw, *Memorials of South Africa*, 37, 32; Whately, "On the Origin of Civilisation," 22; Martin, *History of Southern Africa*, 195.

28. Dugmore, *Reminiscences of an Albany Settler*, 20, 45.

29. Philipps, *Philipps, 1820 Settler*, 117–18; Alexander, *Narrative of a Voyage of Observation*, 1:394–95; Appleyard cited in Thornley Smith, *Memoir of the Reverend John Whittle Appleyard*, 36.

30. Bannister, *Humane Policy*, vi; Alexander, *Narrative of a Voyage of Observation*, 1:398; Stockenstrom, *Autobiography*, 1:423.

31. Buxton, *African Slave Trade*, 509–10. See Bassett, *Life of a Vagrant*; Select Committee, *Report*; and Stocking, "What's in a Name?"

32. Harry Smith, *Autobiography*, 432; Lehmann, *Remember You Are an Englishman*, 189. See Harrington, *Sir Harry Smith*.

33. Godlonton, *Narrative of the Irruption*, 1:229, 231. On Godlonton, see Le Cordeur, "Robert Godlonton." For nineteenth-century reports of *umDali*, see Steedman, *Wanderings and Adventures*, 249; and Kay, *Travels and Researches*, 339.

34. Godlonton, *Narrative of the Irruption*, 1:261; Calderwood, *Caffres*, 33.

35. Godlonton, *Narrative of the Irruption*, 1:212–15.

36. Godlonton, *Narrative of the Irruption*, 1:223–26, 232.

37. Bowker, *Speeches*, 48, 109, 131, 177.

38. Donovan Williams, *When Races Meet*, 60; Peires, *House of Phalo*, 77; Ward, *Five Years in Kaffirland*, 117. On African perceptions of the mission on the eastern Cape frontier, see Fast, "'In One Ear and Out the Other.'"

39. Bowker, *Speeches*, 132; Henry George Grey, *Colonial Policy*, 259.

40. Cole, *Cape and the Kafir*, 185–86.

41. On the Xhosa Cattle-Killing, see Peires, *Dead Will Arise*.

42. Calderwood, *Caffres*, vi, 13, 214, 202.

43. Crais, *Making of the Colonial Order*, 201; Hammond-Tooke, *Command or Consensus*, 2.

44. Donovan Williams, "Missionary Personality," 33; Frank Brownlee, *Transkeian Native Territories*, 24; Warner, "Mr. Warner's Notes," 102.

45. Warner, "Mr. Warner's Notes," 74.

46. Warner, "Mr. Warner's Notes," 103–4, 105–6.

47. Warner, "Mr. Warner's Notes," 79, 75.

48. Warner, "Mr. Warner's Notes," 75.

49. Warner, "Mr. Warner's Notes," 103.

50. Warner, "Mr. Warner's Notes," 75, 79, 81, 73.

51. Holden, *Past and Future*, 284, 292; Thornley Smith, *Memoir of the Reverend John Whittle Appleyard*, 104; Kropf, *Das Volk der Xosa-Kaffern*, 187.

52. Cape of Good Hope, *Blue-book on Native Affairs*, 127; William Thompson, *Nature and Difficulties of the Missionary Enterprise*, 5, 12.

53. Cape of Good Hope, *Report of the Select Committee*, 9, 68–69, 100, 11.

54. Shooter, *Kafirs of Natal*, 217.

4. The Unknown God

1. Webb and Wright, *James Stuart Archive*, 1:243. See Bird, *Annals of Natal*, 1:536.
2. Welsh, *Roots of Segregation*, 12, 19; Shepstone cited in Sullivan, *Native Policy*, 32; Cetshwayo cited in Maylam, *History of the African People*, 78.
3. Webb and Wright, *James Stuart Archive*, 1: 262–63; Brothers, *Correct Account*; John Wilson, *Our Israelite Origins*.
4. Bird, *Annals of Natal*, 1:45; Omer-Cooper, *Zulu Aftermath*, 5. But see Cobbing, "Mfecane as Alibi"; Stuart and Malcolm, *Diary of Henry Francis Fynn*, 86–88; Leverton, *Records of Natal*, 37–40, 247–48; and Wright, "Political Mythology."
5. Isaacs, *Travels and Adventures*, 2:248–49, 1:285–286, 1:98.
6. Gardiner, *Narrative of a Journey*, 152. See Marsh and Stirling, *Story of Commander Allen Gardiner.*
7. Gardiner, *Narrative of a Journey*, 179; Delegorgue, *Voyage*, 2:246–47; Cory, *Diary of Rev. Francis Owen*, 39, 103.
8. Gardiner, *Narrative of a Journey*, 170–171, 314, 316.
9. Brookes, *White Rule in South Africa*, 51; Natal, *Native Affairs Commission*, 1:6.
10. Natal, *Native Affairs Commission*, 3:62–65.
11. Natal, *Native Affairs Commission*, 5:54–55.
12. Shooter, *Kafirs of Natal*, 211, 159–161, 165, 162; Gardiner, *Narrative of a Journey*, 152; Holden, *Past and Future*, 300–301. See Grout, *Zulu-Land*, 136–37.
13. Davies, *Introduction*, 165; Maurice, *Religions of the World*, 2. See Christensen, *Origin and History of Christian Socialism*; Darby, "Soteriology," 66–109; and Maurice, *Life.*
14. Maurice, *Religions of the World*, 255, 7, 98, 159. For the broader context of Maurice's engagement with "other" religions, see Almond, *British Discovery of Buddhism*; and Marshall, *British Discovery of Hinduism.*
15. Colenso, "Diocese of Natal," 243, 246; Colenso, "Church Missions," 2, 17; Colenso, *Ten Weeks in Natal*, 115.
16. Colenso, *Ten Weeks in Natal*, 57, 114, 116–17.
17. Colenso, *Three Native Accounts*, 143; Colenso, *Pentateuch*, 1:vii.
18. Colenso, *Pentateuch*, 1:xxi, 4:117.
19. Colenso, *Pentateuch*, 1:9–10, 4:117; Webb and Wright, *James Stuart Archive*, 1:259.
20. Arnold, "Bishop and the Philosopher," 51. On Colenso's biblical criticism, see Rogerson, *Old Testament Criticism*, 220–37.
21. Rees, *Colenso*, 69, 76, 93; Etherington, *Preachers, Peasants, and Politics*, 137–38; Burnett, *Anglicans in Natal*, 71. For more on Colenso, see Cox, *Life of John William Colenso*; Guy, *Heretic*; and Hinchliff, *John William Colenso.*
22. Milman, *History of the Jews*, 3:iii.
23. *Observer* (14 January 1864); Spohr, *Natal Diaries*, 9. See Bleek, "On the Origin of Theological Concepts," Manuscript Collection, box 1, file 6, South African Library.
24. Thornton, "Elusive Unity," 84; Stocking, *Victorian Anthropology*, 58; Spohr, *Natal Diaries*, 24. See Christian Bunsen, *Outline of a Philosophy of Universal History*; Christian Bunsen, *Egypt's Place*; Christian Bunsen, *God in History*; and Frances Bunsen, *Memoir of Baron Bunsen.*
25. Bleek to Latham, 12 September 1854, Manuscript Collection, box 16, file 59, South African Library; Bleek, "Researches into the Relations," 203.
26. Spohr, *Natal Diaries*, 24, 38.

27. Bleek, "Researches into the Relations," 205; Spohr, *Natal Diaries*, 38; Bleek, *On the Origin of Language*, xiii.
28. Bleek, "Researches into the Relations," 292–93.
29. Bleek, *Zulu Legends*, 3–4.
30. Bleek, "Researches into the Relations," 296; Bleek, "Scientific Reasons," 4.
31. Bleek, "Researches into the Relations," 293; Bleek, *Reynard the Fox*, xv–xvii.
32. Bleek, "On Resemblances," 98. Bleek cites Müller, "Comparative Mythology"; Müller, *Chips from a German Workshop*, 2:1–146; and Müller, *Introduction to the Science of Religion*.
33. Bleek, *Comparative Grammar*, ix.
34. Spohr, *Natal Diaries*, 38; Bleek to Ernst Haeckel, 1874, Special Collections, University of Cape Town Library; Thornton, "'This Dying Out Race,'" 7. Note, however, that Müller also insisted on the importance of studying living spoken dialects; see Müller, *Chips from a German Workshop*, 1:58; and Cox, "Max Müller and the Science of Language."
35. Bleek, *On the Origin of Language*, xv–xvi.
36. Bleek, "Researches into the Relations," 205.
37. Etherington, "Missionary Doctors," 80; Etherington, *Preachers, Peasants, and Politics*, 68, 95, 102.
38. Colenso, "Good Tidings," 38–39; Benham, *Henry Callaway*, 53–54.
39. Benham, *Henry Callaway*, 55; "Bishop Colenso and His Kafir Words."
40. Callaway to Bleek, 8 July 1862, Manuscript Collection, 9.10.c.6, South African Library; Callaway to Bishop Gray, 8 July 1862, Manuscript Collection, 9.10.c.6, South African Library.
41. Callaway, *Polygamy*; Callaway, *Last Word of Modern Thought*, 14.
42. Callaway, *Religious System*, 1–2, 43; with reference to Hardwick, *Christ and Other Masters*, 1:242, 297, 305.
43. Callaway to Bleek, 8 July 1862, Manuscript Collection, 9.10.c.6., South African Library; Etherington, "Missionary Doctors," 86; Benham, *Henry Callaway*, 76.
44. Colenso to Bleek, 20 September 1868, Special Collections, BC151, A111, University of Cape Town Library.
45. Callaway, *Religious System*, 31; Society for Promoting Christian Knowledge, *May, the Little Bush Girl*, 29; Schneider, *Die Religion*, 66; Jenkinson, *Amazulu*, 28.
46. Callaway, *Religious System*, 9–13.
47. Callaway, *Religious System*, 43–44.
48. Callaway, *Religious System*, 33–34, 52–55.
49. Callaway, *Religious System*, 39.
50. Callaway, *Religious System*, 1–6; Hamilton and Wright, "Making of the AmaLala"; Webb and Wright, *James Stuart Archive*, 4:14.
51. Callaway, *Religious System*, 35–36, 56–60, 7–9.
52. Callaway, *Religious System*, 31–33.
53. Callaway, *Religious System*, 49, 51, 38, 86, 96–99.
54. See Etherington, "Missionary Doctors"; Goody, "Religion, Social Change, and the Sociology of Conversion"; Horton, "African Conversion"; and Horton, "On the Rationality of Conversion."
55. Cecil Northcott, *Robert Moffat*, 77.
56. Callaway, *Religious System*, 16–18, 74, 19, 22, 27, 79–80, 94.
57. Callaway, "South African Folk-Lore," 118; Callaway, "Fragment Illustrative of Religious Ideas," 59. See Callaway, "Visit to Pondoland," 262; and Callaway, "On the Religious Sentiment," 96. The divine name—*Qamata*—was recorded as early as 1843; see Donovan Williams, "Missionaries on the Eastern Frontiers," 291.

58. Webb and Wright, *James Stuart Archive*, 1:217, 247, 98.
59. Manuel, *Broken Staff*, 13, 186. See Hodgen, *Early Anthropology*, 338; and Patai, "Ritual Approach to Hebrew-African Culture Contact."
60. Jenkinson, *Amazulu*, 24; Leslie, *Among the Zulus*, 48.
61. Callaway, *Fragment on Comparative Religion*, 12, 24.
62. Webb and Wright, *James Stuart Archive*, 1:261–62.

5. Sacred Animals

1. Weidemann, "Malaboch-oorlog." See Agar-Hamilton, *Native Policy.*
2. Chapman, *Travels in the Interior*, 1:18; Theal, *History of South Africa*, 2:266; Livingstone, *Missionary Travels*, 27. See Boucher, *David Livingstone Correspondence*, 29, 51, 68–69; Cuthbertson, "Missionary Imperialism," 95; and Schapera, *David Livingstone's South African Papers*, 67–95. On British depictions of Boers as ancient Israelites, see Latrobe, *Journal of a Visit*, 295; John Mackenzie, *Ten Years*, 51; and Nixon, *Complete Story*, 71. For a similar French report, see Casalis, *My Life in Basuto Land*, 79. On the "myth of the chosen people" in South Africa, see A. Du Toit, "No Chosen People"; and Gerstner, *Thousand Generation Covenant.*
3. Baines, *Gold Regions*, vi, 66–67; Spoelstra, *Die "Doppers*," 116–17; Tangye, *In New South Africa*, 54–55; Johnston, "Boer Question," 163. On Boers and the supernatural, see John Mackenzie, *Ten Years*, 52; David McKay Wilson, *Behind the Scenes*, 87–88.
4. Pinto, *How I Crossed Africa*, 300–301.
5. Rae, *Malaboch*, 188. See Roberts, "Bagananoa," 254.
6. Ellenberger, *History of the Basuto*, 241–42. See Hoernlé, "Social Organization," 91; and Schapera, *Tswana*, 35.
7. John Barrow, "Account of a Journey," 399–400.
8. Hume, *Natural History*, 81.
9. Lichtenstein, *Foundation*, 70–71.
10. Burchell, *Travels in the Interior*, 2:550, 427, 530–31, 552.
11. Burchell, *Travels in the Interior*, 2:550; Kirby, *Diary of Andrew Smith*, 2:109–10; Bain, *Journey to the North*, 31.
12. John Mackenzie, *Ten Years*, 394. See Casalis, *Basutos*, 248.
13. Richard Cope, *Journal of the Rev. T. L. Hodgson*, 155; Broadbent, *Narrative*, 81–82, 203–4.
14. On Robert Moffat, see J. S. Moffat, *Lives*; Cecil Northcott, *Robert Moffat*; E. W. Smith, *Robert Moffat*; and Walten, *Life and Labours.*
15. Robert Moffat, *Missionary Labours*, 59, 254, 278.
16. Robert Moffat, *Missionary Labours*, 257–60. For similar euhemerist explanations of African religion, see Kay, *Travels and Researches*; and Pringle, *Narrative of a Residence.*
17. Robert Moffat, *Missionary Labours*, 244, 243, 276, 245.
18. Robert Moffat, *Missionary Labours*, 265, 121.
19. Robert Moffat, *Missionary Labours*, 266, 274, 279; Philip, "Letter to the Directors"; Schapera, *David Livingstone's South African Papers*, 100. See Clarke, *Being and Attributes of God*; Clarke, "Unchangeable Obligations"; Byrne, *Natural Religion*, 58–61; and Pailin, *Attitudes to Other Religions*, 23–44.
20. Robert Moffat, *Missionary Labours*, 243–244, 281.
21. Robert Moffat, *Missionary Labours*, 270, 281.
22. Robert Moffat, *Missionary Labours*, 272.

23. Robert Moffat, *Missionary Labours*, 255, 257, 250–51. For a similar comparison between obstacles in Africa and India, see John Mackenzie, *Ten Years*, 488.
24. Robert Moffat, *Missionary Labours*, 305. See Kay, *Travels and Researches*, 209.
25. Robert Moffat, *Missionary Labours*, 247.
26. Robert Moffat, *Missionary Labours*, 260–63, 395. See Setiloane, *Image of God*, 77–86.
27. Robert Moffat, *Missionary Labours*, 264–65, 261; J. Tom Brown, *Among the Bantu*, 103; Comaroff and Comaroff, *Of Revelation and Revolution*, 218.
28. Robert Moffat, *Missionary Labours*, 381, 267; John Mackenzie, *Ten Years*, 338–39.
29. Robert Moffat, *Missionary Labours*, 268, 252; Robert Moffat, *Matabele Journals*, 1:16, 27.
30. Rosalind Shaw, "Invention," 342–43; John Mackenzie, *Ten Years*, 134, 137.
31. John MacKenzie, *Ten Years*, 136, 135 n. 1; see John Mackenzie, *Day-Dawn*, 65–68.
32. Kirby, *Diary of Andrew Smith*, 1:262; see Reyburn, "Missionary as Rainmaker"; and Grove, "Scottish Missionaries." John Mackenzie, *Ten Years*, 378.
33. Edwin W. Smith, *Robert Moffat*, 147; Robert Moffat, *Missionary Labours*, 134.
34. Arbousset and Daumas, *Narrative of an Exploratory Tour*, 165–69; Orpen, *History of the Basutos*, 24.
35. Casalis, *Basutos*, 237; Casalis, *Études de la langue du Béchuana*, xxxviii; Casalis, *Études sur la langue Sechuana*, 22.
36. Rolland, "Idées religieuses," 474; Arbousset and Daumas, *Narrative of an Exploratory Tour*, 176; Lemue, "Coutumes religieuses," 54. See Livingstone, *Missionary Travels*, 13; and Casalis, *Basutos*, 211.
37. Lemue, "Coutumes religieuses," 54; Methuen, *Life in the Wilderness*, 254, 187, 254; see Casalis, *Basutos*, 242; and Arbousset, *Missionary Excursion*, 111. On the myth of the animal messengers, see Zahan, *Religion, Spirituality, and Thought*, 36–52. On European interest in Egypt, see Iversen, *Myth of Egypt*; and Wortham, *Genesis of British Egyptology.*
38. Carlyle, *South Africa*, 48–49, 57; see Merensky, *Beiträge zur Kenntniss*; and Merensky, *Erinnerungen aus dem Missionsleben.* Arbousset and Daumas, *Narrative of an Exploratory Tour*, 104; John Mackenzie, *Ten Years*, 391, 386–87.
39. Holub, *Seven Years*, 1:327–28.
40. Shillington, *Colonisation of the Southern Tswana*, 188.
41. John Mackenzie, *Ten Years*, 394. On John Mackenzie, see Dachs, "Missionary Imperialism"; Hall, "Humanitarianism"; William D. Mackenzie, *John Mackenzie*; William Northcott, "John Mackenzie"; and Sillery, *John Mackenzie.*
42. John Mackenzie, "Native Races of South Africa," 185–86.
43. War Office, *Native Tribes*, 121, 125.
44. Willoughby, *Tiger Kloof*, 28–30. See Haile, "Tiger Kloof"; Haile, *African Bridge-Builders*; and Chirenje, "Church, State, and Education."
45. Willoughby, *Tiger Kloof*, 41; London Missionary Society, *Report on a Visit*, 139.
46. Willoughby, "Notes on Totemism," 264–65, 270–71, 278, 282, 281.
47. Willoughby, "Notes on Totemism," 281; Willoughby, *Tiger Kloof*, 3–4; Willoughby, "Notes on Totemism," 269.
48. Ellenberger, *History of the Basuto*, v, 242–43. On the absence of idolatry, see Robert Moffat, *Missionary Labours*, 243; and Methuen, *Life in the Wilderness*, 304.

49. Ellenberger, *History of the Basuto*, 245, 243, 241, 245.
50. Sonntag, *My Friend Maleboch*, 8–9.
51. Robert Moffat, *Matabele Journals*, 1:17; Winter, "Mental and Moral Capabilities," 371.
52. Bryden, *History of South Africa*, 127. On comparison with "Levitical" laws, see Casalis, *Basutos*, 180; John Mackenzie, *Ten Years*, 393; and Widdicombe, *Fourteen Years*, 45–46.
53. Baines, *Gold Regions*, 71. See Schloemann, "Malepa"; Junod, "BaLemba"; Stayt, "Notes on the Balemba"; and Van Warmelo, *Contributions towards Venda History*, 81–82.
54. Roberts, "Bagananoa," 256, 241.

6. Beyond the Frontier

1. Tooke, "Uncivilised Man," 79, 85. See Fabian, *Time and the Other*.
2. Theal, *Ethnography*, 63, 68, 12; with reference to Skeat and Blagden, *Pagan Races*.
3. Theal, *Ethnography*, 19.
4. Theal, *Ethnography*, 107, 110, 117, 111. See Hahn, *Tsuni-//Goam*.
5. Theal, *Ethnography*, 80.
6. Theal, *Ethnography*, 219–390, 143, 425.
7. Theal, *History of South Africa*, 5:332. On syncretism in the history of religions, see Stewart and Shaw, *Syncretism/Anti-Syncretism*.
8. Theal, *History of South Africa*, 3:482. See Saunders, *Making of the South African Past*, 29; and Schreuder, "Imperial Historian."
9. Le Vaillant, *Travels into the Interior*, 82; Van der Kemp, "Account of the Religion," 435.
10. Gardiner, *Narrative of a Journey*, 314–15; Merriman, *Cape Journals*, 43; Chapman, *Travels in the Interior*, 1:117; John Mackenzie, *Ten Years*, 337.
11. Robert Moffat, *Missionary Labours*, 269, 248.
12. Richard Cope, *Journal of the Reverend T. L. Hodgson*, 357.
13. Lichtenstein, *Foundation*, 72.
14. Bergson, *Laughter*; John Campbell, *Travels in South Africa*, 124.
15. Lévy-Bruhl, *Primitive Mentality*, 22, 36; Philip, *Researches*, 2:116–17.
16. Lévy-Bruhl, *Primitive Mentality*, 23; Arbousset, "Station de Morija," 57.
17. Lévy-Bruhl, *Primitive Mentality*, 24, 26; Burchell, *Travels in the Interior*, 2:295; H. A. Junod, *Life of a South African Tribe*, 2:152.
18. Lévy-Bruhl, *Primitive Mentality*, 368–69; Robert Moffat, *Missionary Labours*, 384; Livingstone and Livingstone, *Narrative of an Expedition*, 557.
19. Lévy-Bruhl, *Primitive Mentality*, 422–23; Dieterlen, "Méfiance," 309.
20. See, for example, Kidd, *Essential Kaffir*; and H. P. Junod, *Bantu Heritage*.
21. Jonathan Z. Smith, *Map Is Not Territory*, 240–64; *Imagining Religion*, 22–26.
22. Callaway, *Fragment on Comparative Religion*, 4; Gardiner, *Narrative of a Journey*, 170–71.
23. Metheun, *Life in the Wilderness*, 296.
24. Benveniste, *Indo-European Language*, 522; Hobbes, *Leviathan*, 69.
25. Philip, *Researches*, 2:116; John Barrow, "Account of a Journey," 399. See Plutarch, *Plutarch's Lives*, 3:15; Sextus Empiricus, *Sextus Empiricus*, 3:13; Hobbes, *Leviathan*, 168–83; Vico, *New Science*, sec. 337; and Hume, *Natural History*, 81.
26. Holden, *Past and Future*, 288; Bowker, *Speeches*, 131.

27. Sextus Empiricus, *Sextus Empiricus*, 3:9–11.
28. Alberti, *Tribal Life*, 47–48; Drachmann, *Atheism*, 19, 43.
29. Frere, "Presidential Address," 1:xxi.
30. Bleek, *On the Origin of Language*, xv–xvi; Spohr, *Natal Diaries*, 24.
31. Robert Moffat, *Missionary Labours*, 305; Kay, *Travels and Researches*, 209. For precedents, see Augustine, *City of God*, 7:33; and William Laurance Brown, *Comparative View of Christianity*, 1:172.
32. See Hodgen, *Doctrine of Survivals*.
33. Van der Kemp, "Account of the Religion," 433; Lichtenstein, *Travels in Southern Africa*, 1:313; De Mist, *Diary of a Journey*, 48–49; Alberti, *Tribal Life*, 47–48; John Campbell, *Travels in South Africa*, 517–18.
34. Lubbock, *Origin of Civilization*, 205–10, 215, 286.
35. Lubbock, *Origin of Civilization*, 287.
36. Clodd, *Myths and Dreams*, 13; Tiele, *Elements of the Science of Religion*, 68, 70, 77.
37. Jevons, *Introduction to the History of Religion*, 28.
38. Schultze, *Psychologie der Naturvölker*, 223; Haddon, *Magic and Fetishism*, 84–85.
39. Andrew Lang, *Making of Religion*, 207; Haddon, "Presidential Address," 519.
40. Schapera, "Present State," 258; see Eiselen and Schapera, "Religious Beliefs and Practices." For political context, see Brian Du Toit, "Missionaries"; Furlong, *Between Crown and Swastika*, 225–26; Robert J. Gordon, "Apartheid's Anthropologists"; and T. Dunbar Moodie, *Rise of Afrikanerdom*, 272–75.
41. Eiselen, "Geloofsvorme"; Eiselen, "Die Seksuele Lewe," 166, 174; Eiselen, "Die Eintlike Reendans"; Eiselen, *Stamskole in Suid Afrika*, 76; South Africa, *Summary of the Report*, 79.
42. Michaelsen, "Significance of the American Indian Religious Freedom Act"; Chidester, *Patterns of Power*, 221–57; Chidester, *Salvation and Suicide*, 24–46.
43. Lawson and McCauley, *Rethinking Religion*, 7; Smart, *Worldviews*.
44. Leakey, *Mau Mau and the Kikuyu*, 93.
45. Leakey, *Defeating Mau Mau*, 41, 40, 43, 52.
46. Rosberg and Nottingham, *Myth of "Mau Mau,"* 336; Berman and Lonsdale, "Louis Leakey's Mau Mau," 194–95.
47. Warner, "Mr. Warner's Notes," 108–9; Lawrence, *Road Belong Cargo*, 272–73. On the significance of cargo movements for the study of religion, see Long, *Significations*.
48. Cook, "Problematic Differences"; Malan, "Cosmological Factor."
49. Needham, "Polythetic Classification"; Poole, "Metaphors and Maps"; Southwold, "Religious Belief". See Chidester, *Shots in the Streets*, 3–5.
50. Hobsbawm and Ranger, *Invention of Tradition*; Anderson, *Imagined Communities*; Clifford, *Predicament of Culture*, 1–17; Rosaldo, *Culture and Truth*, 217. On discourse and force, see Lincoln, *Discourse and the Construction of Society*.
51. Chidester, "Stealing the Sacred Symbols"; Chidester, *Word and Light*, 143–45.
52. Callaway, *Religious System*, 79–80.
53. See Bell, *Ritual Theory, Ritual Practice*.
54. Kolb, *Present State of the Cape of Good Hope*, 29.
55. Kolb, *Present State of the Cape of Good Hope*, 29; Hume, *Treatise of Human Nature*, 1:375; Müller, *Introduction to the Science of Religion*, 9.
56. Jonathan Z. Smith, *Drudgery Divine*, 51.
57. Rowley, *Religion of the Africans*, 15, 43.
58. Mendelssohn, "Judaic or Semitic Legends," 13:395–96, 14:32–33.

BIBLIOGRAPHY

Abe, Stanley K. "Art and Practice in a Fifth-Century Buddhist Cave Temple." *Ars Orientalis* 20 (1991): 1–31.

Ackerman, Robert. *J. G. Frazer, His Life and Work.* Cambridge: Cambridge Univ. Press, 1987.

Agar-Hamilton, J. A. I. *The Native Policy of the Voortrekkers: An Essay in the History of the Interior of South Africa, 1836–1858.* Cape Town: Maskew Miller, 1928.

Alatas, Syed Hussein. *The Myth of the Lazy Native: A Study of the Image of the Malays, Filipinos, and Javanese from the Sixteenth to the Twentieth Century and Its Functions in the Ideology of Colonial Capitalism.* London: Frank Cass, 1977.

Alberti, Ludwig. *Tribal Life and Customs of the Xhosa.* 1807. Trans. William Fehr. Cape Town: Balkema, 1968.

Alexander, James Edwards. *Narrative of a Voyage of Observation among the Colonies of Western Africa, in the Flag-Ship Thalia; and of a Campaign in Kaffir-land.* 2 vols. London: Henry Colburn, 1837.

Allen, D. C. *The Legend of Noah: Renaissance Rationalism in Art, Science, and Letters.* Urbana: Univ. of Illinois Press, 1949.

Almond, Philip C. *The British Discovery of Buddhism.* Cambridge: Cambridge Univ. Press, 1988.

Anderson, Benedict. *Imagined Communities: Reflections on the Origin and Spread of Nationalism.* London: Verso, 1983.

Andrewes, Lancelot. *A Pattern of Catechistical Doctrine.* London: Robert Norton, 1650. Reprint, New York: AMS Press, 1967.

Appadurai, Arjun. "Theory in Anthropology: Center and Periphery." *Comparative Studies in Society and History* 29 (1986): 356–61.

Arbousset, Thomas. "Station de Morija." *Journal des missions évangéliques* 14 (1839): 53–64.

———. *Missionary Excursion into the Blue Mountains.* Trans. David

Ambrose and Albert Brutsch. Morija, Lesotho: Morija Archives, 1991.

Arbousset, Thomas, and François Daumas. *Narrative of an Exploratory Tour to the North-East of the Colony of the Cape of Good Hope.* 1842. Trans. John Croumbie Brown. Cape Town: A. S. Robertson, 1846.

Arnold, Matthew. "The Bishop and the Philosopher." In *Essays, Letters, and Reviews by Matthew Arnold,* ed. Fraser Neiman, pp. 45–58. Cambridge: Harvard Univ. Press, 1960.

Asad, Talal, ed. *Anthropology and the Colonial Encounter.* London: Ithaca Press, 1973.

Aspling, E. *The Malays of Cape Town.* Manchester, 1883.

Astley, Thomas. *A New General Collection of Voyages and Travels.* 4 vols. London: Royal Empire Society, 1745–47.

Augustine. *The City of God.* Trans. Marcus Dods. New York: Modern Library, 1950.

Axtell, James. *The Invasion Within: The Contest of Cultures in Colonial North America.* New York: Oxford Univ. Press, 1985.

Bain, Andrew Geddes. *Journey to the North (to Dithubamba in Molepolole in Bechuanaland).* 1826. Ed. Margaret Hermina Lister. Cape Town: Van Riebeeck Society, 1945.

Baines, Thomas. *The Gold Regions of South Eastern Africa.* London: Edward Stanford; Cape Town: J. W. C. Mackay, 1877.

Bannister, Saxe. *Humane Policy: Or, Justice to the Aborigines of New Settlements.* London: Underwood, 1930.

Baritz, Loren. "The Idea of the West." *American Historical Review* 66 (1960–61): 618–40.

Barnard, Alan. *Hunters and Herders of Southern Africa: A Comparative Ethnography of the Khoisan Peoples.* Cambridge: Cambridge Univ. Press, 1992.

Barrow, John. *An Account of Travels into the Interior of Southern Africa in the Years 1797 and 1798.* 2d ed. 2 vols. London: T. Cadell and W. Davis, 1806.

———. "An Account of a Journey Made in the Years 1801 and 1802, to the Residence of the Chief of the Booshuana Nation, being the remotest point in the interior of Southern Africa to which Europeans have hitherto penetrated." In Barrow, *A Voyage to Cochinchina in the Years 1792 and 1793,* pp. 361–437. London: T. Cadell and W. Davies, 1806.

Barrow, John Henry, ed. *The World's Parliament of Religions.* 2 vols. London: Review of Books, 1893.

Bassett, Josiah. *The Life of a Vagrant, or the Testimony of an Outcast.* London: Charles Gilpin, John Snow, 1850.

Baudet, Henri. *Paradise on Earth: Some Thoughts on European Images of Non-European Man.* Trans. Elizabeth Wenholt. New Haven: Yale Univ. Press, 1965.

Bell, Catherine. *Ritual Theory, Ritual Practice.* New York: Oxford Univ. Press, 1992.

Benham, Marian S. *Henry Callaway M.D., D.D., First Bishop of Kaffraria: His Life History and Work: A Memoir.* London: Macmillan, 1896.

Benveniste, Emile. *Indo-European Language and Society.* Trans. Elizabeth Palmer. London: Faber and Faber, 1973.

Bergson, Henri. *Laughter: An Essay on the Meaning of the Comic.* Trans. Cloudesley Brereton and Fred Rothwell. London: Macmillan, 1911.

Berkhofer, Robert F., Jr. *The White Man's Indian: Images of the American Indian from Columbus to the Present.* New York: Vintage Books, 1978.

Berman, Bruce J., and John M. Lonsdale. "Louis Leakey's Mau Mau: A Study in the Politics of Knowledge." *History and Anthropology* 5 (1991): 143–204.

Berreman, Gerald. *The Politics of Truth: Essays in Critical Anthropology.* New Delhi: South Asian Publishers, 1981.

Bhabha, Homi. *The Location of Culture.* London: Routledge, 1994.

Bird, John. *Annals of Natal.* 2 vols. Pietermaritzburg, South Africa: Davis, 1888. Reprint, Cape Town: Struik, 1965.

"Bishop Colenso and his Kafir Words for the Deity." *South African Christian Watchman,* n.s., 2 (1855): 273–80.

Bleek, W. H. I. *De nominum generibus linguarum Africae Australis, Copticae, Semiticarum aliarumque sexualium.* Bonn: A. Marcus, 1851.

———. "On the Languages of Western and Southern Africa." *Transactions of the Philological Society* 4 (1855): 40–50.

———. "Researches into the Relations between the Hottentots and Kafirs." *Cape Monthly Magazine* 1 (1857): 199–208, 289–96.

———. "South African Languages and Books." *Cape Monthly Magazine* 13, no. 18 (1858): 321–28.

———. *The Library of His Excellency Sir George Grey.* 2 vols. London: Trübner, 1858–59.

———. *Comparative Grammar of the South African Languages.* London: Trübner, 1862.

———. *Reynard the Fox in South Africa; or Hottentot Fables and Tales.* London: Trübner, 1864.

———. *On the Origin of Language: Preface and Treatise.* Ed. Ernst Haeckel and trans. Davidson. 1868. Reprint, New York: L. W. Schmidt, 1869.

————. "Scientific Reasons for the Study of the Bushman Language." *Cape Monthly Magazine*, n.s., 7 (1873): 149–53.

————. "On Resemblances in Bushman and Australian Mythology." *Cape Monthly Magazine*, n.s., 8 (1874): 98–102.

————. *A Brief Account of Bushman Folklore and Other Texts*. Cape Town: J. C. Juta, 1875.

————. *Zulu Legends*. 1857. Ed. J. A. Engelbrecht. Pretoria: Van Schaik, 1952.

Bleek, W. H. I., and Lucy C. Lloyd. *Specimens of Bushman Folklore*. London: George Allen, 1911.

Bogaert, Abraham. *Historische Reizen door d'oostersche Deelen van Asia, zynde eene historische beschryving dier konninkryken en landschappen, door hem bezocht en doorwandelt, beneffens een nauwkeurig ontwerp van de zeden, drachten, wetten en Godtsdienst der zelve inwoners, en wat verder wegens de dieren, planten, Vruchten, enz. in die gewesten aanmerkenswaardig is, etc.* Amsterdam: Nicolaas ten Hoorn, 1711.

Bolling, Frederick Andersen. *Frederici Bollingii, oost-Indisch reisboek, Bevattende Ziyne reis naaar oos Indie, Zoowel als De beschrijving van enige plaatsen, met aan aantal Cermonien der Heidenen, zoowel met betrekking tot hun godsdienst als tot het aangaan van hun huwelijk etc.* Copenhagen: Daniel Paulli, 1678.

Bonsen, R., H. Marks, and J. Miedema, eds. *The Ambiguity of Rapprochement: Reflections of Anthropologists on Their Controversial Relationship with Missionaries*. Nijmegen, Netherlands: Focaal, 1990.

Boorstin, Daniel. *The Discoverers*. New York: Random House, 1983.

Borcherds, Petrus Borchardus. *An Autobiographical Memoir*. Cape Town: Robertson, 1861.

Botha, C. G., ed. *The Wreck of the Grosvenor*. Cape Town: Van Riebeeck Society, 1927.

Boucher, Maurice, ed. *David Livingstone Correspondence in the Brenthurst Library*. Johannesburg: Brenthurst Press, 1985.

Bowker, John Mitford. *Speeches, Letters, and Selections from Important Papers*. 1864. Reprint, Cape Town: C. Struik, 1962.

Brain, J. B., ed. *The Cape Diary of Bishop Patrick Raymond Griffith for the Years 1837 to 1839*. Cape Town: Mariannhill Mission Press, 1988.

Braudel, Fernand. *The Mediterranean and the Mediterranean World in the Age of Philip II*. 2 vols. Trans. Siân Reynolds. London: Collins, 1972.

Brerewood, Edward. *Enquiries Tracing the Diversity of Languages and*

Religions through the Chief Parts of the World. 1613. London: Printed for N. Ranew and J. Robinson, 1671.

Broadbent, Samuel. *A Narrative of the First Introduction of Christianity Among the Baralong Tribe of the Bechuanas, South Africa.* London: Wesleyan Mission House, 1856.

Broberg, Gunnar, ed. *Linnaeus: Progress and Prospects in Linnaean Research.* Stockholm: Almqvist and Wiksell, 1980.

Brookes, Edgar H. *White Rule in South Africa, 1830–1910: Varieties in Governmental Policies Affecting Africans.* Pietermaritzburg, South Africa: Univ. of Natal Press, 1974.

Brothers, Richard. *A correct Account of the invasion and conquest of this Island by the Saxons, necessary to be known by the English Nation, the Descendants of the greater part of the Ten Tribes.* London: Printed for George Riebau, 1822.

Brown, J. Tom. *Among the Bantu Nomads: A Record of Forty Years Spent among the Bechuana.* London: Seeley Service, 1926.

Brown, William Laurance. *A Comparative View of Christianity.* 2 vols. Edinburgh: A. Balfour, 1826.

Brownlee, Frank, ed. *The Transkeian Native Territories: Historical Records.* Lovedale, South Africa: Lovedale Institution Press, 1923.

Brownlee, John. "Account of the Amakosae, or Southern Caffres." In George Thompson, *Travels and Adventures in Southern Africa,* vol. 2, pp. 335–75. London: Henry Colburn, 1827.

Bryden, Henry Anderson. *A History of South Africa: From the First Settlement of the Dutch, 1652, to the Year 1903.* London: William Sands, 1904.

Bunsen, Christian Charles Josias von. *Egypt's Place in a Universal History.* 5 vols. Trans. Charles H. Cottrell. London: Longman, 1848–60.

———. *Outline of the Philosophy of Universal History Applied to Language and Religion.* London: Longman, Brown, Green, and Longman, 1854.

———. *God in History, or the Progress of Man's Faith in the Moral Order of the World.* 3 vols. Trans. Susanna Winckworth. London: Longmans, Green, 1868–70.

Bunsen, Frances. *A Memoir of Baron Bunsen: Drawn chiefly from family papers by his widow.* 2 vols. London: Longmans, Green, 1868.

Burchell, William John. *Travels in the Interior of Southern Africa.* 2 vols. London: Longman, Hurst, Rees, Orme, Brown, and Green, 1824.

Burnett, B. B. *Anglicans in Natal.* Durban: Churchwardens, St. Paul's, n.d.

Burton, Richard F. *The Lake Regions of Central Africa.* 2 vols. London: Longman, Green, Longman, and Roberts, 1860.

Buxton, Thomas Fowell. *The African Slave Trade and its Remedy.* 2d ed. London: John Murray, 1840.

Byrne, Peter. *Natural Religion and the Nature of Religion: The Legacy of Deism.* London: Routledge, 1989.

Caillé, Nicholas Louis de la. *Journal historique du Voyage fait du Cap de Bonne-Espérance.* Paris: Guillyn, 1763.

Caillié, René. *Travels through Central Africa to Timbuctoo; and Across the Great Desert, to Morocco, Performed in the Years 1824–1828.* 2 vols. London: Colburn and Bentley, 1830.

Calderwood, Henry. *Caffres and Caffre Missions.* London: James Nisbet, 1858.

Callaway, Henry. *Polygamy, a bar to admission into the Christian Church.* Durban: John O. Brown, 1862.

———. *The Last Word of Modern Thought: Two Sermons Preached at St. Peter's Cathedral and at St. Andrew's Church, Pietermaritzburg Natal, December 1865.* Springvale, South Africa: J. Blair; Pietermaritzburg, South Africa: Davis, 1866.

———. *Nursery Tales, Traditions, and Histories of the Zulus.* Springvale, South Africa: J. A. Blair; London: Trübner, 1866–68.

———. *The Religious System of the Amazulu.* Springvale, South Africa: Springvale Mission Press, 1868–70.

———. *A Fragment on Comparative Religion.* Natal: Callaway, 1874.

———. "A Visit to Pondoland: Journal of Bp. Callaway." *Mission Field* (June 1875): 161–76 and (September 1875): 257–64.

———. "South African Folk-Lore." *Cape Monthly Magazine* 16, no. 94 (1878): 109–10.

———. "On the Religious Sentiment amongst the Tribes of South Africa: Lecture delivered at Kokstad." *Cape Monthly Magazine,* n.s., 2, no. 5 (1880): 87–102.

———. "A Fragment Illustrative of Religious Ideas Among the Kafirs." *Folklore* 2, no. 4 (1880): 56–60.

Callender, John. *Terra Australis Cognita; or Voyages to the Terra Australis.* 3 vols. Amsterdam: Israel, 1766–68. Reprint, New York: Da Capo, 1967.

Campbell, John. *Travels in South Africa.* London: Black, Parry, 1815. Reprint, Cape Town: Struik, 1974.

Campbell, Mary B. *The Witness and the Other World: Exotic European Travel Writing, 400–1600.* Ithaca: Cornell Univ. Press, 1988.

Cape of Good Hope. *Report of the Select Committee of the House of Assembly on Certain Petitions for Aid from the Public Revenue for Ecclesiastical Purposes, June 15, 1857.* In *Votes and Proceedings of Parliament,* Appendix 2. Cape Town: Saul Solomon, 1858.

———. *Blue-book on Native Affairs.* Cape Town: Saul Solomon, 1875.

Capps, Walter H. "Evaluation of Previous Methods: Commentary." In *Science of Religion: Studies in Methodology,* ed. Lauri Honko, pp. 177–85. The Hague: Mouton, 1974.

Carlyle, J. E. *South Africa and Its Mission Field.* London: James Nisbet, 1878.

Casalis, Eugène. *Études sur la langue Séchuana; precedées d'une introduction sur l'origine et les progres de la mission chez les Bassoutos.* Paris: Comité de la societé des missions évangéliques de Paris, 1841.

———. *Études de la langue du Béchuana.* Paris: Royal Press, 1843.

———. *The Basutos; or, Twenty-Three Years in South Africa.* London: James Nisbet, 1861.

———. *My Life in Basuto Land: A Story of Missionary Enterprise in South Africa.* Trans. J. Brierley. London: Religious Tract Society, 1889.

Chapman, James. *Travels in the Interior of South Africa, 1849–1863.* 2 vols. 1868. Ed. Edward C. Tabler. Cape Town: A. A. Balkema, 1971.

Chidester, David. *Patterns of Power: Religion and Politics in American Culture.* Englewood Cliffs N.J.: Prentice-Hall, 1988.

———. *Salvation and Suicide: An Interpretation of Jim Jones, the Peoples Temple, and Jonestown.* Bloomington: Indiana Univ. Press, 1988.

———. "Stealing the Sacred Symbols: Biblical Interpretation in the Peoples Temple and the Unification Church." *Religion* 18 (1988): 137–62.

———. *Shots in the Streets: Violence and Religion in South Africa.* Boston: Beacon Press, 1991; Cape Town: Oxford Univ. Press, 1992.

———. *Religions of South Africa.* London: Routledge, 1992.

———. *Word and Light: Seeing, Hearing, and Religious Discourse.* Urbana: Univ. of Illinois Press, 1992.

Chirenje, J. Mutero. "Church, State, and Education in Bechuanaland in the Nineteenth Century." *International Journal of African Historical Studies* 9 (1976): 401–18.

Christensen, Torben. *Origin and History of Christian Socialism, 1848–54.* Copenhagen: Aarhuus, 1962.

Clarke, Samuel. *A Discourse Concerning the Being and Attributes of God.* 7th ed. London: Printed by W. Botham for James and John Knapton, 1728.

———. "Discourse Concerning the Unchangeable Obligations of Natural Religion and the Truth and Certainty of the Christian Revelation." In *The Works of Samuel Clarke, D.D.* London: Printed for John and Paul Knapton, 1738. Reprint, New York: Garland, 1978.

Clastres, Helene. "Religion without Gods: The Sixteenth-Century Chroniclers and the South American Savages." *History and Anthropology* 3 (1987): 61–82.

Clifford, James. *The Predicament of Culture: Twentieth-Century Ethnography, Literature, and Art.* Cambridge: Harvard Univ. Press, 1988.

Clifford, James, and George Marcus, eds. *Writing Culture: The Poetics and Politics of Ethnography.* Berkeley and Los Angeles: Univ. of California Press, 1986.

Clodd, Edward. *Myths and Dreams.* London: Chatto and Windus, 1885.

Cobbing, Julian. "The Mfecane as Alibi: Thoughts on Dithakong and Mbolompo." *Journal of African History* 29 (1988): 487–519.

Coetzee, J. M. "Idleness in South Africa." *Social Dynamics* 8 (1982): 1–13.

———. *White Writing: On the Culture of Letters in South Africa.* New Haven: Yale Univ. Press, 1988.

Cole, Alfred W. *The Cape and the Kafir: or, Notes of Five Years' Residence in South Africa.* London: Richard Bentley, 1852.

Colenso, J. W. "The Diocese of Natal." *The Monthly Record of the Society of the Propogation of the Gospel in Foreign Parts* 4 (November 1853): 241–64.

———. "Church Missions Among the Heathen in the Diocese of Natal." 1854. In *Bringing Forth Light: Five Tracts on Bishop Colenso's Zulu Mission,* ed. Ruth Edgecombe, pp. 1–28. Pietermaritzburg: Univ. of Natal Press, 1982.

———. "The Good Tidings of Great Joy, which shall be to all people: A sermon preached in the Cathedral of Norwich, on Sunday August 13 1854, on the occasion of the ordination of Henry Callaway." 1854. In *Bringing Forth Light: Five Tracts on Bishop Colenso's Zulu Mission,* ed. Ruth Edgecombe, pp. 29–41. Pietermaritzburg, South Africa: Univ. of Natal Press, 1982.

———. *Ten Weeks in Natal: A Journal of a First Tour of Visitation among the Colonists and Zulu Kafirs of Natal.* London: Macmillan, 1855.

———. *Three Native Accounts of the Visit of the Bp. of Natal in September and October 1859 to Upande, King of the Zulus.* 3d ed. Pietermaritzburg and Durban, South Africa: Magema, Mubi, 1901.

———. *The Diocese of Natal.* London: Society for Promoting Christian Knowledge, 1860.

———. *The Pentateuch and Book of Joshua Critically Examined.* 7 vols. London: Longman, Robert, and Green, 1862–79.

Collins, David. *Account of the English Colony of New South Wales, 1798–1804.* 2 vols. London: T. Cadell and W. Davies, 1804.

Comaroff, Jean, and John Comaroff. *Of Revelation and Revolution:*

Christianity, Colonialism, and Consciousness in South Africa. Vol. 1. Chicago: Univ. of Chicago Press, 1991.

Cook, S. D. "Problematic Differences between the Cognitive Systems of Christianity, International Business Culture, and the Culture of South African Blacks." Ph.D. diss., Univ. of the North, Sovenga, South Africa, 1987.

Cope, John. *King of the Hottentots.* Cape Town: Howard Timmins, 1967.

Cope, Richard L. "Christian Missions and Independent African Chiefdoms in South Africa in the Nineteenth Century." *Theoria* 52 (1979): 1–23.

Cope, Richard L., ed. *The Journal of the Reverend T. L. Hodgson, Missionary to the Seleka-Rolong and the Griqua, 1821–31.* Johannesburg: Witwatersrand Univ. Press, 1977.

Cory, George, ed. *The Diary of Rev. Francis Owen.* Cape Town: Van Riebeeck Society, 1926.

Cowley, William Ambrose. *Voyage Round the Globe.* In *A Collection of Original Voyages Around the Globe,* ed. William Hacke. London: James Knapton, 1699.

Cox, G. W. "Max Müller on the Science of Language." *Edinburgh Review* 115 (January 1862): 78–79.

———. *The Life of John William Colenso, D. D., Bishop of Natal.* 2 vols. London: W. Ridgway, 1888.

Crais, Clifton C. "The Vacant Land: The Political Mythology of British Expansion in the Eastern Cape, South Africa." *Journal of Social History* 25 (1991): 255–75.

———. *The Making of the Colonial Order: White Supremacy and Black Resistance in the Eastern Cape, 1770–1865.* Johannesburg: Witwatersrand Univ. Press, 1992.

Cuthbertson, Greg. "Missionary Imperialism and Colonial Warfare: London Missionary Society Attitudes to the South African War, 1899–1902." *South African Historical Journal* 19 (1987): 93–114.

———. "Van der Kemp and Philip: The Missionary Debate Revisited." *Missionalia* 17, no. 2 (1989): 77–94.

Dachs, Anthony J. "Missionary Imperialism: The Case of Bechuanaland." *Journal of African History* 13 (1972): 647–58.

Dampier, William. *A New Voyage Round the World. Describing Particularly, the Isthmus of America, Several Coasts and islands in the West Indies, the Isles of Cape Verde, the Passage by Terra del Fuego, the South Sea Coasts of Chili, Peru, and Mexico; the Isle of Guam one of the Ladrones, Mindanao, and other Philippine and East-India Islands near Cambodia, China, Formosa, Luconia, Celebes etc. New Holland, Sumatra, Nicobar Isles; the Cape of Good Hope and Santa Heleena, their Soil, Rivers, Plants, Fruits,*

Animals, and Inhabitants, their Customs, Religion, Government and Trade, etc. London: James Knapton, 1697.

Dapper, Olfert. *Naukeurige Beschryvinge der Afrikaansche Gewesten van Egypten, Barbaryen, Libyen, Biledulgend, Wegroslaat, Guinea, Ethiopien, Abysinie: Verstoort in de Benamingen, Grenspalen, Steden, Revieren, Gewassen, Dieren, Zeeden, Drachten, Tallen, Rijkdommen, Godsdiensten en HeerSchappyn.* Amsterdam: Jacob van Meurs, 1668.

———. *Description de l'Afrique, contenant, les noms, la situation et les confins de toutes ses parties, leurs riviers, leurs plantes et leurs animaux; les moeurs, les coutumes, la langue, les richesses, la religion et la gouvernement de les Peuples, avec Oes Carles des États, des Provinces et des Villes, et des Figures en taille-douce, qui representent les habits et les principales ceremonies des habitants, les plantes et les animaux es moins connus.* Amsterdam: Wolfgang, Waesberge, Boom, and Van Someren, 1686.

Darby, I. D. "The Soteriology of Bishop John William Colenso." Ph.D. diss., Univ. of Natal, Pietermaritzburg, South Africa, 1982.

Daston, Lorraine. "Marvelous Facts and Miraculous Evidence in Early Modern Europe." *Critical Inquiry* 18 (1991): 93–124.

Davids, Achmat. "Muslim-Christian Relations in Nineteenth-Century Cape Town, 1825–1925." *Kronos* 19 (1992): 80–101.

Davies, W. Merlin. *An Introduction to F. D. Maurice's Theology.* London: Society for Promoting Christian Knowledge, 1964.

De Mist, Julie Philippe Augusta Uitenhage. *Diary of a Journey to the Cape of Good Hope and the Interior of Africa in 1802 and 1803.* Cape Town: A. A. Balkema, 1954.

Defert, Daniel. "The Collection of the World: Accounts of Voyages from the Sixteenth to the Eighteenth Centuries." *Dialectical Anthropology* 7, no. 1 (1982): 11–22.

Delegorgue, Adolphe. *Voyage dans l'Afrique Australe.* 2 vols. Paris: A. Renée, 1847.

Diamond, Stanley. *In Search of the Primitive: A Critique of Civilization.* New York: Transaction Books, 1974.

Diderot, Denis. *Supplément à L'Encyclopédie.* Amsterdam: M. M. Rig; Stuttgart: Friedrich Fromann, 1776.

Dieterlen, Henri. "Méfiance." *Journal des missions évangéliques* 83, no. 1 (1908): 307–13.

Diodorus Siculus. *Diodorus of Sicily.* 12 vols. Trans. C. H. Oldfather. Cambridge: Harvard Univ. Press; London: William Heinemann, 1935.

Dowson, Thomas A., and David Lewis-Williams, eds. *Contested Images:*

Diversity in Southern African Rock Art Research. Johannesburg: Witwatersrand Univ. Press, 1994.

Drachmann, A. B. *Atheism in Pagan Antiquity.* London: Gyldendal, 1922.

Dudley, Edward, and Maximilian E. Novak, eds. *The Wild Man Within.* Pittsburgh: Pittsburgh Univ. Press, 1972.

Dugmore, Henry Hare. *The Reminiscences of an Albany Settler.* 1871. Ed. F. G. van der Riet and L. A. Hewson. Grahamstown, South Africa: Grocott and Sherry, 1958.

Du Plessis, J. *A History of Christian Missions in South Africa.* London: Longmans Green, 1911.

Dupuis, C. F. *Origine de tous les cultes, ou religion universelle.* 7 vols. 1795. Paris: E. Babeuf, 1822.

Du Toit, Andre. "No Chosen People: The Myth of the Calvinist Origins of Afrikaner Nationalism and Racial Ideology." *American Historical Review* 88 (1983): 920–52.

Du Toit, Brian M. "Missionaries, Anthropologists, and the Policies of the Dutch Reformed Church." *Journal of Modern African Studies* 22 (1984): 617–32.

Eilberg-Schwartz, Howard. *The Savage in Judaism: An Anthropology of Israelite Religion and Ancient Judaism.* Bloomington: Indiana Univ. Press, 1990.

Eiselen, W. M. "Die Seksuele Lewe van die Bantoe." *Tydskrif vir Wetenskap en Kuns* 2 (1923–1924): 165–74.

———. "Geloofsvorme in Donker Afrika." *Tydskrif vir Wetenskap en Kuns* 3 (1924–1925): 84–98.

———. "Die Eintlike Reendans van die Bapedi." *South African Journal of Science* 25 (December 1928): 387–92.

———. *Stamskole in Suid Afrika: 'n Ondersoek oor die funksie daarvan in die lewe van die Suid-Afrikaanse Stamme.* Pretoria: L. J. van Schalk, 1929.

Eiselen, W. M., and I. Schapera. "Religious Beliefs and Practices." In *The Bantu-Speaking Tribes of South Africa,* ed. Isaac Schapera, pp. 247–70. London: George Routledge, 1937.

Elbourne, Elizabeth. "Concerning Missionaries: The Case of Van der Kemp." *Journal of Southern African Studies* 17 (1991): 153–64.

———. "Early Khoisan Uses of Mission Christianity." *Kronos* 19 (1992): 3–27.

Ellenberger, D., with J. C. MacGregor. *History of the Basuto: Ancient and Modern.* London: Caxton, 1912.

Elphick, Richard. *Kraal and Castle: Khoikhoi and the Founding of White South Africa.* 2d ed. Johannesburg: Ravan Press, 1985.

Elphick, Richard, and V. C. Malherbe. "The Khoisan to 1828." In *The Shaping of South African Society, 1652–1840*, ed. Richard Elphick and Hermann Giliomee, pp. 3–65. Cape Town: Maskew Miller Longman, 1989.

Enklaar, Ido H. *Life and Work of Dr. J. Th. van der Kemp, 1747–1811: Missionary Pioneer and Protaganist of Racial Equality in South Africa.* Cape Town: A. A. Balkema, 1988.

Etherington, Norman. *Preachers, Peasants, and Politics in Southeast Africa, 1835–1880: African Christian Communities in Natal, Pondoland, and Zululand.* London: Royal Historical Society, 1978.

———. "Missionary Doctors and African Healers in Mid-Victorian South Africa." *South African Historical Journal* 19 (1987): 72–92.

Fabian, Johannes. *Time and the Other: How Anthropology Makes Its Object.* New York: Columbia Univ. Press, 1983.

———. "Hindsight: Thoughts on Anthropology upon Reading Francis Galton's *Narrative of an Explorer in Tropical South Africa* (1853)." *Critique of Anthropology* 7, no. 2 (1987): 37–49.

———. "Religious and Secular Colonization: Common Ground." *History and Anthropology* 4 (1990): 339–55.

Fairchild, Hoxie Neale. *The Noble Savage: A Study in Romantic Naturalism.* New York: Columbia Univ. Press, 1928. Reprint, New York: Russel and Russel, 1961.

Fardon, Richard, ed. *Localizing Strategies: Regional Traditions of Ethnographic Writing.* Edinburgh: Scottish Academic Press; Washington DC: Smithsonian Institution Press, 1990.

Fast, Hildegarde H. "'In One Ear and Out the Other': African Responses to the Wesleyan Message in Xhosaland, 1825–1835." *Journal of Religion in Africa* 23 (1993): 47–74.

Fawcett, John. *An Account of Eighteen Months' Residence at the Cape of Good Hope in 1835–1836.* Cape Town: Pike, 1836.

Fleming, Francis. *Kaffraria, and Its Inhabitants.* London: Smith, Elder, 1853.

———. *Southern Africa: A Geography and Natural History of the Country, Colonies, and Inhabitants.* London: Arthur Hall, Virtue, 1856.

Force, Peter, ed. *Tracts and Other Papers, Relating Principally to the Origin, Settlement, and Progress of the Colonies in North America from the Discovery of the Country to the Year 1776.* 4 vols. Washington DC: Printed by P. Force, 1836–47. Reprint, Gloucester MA: Peter Smith, 1963.

Forster, Johann Reinhold. *Observations made during a Voyage round the World on Physical Geography, Natural History, and Ethnic Philosophy.* London: G. Robinson, 1778.

Foucault, Michel. *The Order of Things: An Archaeology of the Human Science.* New York: Random House, 1970.

Frangsmyr, Tore, ed. *Linnaeus: The Man and His Work.* Berkeley and Los Angeles: Univ. of California Press, 1983.

Frantz, R. W. *The English Traveller and the Movement of Ideas, 1660–1732.* Lincoln: Univ. of Nebraska Press, 1934.

Frere, Bartle. "Presidential Address: Native Races of South Africa." *Transactions of the South African Philosophical Society* 1 (1877–80): xii–xxv.

Freund, William B. "The Career of Johannes Theodorus van der Kemp and His Role in the History of South Africa." *Tijdschrift voor Geschiedenis* 86 (1973): 376–90.

Friedman, John Block. *The Monstrous Races in Medieval Art and Thought.* Cambridge: Harvard Univ. Press, 1981.

Frykenberg, Robert Eric. "Constructions of Hinduism at the Nexus of History and Religion." *Journal of Interdisciplinary History* 23 (1993): 523–50.

Furlong, Patrick J. *Between Crown and Swastika: The Impact of the Radical Right on the Afrikaner Nationalist Movement in the Fascist Era.* Hanover NH and London: Wesleyan Univ. Press and Univ. Press of New England, 1991.

Galton, Francis. *The Art of Travel or Shifts and Contrivances available in Wild Countries.* London: John Murray, 1855.

———. *Narrative of an Explorer in Tropical South Africa: Being an Account of a Visit to Damaraland in 1851.* 4th ed. London: Ward, Lock, 1891.

Gardiner, Allen. *Narrative of a Journey to the Zoolu Country in South Africa undertaken in 1835.* London: William Crofts, 1836.

Gardner, James. *The Faiths of the World: An Account of All Religions and Religious Sects, their Doctrines, Rites, Ceremonies, and Customs.* London: A. Fullarton, 1858.

Gerstner, Jonathan Neil. *The Thousand Generation Covenant: Dutch Reformed Covenant Theology and Group Identity in Colonial South Africa.* Leiden: Brill, 1991.

Giliomee, Hermann. "The Eastern Frontier, 1770–1812." In *The Shaping of South African Society, 1652–1840,* ed. Richard Elphick and Hermann Giliomee, pp. 421–71. Cape Town: Maskew Miller Longman, 1989.

Godlonton, Robert. *A Narrative of the Irruption of the Kafir Hordes into the Eastern Province of the Cape of Good Hope, 1834–35.* 2 vols. 1835–36. Cape Town: C. Struik, 1965.

Goerke, Heinz, ed. *Linnaeus.* Trans. Denver Lindley. New York: Scribner, 1973.

itgegewe handskrif [Uitgegee deur] Leo Fouche (O'ergedruk uit "Die Brandwag," 15 Aug en 1 Sep, 1910). Pretoria: Volkstem-Drukkerij, 1910.

Henry, Maureen. *The Intoxication of Power: An Analysis of Civil Religion in Relation to Ideology.* Dordrecht, Netherlands: D. Reidel, 1979.

Henson, Hilary. *British Social Anthropologists and Language: A History of Separate Development.* Oxford: Clarendon Press, 1974.

Herbert, Christopher. *Culture and Anomie: Ethnographic Imagination in the Nineteenth Century.* Chicago: Univ. of Chicago Press, 1991.

Herbert of Cherbury, Edward. *De veritate.* 1624. Trans. Meyrick H. Carré. Bristol: Bristol Univ. Press, 1937.

Herbert, Thomas. *A Relation of Some Yeares Travaile, Begunne Anno 1626 Into Afrique, and the Greater Asia, especially the Territories of the Persian Monarchie and some Points of the Orientall Indies, and Iles adjacent. Of their Religion, Language, Habit, Discent, Ceremonies, and Other Matters Concerning them.* London: William Stansby and Jacob Bloom, 1634.

————. *Some Yeares Travels into Africa and Asia the Great. Describing the Famous Empires of Persia and Industani, as Also Divers Other Kingdoms in the Orientall Indies and Iles Adjacent.* 3d ed. London: R. Everingham for R. Scot, T. Basset, J. Wright, and R. Chiswell, 1677.

Herport, Albrecht. *Riese Nach Java, Formosa, Vorder-Indien und Ceylon, 1659–1668.* 1669. Reprint, The Hague: Martinus Nijhoff, 1930.

Heylen, Peter. *Cosmography.* 5th ed. London: Anne Seile, 1677.

Hezel, Francis X. *The First Taint of Civilization: A History of the Caroline and Marshall Islands in Pre-Colonial Days.* Honolulu: Univ. of Hawaii Press, 1983.

Hinchliff, Peter. *John William Colenso, Bishop of Natal.* London: Nelson, 1964.

Hind, Robert J. "'We Have No Colonies': Similarities within the British Imperial Experience." *Comparative Studies in Society and History* 26 (1984): 3–35.

Hobbes, Thomas. *The English Works of Thomas Hobbes.* Ed. William Molesworth. London: Bohn Publishers, 1839–45.

————. *Leviathan.* Ed. C. B. Macpherson. Hammondsworth, England: Penguin, 1962.

Hobsbawm, Eric, and Terence Ranger, eds. *The Invention of Tradition.* Cambridge: Cambridge Univ. Press, 1990.

Hodgen, Margaret. *The Doctrine of Survivals: A Chapter in the History of Scientific Method in the Study of Man.* London: Allenson, 1936.

——. *Early Anthropology in the Sixteenth and Seventeenth Centuries.* Philadelphia: Univ. of Pennsylvania Press, 1964.

Hodgson, Janet. "A Study of the Xhosa Prophet Nxele (Part 1)." *Religion in Southern Africa* 6, no. 2 (1985): 11–36.

——. "A Study of the Xhosa Prophet Nxele (Part 2)." *Religion in Southern Africa* 7, no. 1 (1986): 3–24.

Hoernlé, A. Winifred. "Certain Rites of Transition and the Conception of *!nau* among the Hottentots." *Harvard African Studies* 2 (1918): 65–82.

——. "A Hottentot Rain Ceremony." *Bantu Studies* 1 (1922): 3–4.

——. "The Expression of the Social Value of Water among the Naman of South-West Africa." *South African Journal of Science* 20 (1923): 514–26.

——. "The Social Organization of the Namaqua Hottentots of South-west Africa." *American Anthropology* 27 (1925): 1–24.

——. "Social Organization." In *The Bantu Speaking Tribes of South Africa*, ed. Isaac Schapera, pp. 67–94. London: Routledge, 1937.

Hoffmann, Johan Christian. *Riese Nach dem Kaaplande, Nach Mauritius und Nach Java, 1671–1676.* 1683. Reprint, The Hague: Martinus Nijhoff, 1931.

Hoge, J. "Personalia of the Germans at the Cape, 1652–1806." *Archives Year Book for South African History.* Cape Town: Government Printer, 1946.

Holden, William C. *The Past and Future of the Kaffir Races.* London: Holden; Port Natal, South Africa: S. C. Cato, 1866.

Holub, Emil. *Seven Years in South Africa: Travels, Researches, and Hunting Adventures between the Diamond Fields and the Zambezi (1872–79).* Trans. Ellen E. Frewer. 2 vols. 2d. ed. London: Sampson Low, Marston, Searle, and Rissington, 1881.

Hondius, Jodocus. *Klare Besgryving van Cabo de Bonna Esperança, Med By-gelegen Kust naar Angola toe, van Cabo Negro af. Vervattende de Ondekking, Benaaming, Gelegendheyd, Verdeling, en Betrekking. Als ook De Hoedanigheden Der Elementen.* Amsterdam: Jodocus Hondius, 1652. Reprint, trans. L. C. van Oordt. Cape Town: Book Exhibition Committee, Van Riebeeck Festival, 1952.

Hopper, John Alan. "Xhosa-Colonial Relations, 1770–1803." Ph.D. diss., Yale Univ., 1980.

Horton, Robin. "African Traditional Thought and Western Science." *Africa* 37 (1967): 50–71.

——. "African Conversion." *Africa* 41 (1971): 85–108.

——. "On the Rationality of Conversion." *Africa* 45 (1975): 219–35, 373–99.

some account of the missionary settlements of the United Brethren near the Cape of Good Hope. London: L. B. Seeley, 1818.

Lawrence, Peter. *Road Belong Cargo: A Study of the Cargo Movement in the Southern Madang District, New Guinea.* Manchester: Manchester Univ. Press, 1964.

Lawson, E. Thomas, and Robert N. McCauley. *Rethinking Religion: Connecting Cognition and Culture.* Cambridge: Cambridge Univ. Press, 1990.

Le Cordeur, Basil A. "Robert Godlonton as Architect of Frontier Opinion (1850–1857)." *Archive Yearbook of South Africa* 22, pt. 2 (1959): vii–170.

Leach, Edmund. "Anthropology and Religion: British and French Schools." In *Nineteenth-Century Religious Thought in the West,* ed. Ninian Smart, John Clayton, Steven Katz, and Patrick Sherry, vol. 3, pp. 215–62. Cambridge: Cambridge Univ. Press, 1985.

Leakey, Louis S. B. *Mau Mau and the Kikuyu.* London: Methuen, 1952.

———. *Defeating Mau Mau.* London: Methuen, 1954.

Legassick, Martin. "The Frontier Tradition in South African Historiography." In *Economy and Society in Pre-Industrial South Africa,* ed. Shula Marks and Anthony Atmore, pp. 44–79. London: Longman, 1980.

Leguat, François. *A New Voyage to the East Indies by Francis Leguat and his Companions, Containing their Adventures in two Desert Islands, And an Account of the most Remarkable Things in Maurice Island, Batavia, at the Cape of Good Hope, the Island of St Helena and Other Places in their way to and from the Desert Islands.* London: R. Bonwicke, W. Freeman, Timothy Goodwin, J. Wathoe, M. Wotton, S. Maship, J. Nicholson, B. Tooke, R. Parker, and R. Smith, 1708.

Lehmann, Joseph H. *Remember You Are an Englishman: A Biography of Sir Harry Smith, 1787–1860.* London: Jonathan Cape, 1977.

Lemue, Prosper. "Coutumes religieuses et civiles des Béchuana." *Journal des missions évangéliques* 19 (1844): 41–58.

Leopold, Joan. *Culture in Comparative and Evolutionary Perspective: E. B. Tylor and the Making of "Primitive Culture."* Berlin: Dietrich Reimer Verlag, 1980.

Léry, Jean de. *History of a Voyage to the Land of Brazil, Otherwise Called America.* Trans. Janet Whatley. Berkeley and Los Angeles: Univ. of California Press, 1990.

Leslie, David. *Among the Zulus and Amatongas.* Ed. W. H. Drummond. Edinburgh: Edmonston and Douglas, 1875.

Le Vaillant, François. *Travels into the Interior Parts of Africa, by way of the Cape of Good Hope in the years 1780–5.* Edinburgh: W. Laine, 1791.

Leverton, Basil. *Records of Natal.* Vol. 1. Pretoria: Government Printers, 1984.

Lévy-Bruhl, Lucien. *Primitive Mentality.* Trans. Lilian A. Clare. London: George Allen; New York: Macmillan, 1923.

Lichtenstein, Martin Karl Heinrich. *Travels in Southern Africa in the Years 1803, 1804, 1805.* 2 vols. 1811–12. Trans. Anne Plumptre. Cape Town: Van Riebeeck Society, 1928.

———. *Foundation of the Cape (1811). About the Bechuanas (1807).* Trans. and ed. O. H. Spohr. Cape Town: A. A. Balkema, 1973.

Lincoln, Bruce. *Discourse and the Construction of Society: Comparative Studies of Myth, Ritual, and Classification.* New York: Oxford Univ. Press, 1989.

Livingstone, David. *Missionary Travels and Researches in South Africa.* London: John Murray, 1857.

Livingstone, David, and Charles Livingstone. *Narrative of an Expedition to the Zambesi and its Tributaries.* London: John Murray, 1865.

London Missionary Society. "Report Concerning the State of Religion in France." *Transactions of the London Missionary Society.* Vol. 1, pp. 509–15. London: Bye and Law, 1804.

———. *Report on a Visit to the South African Missions of the Society, November 1910—April 1911, by Messrs George Cousins and William Dover, and Sir Charles Tarring. Appendix C: Report of the Tiger Kloof Native Institution for 1910.* London: London Missionary Society, 1911.

Long, Charles H. *Significations: Signs, Symbols and Images in the Interpretation of Religion.* Philadelphia: Fortress Press, 1986.

Loubère, Simon de la. *A New Relation of the Kingdom of Siam by Ms. de la Loubere, envoy extraordinary from the French King to the King of Siam, in the Year 1687 and 1688 etc.* 2 vols. 1691. London: Thomas Harne, 1693.

Lovett, Richard. *The History of the London Missionary Society, 1795–1895.* 2 vols. London: Henry Frowde, 1899.

Lubbock, John. *Prehistoric Times.* London: Williams and Norgate, 1865.

———. *The Origin of Civilization and the Primitive Condition of Man.* 5th ed. London: Longmans, Green, 1889.

Luillier. *Voyage du Sieur Luillier aux grandes Indes, avec une instruction pour le commerce des Indes Orientales.* The Hague: Jean Clos, 1706.

MacCormack, Sabine. *Religion in the Andes: Vision and Imagination in Early Colonial Peru.* Princeton: Princeton Univ. Press, 1991.

MacCrone, I. D. *Race Attitudes in South Africa: Historical, Experimental, and Psychological Studies.* London: Oxford Univ. Press, 1937.

Mackenzie, John. *Ten Years North of the Orange River: A Story of Everyday Life and Work among the South African Tribes from 1859 to 1869.* Edinburgh: Edmonston and Douglas, 1871.

———. *Day-Dawn in Dark Places: A Study of Wanderings and Work in Bechuanaland.* London: Cassell, 1883.

———. "Native Races of South Africa and their Polity." In *British Africa,* ed. William Sheowring, pp. 168–94. London: Kegan Paul, Trench, Trübner, 1899.

———. *Papers of John Mackenzie.* Ed. A. J. Dachs. Johannesburg: Witwatersrand Univ. Press, 1975.

Mackenzie, William D. *John Mackenzie: South African Missionary and Statesman.* New York: A. C. Armstrong, 1902.

Macmillan, W. M. *The Cape Colour Question.* London: Faber and Gwyer, 1927.

Malan, J. S. "The Cosmological Factor in Development Programmes." *South African Journal of Ethnology* 11, no. 2 (1988): 61–66.

Malherbe, V. C., and Susan Newton-King. *The Khoikhoi Rebellion in the Eastern Cape, 1799–1803.* Cape Town: Univ. of Cape Town, Centre for African Studies, 1981.

Mandelslo, Johan Albrecht. *De Gedenkwaardige see en Landt Reyse deur Parsen en Indien gedaan van den E. H. Johan Albrecht van Mandelslo.* Amsterdam: Jan Rieuwertsz en Jan Hendricksz, 1685.

Manuel, Frank. *The Eighteenth Century Confronts the Gods.* Cambridge: Harvard Univ. Press, 1959.

———. *The Broken Staff: Judaism through Christian Eyes.* Cambridge: Harvard Univ. Press, 1992.

Marks, Shula. "Khoisan Resistance to the Dutch in the Seventeenth and Eighteenth Centuries." *Journal of African History* 13 (1972): 55–80.

Marsh, John W., and W. H. Stirling. *The Story of Commander Allen Gardiner, R. N..* London: James Nisbet, 1887.

Marshall, P. J., ed. *The British Discovery of Hinduism in the Eighteenth Century.* Cambridge: Cambridge Univ. Press, 1970.

Martin, Robert Montgomery. *History of Southern Africa.* London: Henry G. Bohn, 1843.

Mason, Peter. *Deconstructing America: Representations of the Other.* London: Routledge, 1990.

Maurice, Frederick D. *The Religions of the World and Their Relations to Christianity.* London: John W. Parker, 1847.

———. *The Life of Frederick Denison Maurice chiefly told in his own letters.* 2d ed. London: Macmillan, 1884.

Maylam, Paul. *A History of the African People of South Africa: From the Early Iron Age to the 1970s.* London: Croom Helm, 1986.

Mayson, John Schofield. *The Malays of Capetown.* Manchester: J. Galt, 1861.

McKay, James. *The Origin of the Xosas and Others.* Cape Town: J. C. Juta, 1911.

Meiring, Jane. *The Truth in Masquerade: The Adventures of François le Vaillant.* Cape Town: Juta, 1973.

Meister, Georg. *Der orientalisch-indianische Kunst- und Lust-Gärtner, das ist . . . Beschreibung derer meisten indianischen als auf Java Major, Malacca und Jappon, wachsenden Gewürtz-Frucht-und Blumen-Bäume . . . wie auch noch andere denckwürdige Ammerckungen was bey des Autoris zweymahlige Reise nach Jappon, von Java Major, oder Batavia, längst der Küsten Sina, Siam und rüchwertz über Malacca etc.* Dresden: Johan Riedel, 1692.

Mendelssohn, Sidney. "Judaic or Semitic Legends and Customs amongst South African Natives." *Journal of the African Society* 13 (1914): 395–406; 14 (1914): 24–34.

Mentzel, O. F. *A Geographical and Topographical Description of the Cape of Good Hope.* 1785–87. Trans. G. V. Marais and J. Hoge. Ed. H. J. Mandelbrote. Cape Town: Van Riebeeck Society, 1944.

Merensky, Alexander. *Beiträge zur Kenntniss Süd-Afrikas.* Berlin: Evangelical Missionshaus, 1875.

———. *Erinnerungen aus dem Missionsleben in Transvaal.* Berlin: Evangelical Missionshaus, 1899.

Merriman, N. J. *The Cape Journals of Archdeacon N. J. Merriman, 1848–1855.* Ed. Douglas Harold Varley and H. M. Matthew. Cape Town: Van Riebeeck Society, 1957.

Metheun, Henry H. *Life in the Wilderness, or Wanderings in South Africa.* London: Richard Bentley, 1846.

Michaelsen, Robert S. "The Significance of the American Indian Religious Freedom Act of 1978." *Journal of the American Academy of Religion* 52 (1984): 93–115.

Miller, Christopher L. *Blank Darkness: Africanist Discourse in French.* Chicago: Univ. of Chicago Press, 1985.

Milman, Henry Hart. *History of the Jews.* 3 vols. London: J. Murray, 1829.

M'Lennan, John Fergusson. "The Worship of Plants and Animals." *Fortnightly Review* 7 (1869–1870): 194–216.

Moffat, John S. *The Lives of Robert and Mary Moffat.* New York: A. C. Armstrong, 1886.

Moffat, Robert. *Missionary Labours and Scenes in Southern Africa.* London: John Snow, 1842.

———. *The Matabele Journals of Robert Moffat, 1829-1860.* 2 vols. London: Chatto and Windus, 1945.

Moodie, John W. D. *Ten Years in South Africa, including a particular description of the Wild Sports of that Country.* 2 vols. London: Richard Bentley, 1835.

Moodie, T. Dunbar. *The Rise of Afrikanerdom: Power, Apartheid, and Afrikaner Civil Religion.* Berkeley and Los Angeles: Univ. of California Press, 1975.

Morton, Thomas. *New English Canaan, or New Canaan.* Amsterdam: Printed by J. F. Stam, 1637.

Müller, F. Max. "Comparative Mythology." *Oxford Essays.* 4 vols. London: John W. Parker, 1856.

———. *Chips from a German Workshop.* Vol. 2. London: Longmans, Green, 1872.

———. *Introduction to the Science of Religion.* London: Longmans, Green, 1873.

Napier, Edward Pelaval. *Excursions in Southern Africa, including a History of the Cape Colony, an Account of the Native Tribes.* 2 vols. London: Schoberl, 1849.

Natal. *Native Affairs Commission: Proceedings of the Commission appointed to inquire into the Past and Present State of the Kafirs in the District of Natal.* 7 parts. Pietermaritzburg, South Africa: Archbell, 1852–53.

Needham, Rodney. "Polythetic Classification: Convergence and Consequences." *Man,* n.s., 10 (1975): 347–69.

———. *Exemplars.* Berkeley and Los Angeles: Univ. of California Press, 1985.

Newton-King, Susan. "The Enemy Within: The Struggle for Ascendancy on the Cape Eastern Frontier, 1760–1799." Ph.D. diss., Univ. of London, 1992.

Nieuhof, Johan. *Gedenkweerdige Brasiliaense zee-en Lant Reize Behelzende Afhetgeen opdegelvde is voorgevallen beneffens Een bondige beschrijving van gantsch Neerlants Brasil etc.* Amsterdam: Jacob van Meurs, 1682.

Nixon, John. *The Complete Story of the Transvaal: From the "Great Trek" to the Convention of London.* London: Sampson, Law, Marson, Searle, and Rissington, 1885.

Northcott, Cecil. *Robert Moffat: Pioneer in Africa, 1817–1870.* London: Lutterworth, 1961.

Northcott, William C. "John Mackenzie and Southern Africa." *History Today* 22 (1972): 656–63.

O'Gorman, Edmundo. *The Invention of America: An Inquiry into the*

Historical Nature of the New World and the Meaning of Its History. Bloomington: Indiana Univ. Press, 1961.

Omer-Cooper, J. D. *The Zulu Aftermath: A Nineteenth-Century Revolution in Bantu Africa.* London: Longmans, 1966.

Orpen, J. M. *History of the Basutus of South Africa.* 1857. Reprint, Mazenod, Lesotho: Mazenod Book Centre, 1979.

Ovington, John. *A Voyage to Suratt, in the year, 1689. Giving a large account of that city, and its inhabitants, and of the English factory there. Likewise a description of Madeira, St. Jago, Annobon, Cabenda and Malemba (upon the Coast of Africa), St. Helena, Johanna, Bombay, the city of Muscatt, and its Inhabitants in Arabia Felix, Mocha, and other maritime towns upon the Red-Sea, the Cape of Good Hope, and the Island Ascension.* London: Jacob Tonson, 1696.

Pagden, Anthony. *The Fall of Natural Man: The American Indian and the Origins of Comparative Ethnology.* Cambridge: Cambridge Univ. Press, 1982.

———. *European Encounters with the New World: From Renaissance to Romanticism.* New Haven: Yale Univ. Press, 1993.

Pailin, David, ed. *Attitudes to Other Religions: Comparative Religion in Seventeenth-and Eighteenth-Century Britain.* Manchester: Manchester Univ. Press, 1984.

Park, Katherine, and Lorraine Daston. "Unnatural Conceptions: The Study of Monsters in Sixteenth-and Seventeenth-Century France and England." *Past and Present* 92 (August 1981): 20–54.

Patai, Raphael. "The Ritual Approach to Hebrew-African Culture Contact." *Jewish Sociological Studies* 24 (1962): 86–96.

Peires, J. B. "Nxele, Ntsikana and the Origins of the Xhosa Religious Reaction." *Journal of African History* 20 (1979): 51–62.

———. *The House of Phalo: A History of the Xhosa People in the Days of Their Independence.* Johannesburg: Ravan Press, 1981.

———. *The Dead Will Arise: Nongqawuse and the Great Xhosa Cattle-Killing Movement of 1856–7.* Johannesburg: Ravan Press, 1989.

Penn, Nigel. "Land, Labour, and Livestock in the Western Cape during the Eighteenth Century." In *The Angry Divide,* ed. Wilmot James and Mary Simons, pp. 2–19. Cape Town: David Philip, 1989.

Percival, Robert. *An Account of the Cape of Good Hope.* London: Baldwin, 1804.

Philip, John. *Researches in South Africa.* 2 vols. London: James Duncan, 1828. Reprint, New York: Negro Univ. Press, 1969.

Philip, John. "Letter to the Directors of the L.M.S." *British Quarterly Review* 14 (1851): 106–13.

Philipps, Thomas. *Scenes and Occurences in Albany and Cafferland, South Africa.* London: William Marsh, 1827.

———. *Philipps, 1820 Settler, His Letters.* Ed. A. Keppel-Jones. Pietermaritzburg, South Africa: Shuter and Shooter, 1960.

Pietz, William. "The Problem of the Fetish, I." *Res: Anthropology and Aesthetics* 9 (spring 1985): 5–17.

———. "The Problem of the Fetish, II." *Res: Anthropology and Aesthetics* 13 (spring 1987): 23–45.

———. "The Problem of the Fetish, IIIa." *Res: Anthropology and Aesthetics* 16 (autumn 1988): 105–23.

Pinkerton, John. *A General Collection of the Best and Most Interesting Voyages and Travels in all Parts of the World.* London: Longmans, 1814.

Pinto, Serpa. *How I Crossed Africa from the Atlantic Ocean, through Unknown Continent, etc.* Vol. 2. London: Sampson Low, Marston, Searle, and Livington, 1881.

Plutarch. *Plutarch's Lives.* 11 vols. Trans. Bernadette Perin. London: Heinemann, 1914–26.

Poole, Fitz John Porter. "Metaphors and Maps: Towards Comparison in the Anthropology of Religion." *Journal of the American Academy of Religion* 54 (1986): 411–57.

Pratt, Mary Louise. "Scratches on the Face of the Country; or, What Mr. Barrow Saw in the Land of the Bushmen." In *"Race," Writing, and Difference,* ed. Henry Louis Gates Jr., pp. 135–62. Chicago: Univ. of Chicago Press, 1985.

———. *Imperial Eyes: Travel Writing and Transculturation.* London: Routledge, 1992.

Preus, J. Samuel. *Explaining Religion: Criticism and Theory from Bodin to Freud.* New Haven: Yale Univ. Press, 1987.

Pringle, Thomas. *Narrative of a Residence in South Africa.* London: Moxon, 1835.

Purchas, Samuel. *Purchas his Pilgrimage or Relations of the World and the Religions Obscured in all the Ages and Places, Discoursed, from the Creation unto the Present, Containing a Theological and Geographical Historie of Asia, Africa and America, with the lands adjacent. Declaring the ancient Religions before the Flood, the Heathenisn, the Jewish, and Saracenicall in all Ages since, in those parts profesed, with their several opinions, Idols, Oracles, Temples, Priests, Fasts, Feasts, Sacrifices and Rites Religious. Their beginning, sects, orders, and successions etc.* 1626. Reprint, Glasgow: James MacLehose, 1905.

Rae, Colin. *Malaboch, or Notes from a Diary on the Boer Campaign of 1894 against the Chief Malaboch, etc.* London: Sampson, Low, Master; Cape Town: Juta, 1898.

Rau, Charles, ed. *Articles on Anthropological Subjects contributed to the Annual Reports of the Smithsonian Institution from 1863 to 1877.* Washington DC: Smithsonian Institution, 1882.

Raven-Hart, R., ed. and trans. *Before Van Riebeeck: Callers at South Africa from 1488 to 1652.* Cape Town: C. Struik, 1967.

———. *Cape of Good Hope, 1652–1702: The First Fifty Years of Dutch Colonisation as Seen by Callers.* 2 vols. Cape Town: A. A. Balkema, 1971.

Rees, Wyn, ed. *Colenso: Letters from Natal.* Pietermaritzburg, South Africa: Schuter and Shooter, 1958.

Reyburn, H. A. "The Missionary as Rainmaker." *The Critic* 1 (1933): 146–53.

Ricards, James. *The Catholic Church and the Kaffir.* London: Burns and Oates, 1879.

Roberts, Noel. "The Bagananoa or Ma-Laboch: Their Early History, Customs, and Creed." *South African Journal of Science* 13 (1915): 241–56.

Rogerson, John. *Old Testament Criticism in the Nineteenth Century: England and Germany.* London: Society for Promoting Christian Knowledge, 1984.

Rolland, Samuel. "Idées religieuses et coutumes des Béchuanas." *Journal des missions évangéliques* 18 (1843): 473–79.

Rosaldo, Renato. "The Rhetoric of Control: Illongots Viewed as Natural Bandits and Wild Indians." In *The Reversible World: Symbolic Inversion in Art and Society,* ed. Barbara Babcock, pp. 240–57. Ithaca: Cornell Univ. Press, 1978.

———. *Culture and Truth: The Remaking of Social Analysis.* Boston: Beacon Press, 1989.

Rosberg, Carl G., Jr., and John Nottingham. *The Myth of "Mau Mau": Nationalism in Kenya.* New York: Meridian Books, 1966.

Rose, Cowper. *Four Years in Southern Africa.* London: Henry Colburn and Richard Bentley, 1829.

Ross, Andrew. *John Philip (1775–1851): Missions, Race and Politics in South Africa.* Aberdeen: Aberdeen Univ. Press, 1986.

Roussier, Paul. *L'Establissement d'Issiny.* Paris: Larose, 1935.

Rowley, Henry. *The Religion of the Africans.* London: W. Wells Gardner, 1877.

Rutherford, J. *Sir George Grey, K.C.B., 1812–1898: A Study in Colonial Government.* London: Cassell, 1961.

Ryan, Michael T. "Assimilating New Worlds in the Sixteenth and Seventeenth Centuries." *Comparative Studies in Society and History* 23 (1981): 519–38.

Said, Edward W. *Orientalism.* New York: Vintage Books, 1978.

Sales, Jane. *Mission Stations and the Coloured Communities of the Eastern Cape, 1800–1852.* Cape Town: Balkema, 1975.

Saunders, Christopher. "The Hundred Years' War: Some Reflections on African Resistance on the Cape-Xhosa Frontier." In *Profiles of Self-Determination,* ed. David Chanaiwa, pp. 55–77. Northridge: California State Univ. Foundation, 1976.

———. *The Making of the South African Past: Major Historians on Race and Class.* Cape Town: David Philip, 1988.

Schapera, Isaac. *The Khoisan Peoples of South Africa: Bushmen and Hottentots.* London: George Routledge, 1930.

———. "The Present State and Future Development of Ethnographical Research in South Africa." *Bantu Studies* 8 (1934): 219–342.

———. *The Tswana.* Rev. ed. London: International Institute, 1976.

Schapera, Isaac, ed. *The Early Cape Hottentots.* Cape Town: Van Riebeeck Society, 1933.

———. *David Livingstone's South African Papers, 1849–53.* Cape Town: Van Riebeeck Society, 1974.

Schloemann. "Die Malepa in Transvaal." *Zeitschrift für Ethnologie* 26 (January 1894): 64–70.

Schneider, Wilhelm. *Die Religion der afrikanischen Naturvölker.* Münster: Aschendorff, 1891.

Scholte, Bob. "Discontents in Anthropology." *Social Research* 38 (1971): 777–807.

Schreuder, Deryck. "The Imperial Historian as Colonial Nationalist: George McCall Theal and the Making of South African History." In *Studies in British Imperial History,* ed. Gordon Martel, pp. 95–158. New York: St. Martin's Press, 1986.

Schreyer, Johan Chirvgi. *Neue Ost-Indianische Reisz-Beschreibung, 1669–1677, Handelnde von unterschiedenen africanischen und barbarischen Völkern, sonderlich derer an dem VorGebürge Caput bonae spei sich enthaltenden. so genanten Hottentoteten, Lebens-Art, Kleidung, Haushaltung etc.* Leipzig: Johann Christian Wohlfart, 1681.

Schultze, Fritz. *Psychologie der Naturvölker: Entwicklungspsychologische Charakteristik des Naturmenschen in Intellektueller, Aesthetischer, Ethischer und Religiöser Beziehung.* Leipzig: Verlag Von Veit, 1900.

Schweitzer, Christophorus, and Christopher Fryke. *A Relation of Two Several Voyages Made in the East-Indies, Containing an Exact Ac-*

count of Their Customs, Description, Manners, Religion etc, of the several kingdoms and Dominions in those parts of the World in General: But in a more particular Manner, Describing those Countries which are under the Power and Government of the Dutch. London: D. Brown, S. Crouch, J. Knapton, R. Knaplock, J. Wyate, B. Tooke, and S. Buckley, 1700.

Select Committee. *Report of the Parliamentary Select Committee.* London: Aborigines Protection Society, 1836–37.

Setiloane, Gabriel M. *The Image of God among the Sotho-Tswana.* Rotterdam: A. A. Balkema, 1976.

Sextus Empiricus. *Sextus Empiricus.* 3 vols. Trans. G. Bury. London: Heinemann, 1936.

Sharpe, Eric J. *Comparative Religion: A History.* 2d ed. La Salle Il: Open Court, 1986.

Shaw, Barnabas. *Memorials of South Africa.* 1839. Cape Town: C. Struik, 1970.

Shaw, Rosalind. "The Invention of 'African Traditional Religion.'" *Religion* 20 (1990): 339–53.

Shaw, William. *The Story of My Mission in South Eastern Africa.* London: Hamilton Adams, 1860.

Shillington, Kevin. *The Colonisation of the Southern Tswana, 1870–1900.* Johannesburg: Ravan Press, 1985.

Shooter, Joseph. *The Kafirs of Natal and the Zulu Country.* London: E. Stanford, 1857.

Sillery, Anthony. *John Mackenzie of Bechuanaland, 1835–1899: A Study in Humanitarian Imperialism.* Cape Town: Oxford Univ. Press, 1971.

Skeat, Walter, and Charles Otto Blagden. *The Pagan Races of the Malay Peninsula.* 2 vols. London: Macmillan, 1906.

Smart, Ninian. *Worldviews: Crosscultural Explorations of Human Beliefs.* New York: Charles Scribner, 1983.

Smith, A. B. "The Disruption of Khoi Society in the Seventeenth Century." In *Africa Seminar: Collected Papers,* vol. 3, pp. 257–71. Cape Town: Univ. of Cape Town, Centre for African Studies, 1983.

Smith, A. B. "On Becoming Herders: Khoikhoi and San Ethnicity in Southern Africa." *African Studies* 49, no. 2 (1990): 51–73.

Smith, Bernard. *European Vision and the South Pacific, 1768-1850.* 2d ed. New Haven: Yale Univ. Press, 1985.

Smith, Edwin W. *Religion of the Lower Races (as Illustrated by the African Bantu).* New York: Macmillan, 1923.

———. *Robert Moffat, One of God's Gardeners.* London: Church Missionary Society, 1925.

Smith, Harry. *The Autobiography of Lt. Gen. Sir Harry Smith.* Ed. G. C. Moore Smith. London: John Murray, 1903.

Smith, Jonathan Z. *Map Is Not Territory: Studies in the History of Religions.* Leiden: E. J. Brill, 1978.

———. *Imagining Religion: From Babylon to Jonestown.* Chicago: Univ. of Chicago Press, 1982.

———. *Drudgery Divine: On the Comparison of Early Christianities and the Religions of Late Antiquity.* Chicago: Univ. of Chicago Press, 1990.

Smith, Thornley. *Memoir of the Reverend John Whittle Appleyard, Wesleyan Missionary in South Africa.* London: Wesleyan Missionary Society, 1881.

Smith, William. *A New Voyage to Guinea.* London: Nourse, 1744.

Smith, William Robertson. *Lectures on the Religion of the Semites.* Edinburgh: A. and C. Black, 1889.

Snowden, Frank M. *Blacks in Antiquity.* Cambridge: Harvard Univ. Press, 1970.

Society for Promoting Christian Knowledge. *May, the Little Bush Girl.* London: SPCK, 1875.

Solomon, Saul, ed. *The Progress of His Royal Highness Prince Alfred Ernest Albert through the Cape Colony, British Kaffraria, the Orange Free State, and Port Natal in the Year 1860.* Cape Town: Saul Solomon, 1861.

Somerville, William. *Narrative of His Journeys to the Eastern Cape Frontier and to Lattakoe, 1799–1802.* Ed. Edna Bradlow and Frank Bradlow. Cape Town: Van Riebeeck Society, 1979.

Sonntag, Christopher. *My Friend Maleboch: Chief of the Blue Mountains (An Eyewitness Account of the Maleboch War of 1894).* Pretoria: Sigma Press, 1983.

South Africa. *Summary of the Report of the Commission for the Socio-Economic Development of the Bantu Areas within the Union of South Africa.* Pretoria: Government Printers, 1955.

Southwold, Martin. "Religious Belief." *Man,* n.s., 14 (1979): 628–44.

Sparrman, Anders. *A Voyage to the Cape of Good Hope, Towards the Antarctic Polar Circle, and Round the World, But Chiefly into the Country of the Hottentots and Caffres. From the Year 1772, to 1776.* Vol. 1. 2d ed. London: C. G. J. and J. Robinson, 1786.

Spoelstra, Bouke. *Die "Doppers" in Suid Afrika, 1760–1899.* Cape Town: Nasionale Boekhandel, 1963.

Spohr, O. H. *The Natal Diaries of Dr. W. H. I. Bleek, 1855–1856.* Cape Town: A. A. Balkema, 1965.

Stayt, H. A. "Notes on the Balemba (An Arabic-Bantu tribe living among the BaVenda and other Bantu tribes in the Northern Transvaal and

Southern Rhodesia)." *Journal of the Royal Anthropological Institute* 61 (1931): 231–38.

Steedman, Andrew. *Wanderings and Adventures in the Interior of Southern Africa.* 2 vols. London: Longman, 1835.

Stewart, Charles, and Rosalind Shaw, eds. *Syncretism/Anti-Syncretism: The Politics of Religious Synthesis.* London: Routledge, 1994.

Stockenstrom, Andries. *The Autobiography of the Late Sir Andries Stockenstrom.* 2 vols. Ed. C. W. Hutton. Cape Town: J. C. Juta, 1887.

Stocking, George. "What's in a Name? The Origins of the Royal Anthropological Institute (1837–71)." *Man,* n.s., 6 (1971): 369–90.

Stocking, George W., Jr. *Victorian Anthropology.* New York: The Free Press, 1987.

Stocking, George, Jr., ed. *Colonial Situations: Essays in the Contextualization of Ethnographic Knowledge.* Madison: Univ. of Wisconsin Press, 1991.

Stoler, Ann L. "Rethinking Colonial Categories: European Communities and the Boundaries of Rule." *Comparative Studies in Society and History* 31 (1989): 134–61.

Strangman, Edward. *French Callers at the Cape.* Cape Town: Juta, 1936.

Streak, Michael. *The Afrikaner as Viewed by the English, 1715-1854.* Cape Town: Struik, 1974.

Stuart, James, and D. M. Malcolm, eds. *The Diary of Henry Francis Fynn.* Pietermaritzburg, South Africa: Shuter and Shooter, 1950.

Sullivan, J. R. *The Native Policy of Sir Theophilus Shepstone.* Johannesburg: Walker and Snashall, 1928.

Sutherland, John. *Original Matter Contained in Lt. Col. Sutherland's Memoir of the Kaffers, Hottentots, and Bosjemans of South Africa.* Cape Town: Pike and Philip, 1847.

Tachard, Gui. *Voyage de Siam, des peres jesuitses, envoyaz par les Roy aux Indes et à la Chine. Avec leurs observations astronomiques, et leurs remarques de physique, de géographic, d'hydrographic et d'historie.* 2 vols. Paris: Arnould Senenze et Daniel Horthemels, 1686.

———. *A Relation of the Voyage to Siam.* London: F. Robinson and A. Churchill, 1688.

Tangye, H. Lincoln. *In New South Africa: Travels in the Transvaal and Rhodesia.* London: Horace Cox, 1896.

Tavernier, Jean Baptiste. *The Six Voyages of John Baptista Tavernier, a noble man of France now living, through Turkey, into Persia, and the East Indies, finished in the Year 1670.* 2 vols. 1676. London: John Starkey and Moses Pitt, 1678.

Taylor, Isaac. *Scenes in Africa for Little Tarry-at-Home Travellers*. 1820. Reprint, London: Harris, 1821.

Terry, Edward. *A Voyage to East India Wherein Some things are Taken Notice of, In our Passage Thither, But Many More in our Abode There etc.* 1655. London: J. Wilkie, 1777.

Theal, George McCall. *History of South Africa*. 11 vols. London: George Allen and Unwin, 1892–1919.

———. *Ethnography and Condition of South Africa before* A.D. *1505.* London: George Allen and Unwin, 1919.

Thomas, Keith. *Man and the Natural World: Changing Attitudes in England, 1500–1800*. London: Allen Lane, 1983.

Thompson, George. *Travels and Adventures in Southern Africa: Eight Years a Resident at the Cape*. London: Henry Colburn, 1827.

Thompson, William. *The Nature and Difficulties of the Missionary Enterprise among Barbarous Tribes, and the Way to Obtain Success*. Cape Town: Saul Solomon, 1880.

Thornton, Robert J. "'This Dying Out Race': W. H. I. Bleek's Approach to the Languages of Southern Africa." *Social Dynamics* 9, no. 2 (1983): 1–10.

———. "The Elusive Unity of Sir George Grey's Library." *African Studies* 42, no. 1 (1983): 79–89.

———. "Narrative Ethnography in Africa, 1850–1920: The Creation and Capture of an Appropriate Domain for Anthropology." *Man*, n.s., 18 (1983): 502–20.

Thorowgood, Thomas. *Jews in America, or Probabilities that the Americans are of that Race*. London, 1650.

Thunberg, C. P. *Travels in Europe, Africa, and Asia made between the years 1770 and 1779*. 4 vols. London: Printed for F. and C. Rivington, 1793–95.

Thwaites, Reuben Gold, ed. *The Jesuit Relations and Allied Documents: Travels and Explorations of the Jesuit Missionaries in New France, 1610–1791*. 73 vols. Cleveland: Burrows, 1896–1901.

Tiele, C. P. *Elements of the Science of Religion*. Vol. 1. Edinburgh and London: William Blackwood, 1897.

Tooke, W. Hammond. "Uncivilised Man South of the Zambesi." In *Science in South Africa: A Handbook and Review*, ed. W. Flint, pp. 79–101. Cape Town: T. Maskew Miller, 1905.

Trouillot, Michel-Rolph. "Anthropology and the Savage Slot: The Poetics and Politics of Otherness." In *Recapturing Anthropology: Working in the Present*, ed. Richard G. Fox, pp. 17–44. Sante Fe: School of American Research Press, 1991.

Van der Geest, Sjaak. "Anthropologists and Missionaries: Brothers under the Skin." *Man*, n.s. 25 (1990): 588–601.

Van der Kemp, J. T. "Transactions of Dr. Vanderkemp in the Year 1800." *Transactions of the [London] Missionary Society.* Vol. 1, pp. 412–31. London: Bye and Law, 1804.

————. "An Account of the Religion, Customs, Population, Government, Language, History, and Natural Productions of Caffraria." *Transactions of the [London] Missionary Society.* Vol. 1, pp. 432–41. London: Bye and Law, 1804.

Van Warmelo, N. J. *Contributions towards Venda History, Religion and Tribal Ritual.* Pretoria: Government Printers, 1932.

Varley, D. H. "A Note on Coree the Saldanian." *Quarterly Bulletin of the South African Library* 1, no. 3 (1947): 78–81.

Vaughan, Alden T. "'Expulsion of the Salvages': English Policy and the Virginia Massacre of 1622." *William and Mary Quarterly* 35 (1978): 57–84.

Vespucci, Amerigo. *Mundus Novus: Letters to Lorenzo Pietro di Medici.* Trans. George Tyler Northrup. Princeton: Princeton Univ. Press, 1916.

Vico, Giovanni Giambattista. *The New Science of Giambattista Vico.* Trans. Thomas Goddard Bergin and Max Harold Frisch. Ithaca: Cornell Univ. Press, 1948.

Vogel, Johan Wilhelm. *Oost-Indianische Reise-Beschreibung, in drey Thiele abgetheilet. Deren der Erste, des Autoris Abreise nach Holland und Oos-Indien, nebst einem Bericht von unterschiedlichen Oertern und deren merckwürdigen Sachen in sich begreifft. Der Andere des Autoris in Indien verrichtete Dienste.* Altenburg, Germany: J. Ludwig Richters, 1716.

Wallerstein, Immanuel. *The Modern World System: Capitalist Agriculture and the Origin of the European World-Economy in the Sixteenth Century.* New York: Academic Press, 1974.

Walten, William. *Life and Labours of Robert Moffat.* London: Walter Scott, 1885.

War Office. *The Native Tribes of the Transvaal, Prepared for the General Staff, War Office, 1905.* London: Majesty's Stationery Office, 1905.

Ward, Harriet. *Five Years in Kaffirland with Sketches of the Late War in that Country, to the Conclusion of Peace, written on the Spot.* 2d ed. Vol. 1. London: Henry Colburn, 1848.

Warner, J. C. "Mr. Warner's Notes." In *A Compendium of Kafir Laws and Customs,* ed. John Maclean, pp. 57–109. Mount Coke, South Africa: Wesleyan Mission Press, 1858.

Webb, C. de B., and J. B. Wright. *The James Stuart Archive of Recorded Oral Evidence Relating to the History of the Zulu and Neighbouring Peoples.* Vols. 1 and 4. Pietermaritzburg, South Africa: Univ. of Natal Press; Durban: Killie Campbell Africana Library, 1976, 1986.

Weidemann, N. C. "Die Malaboch-oorlog (1894)." *Historiese Studies* 7 (1946): 1–48.

Welsh, David. *The Roots of Segregation: Native Policy in Colonial Natal, 1845–1910.* Cape Town: Oxford Univ. Press, 1971.

Whately, Richard. "On the Origin of Civilisation." In *Lectures Delivered before the Young Men's Christian Association from November 1854 to February 1855,* pp. 3–36. London: Nisbet, 1879.

Widdicombe, John. *Fourteen Years in Basutoland: A Sketch of Mission Life.* London: Church Printing, 1891.

Williams, Donovan. "The Missionaries on the Eastern Frontiers of the Cape Colony, 1799–1853." Ph.D. diss., Univ. of the Witwatersrand, 1959.

————. *When Races Meet: The Life and Times of William Ritchie Thomson, Glasgow Society Missionary, Government Agent, and Dutch Reformed Church Minister, 1794–1891.* Johannesburg: APB Publishers, 1967.

————. "The Missionary Personality in Caffraria, 1799–1853: A Study in the Context of Biography." *Historia* 34, no. 1 (1989): 15–35.

Williams, Glyndwr, and P. J. Marshall. *The Great Map of Mankind: British Perceptions of the World in the Age of Enlightenment.* London: Macmillan, 1982.

Willoughby, W. C. "Notes on the Totemism of the Becwana." *Addresses and Papers Read at Joint Meeting of the British and South African Associations for the Advancement of Science* 3 (1905): 263–93.

————. "Notes on the Initiation Ceremonies of the Becwana." *Journal of the Royal Anthropological Institute* 39 (1909): 228–45.

————. *Tiger Kloof: The London Missionary Society's Native Institution in South Africa.* London: London Missionary Society, 1912.

————. *Race Problems in the New Africa.* Oxford: Clarendon Press, 1923.

————. *The Soul of the Bantu: A Sympathetic Study of the Magico-Religious Practices and Beliefs of the Bantu Tribes of Africa.* London: SCM Press; New York: Doubleday, 1928.

————. *Nature Worship and Taboo: Further Studies in "The Soul of the Bantu".* Hartford: Hartford Seminary Press, 1932.

Wilson, David McKay. *Behind the Scenes of the Transvaal.* London: Cassel, 1901.

Wilson, John. *Our Israelite Origins.* 1840. Reprint, Philadelphia: Daniels and Smith, 1850.

Wilson, M. L. "Khoisanosis: The Question of Separate Identities for Khoi and San." In *Variation, Culture, and Evolution in African Populations,* ed. Ronald Singer and John K. Lundy, pp. 13–25. Johannesburg: Witwatersrand Univ. Press, 1986.

Winter, Johannes August. "The Mental and Moral Capabilities of the Natives, Especially of Sekukuniland (Eastern Transvaal)." *South African Journal of Science* 11 (1914): 371–83.

Wintergerst, Martin. *Reisen auf dem mittelandischen meere, der wordsee, Nach Ceylon, und nach Java, 1688–1690.* 2 vols. 1712. Reprint, The Hague: Martinus Nijhoff, 1932.

Wittkower, Rudolph. "Marvels of the East: A Study in the History of Monsters." *Journal of the Warburg and Courtauld Institutes* 5 (1942): 159–97.

Wolf, Eric R. *Europe and the People without History.* Berkeley and Los Angeles: Univ. of California Press, 1982.

Wortham, John David. *The Genesis of British Egyptology, 1549-1906.* Norman: Univ. of Oklahoma Press, 1971.

Wright, John. "Political Mythology and the Making of Natal's Mfecane." *Canadian Journal of African Studies* 23 (1989): 272–91.

Wroth, Lawrence C. *The Voyages of Giovanni da Verrazzano, 1524-1528.* New Haven: Yale Univ. Press, 1970.

Zahan, Dominique. *The Religion, Spirituality and Thought of Traditional Africa.* Chicago: Univ. of Chicago Press, 1979.

INDEX

Aborigines' Protection Society, 97, 102

Adamson, James R., 222

African religion: representations of, 235–37; as Roman Catholicism, 85–86

Alberti, Ludwig, 78, 86, 233, 237, 243–44, 245

Alexander, James, 95–96

Allison, James, 134

ancestors: as demons, 194–95; Sotho-Tswana, 194–95; Xhosa, 103–4, 108–10; Zulu, 126, 157, 166

ancestor worship: Bantu, 220; as most ancient religion, 145; Sotho-Tswana, 205; southern African, 27; Xhosa, 108–10, 115; Zulu, 126–28, 145–48, 150–52, 157, 166, 170–71

anchor: as evidence for the absence of religion, 75–78, 243–44; as evidence for the origin of religion, 244–50

ancient Egypt: and Khoikhoi, 27, 133, 142, 148–49, 184, 222–23; and San, 71; and Sotho-Tswana, 27, 202–3, 213, 215–18

ancient Greece: mythology, 90; ritual, 236; and Stephanos the Pole, 33; theories of religion, 236–37; and Zulu, 118

ancient Israel: and Boers, 173–75; and Khoikhoi, 50–56; and Zulu, 124–27. *See also* Judaism

Andrewes, Lancelot, 14

angekoks, 192

animal emblems (Sotho-Tswana), 176–78, 200–203; as gods, 200–201; summary of theories,

215–16; as system of difference, 197–99

animal worship: Bushman, 220; as iconology, 212–14; as totemism, 209–11; War Office on, 206–7

animism, 86, 211, 251

Appadurai, Arjun, 70

Appleyard, John, 92

Arawaks, 11

Arbousset, Thomas, 201, 203

Arnold, Matthew, 139

atheism: endemic, 199–200; original, 244

Australia, 9, 12

Aztecs, 12

Bagananoa. *See* Malaboch

Bain, Andrew Geddes, 181

Baines, Thomas, 174

Bannister, Saxe, 96

Bantu religion: and closed frontier, 26; Eiselen on, 252–53; Theal on, 223–25; at Tiger Kloof, 209, 211; War Office on, 206–7, 218

baptism: compared to circumcision, 198; compared to excision of testicle, 41

Barrow, John: and "fear theory" of religion, 179, 201, 235; and Khoisan, 58, 70; and Sotho-Tswana, 178–79; and Stephanos the Pole, 30–31, 33; and Xhosa, 74–75

Basutos. *See* Sotho-Tswana

Batavian Republic, 24

Bechuanas. *See* Sotho-Tswana

Benveniste, Emile, 234

Bergson, Henri, 229–30

Berlin Missionary Society, 202, 215

Roger Poole
Kierkegaard: The Indirect Communication

John D. Barbour
Versions of Deconversion: Autobiography and the Loss of Faith

Gary L. Ebersole
*Captured by Texts: Puritan to Postmodern
Images of Indian Captivity*

David Chidester
*Savage Systems: Colonialism and Comparative
Religion in Southern Africa*

Laurie L. Patton and Wendy Doniger, editors
Myth and Method